BEGINNER'S GUIDE TO drawing the FUTURE

3dtotal Publishing

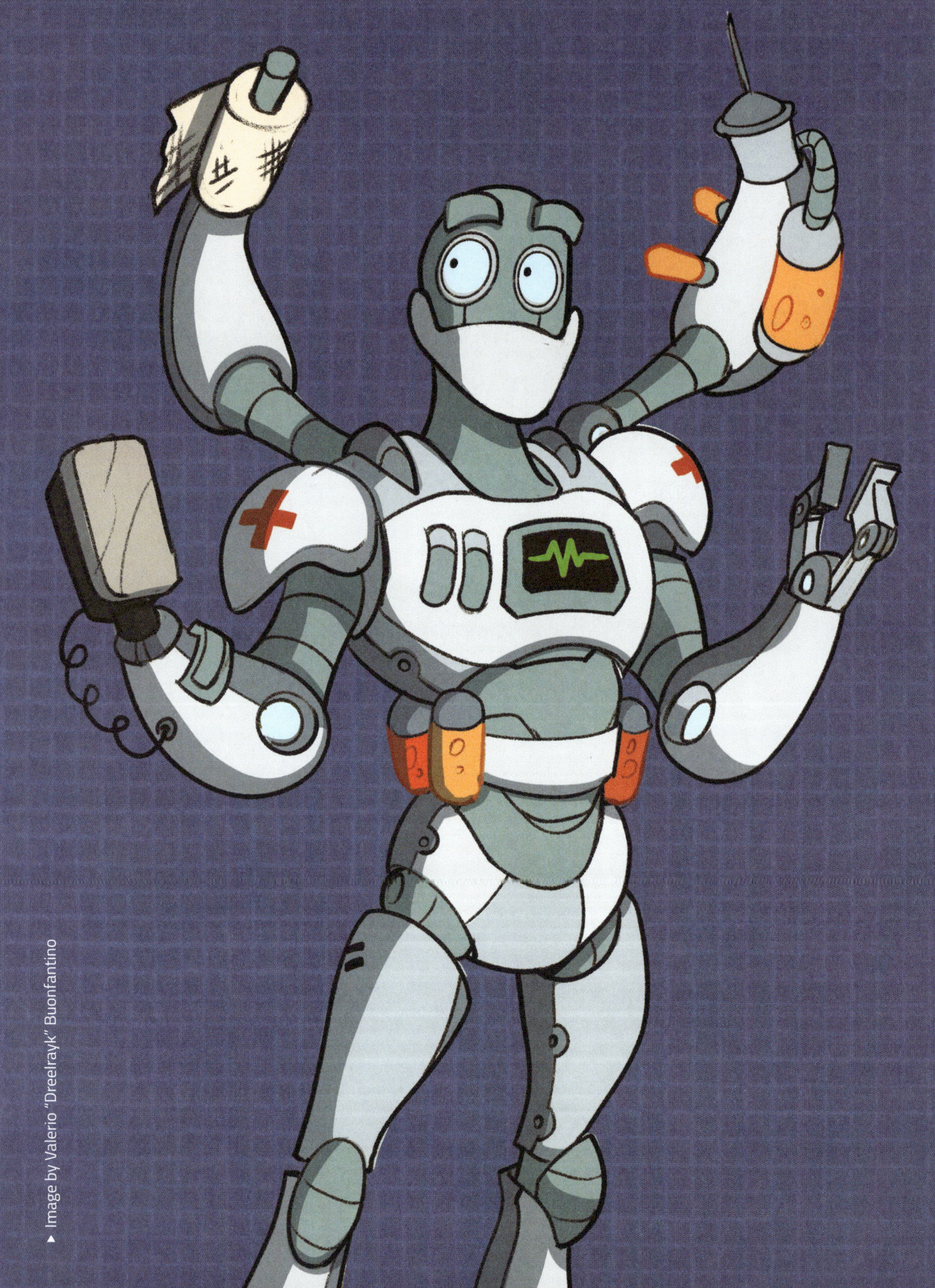

▶ Image by Valerio "Dreelrayk" Buonfantino

3dtotalPublishing

Correspondence: publishing@3dtotal.com
Website: www.3dtotal.com

Every effort has been made to ensure the credits and contact information listed are present and correct. In the case of any errors that have occurred, the publisher respectfully directs readers to the www.3dtotalpublishing.com website for any updated information and/or corrections.

First published in the United Kingdom, 2022, by 3dtotal Publishing.

Address: 3dtotal.com Ltd, 29 Foregate Street, Worcester, WR1 1DS, United Kingdom.

Soft cover ISBN: 978-1-912843-54-1
Printing and binding: Gutenberg Press Ltd (Malta)
www.gutenberg.com.mt

Visit www.3dtotalpublishing.com for a complete list of available book titles.

Managing Director: Tom Greenway
Studio Manager: Simon Morse
Lead Designer: Joseph Cartwright
Lead Editor: Samantha Rigby
Editor: Philippa Barker
Designer: Matthew Lewis

Front cover artwork by Valerio "Dreelrayk" Buonfantino, based on designs by individual artists as listed throughout the book. Back cover artwork © Individual artists as listed throughout the book.

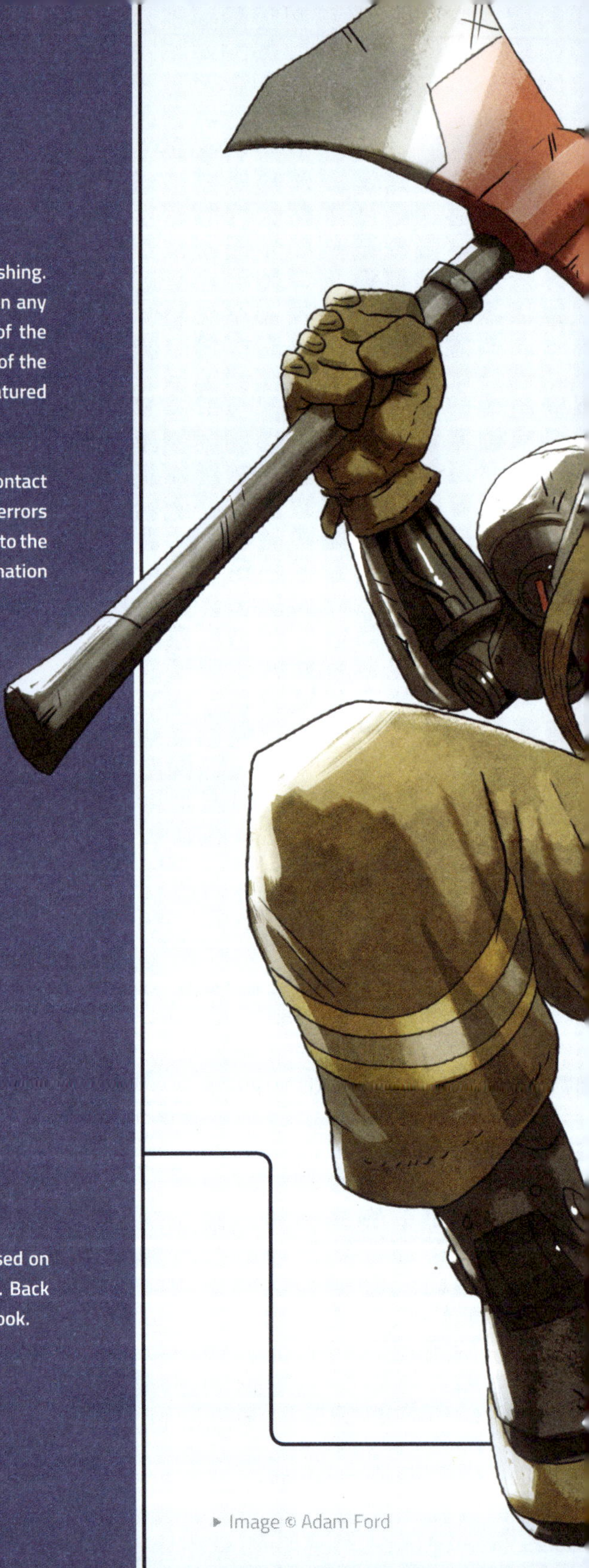

▶ Image © Adam Ford

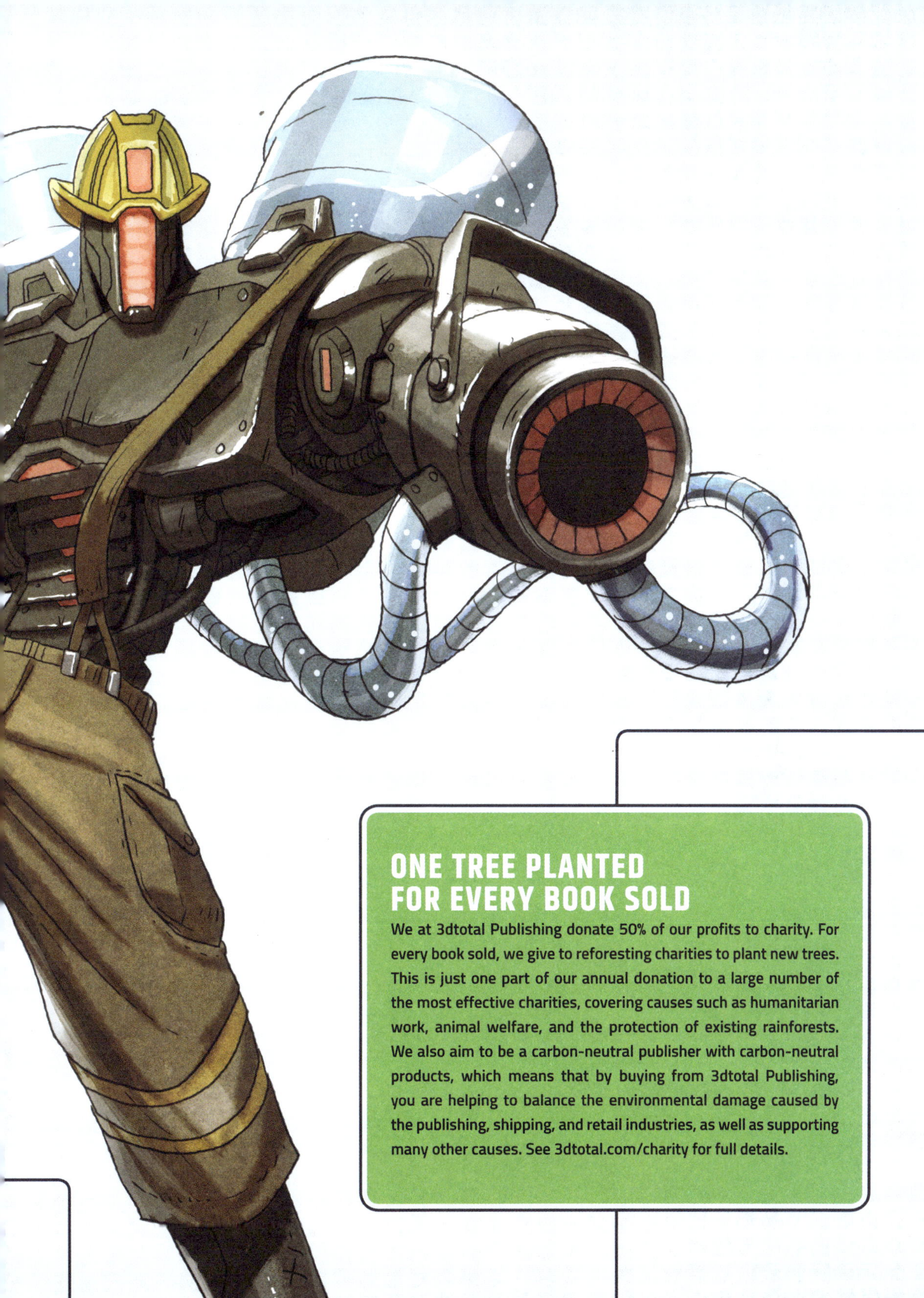

ONE TREE PLANTED
FOR EVERY BOOK SOLD

We at 3dtotal Publishing donate 50% of our profits to charity. For every book sold, we give to reforesting charities to plant new trees. This is just one part of our annual donation to a large number of the most effective charities, covering causes such as humanitarian work, animal welfare, and the protection of existing rainforests. We also aim to be a carbon-neutral publisher with carbon-neutral products, which means that by buying from 3dtotal Publishing, you are helping to balance the environmental damage caused by the publishing, shipping, and retail industries, as well as supporting many other causes. See 3dtotal.com/charity for full details.

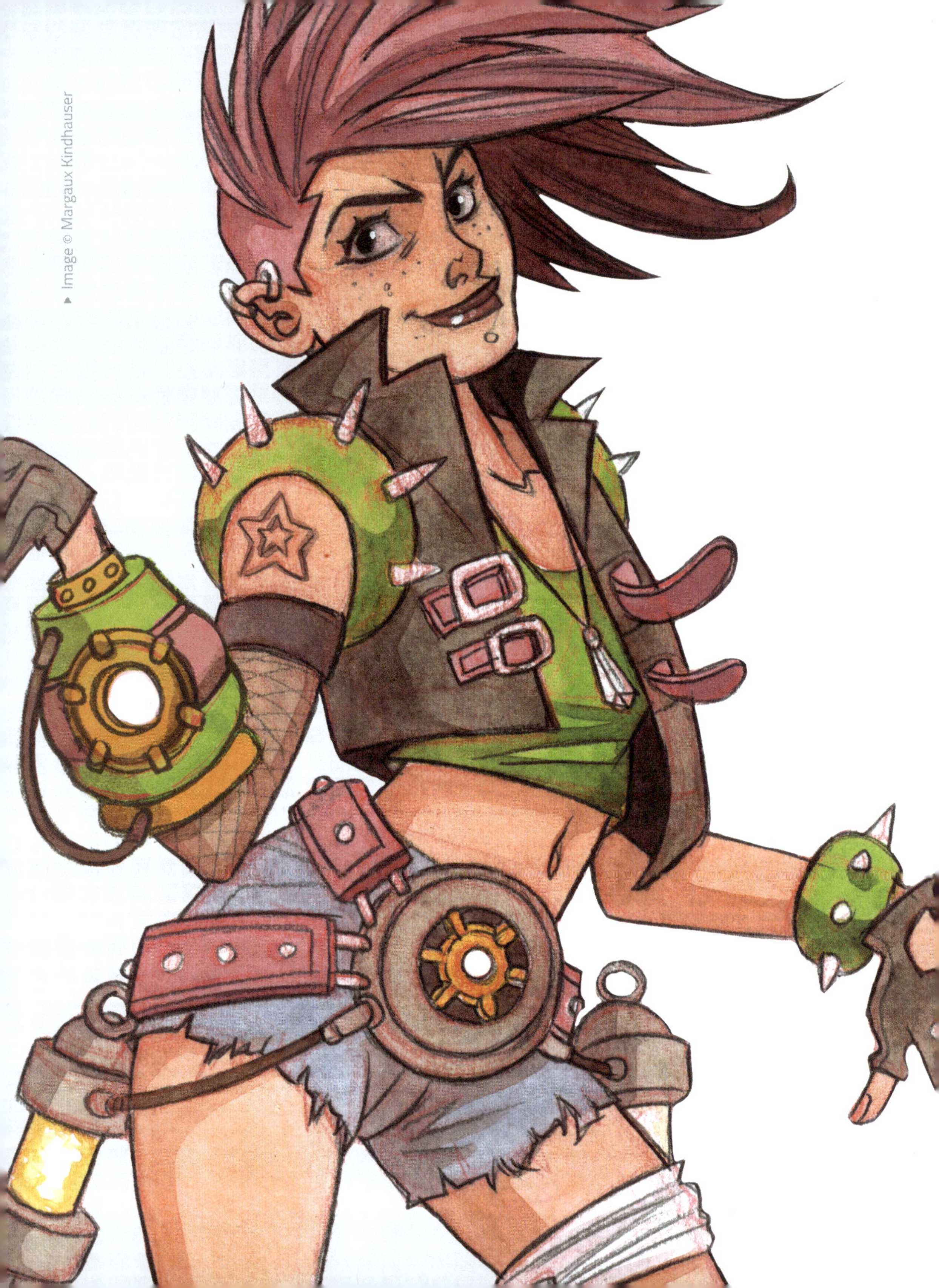

CONTENTS

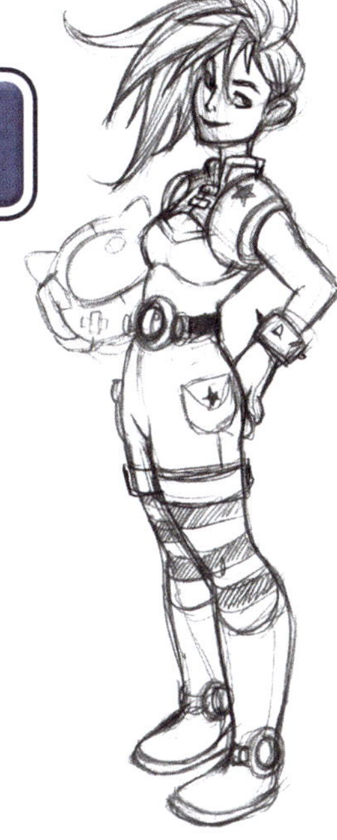

INTRODUCTION

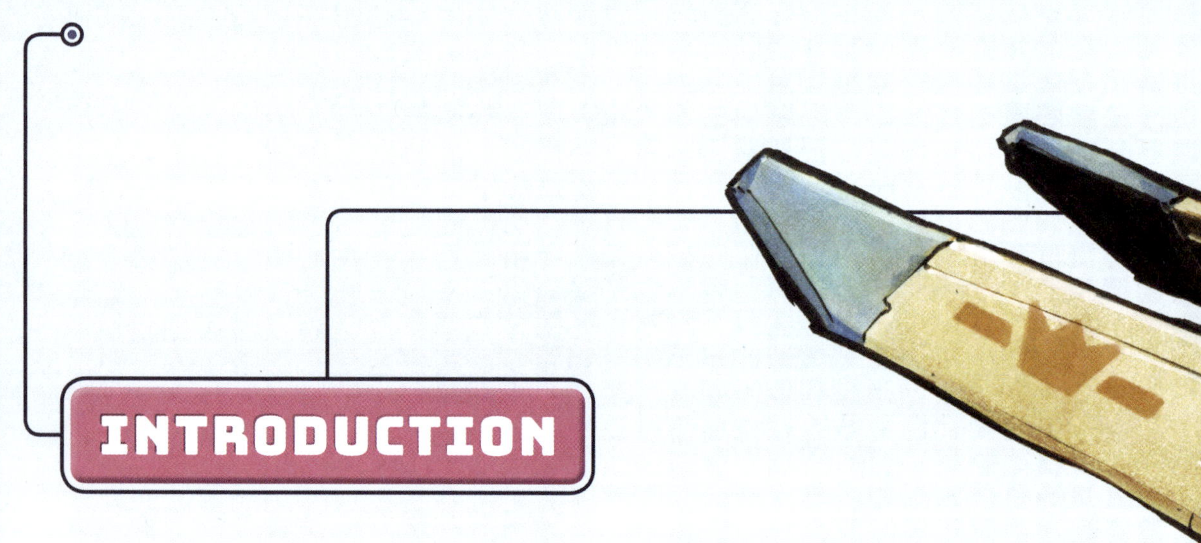

From *Star Wars* to *Stranger Things*, science fiction has captivated audiences for decades. A genre known for its sense of wonder, it invites audiences to look to the future and ask *what if…?*

As you begin your journey into drawing sci-fi crafts and characters, you are bound to come across challenges. Whether drawing incredible droids or human space travelers, high-tech space crafts or futuristic weapons, illustrating your imaginings on paper can take a lot of practice. If you find yourself losing your motivation, or just don't know where to begin, let this book be your guide.

In *Beginner's Guide to Drawing the Future*, a team of professional artists from around the world will show you how to bring your sci-fi imaginings to life. The four *Getting Started* chapters will introduce you to fundamental skills and foundations that you should try to bring into your regular drawing practice. The *Tutorials* will then demonstrate how to apply this knowledge to create your own impressive pieces of sci-fi art, with different subjects and styles to explore. Each artist shares invaluable tips and advice as they present their unique approach to the drawing and coloring process.

Whether your preference is for pencils or pens, markers or paints, take the time to try out each skill and technique before following each tutorial in turn. This will equip you with the tools and preparation you need to make your imagined futuristic sci-fi worlds a reality on the page.

PHILIPPA BARKER
EDITOR

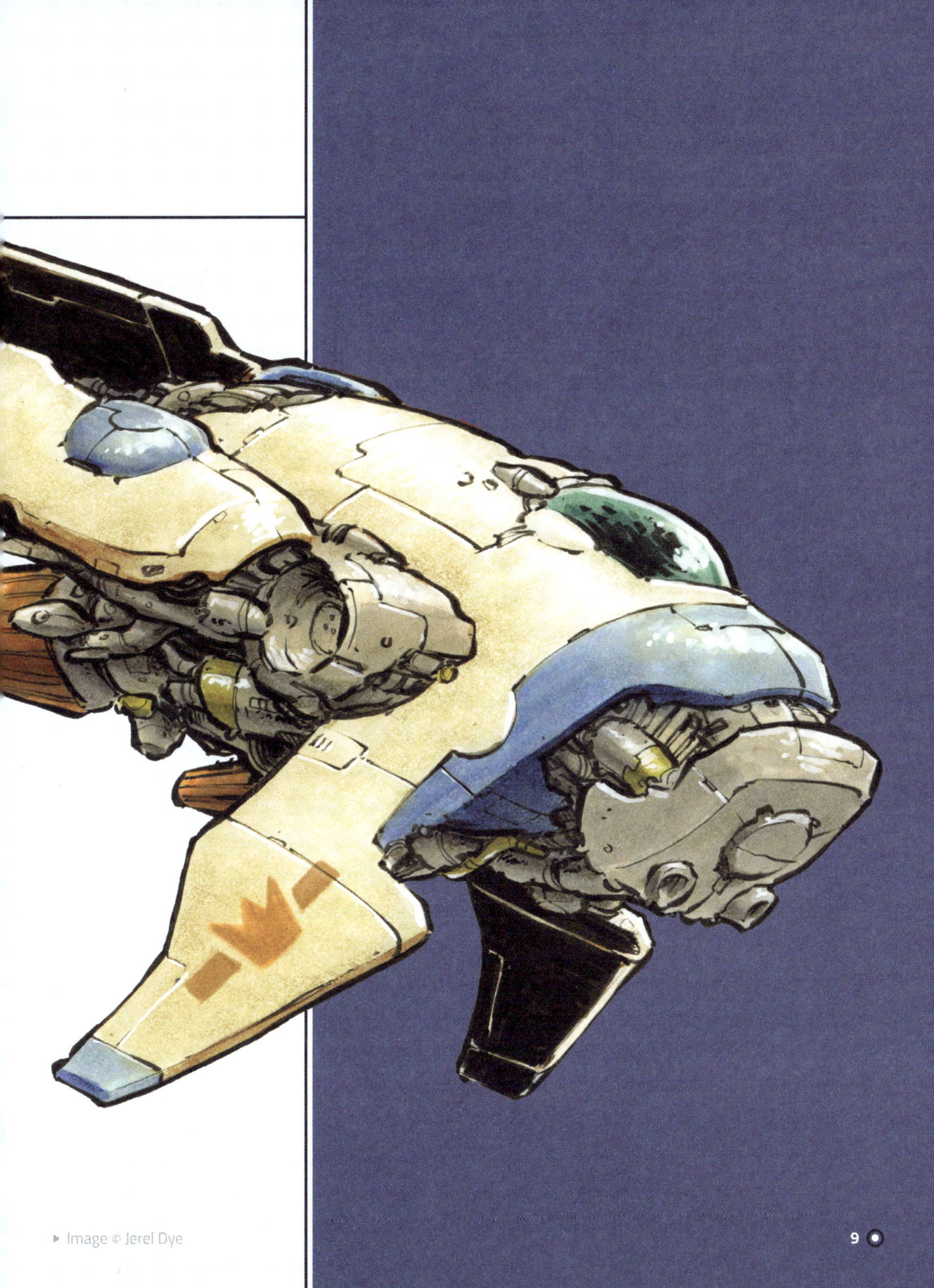

GETTING STARTED

Before you begin drawing imaginative spacecrafts and futuristic droids, it's important to take the time to learn the basics. What tools and equipment will you need to bring your ideas to life on paper? What do you need to know about the sci-fi genre? And what design techniques – from perspective to lighting – can be used to make your drawings more engaging and believable? This chapter is divided into four sections, each of which will introduce you to key principles to remember as you prepare for the tutorials that follow.

TOOLS & TECHNIQUES 12

An understanding of drawing tools, shading techniques, and basic color theory should form the foundation of your journey into drawing, whatever your subject matter. This section explores these core topics – as well as surfaces, material, and light – providing you with the knowledge needed to begin.

TOOLS & TECHNIQUES

BY VALERIO "DREELRAYK" BUONFANTINO

Before you set pencil to paper, it can help to grasp a basic understanding of the equipment and skills you will need to help make your imaginings a reality. The following chapter will explore a range of simple tools and creative techniques, including artwork that demonstrates how these can be used in a science fiction context. Arming yourself with patience and determination, experiment with each tool and technique as you go to see the effects you can create.

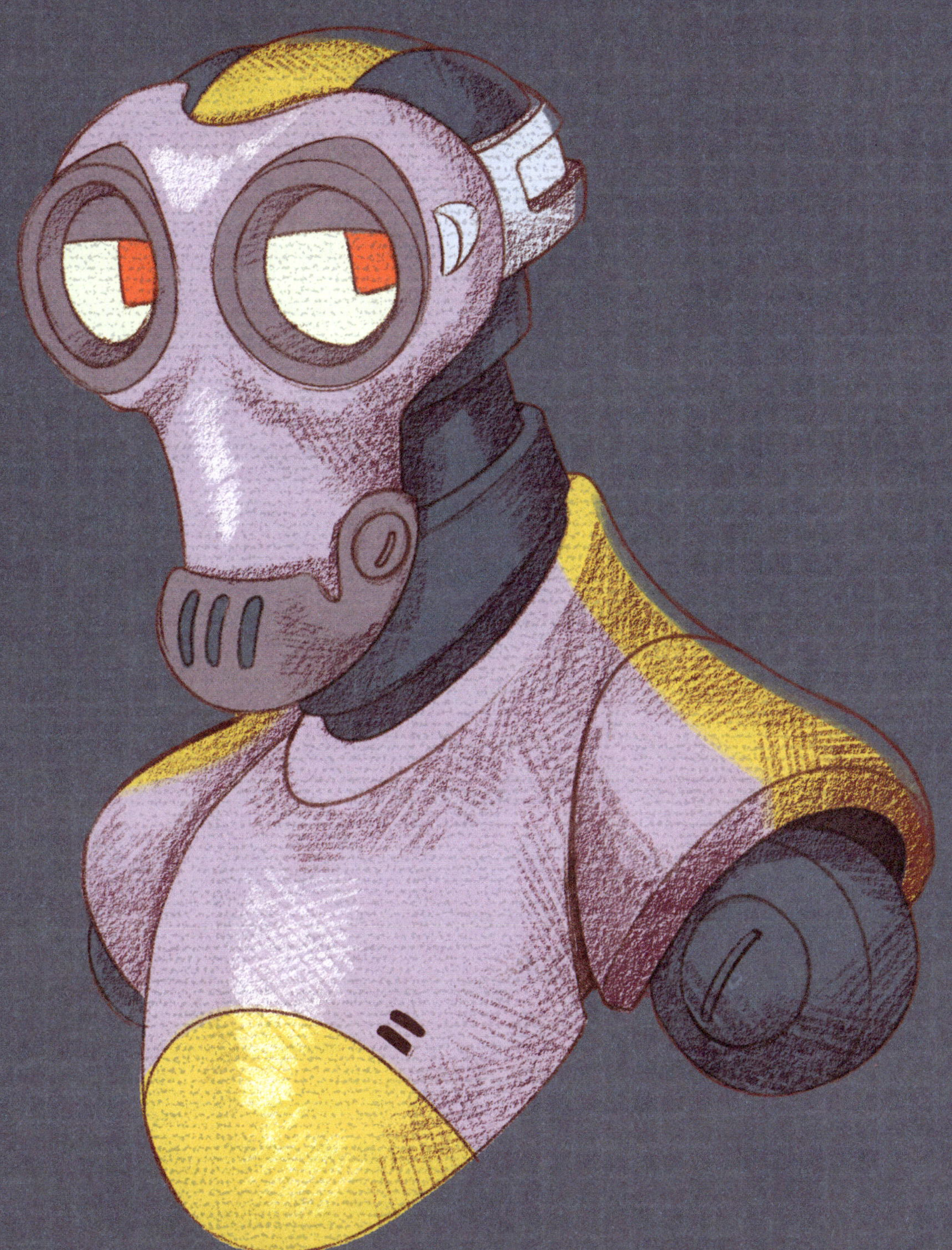

DRAWING TOOLS
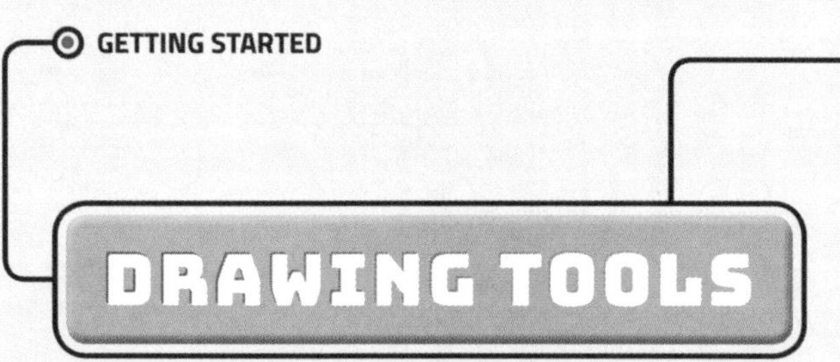

Pencils, pens, and brushes are just some of the tools available to you when you start drawing. Some are easier and more intuitive to use than others, but with a little patience and practice it's possible for anyone to create great sci-fi artwork with a range of different materials. Whether drawing in a cartoon, comic, or more realistic style, it's first important to familiarize yourself with the basic tools and how to use them.

PAPER

Choosing the right paper is a fundamental step in the creation of a drawing. There are many different types of paper, each with qualities more or less suitable for the tools you wish to work with. **Textured papers**, for example, are often preferred by artists who use watercolor. Watercolorists should take care to choose specific types of paper that are manufactured to withstand the generous use of water, and therefore work well with the watercolor technique. Other artists may prefer **smooth paper**, which is better suited for drawing fine details with pen or pencil.

It's also essential to pay attention to the quality of the paper. A good product can make a difference to the quality of the drawing.

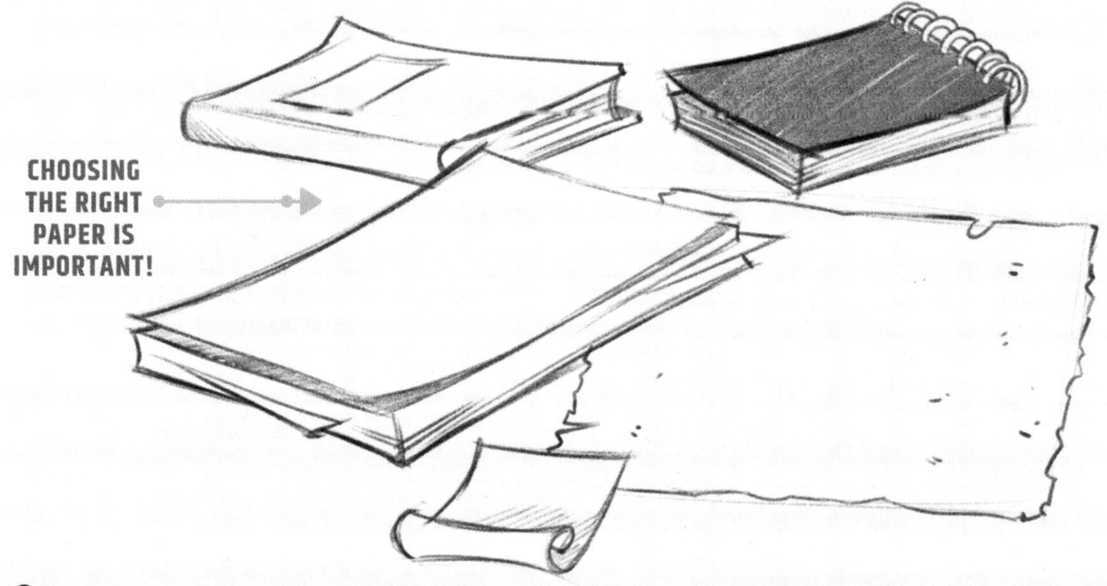

PENCILS

▸ Traditional **graphite pencils** are a good starting point for any artist. There are a variety of pencil grades to choose from, ranging from hard and light (H grades) to dark and soft (B grades). An HB pencil is a standard, versatile pencil that's neither too hard nor soft. A 2B pencil, for example, possesses a good level of darkness, without being excessively so.

▸ **Mechanical pencils** create a thin, uniform line and don't need sharpening.

▸ **Non-photographic blue pencils** are blue colored pencils that are easier to erase from a captured image or digital scan, leaving clean line art behind. This makes them an ideal tool for sketching drafts that will then be erased during the definition phase.

▸ **Colored pencils** are ideal for coloring drawings and adding final details. There are many types and qualities available that allow artists to use different drawing techniques, including water-soluble and erasable varieties.

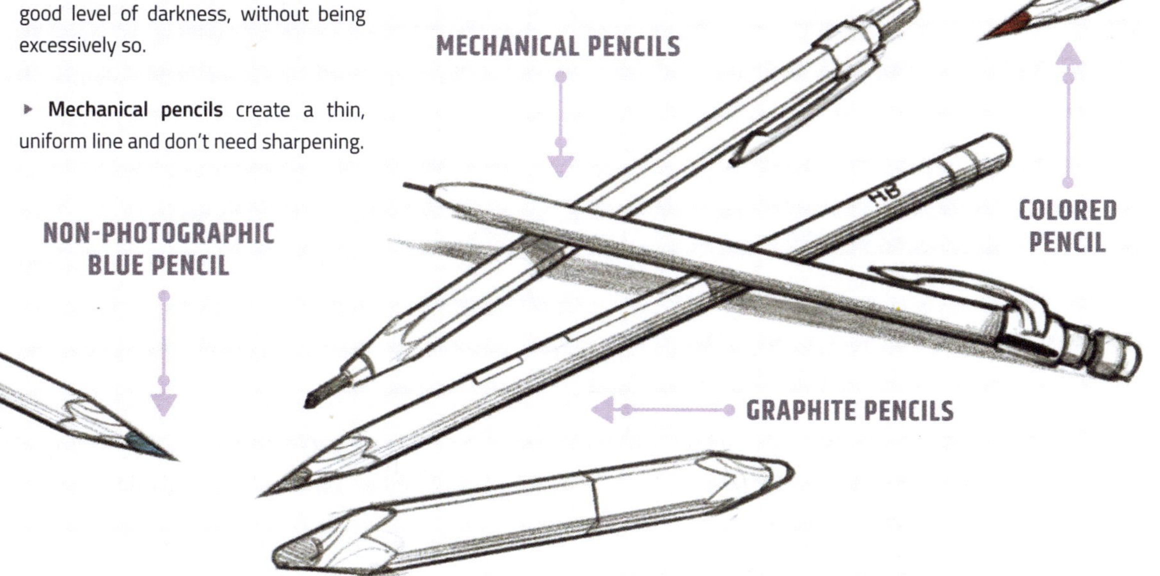

ERASERS

There are many different types of erasers, ranging from hard to soft. Take care in which one you choose, as some may not be suitable for the type of pencil you are working with.

▸ Darker pencils need to be erased by **soft plastic erasers**, while lighter pencils require **hard plastic erasers**.

▸ Another option is a **putty, or kneadable, eraser**. Being malleable, it allows you to adjust the level of erasure to your liking. Unlike a plastic eraser, it will not leave rubbings on the page, but will get dirty with use.

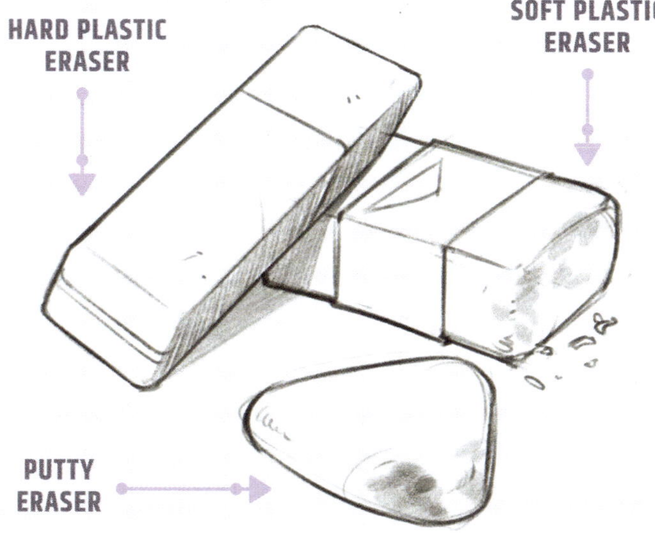

PENS

Pens are useful tools for drawing sketches as well as for fine detailing work. There are several types, each with specific characteristics:

▸ **Fineliner pens** are ideal for inking drawings and working on details, because the tips, while they come in various sizes, are typically quite thin.

▸ The **ballpoint pen** is a basic tool that is widely accessible. Not only is it useful for creating quick sketches, but it can also be used to define and add detail.

▸ **Brush pens** have a flexible felt tip, similar to brushes. They are available in various sizes and are a great tool for inking, as well as adding color.

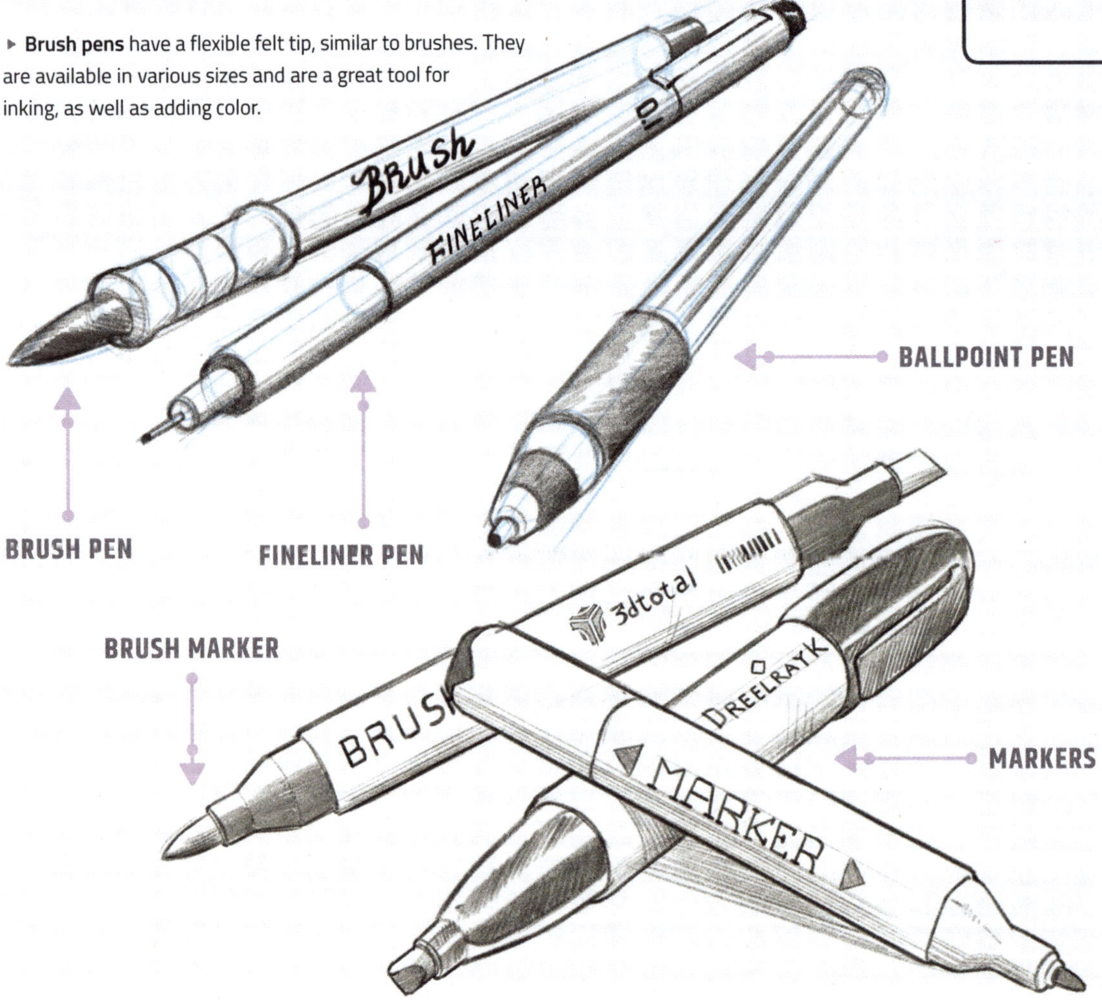

BRUSHES

Choosing the correct brush is essential for inking. It can be helpful to work out in advance what drawing technique you wish to use, as this will help determine what size and type of brush you need. As with pencils and markers, there are a variety of different types that can be used for each stage of the drawing process.

▸ **Thin, round-tipped brushes** are ideal for line art and detailing, as they allow for much finer and more accurate line control.

▸ **Flat-tipped brushes** are useful for bold strokes, large space fills, or blended effects.

▸ **Angled brushes** provide excellent line control and are therefore good for coloring at the edges. Similar to the flat-tipped brushes, they can also be used to fill large backgrounds.

MARKERS

Whether thin or thick tip, brush or chisel tip, Sharpie or Copic, there are a variety of different markers to choose from. They have many different uses, from drawing line art to coloring an image. For example, thin-tipped markers can be useful for drawing with a colored line.

Take care when using markers, as they are practically impossible to erase. Errors can sometimes be covered with brushstrokes or correcting pens.

▸ Markers can either be **water-based** or **alcohol-based**, both of which are useful for creating intense color fills or simple shades.

▸ **Brush markers** have a flexible tip, similar to that of a brush, which allows you to create a wide range of mark-making. They come in a wide variety of colors and are made to be blended. Try layering colors and experiment with the effects you can create.

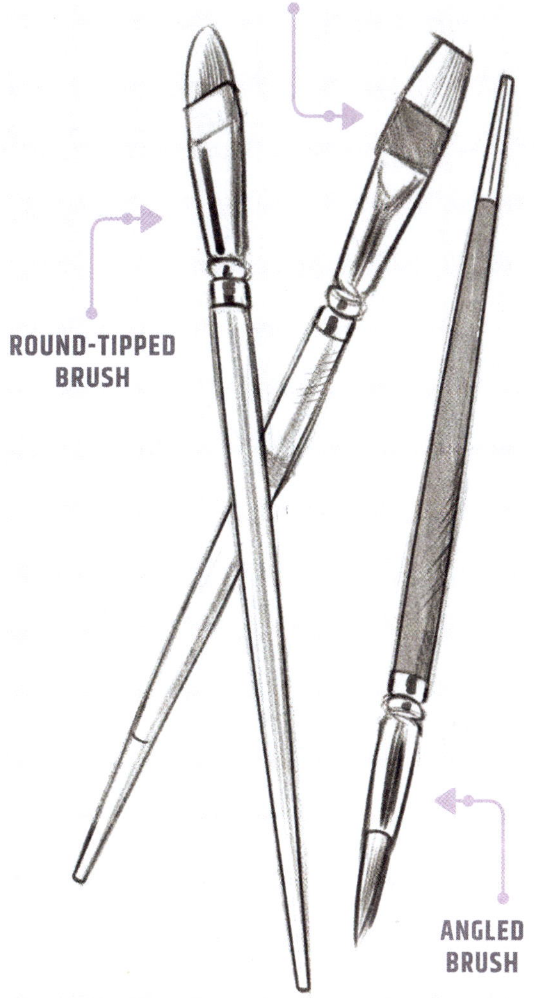

BRUSH MAINTENANCE

The brush is a very delicate tool and requires careful drying and storage to preserve its condition. A damaged brush won't work as well as one that has been looked after.

PENCIL TECHNIQUES

The pencil is an extremely versatile tool. Whether you want to create a clean-lined drawing or wish to color it in, there will be a pencil suitable for the task. The following techniques can be achieved with either classic graphite pencils or colored pencils. They could also be combined with the use of other tools – such as pens, brushes, or markers – to produce interesting effects and styles.

SKETCHING

Pencil is the perfect tool for creating quick sketches that act as rough first drafts of a drawing. These sketches can be used as basic structures that are later erased during the clean-up phase. Sketching is useful for creating quick, approximate ideas that don't waste time on attention to detail. Don't be too neat or meticulous at this stage, but give free rein to your creativity.

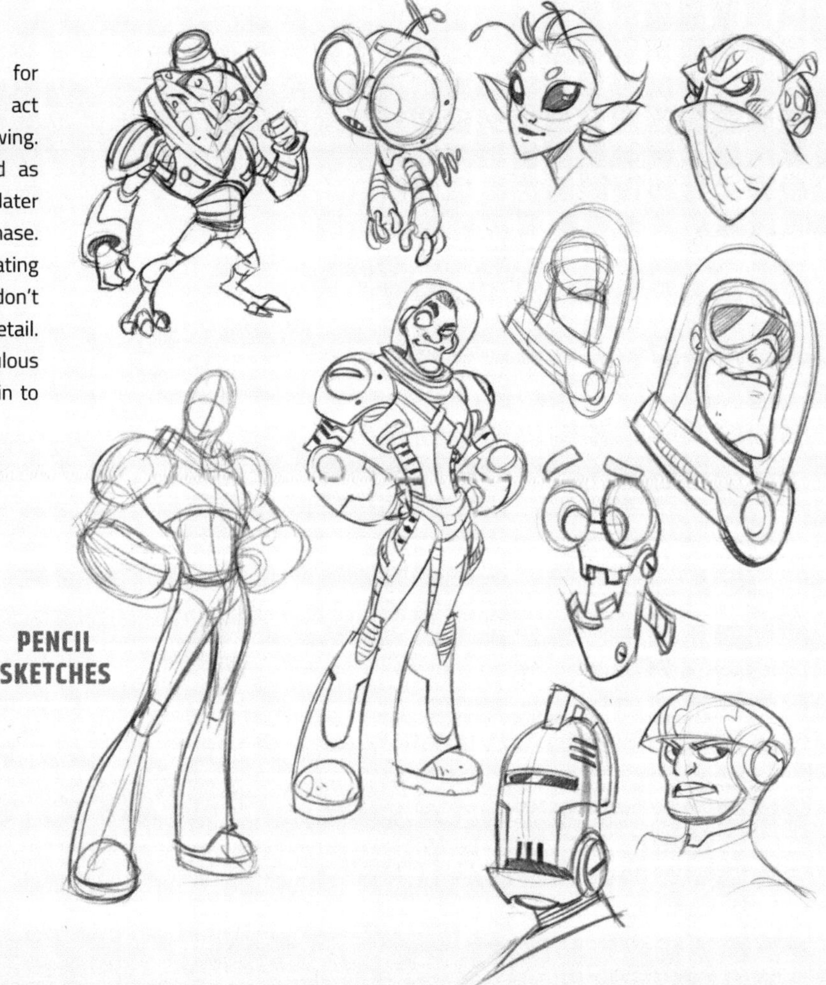

PENCIL SKETCHES

CLEAN LINE

To create precise, clean **line work**, it's necessary to start from a clear, well-structured sketch that can be erased before the cleaning-up phase. Start by drawing a faint sketch using a 2H or HB pencil, taking care not to be too heavy-handed with the line. Next, use a darker pencil, such as a 2B, to finalize the line with the utmost attention to detail. Try to be as precise as possible, as too many erasures can dirty the paper and give the drawing a messy look.

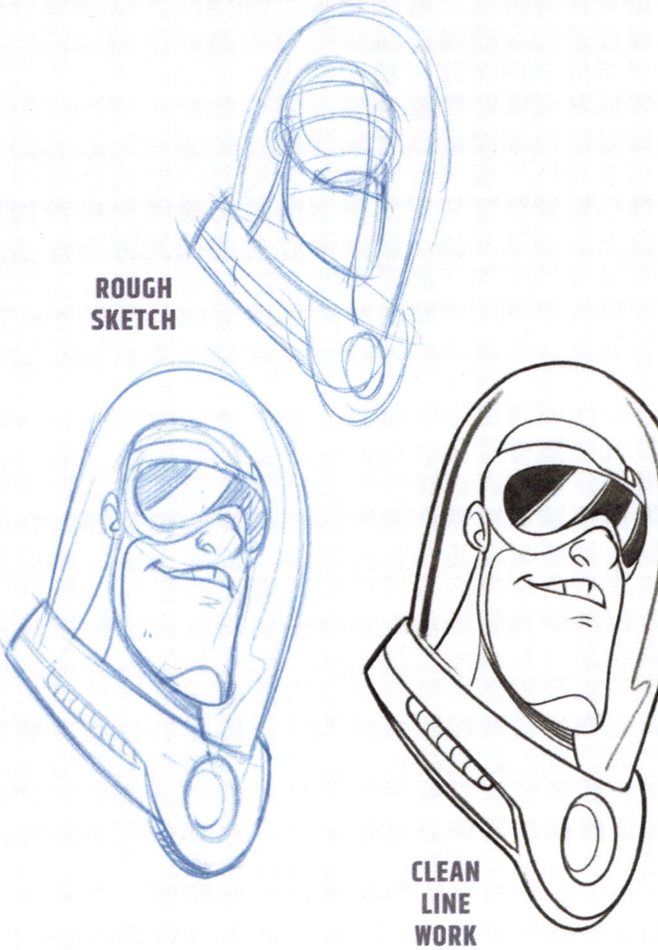

SCRIBBLING

Small circular motions, similar to a child's scribbles, can be used to produce a variety of interesting effects, both for creating shadows and conveying particular textures. Applying a slightly greater pressure on the paper, draw small, very dense scribbles to create the look of darker shadow areas. Next, use a lighter pressure to draw sparser, fainter scribbles for the lighter areas. If you have difficulty controlling the pressure of the line, try changing your pencil for one that is darker or lighter, depending on the areas you are working on.

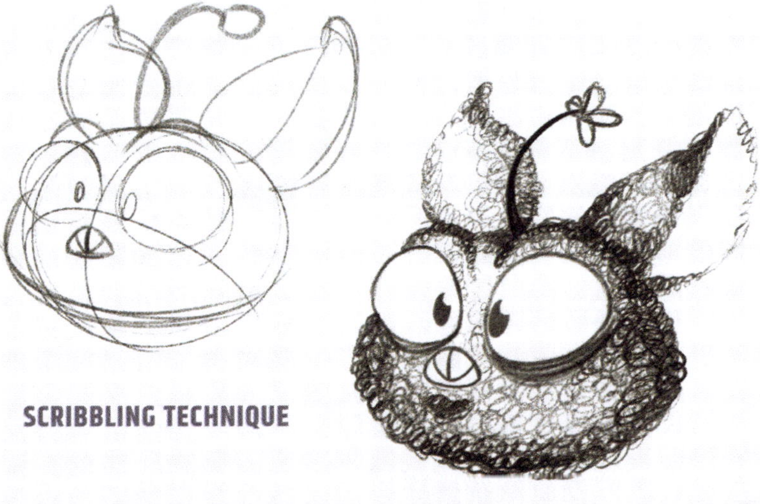

ROUGH
SKETCH

CLEAN
LINE
WORK

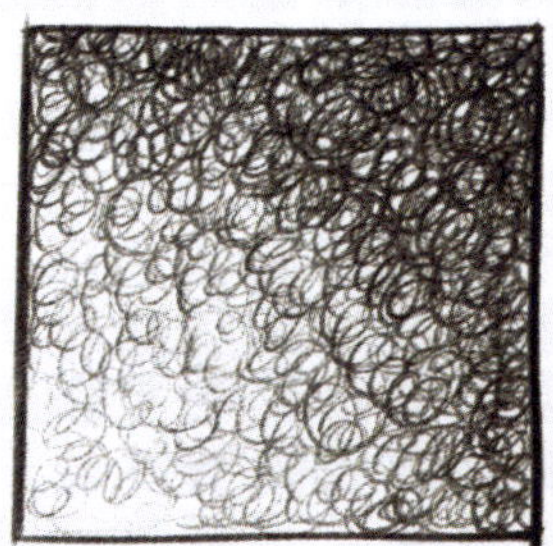

SCRIBBLING TECHNIQUE

HATCHED SHADOWING

Hatching is a useful technique for creating the illusion of light and shadow with straight or curved parallel lines. Draw lines closer together to create dark values, or farther apart to create highlights and midtones. Applying more pressure on the pencil will thicken the lines for added darkness. **Cross-hatching** lines on top of one another, in different directions, will allow you greater control over the light and dark areas. Cross-hatch and layer more lines at the darker points and fewer in the lighter areas.

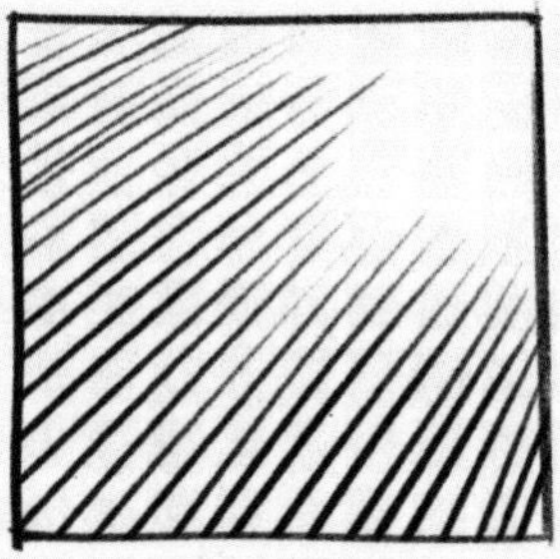

HATCHING

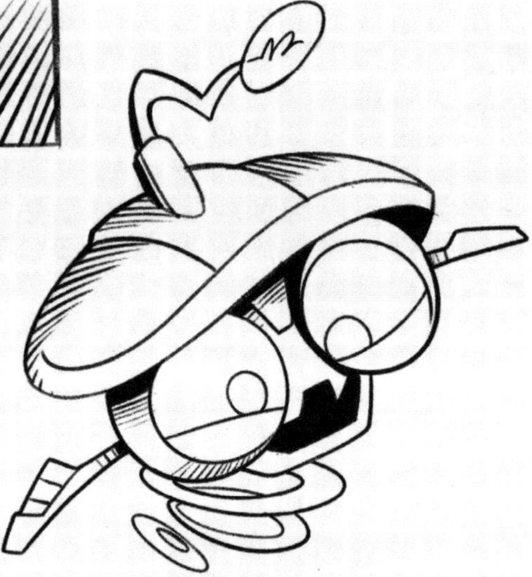

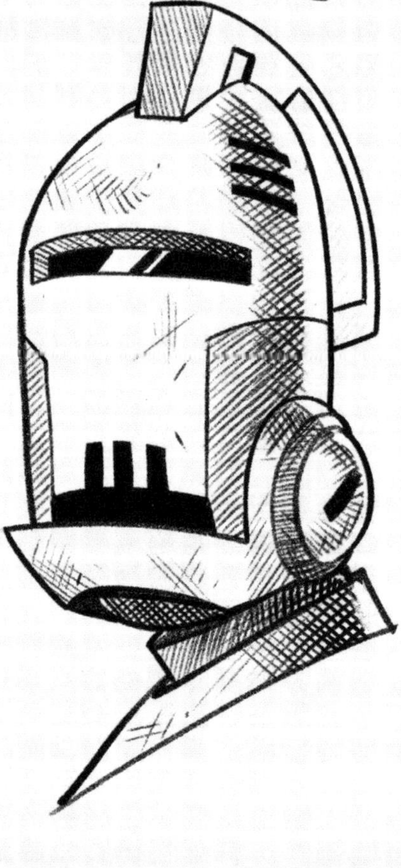

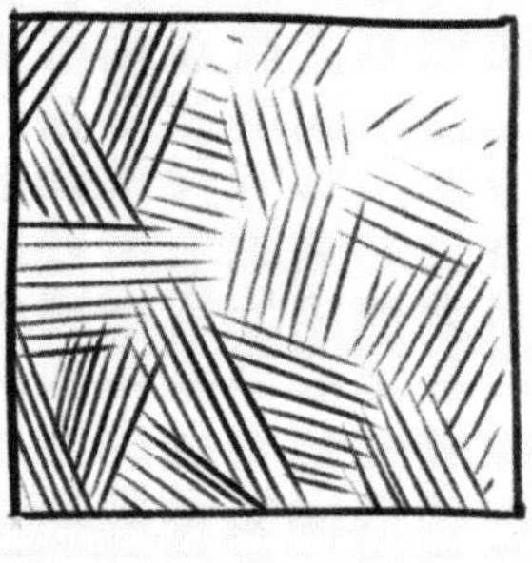

CROSS-HATCHING

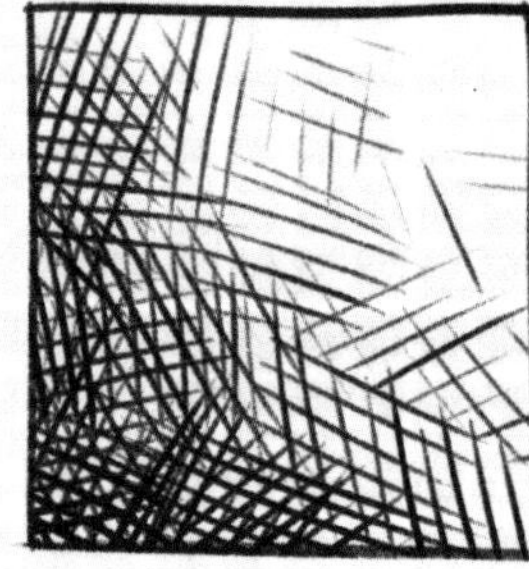

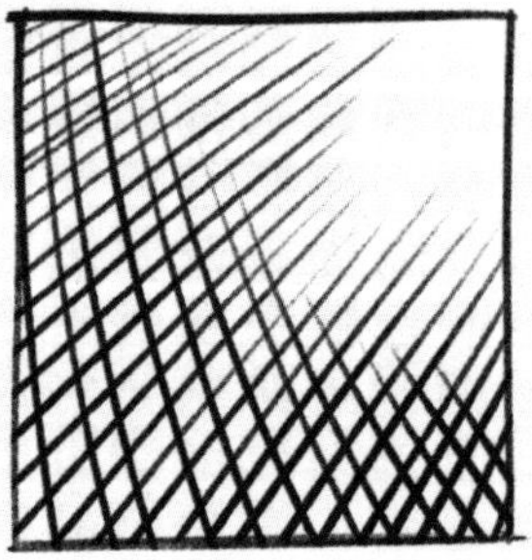

SMOOTHED SHADING

This technique requires a little more patience and pencil-pressure control. Hold the pencil at a slight angle and ensure the tip is not too sharp. Start from the darker tones and apply a good amount of pressure on the paper, before moving toward the lighter areas as you ease the pressure. Pay close attention to the direction in which you move your hand. Always try to draw on the external side of the drawing without touching it with your palm; otherwise you could blur the lines and smudge or dirty the work.

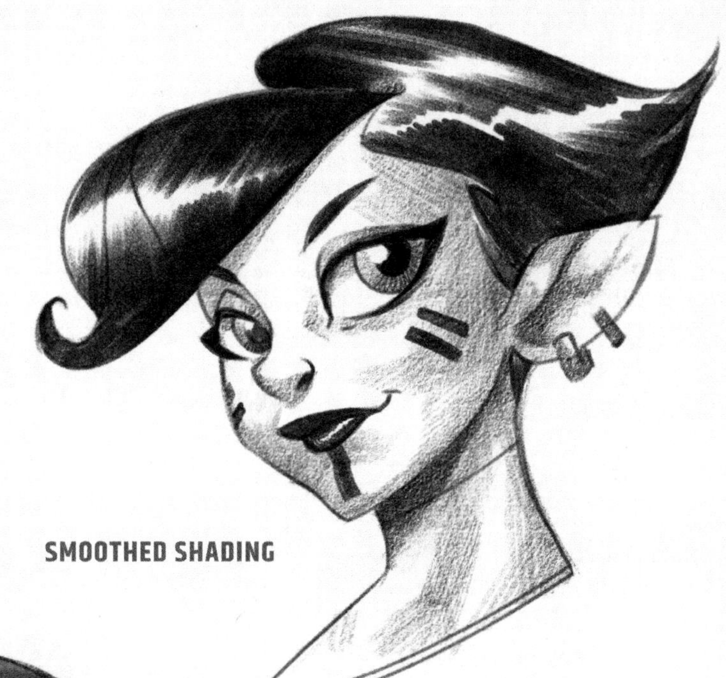

SMOOTHED SHADING

FINGER BLENDING

This technique is useful for larger drawings. Start by creating a lightly shaded area, perhaps with a soft, greasy pencil, being careful not to use too much pressure. Run a finger over the stroke, from the darkest area to the direction in which the shadow lightens. Your hands may become very dirty, but with the right control and care so as not to smudge the rest of the drawing, you can achieve soft, nuanced effects.

FINGER BLENDING

MARKER TECHNIQUES

Markers are a great tool for any artist to have in their toolkit, whether used to create vivid colorful tones or for inking purposes. Knowing how to use them well can make for eye-catching illustrations. They come in a wide range of colors, from the most subtle, muted tones to bright, even fluorescent, shades. While you don't need too much preparation to use them, some stroke control is required to avoid making mistakes that can prove very difficult to erase.

TECHNIQUES

▸ Inking

▸ Hatching

▸ Flat shadowing

▸ Shading

▸ Full black and white

▸ Water marker shades

INKING

Inking with markers is a technique that requires attention to detail and good line control. It's a useful technique for making a drawing cleaner and neater, while achieving dynamic, varied line weights. Inking allows you to make a focal point of certain areas and can even accentuate the highlights and shadows. Fine-tipped markers will create thinner lines, while thicker-tipped markers can be used to highlight certain areas, such as outlines. A chisel-tipped marker is useful for filling in any parts that require the heavy use of black.

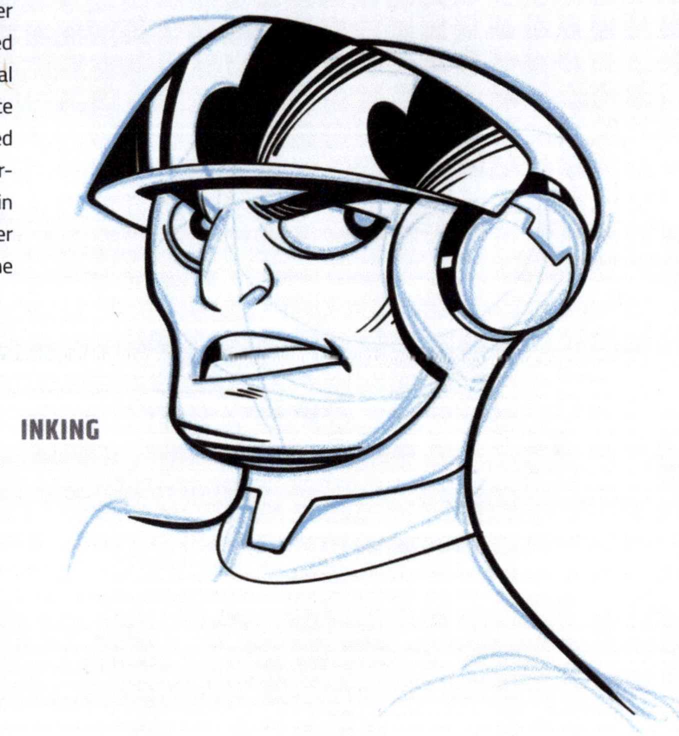

INKING

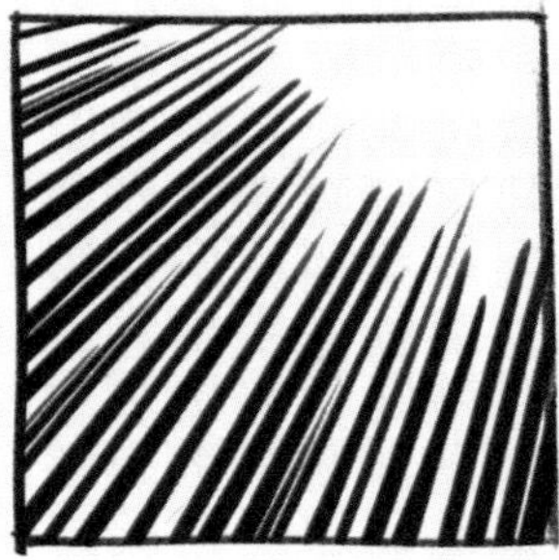 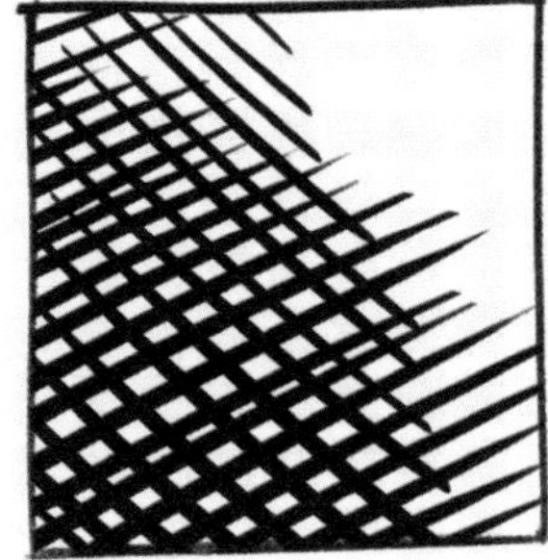 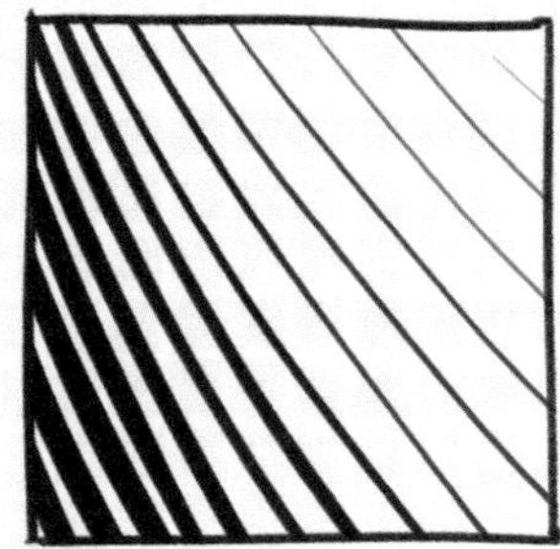

HATCHING WITH MARKERS

HATCHING

As with pencil, you can use markers to achieve tonal variations through the use of parallel or crisscrossing strokes. A lighter pressure will make the line less thick, but unlike pencil, the intensity of the stroke will remain the same. To make the tonal change more evident, try to decrease the thickness of the stroke as you get closer to the lighter area. Experimenting with different hatching techniques before you start will allow you to train your hand to maintain the desired pressure.

FLAT SHADOWING

Flat shadows can be created by overlapping several layers of shade on a flat base. The more layers you add, the darker the tone will become. Start with a light shade of gray that allows you to darken areas as needed. If you start with a gray that is too dark, you won't have maximum control of the hue. Take care to wait a few minutes between moving from one layer to the next, as application on a color that is still wet could cause unexpected shades.

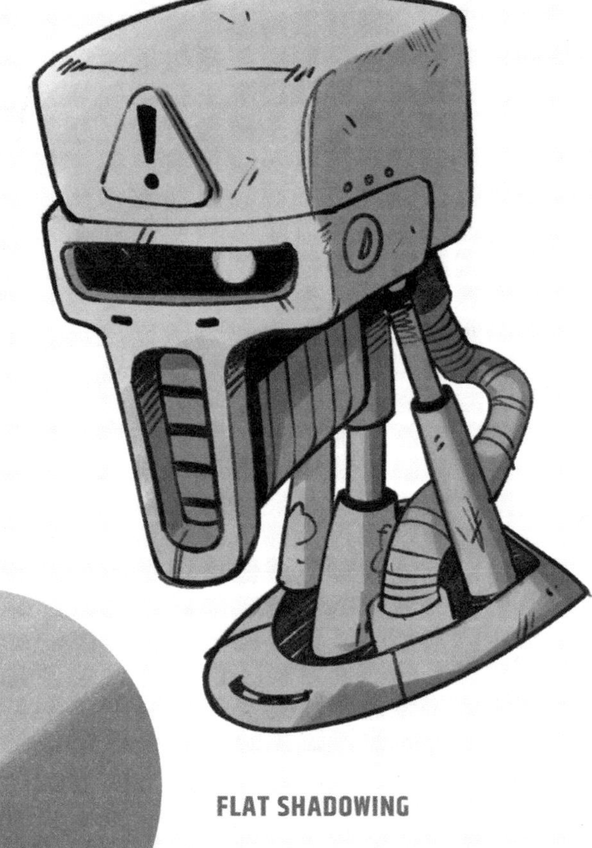

FLAT SHADOWING

SMOOTH GRADIENTS

To achieve shading with a smooth, uniform texture, use markers with different tones, transitioning from the darkest to the lightest. Start with the lightest tone, then as you get closer to the areas to be darkened, change to a slightly darker marker, until you reach the desired level of darkness. To obtain smoother gradients, apply each shade while the previous layer is still wet, allowing the two colors to blend more evenly. This technique requires a little practice to attain a smooth, gradual finish.

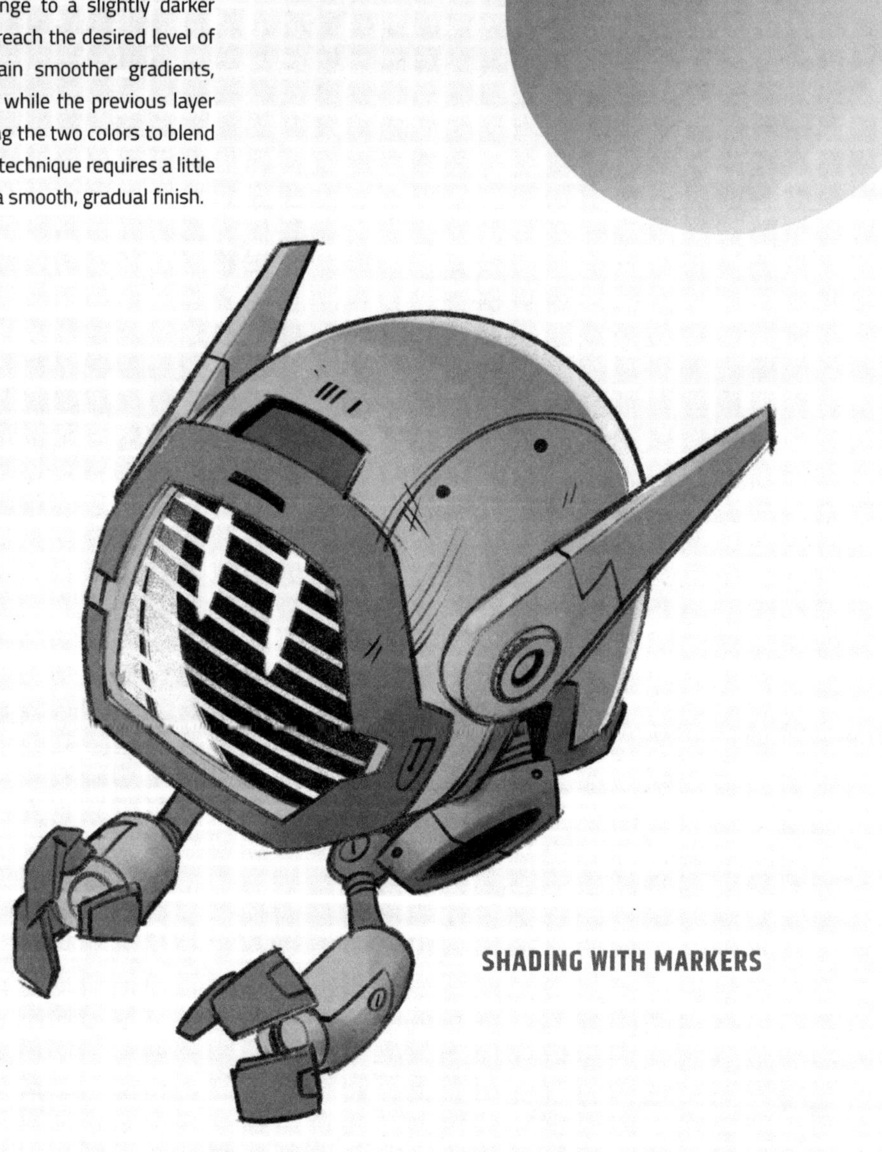

SHADING WITH MARKERS

FULL BLACK AND WHITE

With clever control of lights and shadows, it's possible to create drawings without the use of tones and blending, simply alternating large black areas with large white spaces instead. If you don't wish your illustration to contain white, this technique can be used with flat colors instead to create a dark, intense atmosphere. With an informed use of lights and shadows, you can create an ominous or mysterious mood in your illustrations.

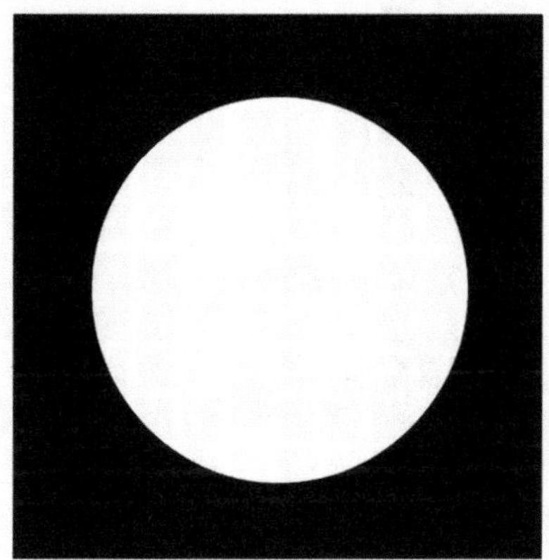

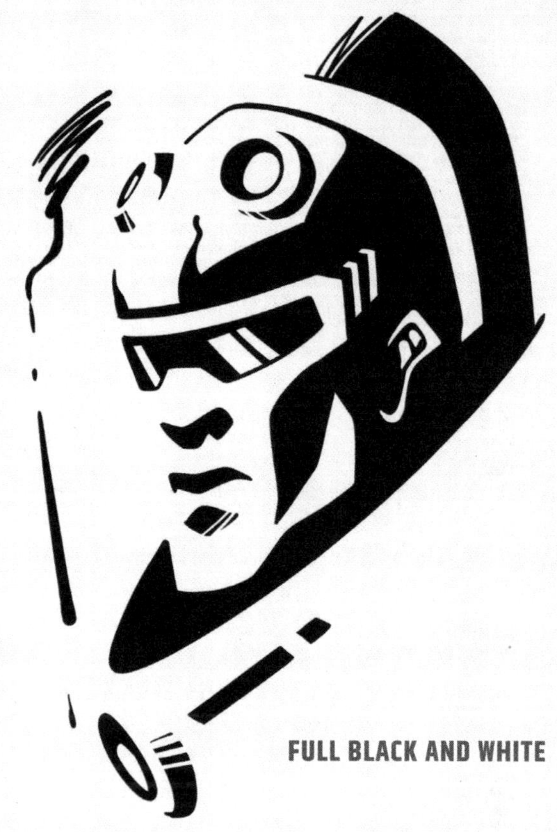

FULL BLACK AND WHITE

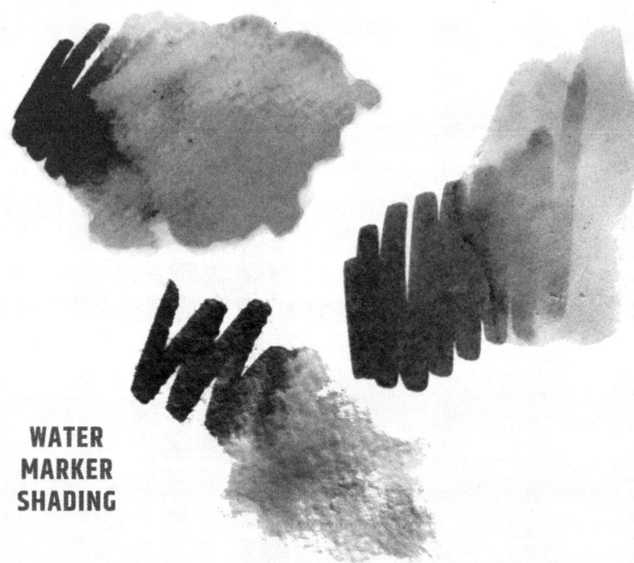

WATER
MARKER
SHADING

WATER-MARKER SHADING

Water markers allow artists to create fluid effects and varied colors. Start by making shades using different tones, then pass a thin layer of water over them using a wet brush. This will allow the strokes to blend together, producing effects similar to watercolors. If you want to add sharp tone overlaps, remember to wait until the previously colored surface is completely dry to avoid unwanted shades or smudging. This technique is very useful for giving an illustration a more painterly look, but it can also be used in combination with other techniques to obtain original effects.

SURFACES, MATERIALS, & LIGHT

The ability to realistically capture various surfaces and materials, plus different lighting, will help you to take your sci-fi designs to the next level. While there are certain materials that are typical to the science-fiction genre, factors such as lighting or wear-and-tear will determine how you draw these. Making time to research reference imagery to inspire your designs will equip you to reproduce a variety of effects.

SURFACES & MATERIALS

CHROME

Chrome is a shiny material often found on parts of sci-fi weapons and spaceships, or in sci-fi environments. As chrome is very reflective, before putting pencil to paper you must first identify the light source and surrounding environment. Chrome reflects nearby objects and light, like a mirror. These reflections will be deformed by the shape of the chrome surface, and can be rendered using clear, defined values and colors. Any part of the chrome surface that is facing a light source should be drawn lighter, while any parts in shadow or reflecting solid objects will be darker.

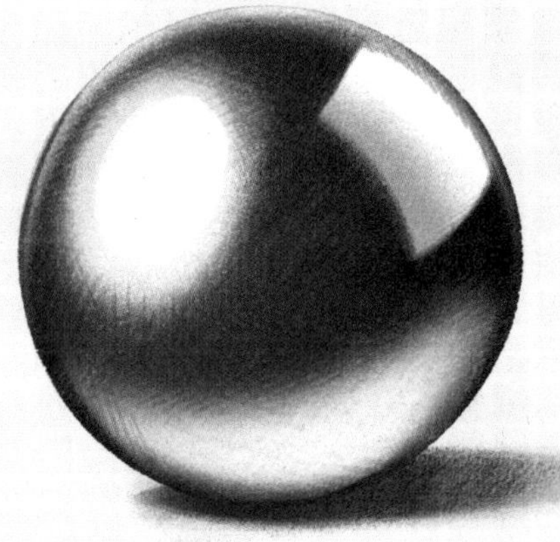

MATTE METAL

There are many different types of metals with varying levels of reflectivity. Matte metal surfaces, such as brushed steel, don't reflect their surroundings as sharply as a highly reflective chrome. The shapes reflected in the material are less recognizable and can therefore be given a softer treatment. Shading with the finger is a useful technique for giving the shades a more homogeneous look, as explained in Pencil Techniques (page 21).

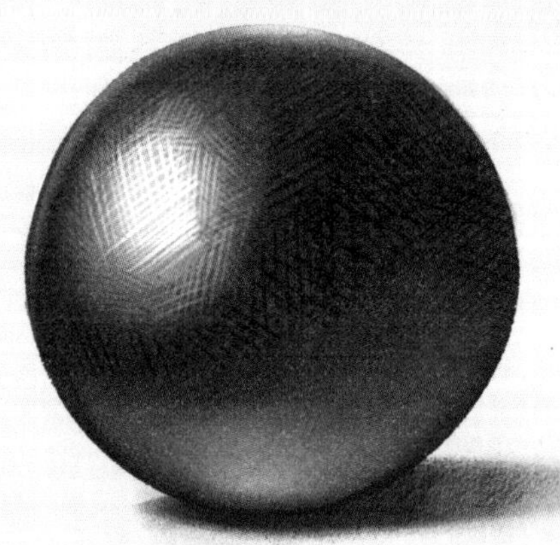

WEATHERED SURFACE

Science fiction isn't always clean, polished, and minimalistic. Sci-fi worlds can also contain weathered, dirty, or aged surfaces. To capture this, start by considering how the material would have looked originally, followed by why it is now dirty or damaged. Has it been through a fierce battle? Is it old and worn? Did it land in a muddy space swamp? This context will dictate how you draw it. For example, if it's a reflective metal, you could start by progressively reducing the brightness on some areas, then adding burns or scratches.

GLOSSY SURFACE

While a glossy surface is similar to chrome, its surface does not reflect the surrounding space like a perfect mirror. To create a shiny appearance on a material that is not excessively reflective, begin by considering the main light source, as it will be the sharpness of the light's reflection that captures the look of the surface. Although nearby objects may partially reflect on the surface, they will not be as noticeable as on chrome.

TRANSLUCENT & TRANSPARENT MATERIALS

Transparent materials, such as clear glass in the cockpit of a spaceship, allow you to see right through them. Translucent materials, such as gloopy alien materials or frosted glass, are semi-transparent but have more texture and density. A translucent surface may be glossy or textured, misty or reflective. Transparent and translucent materials allow light to pass through them, rather than reflecting it, and can often appear to assume the color of nearby objects.

SKIN

Whether human or alien skin, it's important to differentiate this fleshy surface from others. Consider the story of the character it belongs to. Is their skin smooth and young, or old and weathered? Is it scaly, hairy, or freckled? It's also worth noting that, like many organic materials, skin is slightly translucent. At the outermost areas or parts where the skin is less dense, such as the outer ear, light may be able to shine through the edges, creating a reddish tone in the case of human skin. If an alien, this could be a different color or body part entirely.

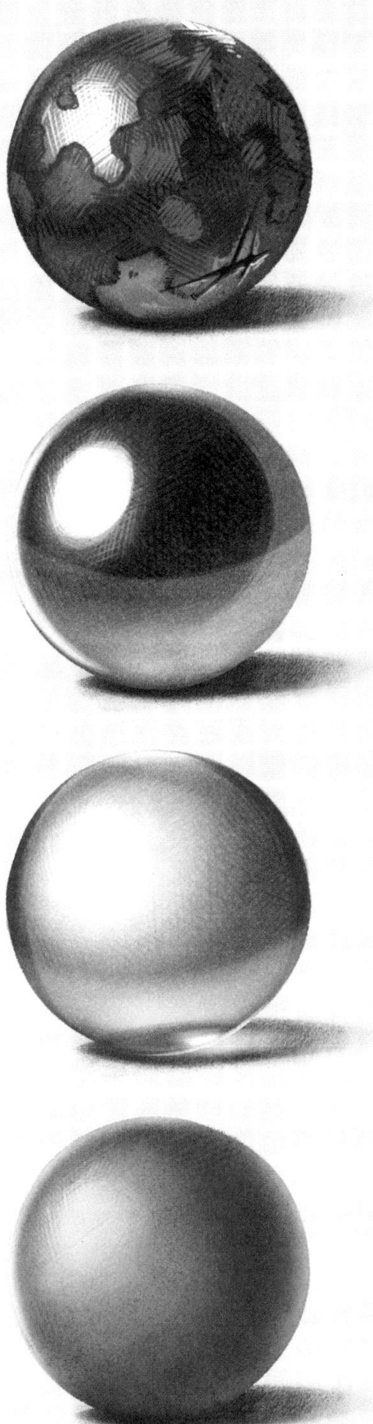

LIGHT

AMBIENT LIGHT

Ambient light is the soft, indirect light that illuminates the whole scene. It is usually sunlight, but can sometimes come from an artificial source. It shines from no particular direction and does not cast distinct shadows. Overcast light on a cloudy day is the perfect, natural example of ambient lighting.

BOUNCED LIGHT

Light will often reflect off a nearby surface and back onto an object, creating a "bounced" light that brightens the object's shadowed side. The reflected light can be dull or bright, depending on the proximity between the objects and the shininess of the reflecting surface. For example, light reflected off a glossy floor directly below an object will be much brighter than if the object were floating far above the floor. Additionally, this type of light takes on the color of the object that reflects it.

PRIMARY & SECONDARY LIGHTS

The primary light, or key light, is the single strongest directional light in a scene. It could be a bright lamp, illuminating the object and casting a strong shadow. The secondary light, or fill light, is a weaker directional light source that can highlight areas that would otherwise be in shadow. An example is faint light coming through a window. You can create engaging contrast by using primary and secondary lights with different colors. Adding a secondary light to the environment can be a useful method for creating a cooler atmosphere, or to give it a more three-dimensional and visually interesting look.

RIM LIGHT

Placing a light source behind an object in a dark environment will create a rim light around it. This will illuminate the contours of the object, producing a dramatic and mysterious look. You can decide to use one or more lights to illuminate the entire outline or just a part of the object. It's also possible to combine other lighting methods to create a variety of interesting moods and effects.

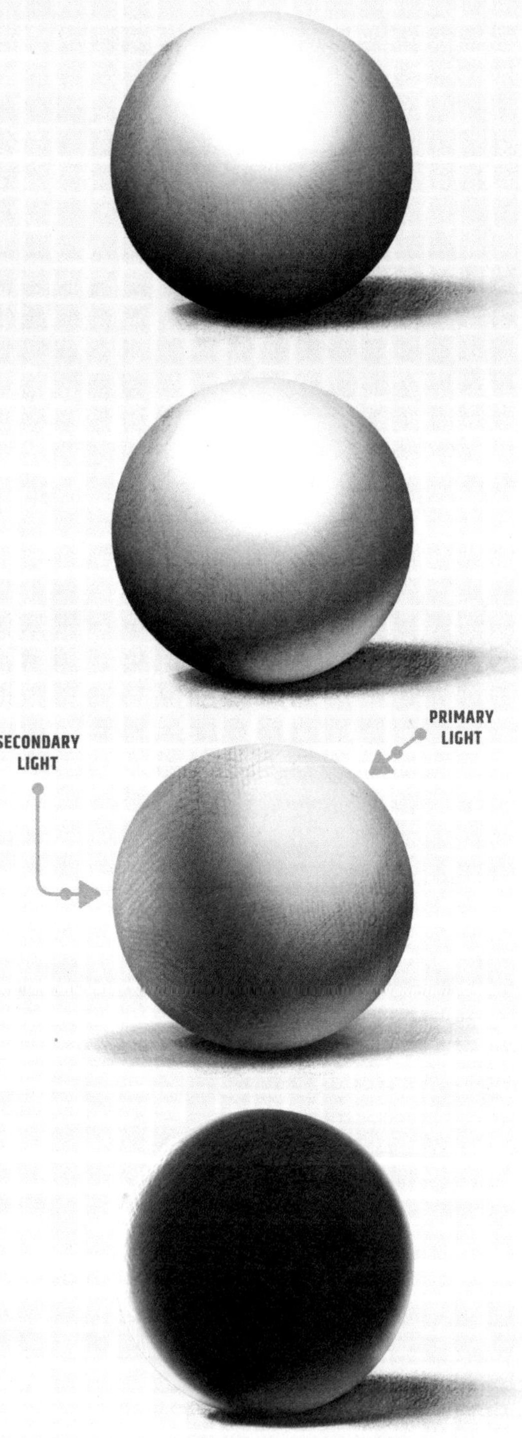

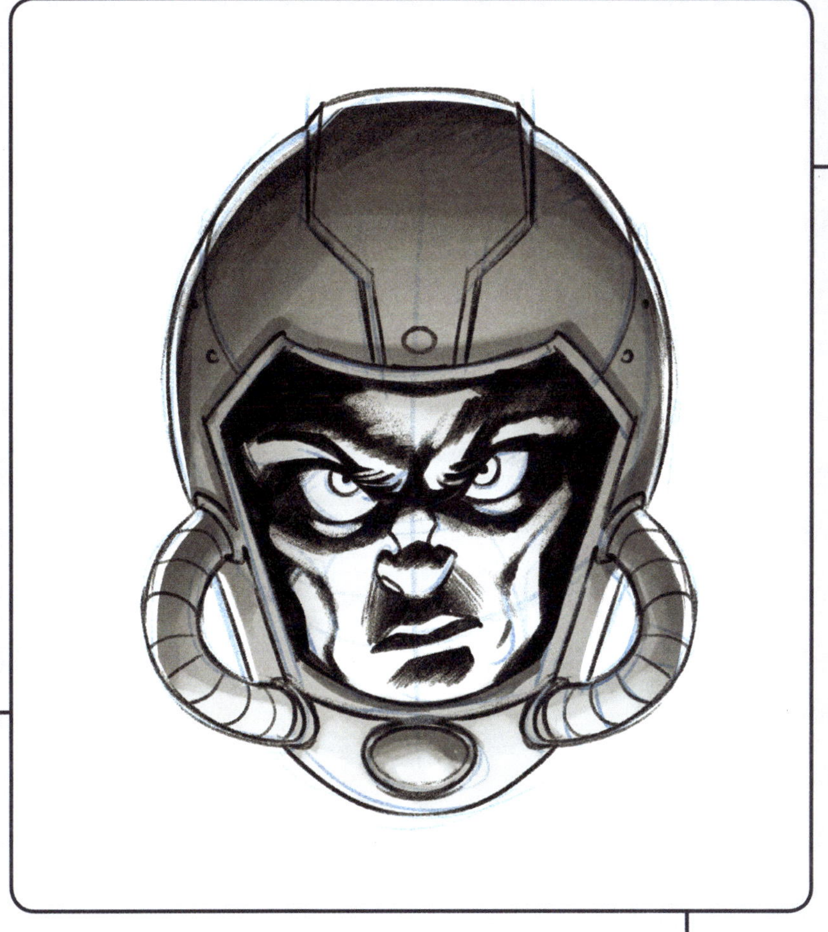

CREATING THE RIGHT MOOD

Lighting is the key ingredient for creating different atmospheres and conveying an intended mood in your sci-fi artwork. Consider carefully what feeling you want to create before choosing the type of light for your drawing. Have you ever told a scary ghost story in a dark room with a torch held under your chin? Light shining from below can represent anguish and fear, whereas a light shining down from above can inspire power and heroism.

ADDING COLOR

While excellent results can be achieved in black and white, color is an incredibly important part of bringing your sci-fi artwork to life. In addition to allowing artists to produce a myriad of different effects and material textures, it is also an ideal tool for creating various atmospheres, moods, and emotions in a sci-fi design. Certain colors communicate specific feelings. Red, for example, can express danger and fear, but also passion and love. While blue can convey peace and tranquility, it can also suggest coldness and distance. Cool colors are often used in science-fiction artwork, enhancing the cold, metallic surfaces and futuristic advanced technology.

This section will cover basic techniques for adding color to your drawings. Practice, experimentation, and patience will take you the rest of the way.

COLORED PENCILS

Colored pencils are a great choice when you want to start experimenting with color, as they are among the easiest and most intuitive tools for beginners. They still require practice, however, and it is worth choosing good-quality materials to achieve the best results. Try mixing various shades and using different graphic styles to create a wide range of results. There are also watercolor pencils, which you can blend with water to create results similar to watercolor paints.

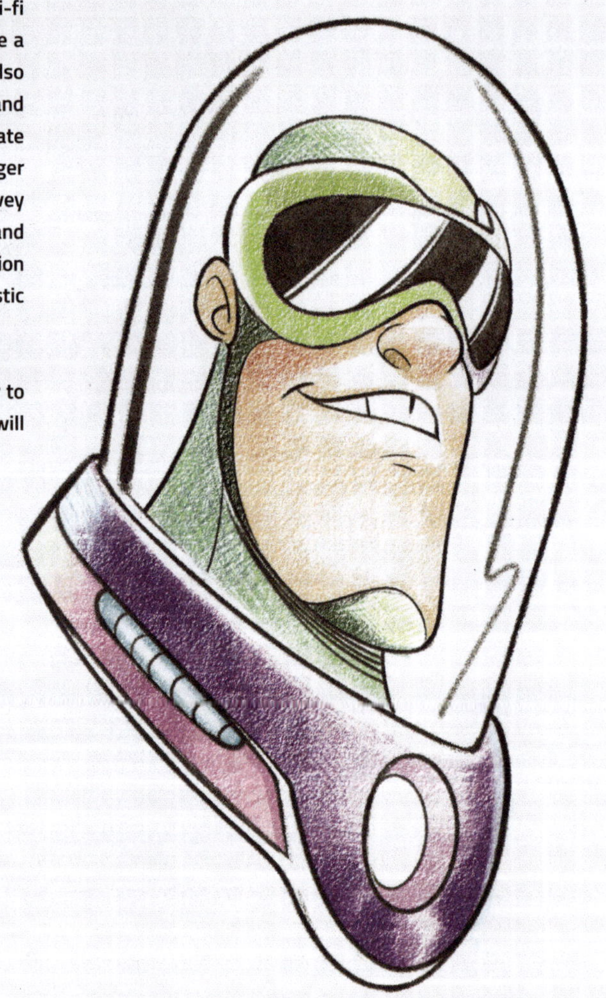

COLORED LINE ART

If you want to give your drawing a fresher, brighter look, consider using colored line art instead of black markers or inks. Fine-tipped felt-tip pens, brushes, or markers can be used for this. To ensure the line art is clearly visible, select colors that are slightly darker than the main color of the subject. If you decide to color the drawing with techniques that require the use of water, remember that you will need to color the design before inking the line art, as the water could dilute the ink and ruin the drawing.

FLAT COLORS

Coloring with flat, uniform tones is a technique that lends itself well to comic or cartoonlike styles that are not overly realistic. It's also an effective method for creating a clean, graphic look to your illustrations. Colored chisel-tip markers are perfect for this technique. Simply move the wide side of the tip smoothly in one continuous motion without lifting it off the paper. Dry colors appear lighter than when first applied, so keep this in mind when choosing shades. It's always beneficial to test out colors on a separate piece of paper before using them on your drawing.

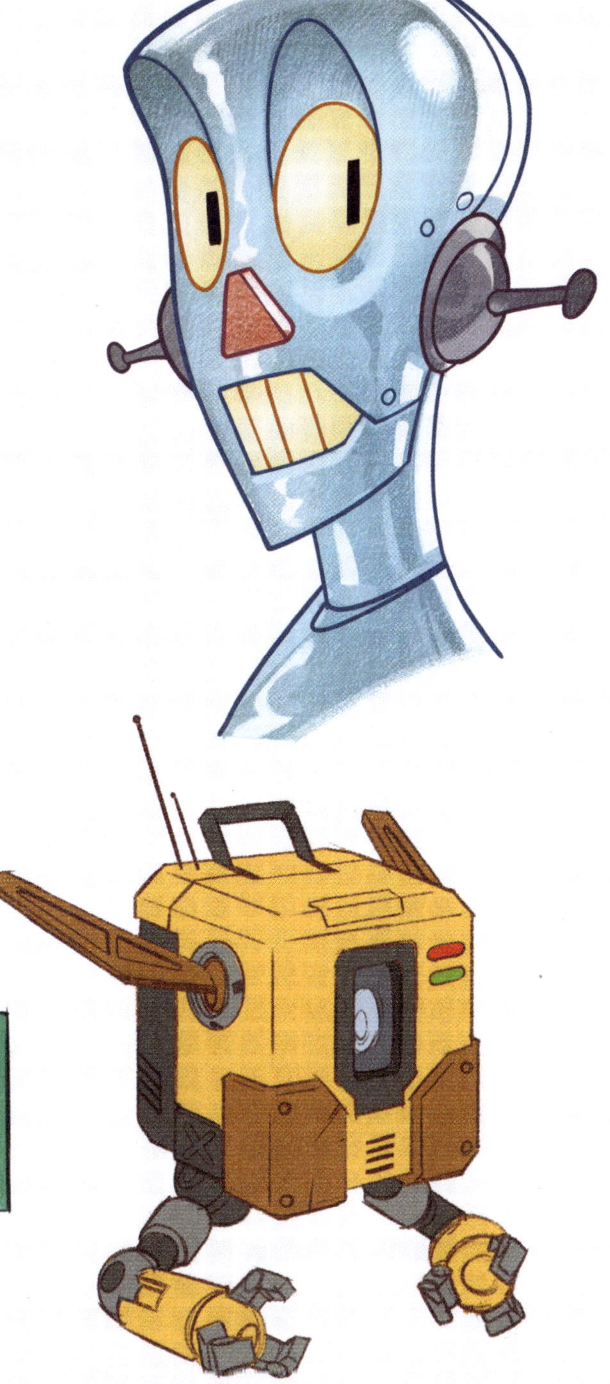

MARKER SHADES

To achieve uniform blocks of color, use multiple markers in different shades of the same color, from the lightest to the darkest. Start by coloring with the lightest shade, then as you get closer to the areas to be darkened, change the marker to one of a slightly darker shade, and so on, until you reach the desired level of darkness. Apply each shade while the previous one is still damp to allow the two colors to blend more evenly and create a smoother appearance.

WATERCOLOR PAINTS

Watercolors are a versatile tool, but require a lot of practice as you learn how to control the brushstroke. There are many different ways to use watercolors to color your sci-fi designs. Using a dry brush will create rough, scratched strokes that are great for making smudges or simulating weathered-looking surfaces. Alternatively, using a wet brush on dry paper will allow you to produce flat, clear colors. Applying a wet brush on wet paper will open up the possibility for even more interesting and nuanced colorful effects, which can prove very useful for creating scenic sci-fi effects and ethereal shades.

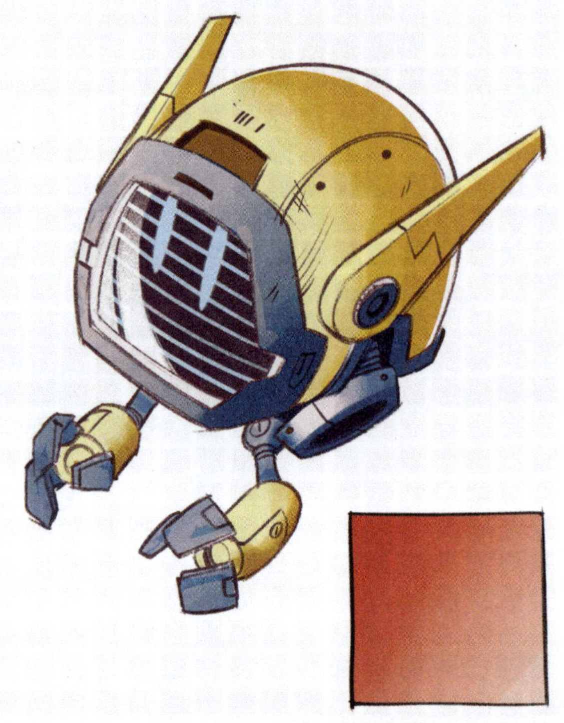

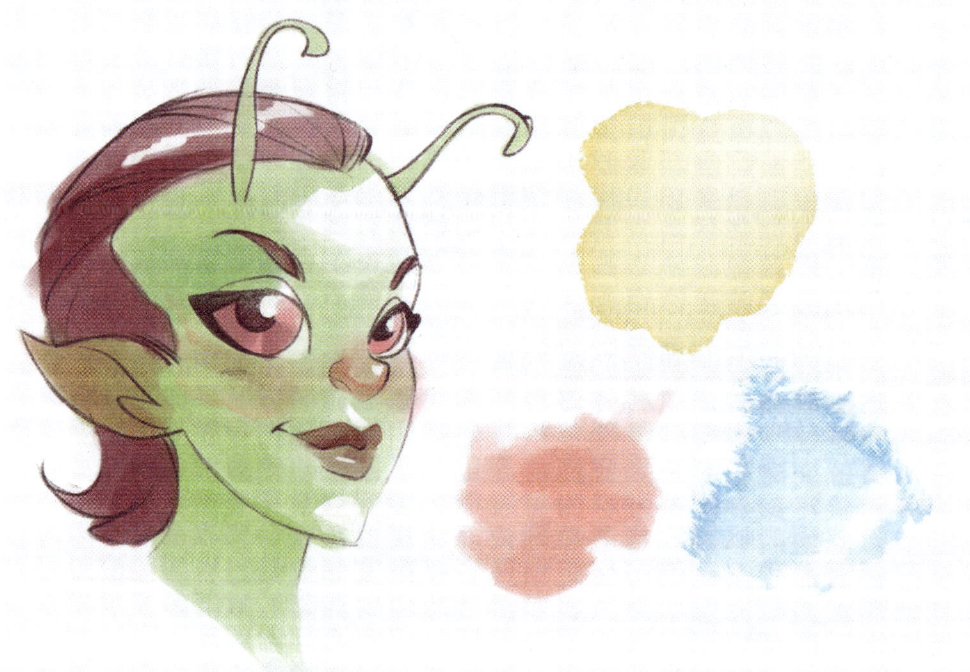

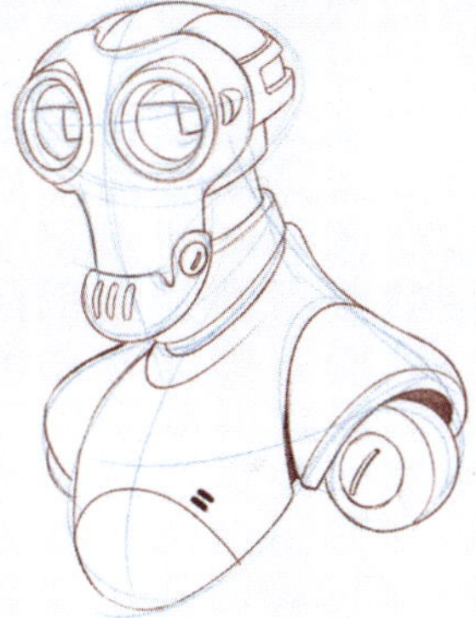
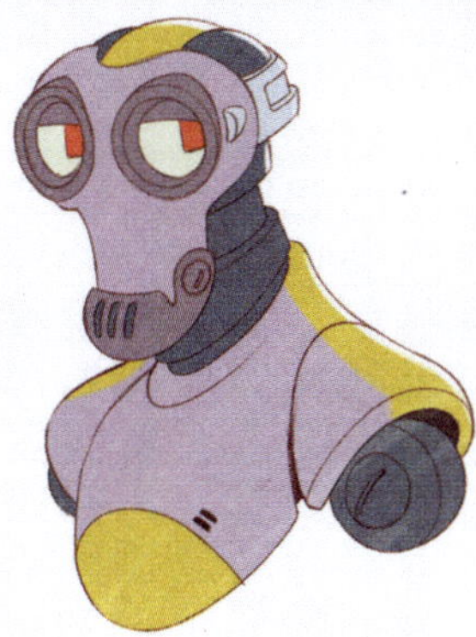
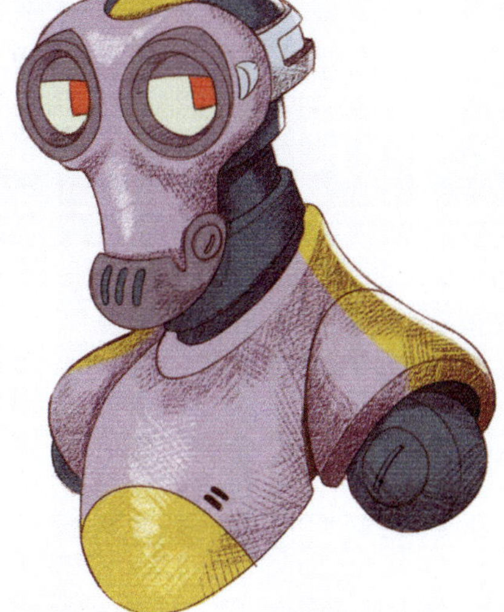

COMBINED TECHNIQUES

Make time to experiment with various coloring techniques using different tools. The combinations are endless! For example, you may choose to use markers on textured paper to produce flat color bases, then create the different shades using colored pencils on top to accentuate the roughness of the paper, creating a visual contrast between the basic flat colors and the rougher shadows.

CHOOSING A COLOR PALETTE

Resist the temptation to use every color available. Limiting yourself to making precise, accurate color choices will lead to a more balanced and visually pleasing final image. There are various color groups and pairings that you should refer to when building a color palette.

▶ The primary colors are red, blue, and yellow (or sometimes referred to as magenta, cyan, and yellow). From these three basic colors you are able to mix and create all other colors.

▶ The secondary colors are purple, green, and orange. These are created by mixing different pairs of primary colors.

▶ Complementary colors sit opposite one another on the color wheel. These pairings include yellow and purple, magenta and green, and cyan and orange. Pairing these colors together creates a high contrast, which is perfect for creating visual impact in your artwork.

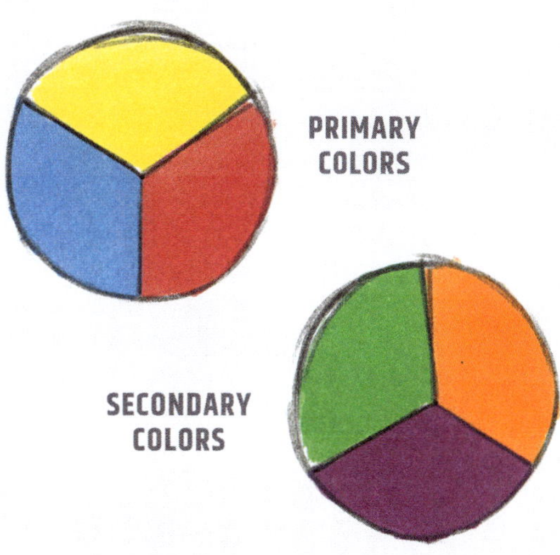

COMPLEMENTARY COLORS

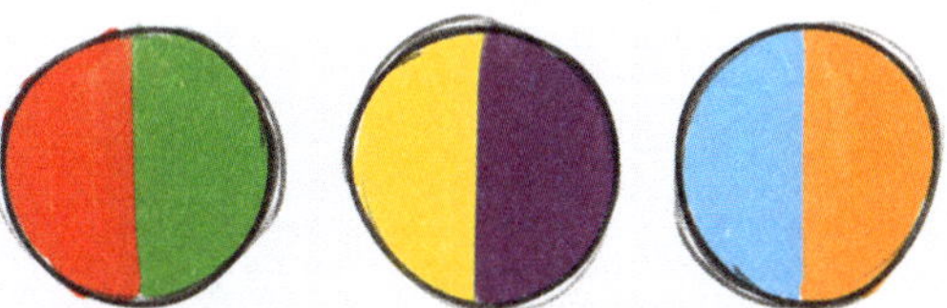

SCI-FI BASICS

BY VALERIO "DREELRAYK" BUONFANTINO

It's time to delve into the boundless world of science fiction. Whether you want to dream up exciting new technologies of the future, or perhaps imagine alien worlds, spacecrafts, and intergalactic battles, this genre can be represented in a wide range of creative ways. You could take a more realistic and plausible approach, grounded in familiar technology and a near-future setting. Or maybe you'd prefer to immerse yourself in the fantastical, imagining endless realms of outlandish sci-fi creatures and gadgets that push your imagination to its limits. This chapter will explore some of the elements you will need to create when bringing your sci-fi imaginings to life on the page.

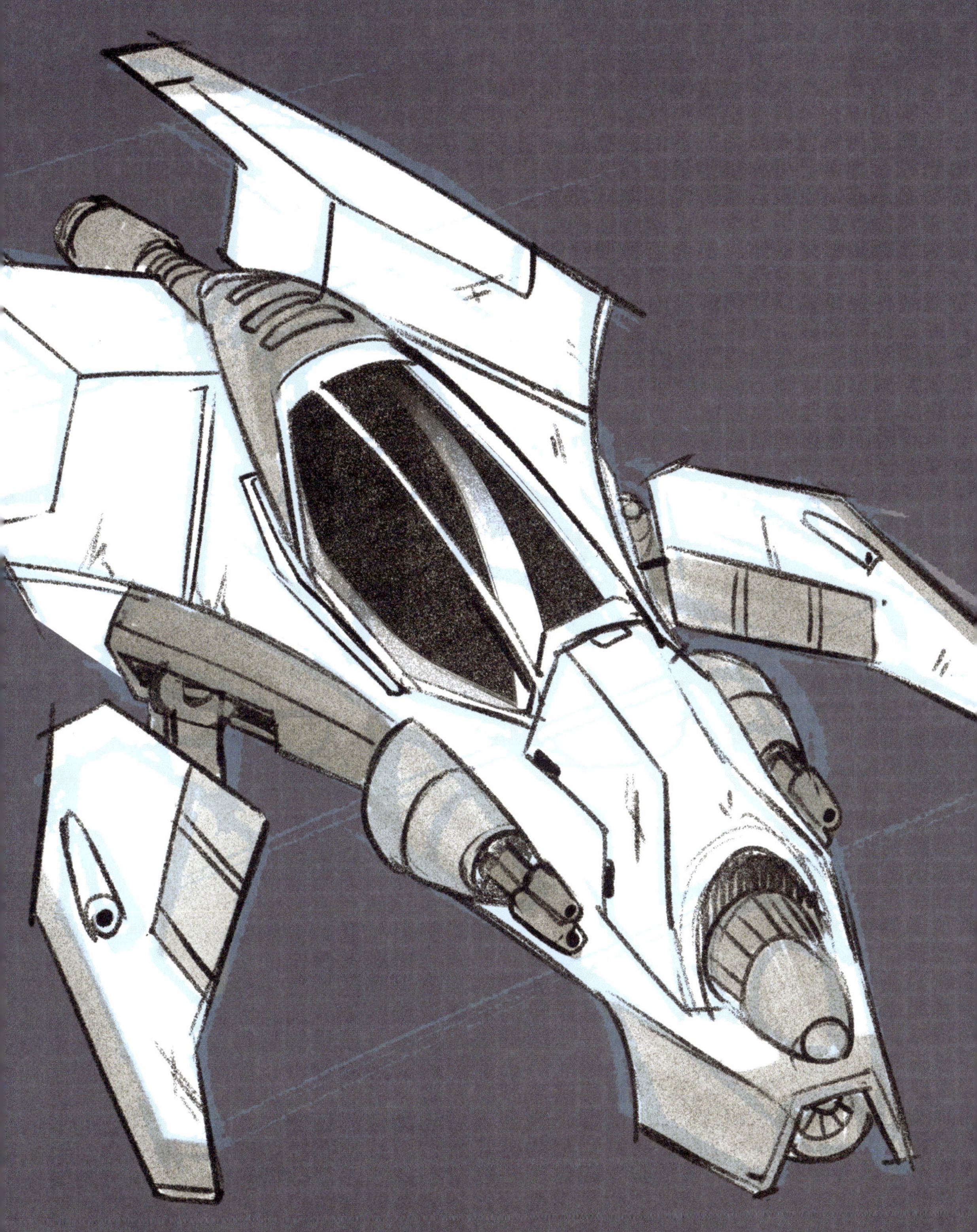

HUMAN-TO-ROBOT ANATOMY

Robots and droids feature throughout the science-fiction genre in many variations. They can be anthropomorphic characters, or more angular and machinelike. They may possess a range of spirited personalities, or exist as simple calculators without emotions and feelings. Being fictional characters, the ways to represent them are unlimited, though you may consider using existing technologies as a reference to add believability to your designs. This section will explore different types of robots and the things you should consider when drawing them.

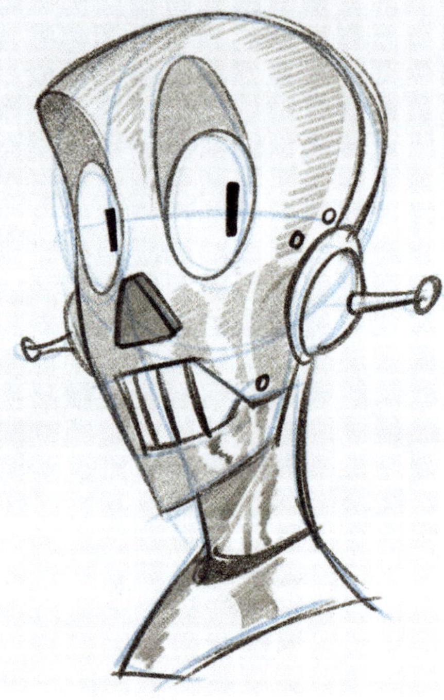

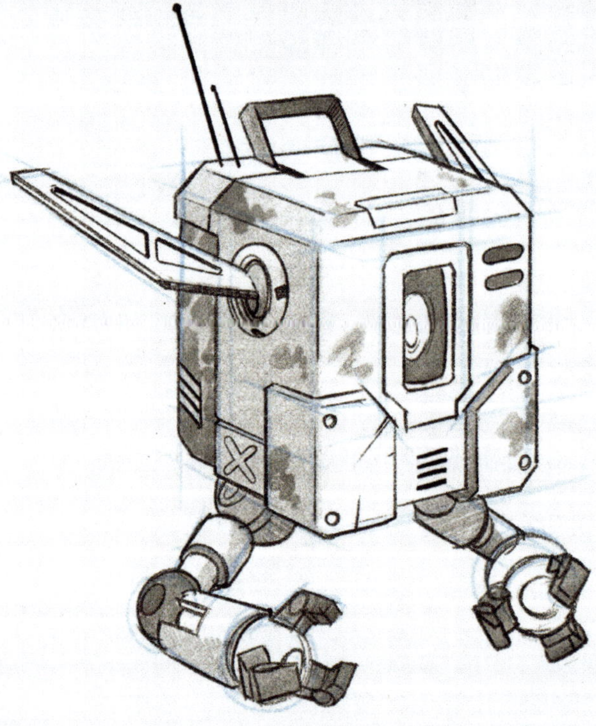

CONTEXT

Does the robot exist in the future, or present-day but in space? Do they live in a wealthy, technological world, or a devastated, apocalyptic one? Ask yourself such questions before starting to design any droid. Considering their story and context will allow you to create a more accurate and plausible representation of the character. For example, if the robot lives on an impoverished planet, this should be reflected in the materials and technology it's built from. Perhaps it would be crafted from waste materials and assembled in a rough manner, whereas a robot living on a wealthy planet would look much sleeker, cleaner, and more advanced.

ROBOT

There are many variations of robot and numerous ways to construct them. A robot is usually created for a specific function. Whether it's a service or battle robot, its appearance should be functional and influenced by its use, with tools or accessories necessary for the performance of its duties.

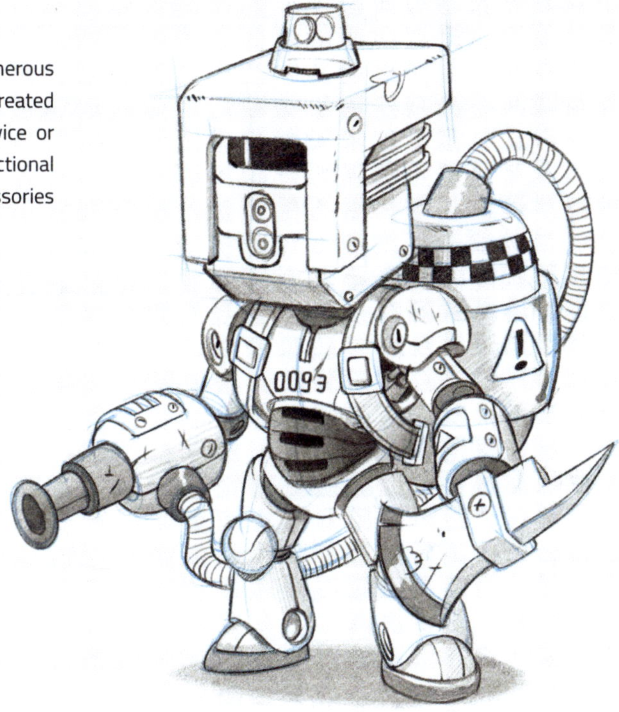

ALIEN ROBOTS

If the robot was created by an alien race, you should try to make it look as different as possible from human technologies. The basic anatomy could instead be similar to the alien species that created it. This allows more space for creativity as you imagine unlikely materials or power sources that do not exist on Earth.

HUMAN ANATOMY

If you want to give a robot a more empathic look, making it easier for human characters to interact with, consider drawing it with anthropomorphic forms, using human anatomy as a reference. Here the muscles are replaced with hydraulic pistons and the skin with metal plates, some with very organic shapes and some less so.

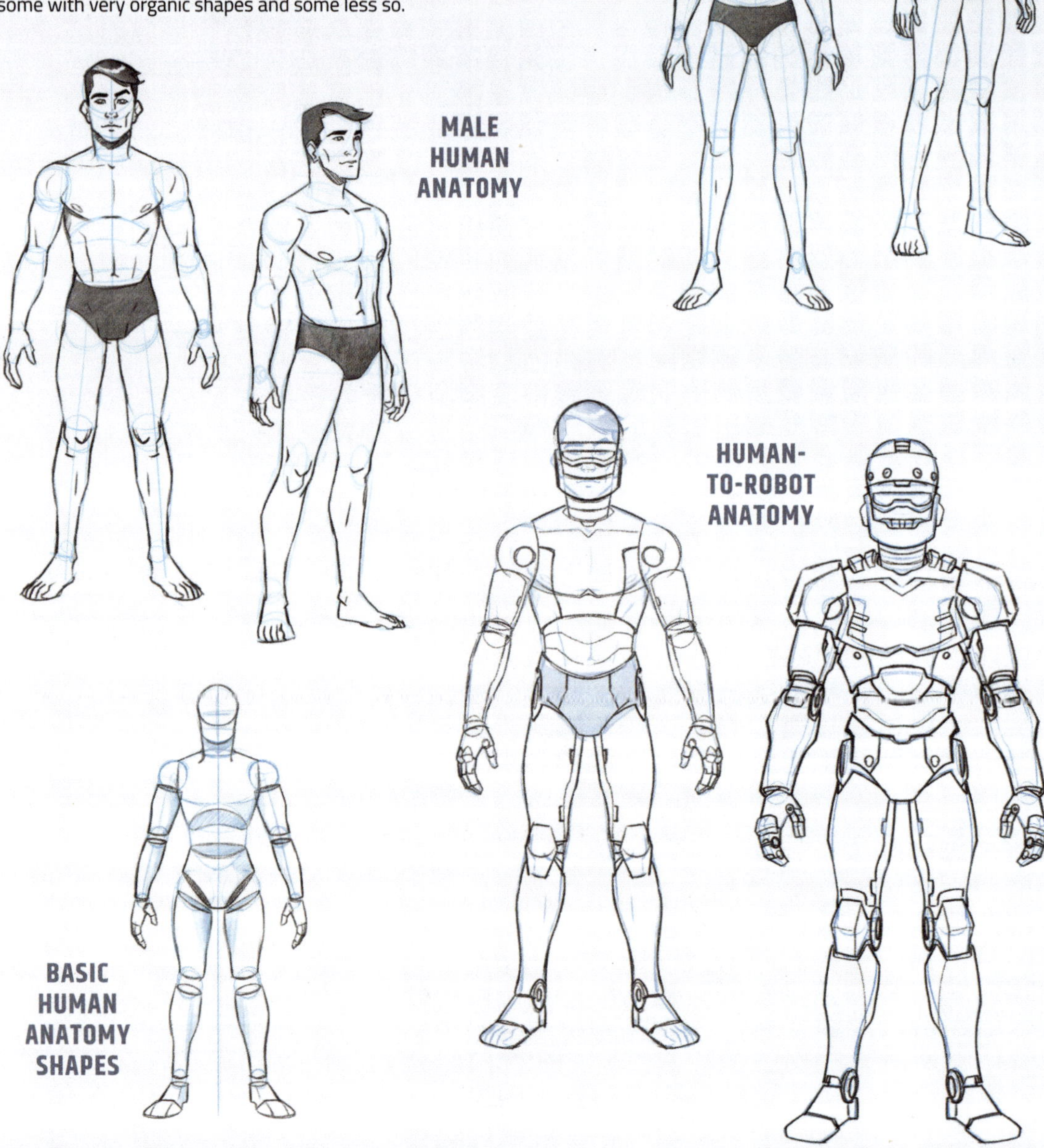

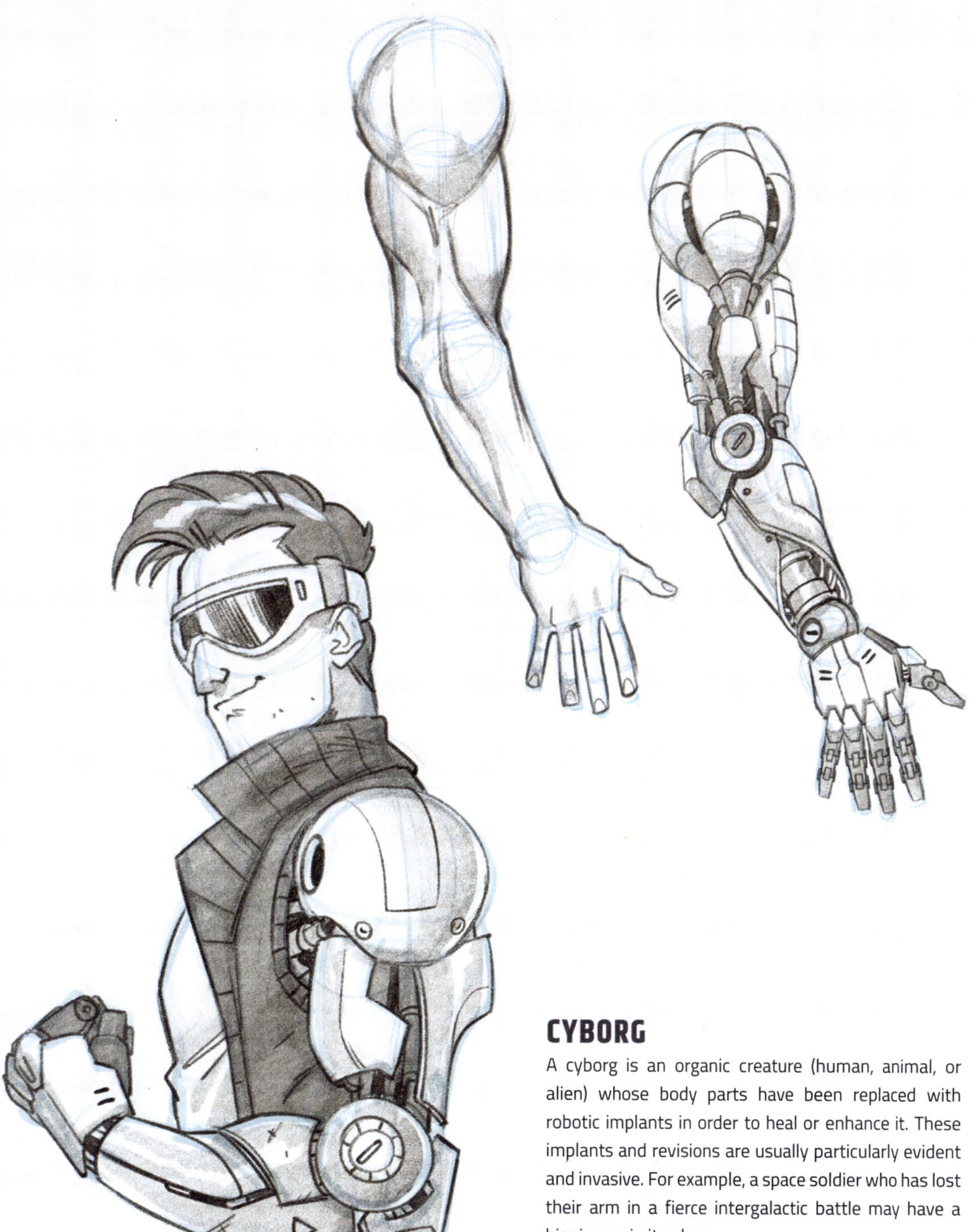

CYBORG

A cyborg is an organic creature (human, animal, or alien) whose body parts have been replaced with robotic implants in order to heal or enhance it. These implants and revisions are usually particularly evident and invasive. For example, a space soldier who has lost their arm in a fierce intergalactic battle may have a bionic arm in its place.

VEHICLE DESIGN

Science-fiction stories are often full of strange and stylish high-tech vehicles. While some may be designed to travel short distances, others will be built for interstellar or even intergalactic travel. Knowing your vehicle's use is essential for creating a coherent appearance. This section will explore typical sci-fi vehicles and the main elements to keep in mind when designing them.

CARS AND MOTORCYCLES

Cars and motorcycles are typically used for shorter distances. In a science-fiction context, they may also have the ability to fly and hover. Rather than drawing the usual wheels, you could add small combustion reactors similar to those on jet planes, or even more futuristic antigravity magnetic reactors.

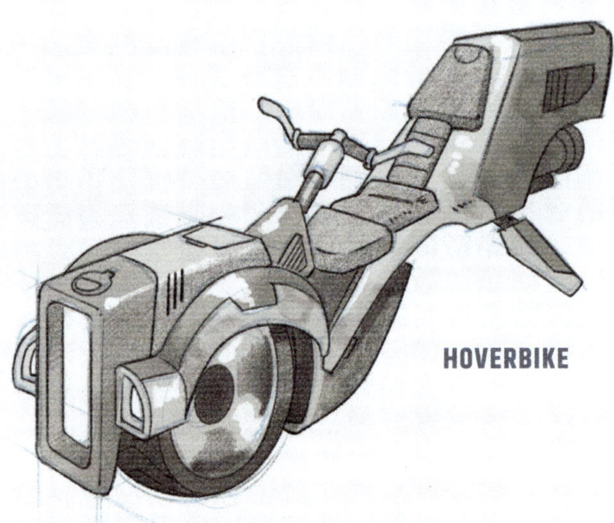

HOVERBIKE

FLYING CAR

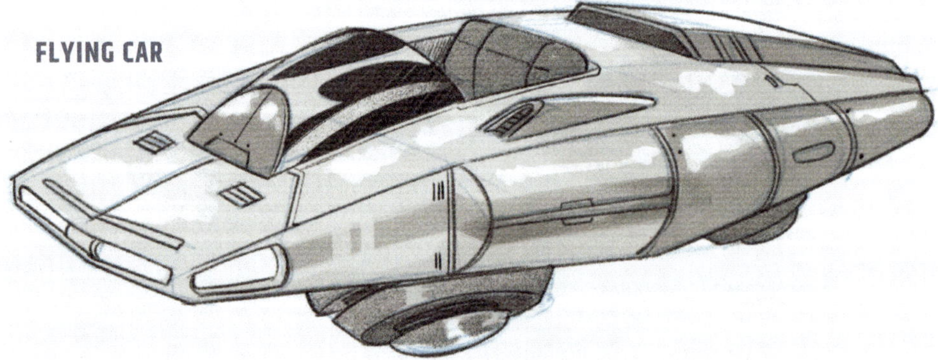

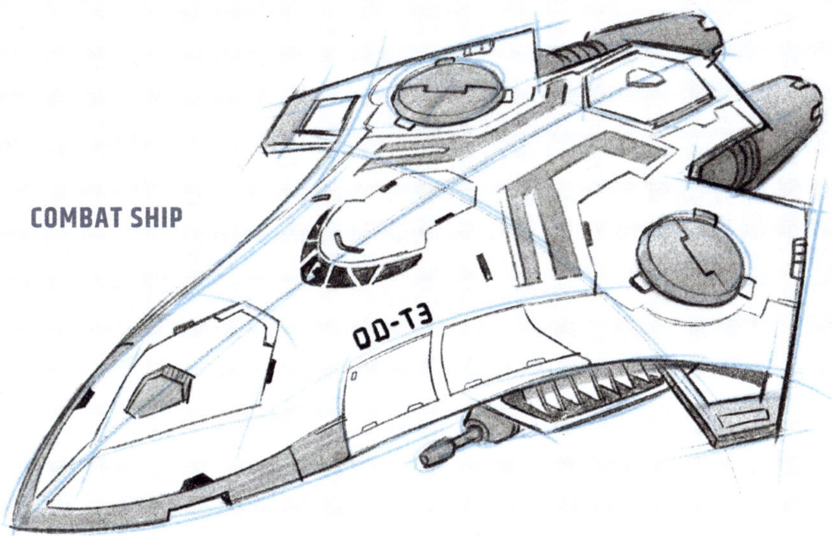

COMBAT SHIP

SPACESHIPS

Spaceships are built to travel interplanetary distances, so for a realistic and functional design, consider adding powerful reactors that can handle this type of travel. In addition, as they travel through space with the absence of an atmosphere, it's essential they don't have any open or non-pressurized areas.

ROYAL SHIPS

In a universe full of alien civilizations, the royal elite may travel around in a grand spaceship that shows off their importance and royalty. Using shiny, reflective materials will give the vehicle a clean, wealthy look. It may also have defensive weapons, but these should be subtle and non-invasive, to avoid conveying an aggressive, combative message.

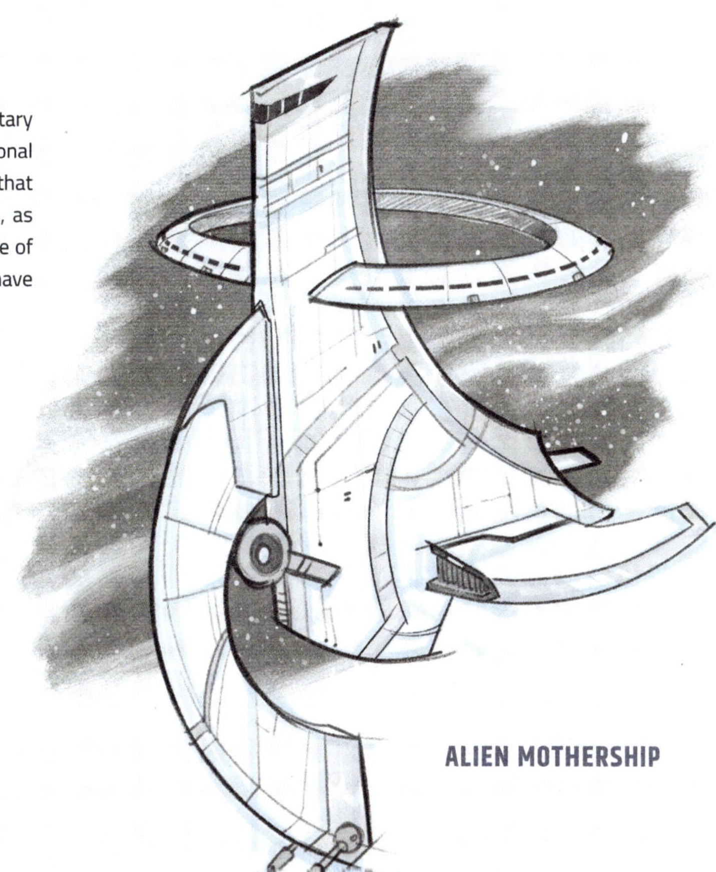

ALIEN MOTHERSHIP

SPACE FIGHTERS

Space fighter ships are used for space battles and don't typically travel long distances. Operating in space, they require pressurized cockpits, which might seat one or two pilots. As they are battle vehicles, they will need to be armed, so take the time to explore advanced weaponry capable of operating in space, such as laser or plasma cannons.

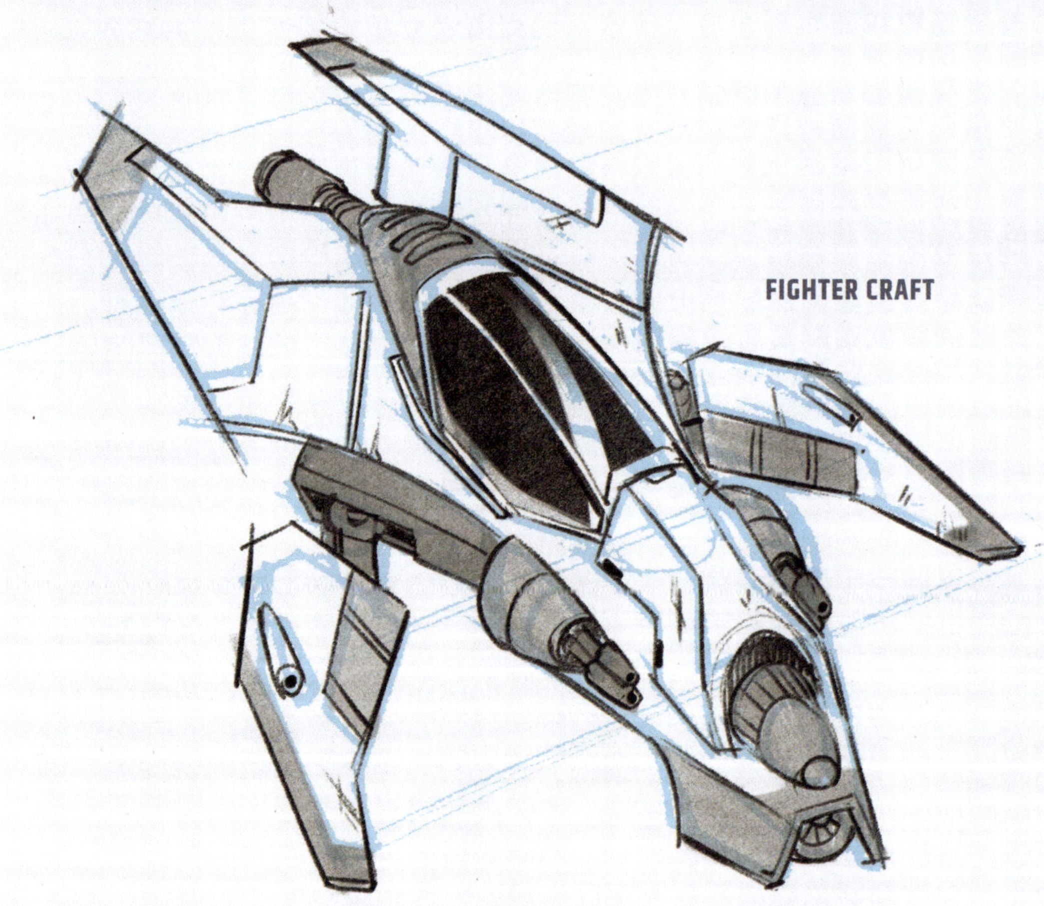

FIGHTER CRAFT

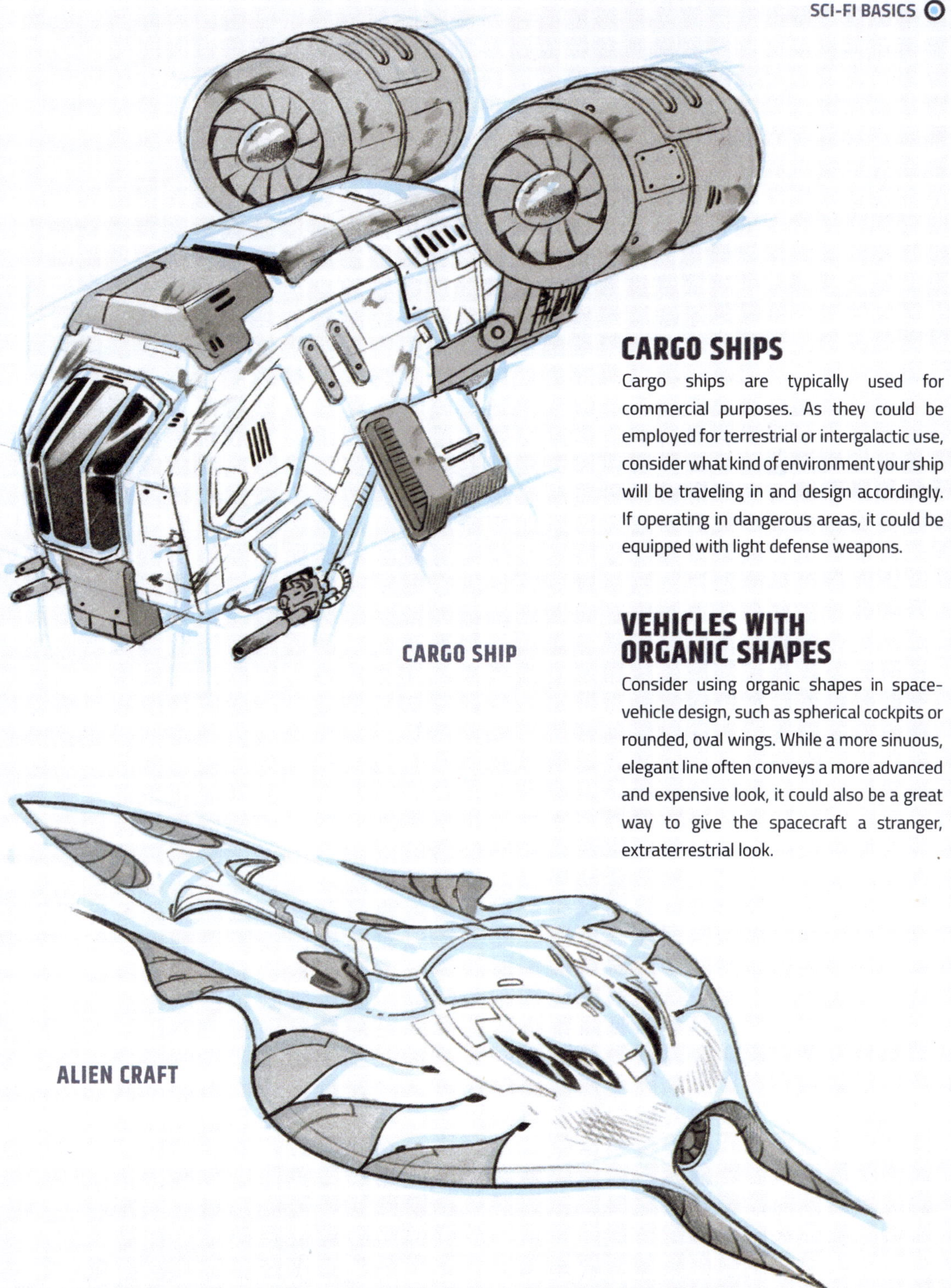

CARGO SHIPS

Cargo ships are typically used for commercial purposes. As they could be employed for terrestrial or intergalactic use, consider what kind of environment your ship will be traveling in and design accordingly. If operating in dangerous areas, it could be equipped with light defense weapons.

VEHICLES WITH ORGANIC SHAPES

Consider using organic shapes in space-vehicle design, such as spherical cockpits or rounded, oval wings. While a more sinuous, elegant line often conveys a more advanced and expensive look, it could also be a great way to give the spacecraft a stranger, extraterrestrial look.

BUILDINGS

This section will cover how to design science-fiction environments. Think futuristic structures with sliding doors and fishbowl windows, hyper-technological solar-powered cities, and lonely gas stations hovering on the edge of outer space. Start by researching real-life buildings and cities for inspiration, then stylize and exaggerate to give them a sci-fi look. Combining your imagination with real-world references will make them appear more believable and realistic.

FUTURISTIC SKYSCRAPER CITY

When designing a futuristic city, look to modern cities packed with skyscrapers and innovative architecture, such as New York, Dubai, and Tokyo. Start by recreating the basic structures before making the design more advanced by adding landing platforms and subway tunnels that run between the buildings.

FUTURISTIC SKYSCRAPER CITY

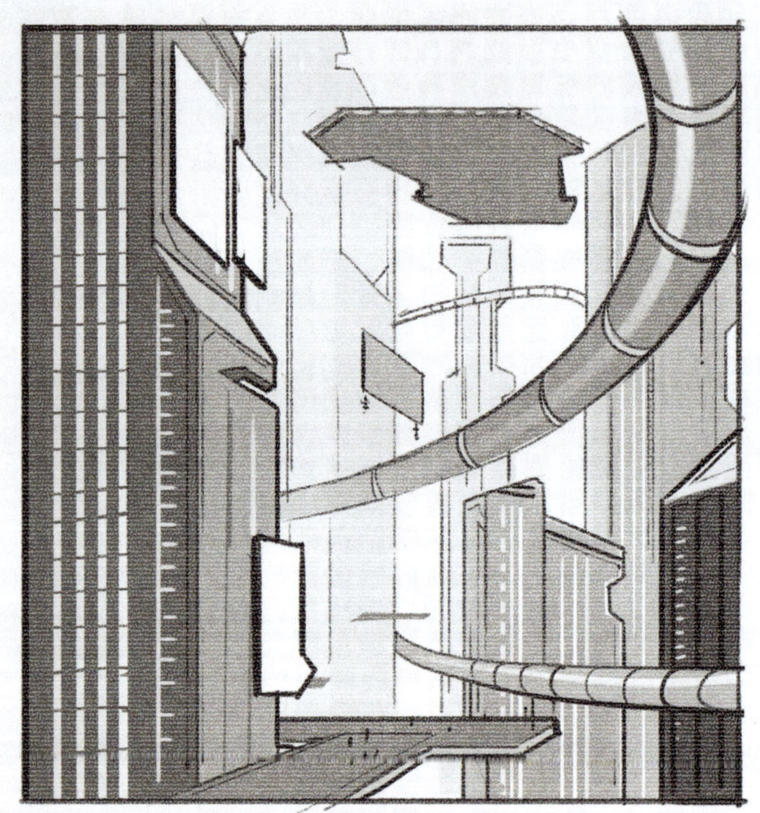

FUTURISTIC DOWNTOWN

The slums of a futuristic city might be gloomy and polluted, with garbage tossed down from the polished walkways above. Alien graffiti may be scrawled across walls, radioactive garbage and toxic fumes could fester through the streets, neon signage might flicker outside seedy clubs, and faceless criminals might lurk in the shadows.

SPACE FACTORY

A highly technological city means plenty of industrialization. Factories occur frequently in sci-fi worlds. When designing a factory, first decide what product is being made or processed, such as weapons, robots, minerals, spacecrafts, scrap metal, or food. Common elements could include conveyor belts, huge flues, and large pipes for discharging waste materials.

FUTURISTIC DOWNTOWN

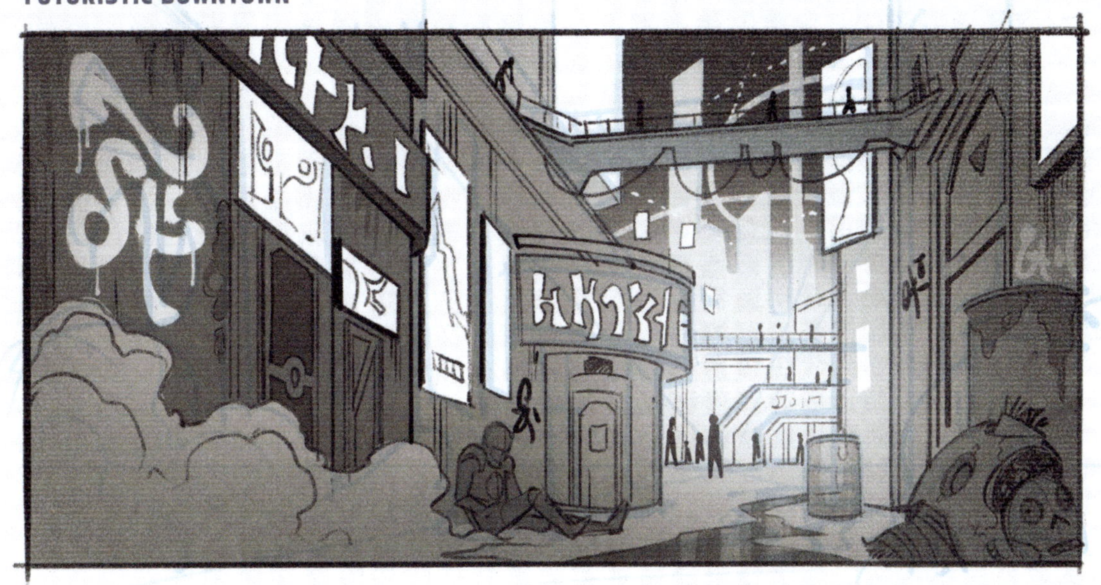

SPACE FACTORY

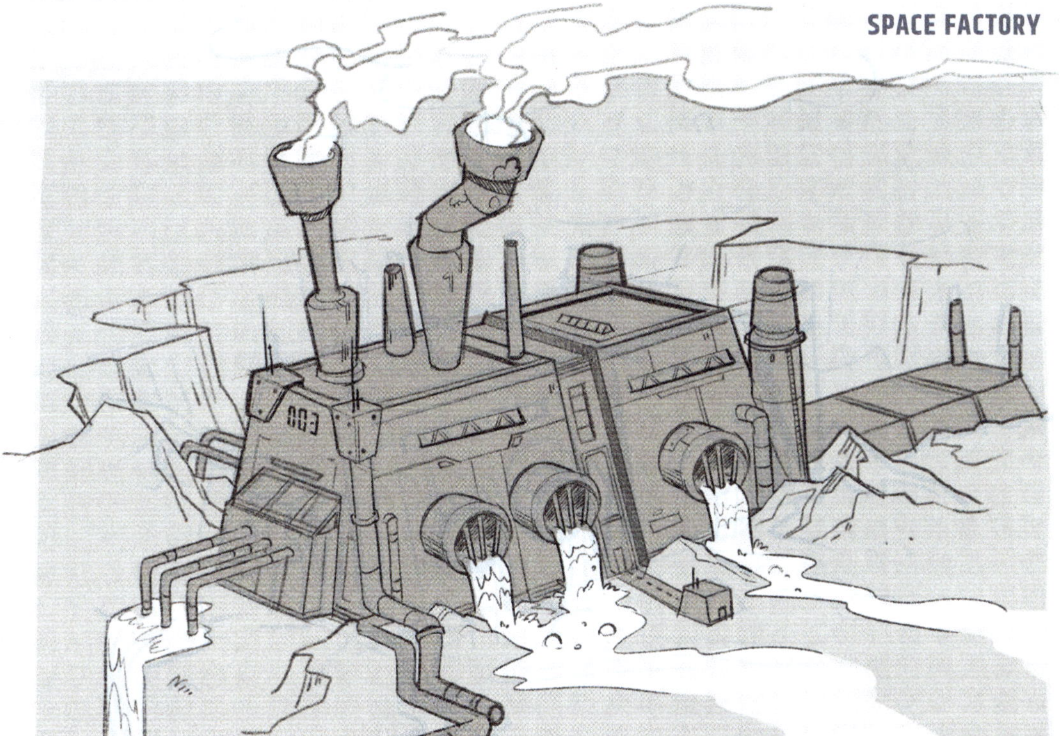

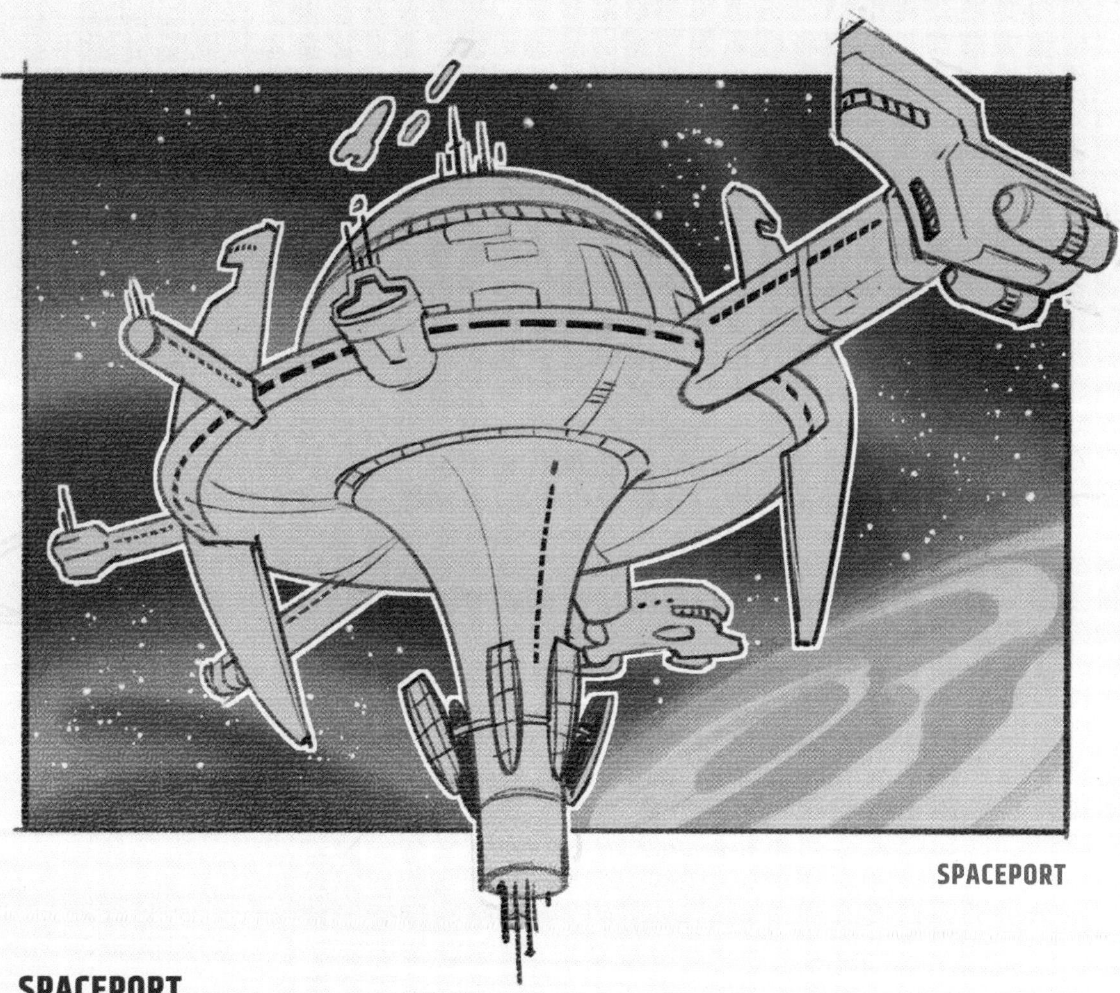

SPACEPORT

SPACEPORT

Whether intended for small spaceships or large interstellar cruisers, spaceports should allow the docking of spacecrafts of various sizes. As they have to float in space, avoid designing open areas, instead considering pressurized docking doors that can safely accommodate passing crews.

LABS

Laboratories are another typical environment in sci-fi worlds. Consider what kind of research is being carried out in the laboratory. Maybe it is for researching alien plant life or a new type of robot. Starting with this question, imagine what tools and machinery could be useful for that research, such as microscopes, tanks, or test tubes.

ROYAL PALACES

Future or alien technologies could allow for the construction of grand buildings that showcase the importance of their royal family or ruling class. Research other impressive monuments – such as the Pyramids of Giza in Egypt, the Taj Mahal in India, or the Colosseum in Rome – imagining how they could be built using futuristic technologies.

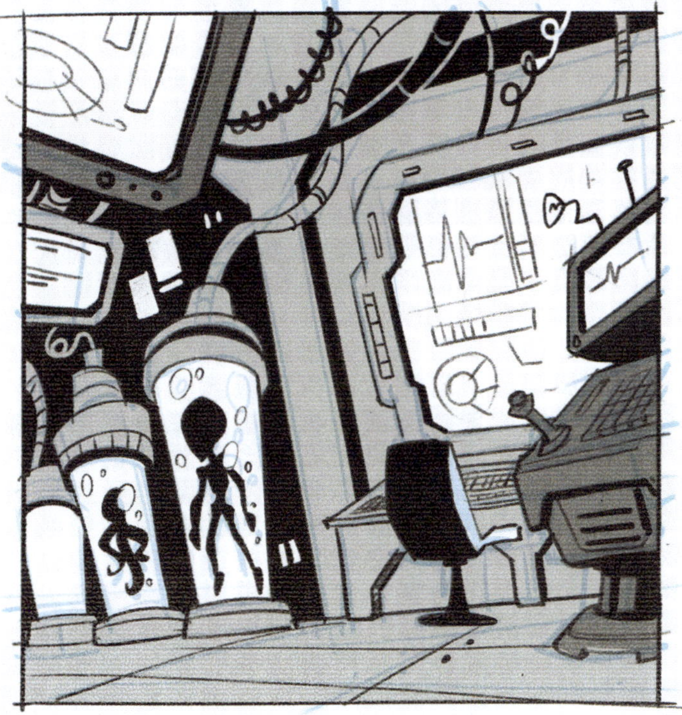

LAB

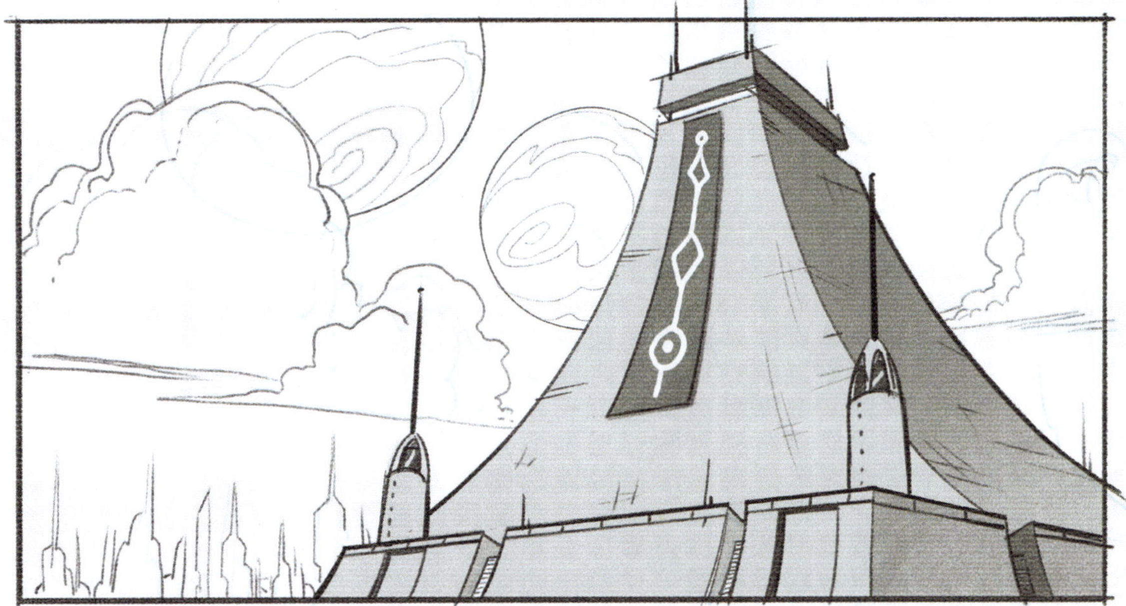

ROYAL PALACE

DESIGN TECHNIQUES

BY VALERIO "DREELRAYK" BUONFANTINO

To take your sci-fi drawings to the next level, it's useful to experiment with different techniques to frame, pose, and light your designs. Each technique will influence the mood of the artwork in a different way, so you must first consider what feeling or emotion you wish to provoke in the viewer in order to decide which technique will be most suitable. The following section will explore some of the more helpful and frequently used techniques in science-fiction artwork.

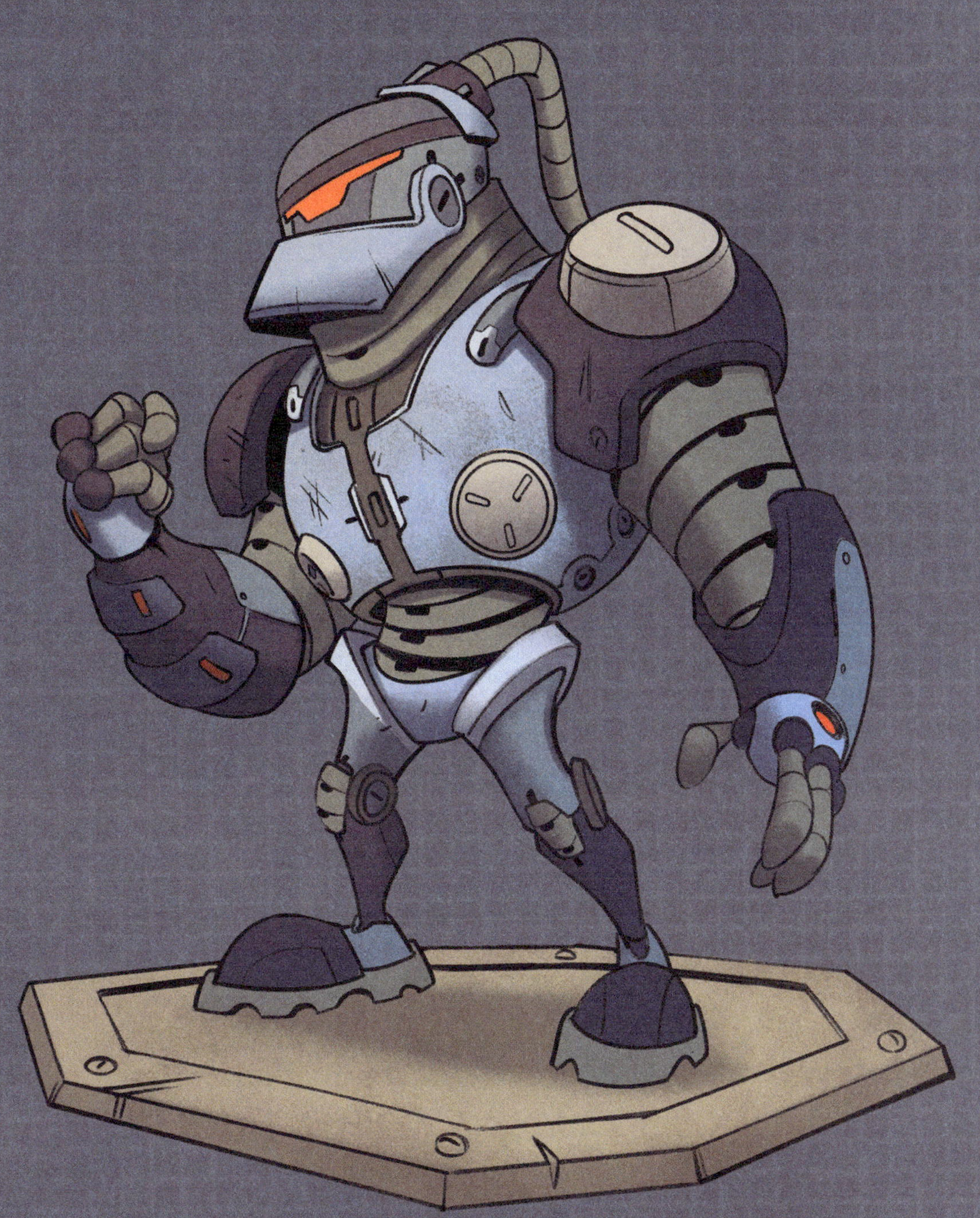

FORESHORTENING

Foreshortening is a way of conveying perspective in an image by distorting, shortening, or enlarging shapes. When the foreshortened object is close to the viewer, the closest parts will appear larger while the parts farthest away will look smaller. This technique can be used to make a character appear more dynamic and engaging. Without foreshortening, they can appear flat and lifeless.

Study this robot. The eye-level version on the left shows the robot's real proportions. In the foreshortened version on the right, viewed from above, the upper section of the robot looks larger than it actually is, while the body appears shorter and more compacted. Maybe he is looking up at a larger, more menacing robot? Or perhaps, with some motion lines added, he could be flying off on a mission?

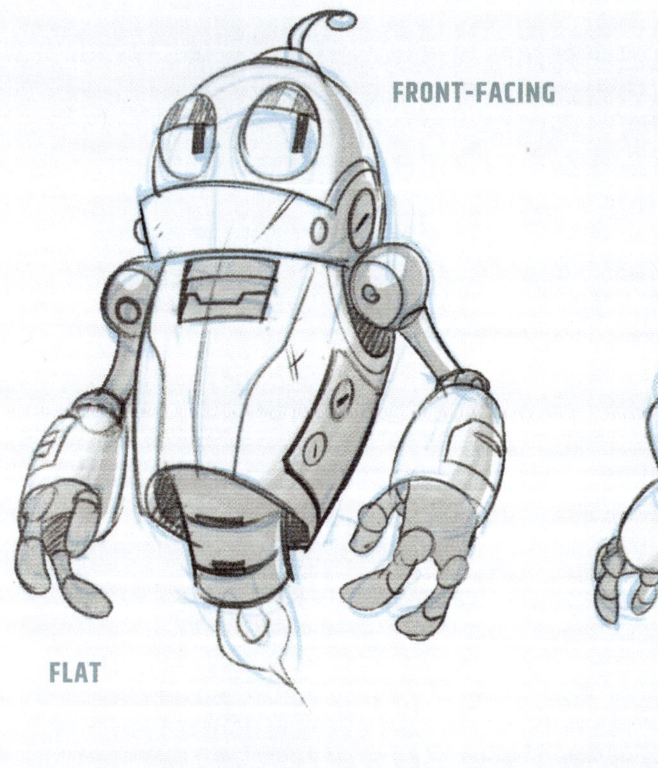

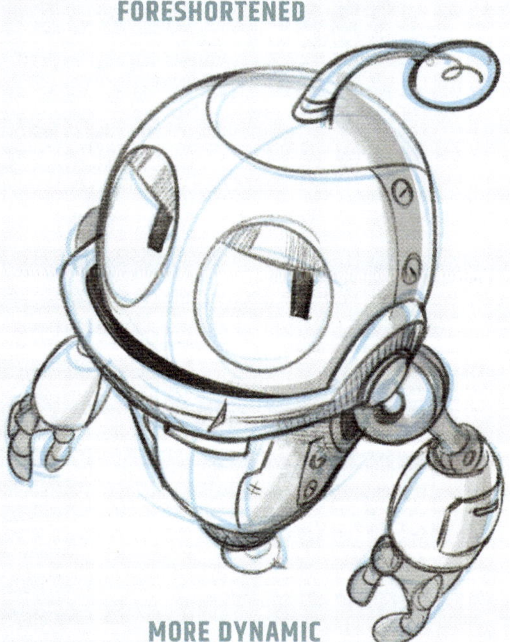

STANDING POSE

A standing pose can be very useful for showing a character in its entirety, ensuring essential parts of the design are not hidden from view. A front-facing standing pose will provide a static and unexpressive image. While this may be perfect for a robot on standby or waiting for orders, a foreshortened standing pose will create a more interesting design that is fitting of dynamic, heroic, or dangerous characters.

DRAMATIC FORESHORTENING

Dramatic foreshortening can be used to spark certain emotions in the viewer, as well as to add a particular mood to a design. A character viewed from below can convey dominance, grandeur, royalty, danger, and power. On the contrary, a character viewed from above can provoke fear, despair, frailty, and helplessness. But context is everything – the top-down foreshortening below makes this fierce robot look ready for action, facing down a bigger opponent. In science fiction, dramatic foreshortening can be used to add a feeling of danger to aliens, heroism to space warriors, and much more.

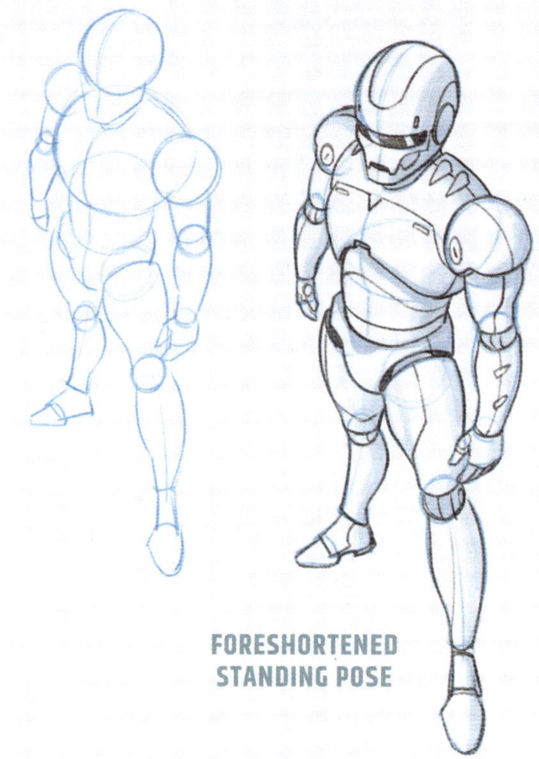

FORESHORTENED
STANDING POSE

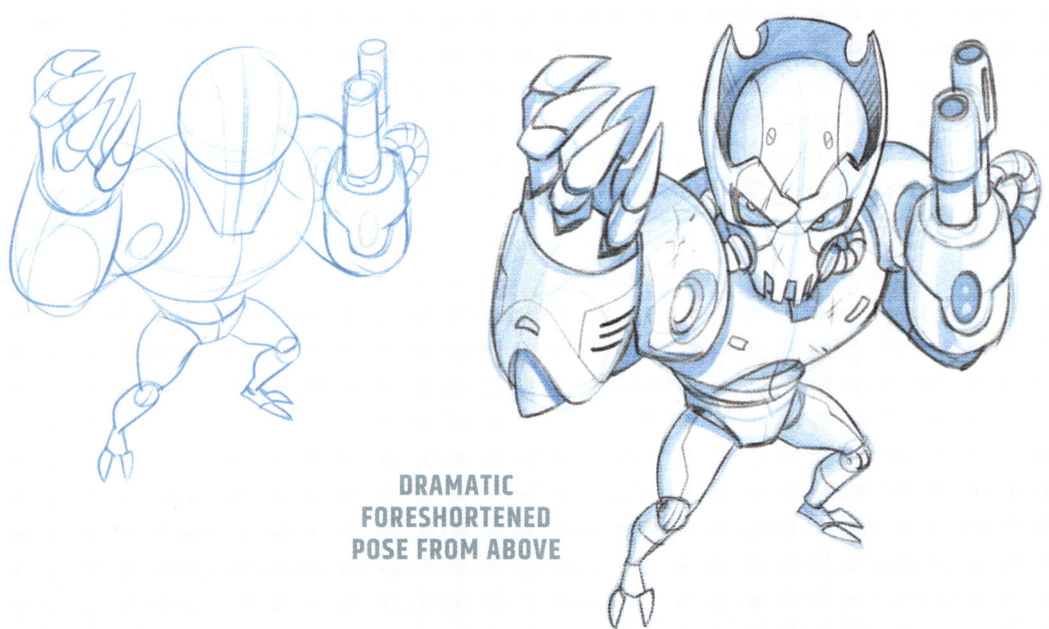

DRAMATIC
FORESHORTENED
POSE FROM ABOVE

POSES

If you want to immerse a character in an action scene, you must first be able to draw them in interesting, dynamic poses. This will make your character designs more animated and captivating, and give personality and life to the character. It's also worth remembering that a character's personality and backstory will affect their posture, body language, and how they assume different poses.

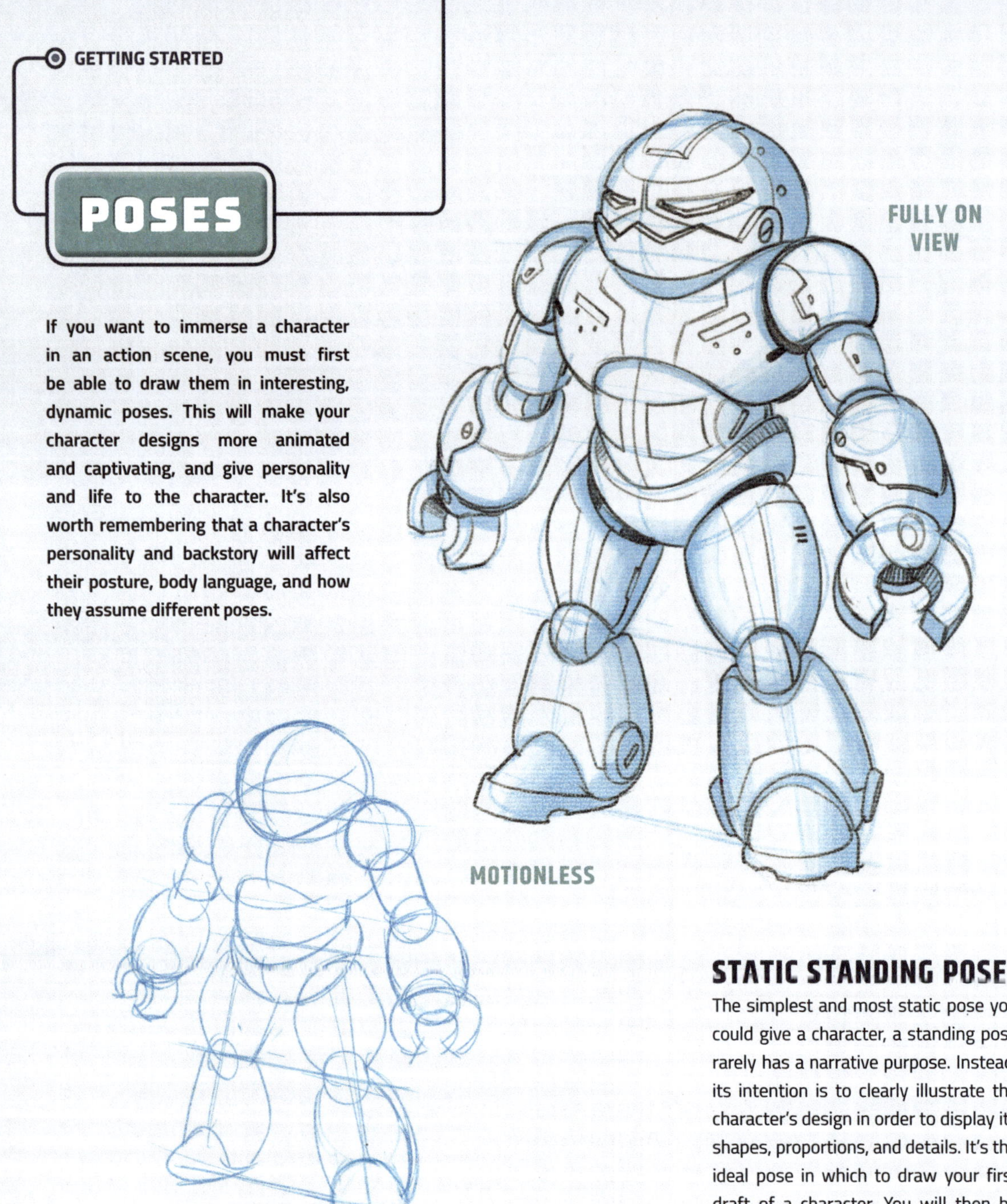

STATIC STANDING POSE

The simplest and most static pose you could give a character, a standing pose rarely has a narrative purpose. Instead, its intention is to clearly illustrate the character's design in order to display its shapes, proportions, and details. It's the ideal pose in which to draw your first draft of a character. You will then be able to refer back to it when drawing the character in more interesting, dynamic poses that better tell their story.

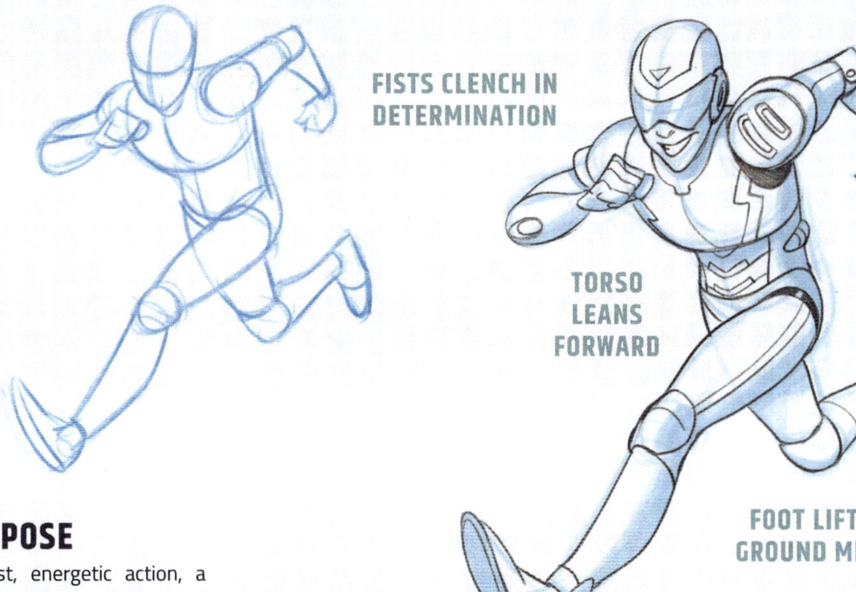

RUNNING POSE

Depicting a fast, energetic action, a running pose should be as dynamic as possible. The character's torso should lean forward into the movement. To adequately balance the weight of the body, the arms and legs should move in opposite directions. For example, here the left leg and right arm are extended forward, while the right leg and left arm are behind.

SITTING POSE

There are numerous different ways to sit, each one suited to different situations. Relaxed or tense, graceful or slumped; a character's personality will dictate the way they sit and hold themselves. For example, a regal space princess will likely have an elegantly composed way of sitting, while a rough bounty hunter may prefer a more slouched sitting position. A robot, on the other hand, might possess a stiff, static posture and perch on the edge of their seat. Imbuing the action with the character's personality will make a simple sitting pose much more credible.

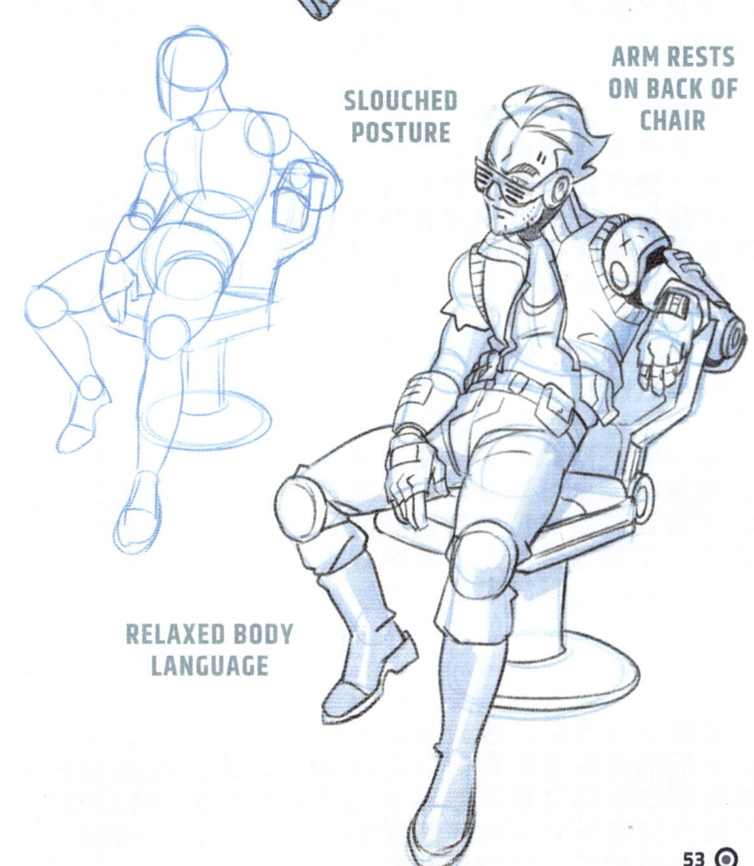

READY FOR ACTION

To depict an action pose, keep in mind the type of action being performed along with the mood of the scene. Drawing parts of the body angled in slightly different directions can help to instill the pose with a more dynamic feel. Here the character's head faces in a different direction to her torso, giving the impression that she's had to turn back to face an opponent.

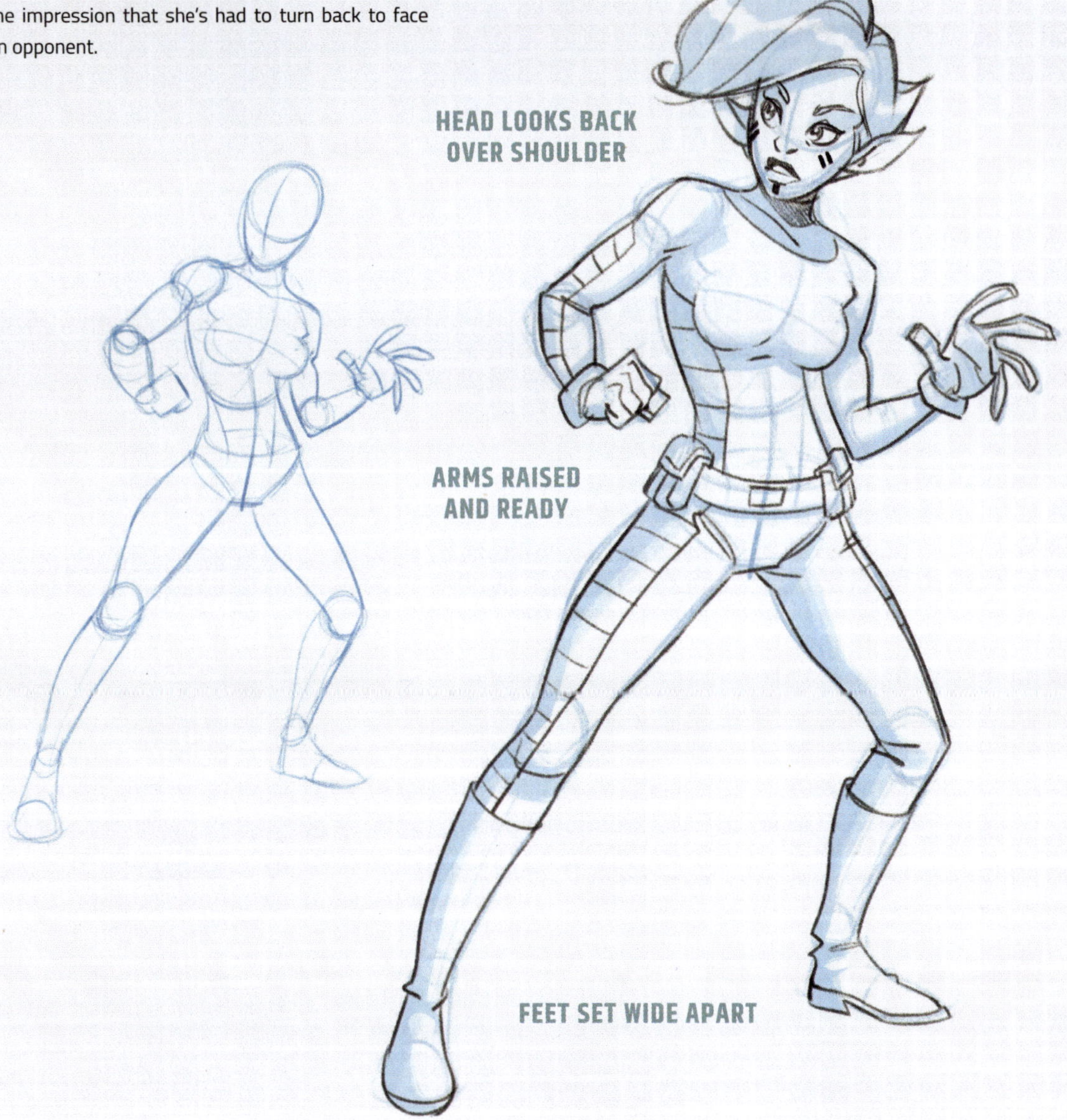

RELAXED POSE

Your posture is only ever symmetrical when you stand up straight. When relaxed, it becomes more uneven. Imagine two lines that run across the shoulders and pelvis. In a relaxed posture, they will likely slant in opposite directions to balance the weight on the whole body, making the pose less tiring to hold. An arm on the hip or in a pocket can help make a pose look more natural. Or maybe the character could take a simple action, like taking a look at their data pad or space gun.

HERO POSE

A space warrior may want to show off their strength and power to assert their dominance. A hero pose requires the opposite posture and body language to that of a relaxed pose. In this case, the muscles should be tense and flexed. Here the character puffs out his chest, plants his arms on his hips, and looks off into the horizon, expressing little interest in his immediate surroundings. To enhance the pose, consider drawing the character from a slightly lower angle to create an air of heroism and authority.

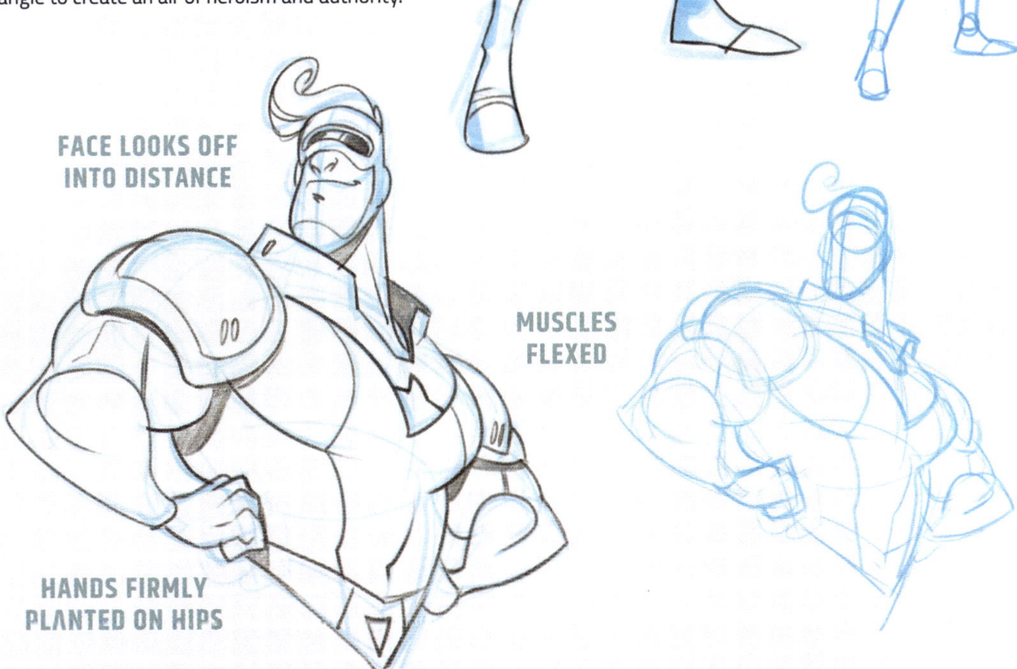

PERSPECTIVE

Perspective is used to create the illusion of three-dimensionality on a two-dimensional surface. It's essential in science-fiction artwork to effectively capture the height, width, and depth of objects, such as the colossal size of a spaceship next to a tiny astronaut. It's also useful for recreating believable environments, showing how objects appear smaller as they move further away.

There are two important elements to remember. Firstly, the horizon line, which is an imaginary horizontal line that represents the viewer's eye level. Secondly, the vanishing point, which is where the lines and objects appear to converge, as if receding into the distance.

ONE-POINT PERSPECTIVE

One-point perspective is typically used when a subject is viewed from the front, when looking directly at the frontal plane. Surfaces that move away from the viewer converge toward a single vanishing point on the horizon line at the viewer's eye level. Surfaces on the frontal plane appear as their true shape, with little distortion.

TWO-POINT PERSPECTIVE

For two-point perspective, two vanishing points are placed on the horizon line. These two points should be far apart from one another to prevent distortion. It's possible that the two vanishing points could be outside of the picture plane, off the side of the paper on which you draw, but they must remain on the horizon line, which continues off the picture plane in both directions. This technique creates a more dynamic, natural look than one-point perspective, and is useful for drawing foreshortened elements with a view that is not front facing.

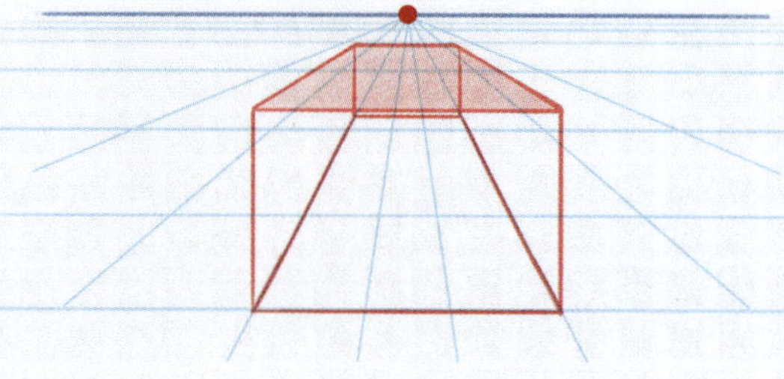

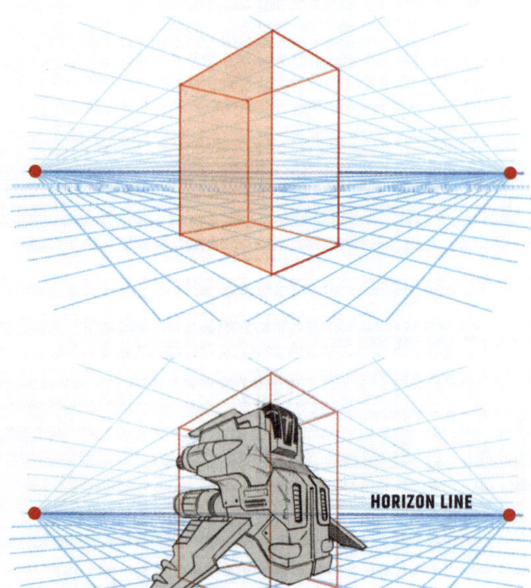

THREE-POINT PERSPECTIVE

FOUR-POINT PERSPECTIVE

THREE-POINT PERSPECTIVE

To draw an object in three-point perspective, start by drawing a horizon line with a vanishing point at either end. Draw the horizon line toward the top of your page if the viewer will be looking down onto the object, or toward the bottom of your page if the viewer will be looking up at it. Next, place a third vanishing point either above or below the horizon line. Three-point perspective can be used to create more dynamic artwork and extreme viewpoints, such as looking up at a towering alien skyscraper.

FOUR-POINT PERSPECTIVE

Four-point perspective is useful when you want to show large objects in their entirety, such as huge spaceships or a very tall palace, to capture their size and grandeur. The method is the same as for three-point perspective, but in addition, a fourth vanishing point is added on the other side of the horizon line to the third vanishing point, creating a fish-eye lens effect.

LIGHTING

Knowing how to use light to your advantage is essential for narrative and storytelling in your artwork. Each type of lighting situation can convey different moods and emotions, whether energy and cheerfulness, or fear and mystery. The science-fiction genre allows for much experimentation with light, such as using it to create atmosphere, or as a decorative medium for landscapes and spaceships. This chapter will explore different types of lighting and how to use them.

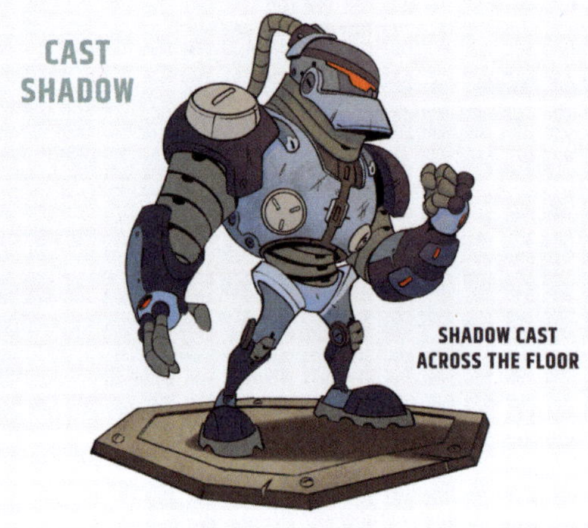

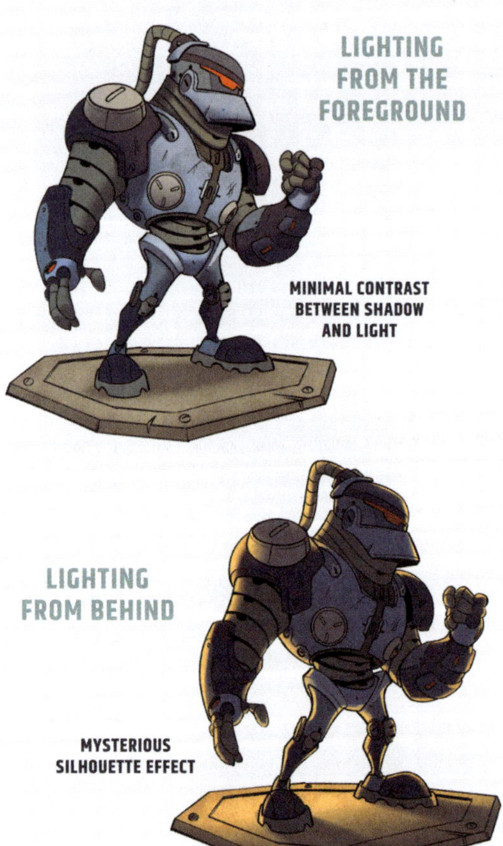

CAST SHADOW

Where there are sources of light, there are almost always shadows. These typically replicate the shapes of the objects that are causing them and are deformed by the surfaces they hit. The stronger the ambient light, the sharper the shadow that will be cast. The solid blacks technique (see Marker Techniques, page 25) can be used to depict sharp, dark shadows, creating a dark, dangerous mood to the artwork.

LIGHTING FROM THE FOREGROUND

A basic ambient light is useful when you don't wish to create a specific atmosphere in the scene. Take care not to increase the contrast between the areas in shadow and those in light too much, keeping the lighting soft and subtle. This type of lighting allows you to clearly see the details of the character, so is an ideal choice when working on a character design.

LIGHTING FROM BEHIND

Lighting a character from behind almost creates a silhouette, with the front of the character cast in shadow while a rim light shines around their outline. This gives a character a mysterious, even dangerous appearance. To create this effect, draw the character with all of their details, even if these will be hidden in shadow. This will allow you to follow the contours with thin lines of light that will help to convey the shapes in a subtle way.

LIGHTING FROM BELOW

Spaceships often feature floor tiles lit from below, or ground-level spotlights that run the length of corridors. Characters are therefore illuminated from below, giving them an ominous or dangerous look. This lighting situation can also create a threatening, scary atmosphere, as if danger is lurking around every corner and could strike at any moment. You can create an even more sinister feel in a scene by coloring the floor lamps red, like the emergency floor lighting illuminated in blackouts.

LIGHTING FROM THE SIDE

A light shining from one side can spark curiosity in the viewer. Where is the light coming from? Maybe a spaceship has landed and is aiming its headlights at the character, or perhaps there's an explosion that has emitted a burst of bright cosmic energy and stardust. The color of the light can also add atmosphere. Cold colors, such as blue or gray, typically found in the interior of a laboratory or spaceship, are perfect for creating a clinical sci-fi atmosphere.

LIGHTING FROM ABOVE

A light shining down from above will make the upper parts of a character more visible, while leaving the lower parts in shadow. Always consider the source of the light. A sun, for example, will illuminate a wider area in a more homogeneous way. A small light bulb, on the other hand, will light a much smaller area, creating a greater contrast between areas in light and areas in shadow, as demonstrated in the example on this page.

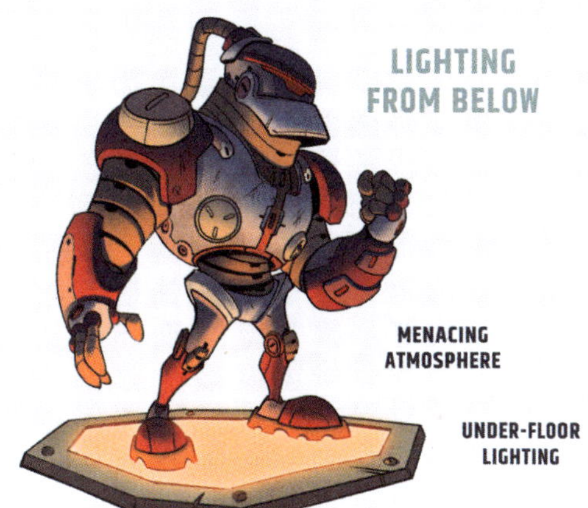

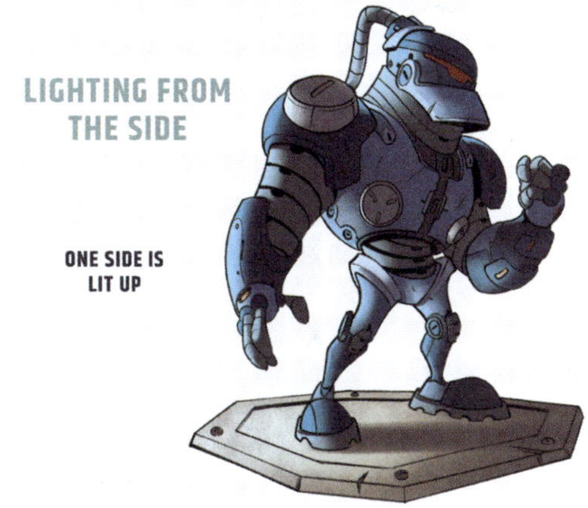

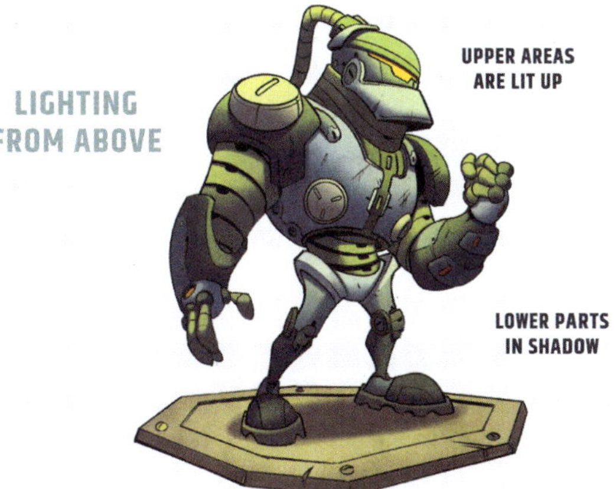

DESIGN VARIATIONS

Science-fiction stories are full of interesting characters, inviting you to imagine and adapt them into a wide range of different situations and scenarios. Starting with a basic idea or familiar premise, you can use your imagination to explore virtually unlimited narratives. This chapter will make small changes to a service-droid design to illustrate just some of the variations possible. Thinking outside the box will always lead to the most unique designs.

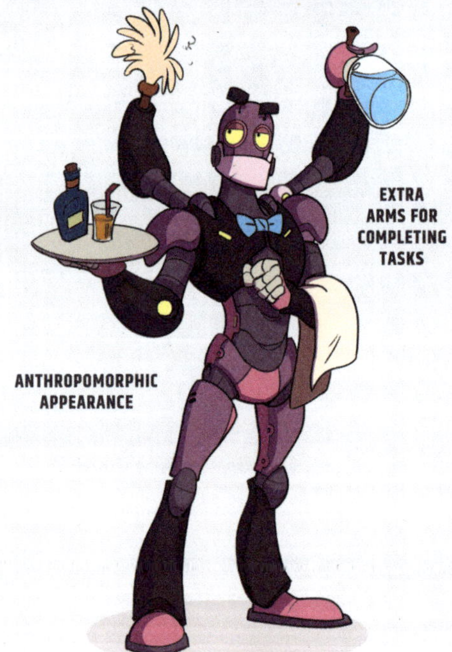

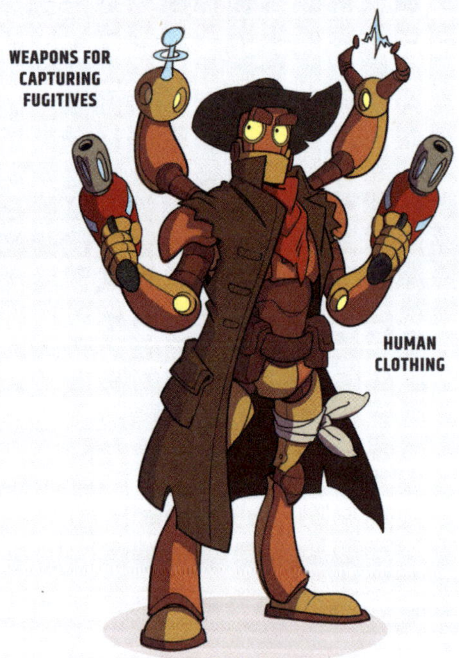

SERVICE DROID

A service robot could be programmed to complete a host of different domestic tasks, such as cleaning rooms, servicing appliances, or cooking food. It therefore needs to be equipped with the appropriate tools for carrying out these tasks, perhaps incorporated into extra arms. An anthropomorphic look is beneficial if the droid works in the service of humanoid creatures, making it easier for it to interact with its masters.

BOUNTY-HUNTER DROID

This design adapts the service-droid design for a new purpose and story. Redesigned as a bounty-hunter droid, it still has the anthropomorphic appearance to allow it to disguise itself and move unnoticed in a crowd when following a fugitive. It dresses in human clothing to blend in with its surroundings and is equipped with weapons, such as handcuffs, electric stun weapons, and metal detectors, capable of capturing the most hostile prey.

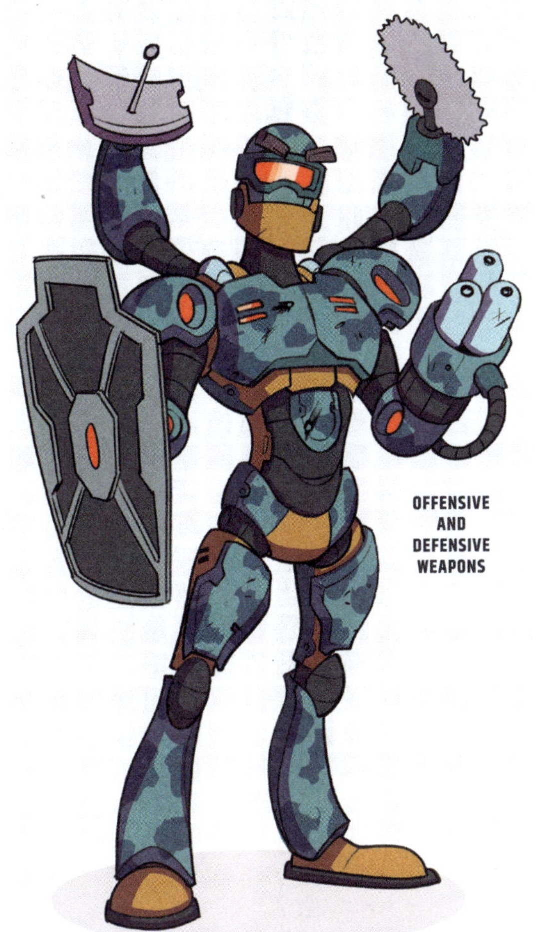

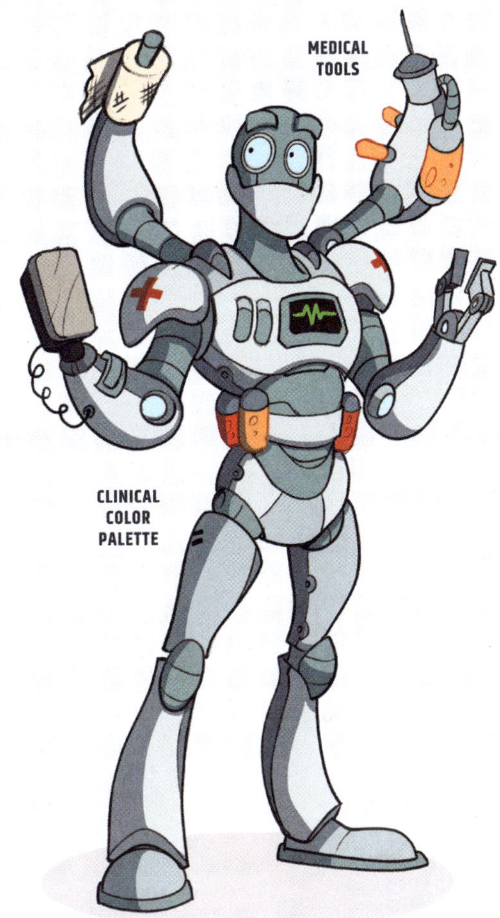

SOLDIER DROID

Here the droid is redesigned as a high-tech soldier robot, with weapons and armor necessary for fighting in battle. This includes offensive weaponry, such as laser or plasma cannons, as well as defensive weapons, such as deflector-shield emitters. Its body is coated with larger plates that protect its more delicate circuits from the blows it could suffer in battle. No longer holding cleaning tools, the droid's additional arms are equipped with antennae that pick up the signal for contacting allied warriors.

MEDIC DROID

This medic droid is the opposite of the battle robot – its tools and equipment are only for medicinal and healing purposes. It carries bandages, a defibrillator, and an anesthetizing syringe. It's also important that it has a calm, reassuring demeanor to comfort patients in distress. A clinical white-and-blue color palette, paired with the typical symbols of medical services, make it easy to recognize the droid's function.

PROCESS TIPS

BY VALERIO "DREELRAYK" BUONFANTINO

Drawing can sometimes be hard work, but following a logical way of working will make the whole process a lot easier and more enjoyable. This chapter will cover ideal habits to practice to achieve the best results and suggest ways to improve your design and drawing process.

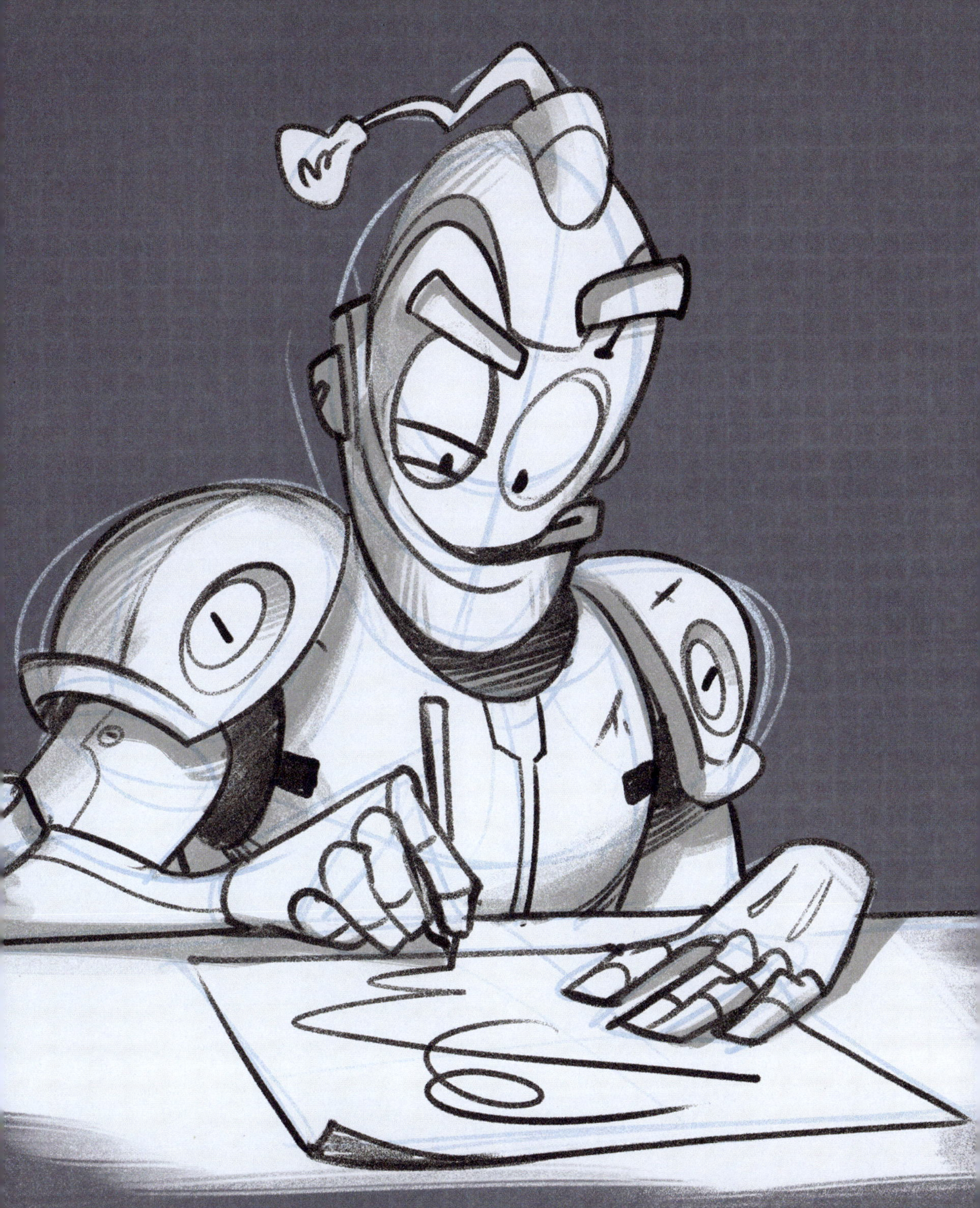

DRAWING HABITS

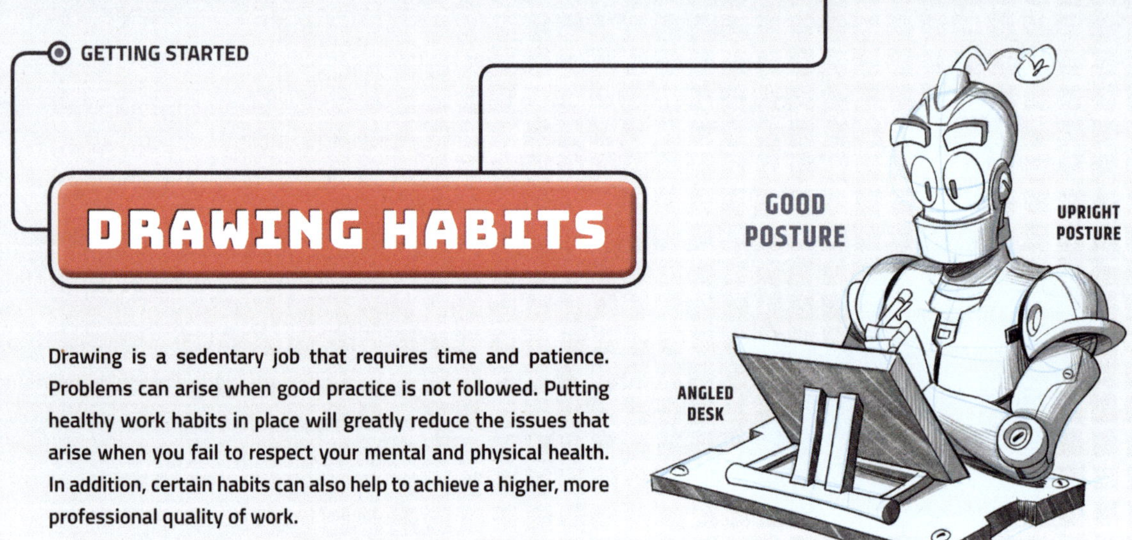

Drawing is a sedentary job that requires time and patience. Problems can arise when good practice is not followed. Putting healthy work habits in place will greatly reduce the issues that arise when you fail to respect your mental and physical health. In addition, certain habits can also help to achieve a higher, more professional quality of work.

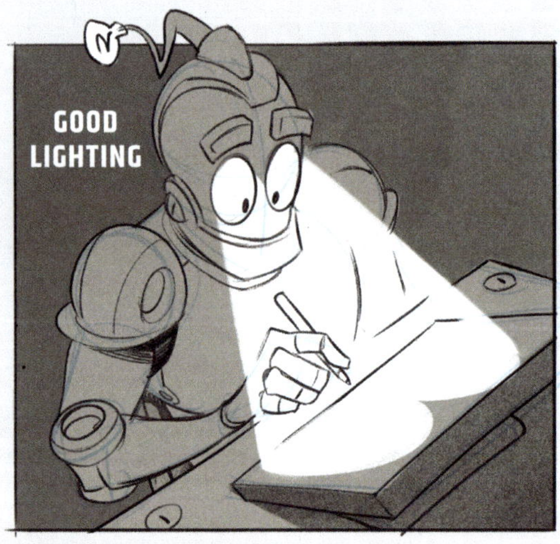

GOOD POSTURE

Maintaining a healthy posture is essential to avoid long-term back problems. Try to keep your back straight rather than hunched over your work, perhaps with the help of an angled drawing board or easel. By not working on a completely horizontal surface, you are less likely to draw a distorted image, caused by viewing the image from an awkward angle. While an upright posture may seem uncomfortable at first, it will benefit both your health and the quality of your work.

GOOD LIGHTING

Make sure your work environment is well lit. This will prevent excessive strain on your eyesight and will protect it long-term. Whether using a lamp or natural light source, ensure it's on the opposite side to the hand you draw with, to avoid shadows falling across your drawing. If you are planning to color your artwork, it's advisable to use a neutral or natural type of lighting. Colored lights, whether too hot or too cold, could change your perception of the colors you use, leading to a different result from the one you intended.

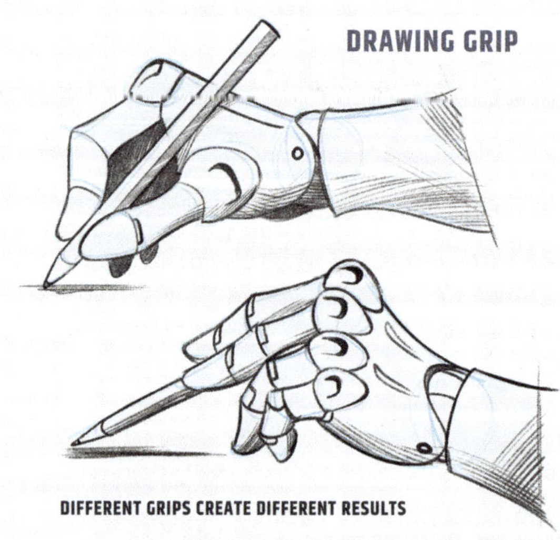

TAKE BREAKS

If you begin to feel tired or are struggling to come up with new ideas, put down your tools and take a break. It's important to schedule in regular breaks, especially if you've been working for a long period of time. Time away will allow your mind to relax, which can help to stimulate your imagination. Taking a walk outside in the fresh air will also allow your body to stretch and de-stress, avoiding problems that arise from sitting still for too long.

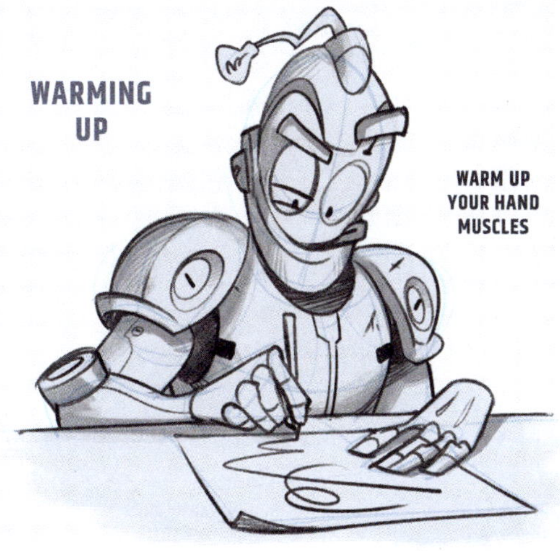

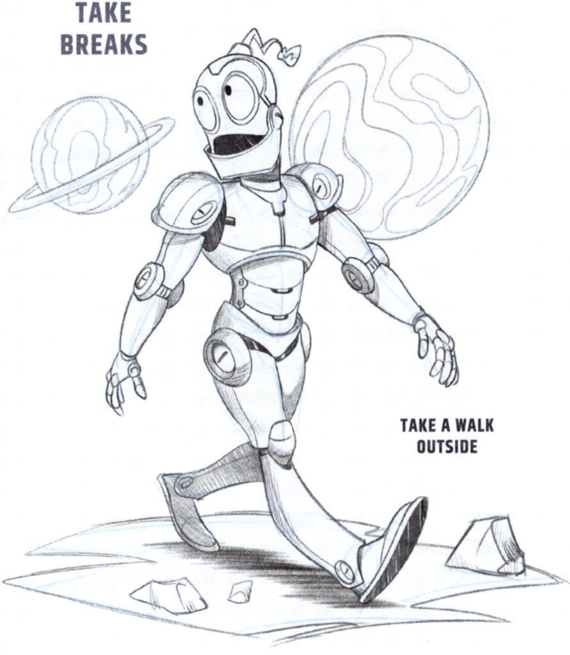

WARMING UP

The hand has muscles that you use when you draw. As with any exercise, it's important to warm up the hand muscles before starting to sketch. Drawing a series of scribbles or a few curved lines, trying to make them as precise as possible, will prepare your hand for handling this type of work, enabling you to draw even more precise lines when you begin your artwork.

IDEA EXPLORATION

Sharing your work with a friend or colleague can be a great way to come up with ideas you may have struggled to arrive at on your own. Try creating a co-working space, or maybe just ask for some advice. Bringing different points of view together can open up new possibilities and a produce a greater variety of ideas, which may highlight concepts you had missed.

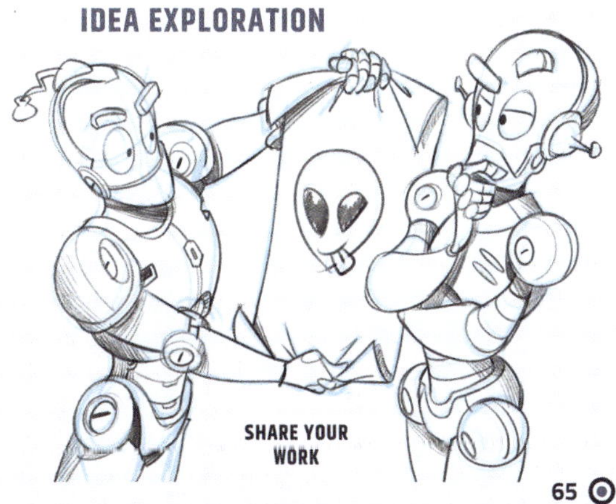

DRAWING GRIP

Depending on the techniques you plan to use and effects you wish to create, there are different ways to grip your tool. Holding the instrument close to the tip enables greater control of the line for capturing small details, while a grip further away from the tip, alongside freer movement of the wrist, is better for the creation of larger curved lines. Holding the tool semi-parallel to the paper allows you to move the pencil more freely, making the lines rougher and looser to create spontaneous and dynamic sketches.

RESEARCH

Whatever type of artwork you wish to create, and whatever your skill or experience level, it's always important to take the time to look for references. The sci-fi genre contains numerous elements that are impossible to draw without using reference imagery for inspiration and instruction. You can use real-life references, such as photographs and videos, or draw inspiration from the work of other artists. Doing this research will enrich your technical and artistic knowledge, making your artwork more interesting and plausible.

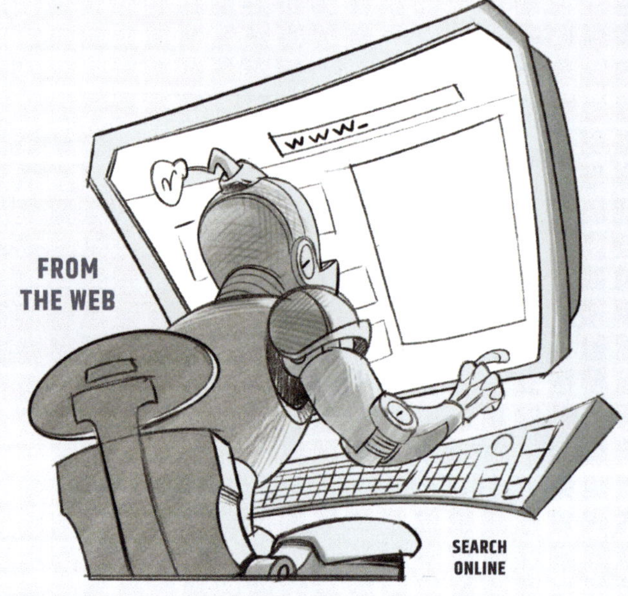

FROM THE WEB

The internet is probably the largest and most complete resource you can draw from when looking for references. It provides access to an unlimited amount of information! There are numerous websites that specialize in collecting images and videos, offering a wide variety of reference material. Gather these references in digital folders to consult when looking for inspiration in the future.

SURROUNDING OBJECTS

STUDY SHAPES

SURROUNDING OBJECTS

Look around and study your immediate environment. You will notice that you are surrounded by a variety of different objects of all shapes and sizes. This is an unlimited source of inspiration, especially in a sci-fi context. An iron, for example, could be a perfect foundation for building an alien spaceship, or perhaps a robot head. By viewing the shapes that surround you with fresh eyes, you can stimulate your imagination to create a diverse array of original ideas.

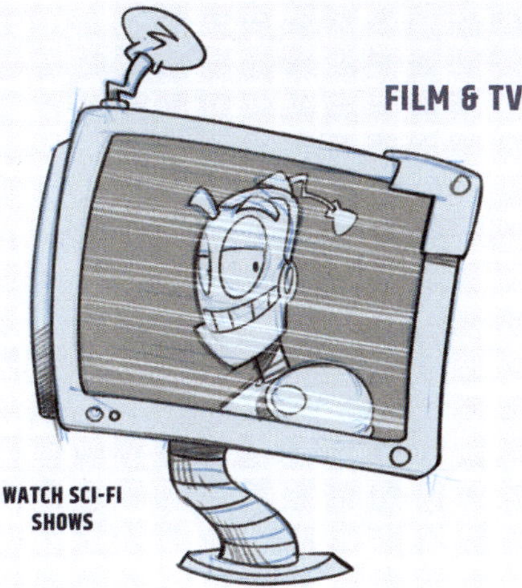

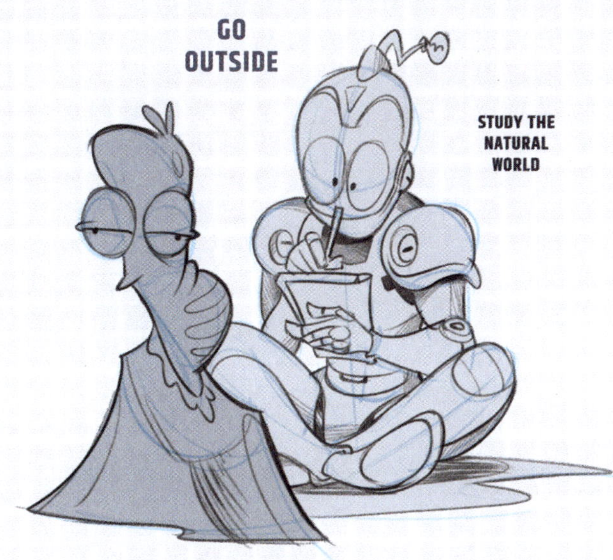

FILM & TV

Movies and television are among the best sources of inspiration. You will also find that documentaries can prove incredibly valuable when searching for ideas. Take the time to watch sci-fi media, using it as an introduction to the different types of characters and worlds that have already been created. In addition, a good knowledge of genre cinematography is useful, to familiarize yourself with the sci-fi genre and understand what to avoid and what to aim for.

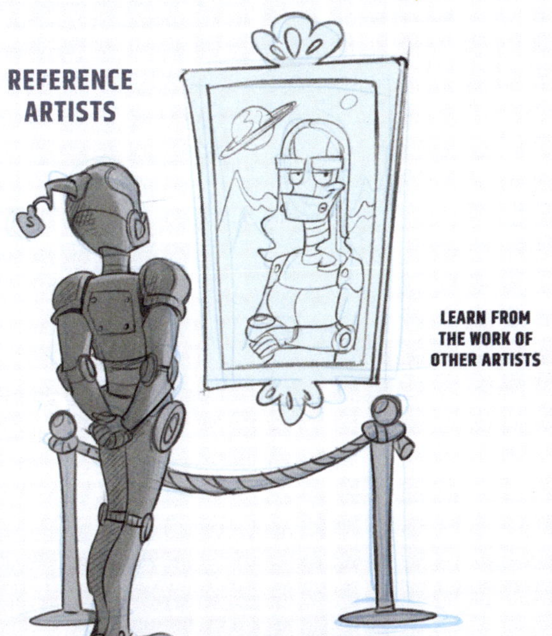

GO OUTSIDE

You will also find great reference material by stepping outside and exploring the world around you. Wherever you are – whether a big city or a country road – there will be many natural or man-made elements that can act as inspiration. Maybe there is an interesting architectural structure, or a tree with a bizarre shape. Any of these objects could be reworked for a science-fiction world. You can also photograph them for later, collating an album of photos to pull ideas from.

REFERENCE ARTISTS

Look to the work of more experienced artists for inspiration. Whether you need ideas for graphic style, or want to understand how they solved some of the problems you're struggling with, it can be helpful to try to understand their process and way of working. However, while you may take inspiration from other artists, it's bad practice to copy them completely. Always try to instill your artwork with your own personality and artistic style. This will allow you to create original artwork that's unique to you.

THUMBNAILS

Thumbnails play a crucial role when creating a new artwork, allowing you to quickly sketch out small, rough versions of your idea before you've decided on any one direction. The fast nature of the process enables you to create a lot of them in a short space of time, making it possible to view different variations of your idea before you commit to one design.

SCRIBBLED SKETCHES

When you're not sure what to draw and need to get your creative juices flowing, you can jumpstart your creativity by sketching several quick doodles. Once you have a few, study them carefully to work out which contain the most interesting shapes. Single out one that could form a foundation on which to create a character or vehicle, then begin to draw more precise lines over the top to develop the design.

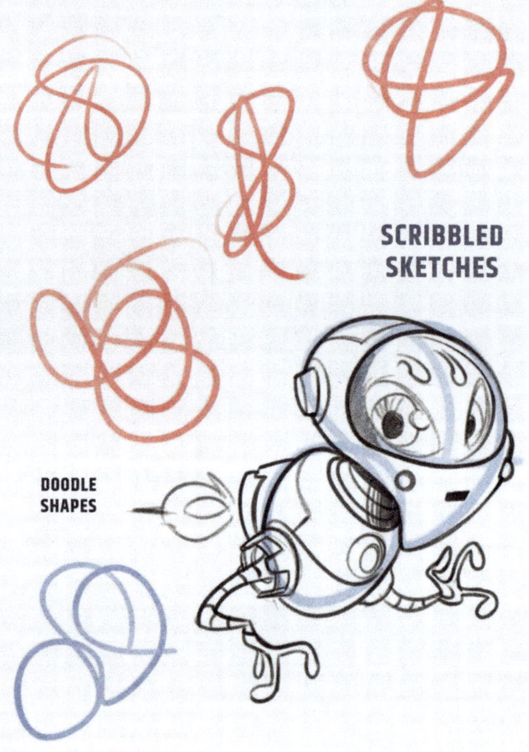

BLOBS

Similar to the scribbled sketch approach, drawing blobs of varying shapes is a fun and useful exercise to spark your imagination. Once you have a series of blobs, try creating characters or vehicles within the shapes, drawing details on top while sticking to the outline. This is a great way to create a collection of original characters that are different from each other. Plus, it allows you to come up with new ideas.

MINIATURES

Don't settle for the first thumbnail. To create a strong design, take the time to try out different variations of an idea. Create a series of small, fast sketches, varying the pose, gesture, shape language, and composition. You may find that your initial idea doesn't work as well as you imagined. Only once you have found a thumbnail you're happy with should you move on to the next stage of adding detail.

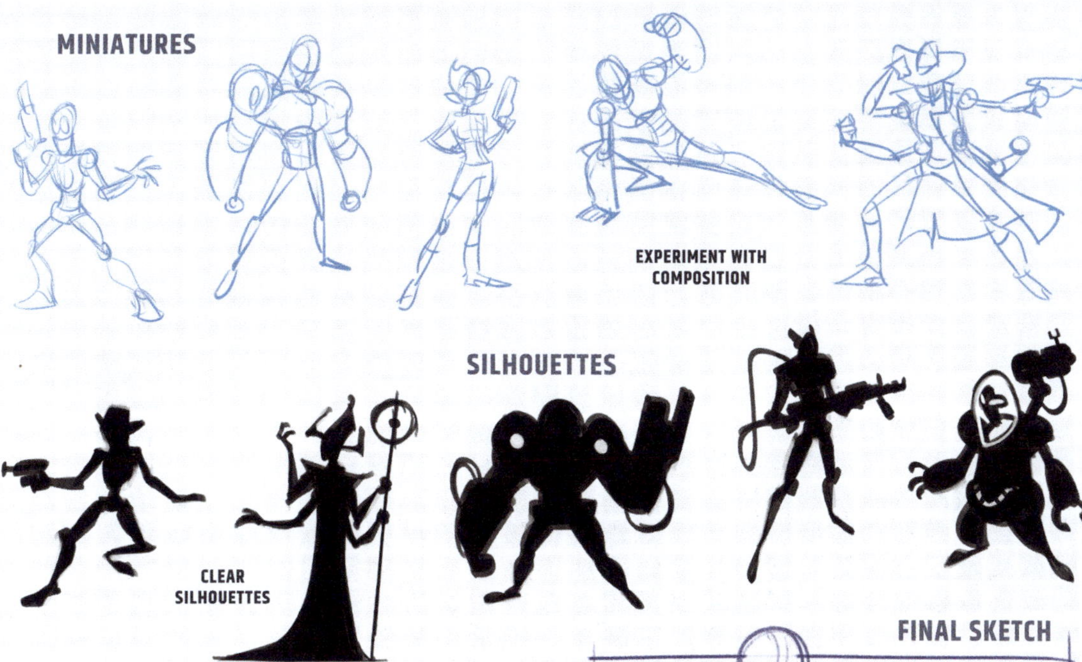

SILHOUETTES

A clear and interesting silhouette is the backbone of any good character or vehicle design. Before moving on to the detailing stage of a drawing, quickly draw a silhouette of your design using a marker or a brush. A strong silhouette is both intriguing and clearly legible. The main parts of the design should be easy to read, with no confusion or unsightly overlaps. Try to break the symmetry also. This will make the design more natural and dynamic.

FINAL SKETCH

Once you have chosen your preferred character or vehicle design from your thumbnails and have found the ideal composition, you can start to define the illustration. Pin down the right proportions and begin to sketch in the details in order to visualize the final illustration more clearly. This sketch will be the foundation for everything that follows, so don't rush – take the time to define the details.

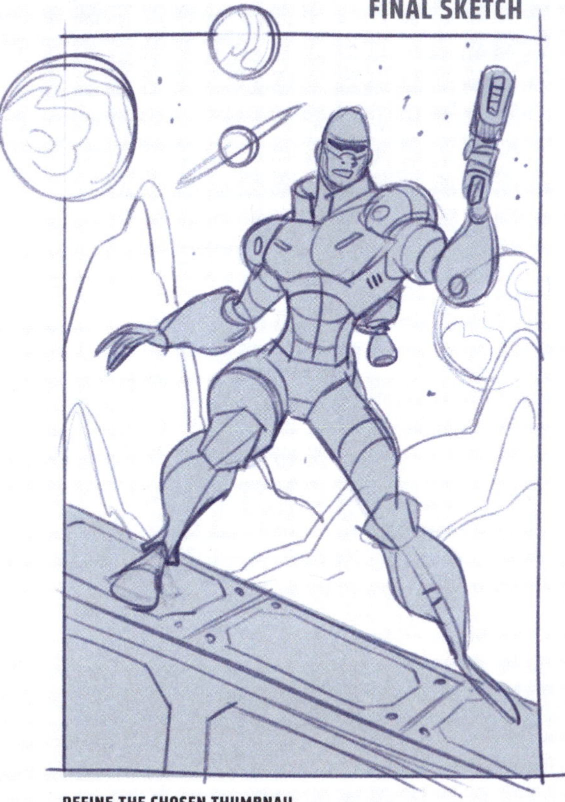

FINAL SKETCH

DEFINE THE CHOSEN THUMBNAIL

STORYTELLING

Every artwork you create should be supported by a narrative component. Each time you draw a new character or vehicle design, take the time to think about its origins and story before you put pencil to paper. This will help you to form an idea of which direction to take the design in, and will also add interest to the artwork.

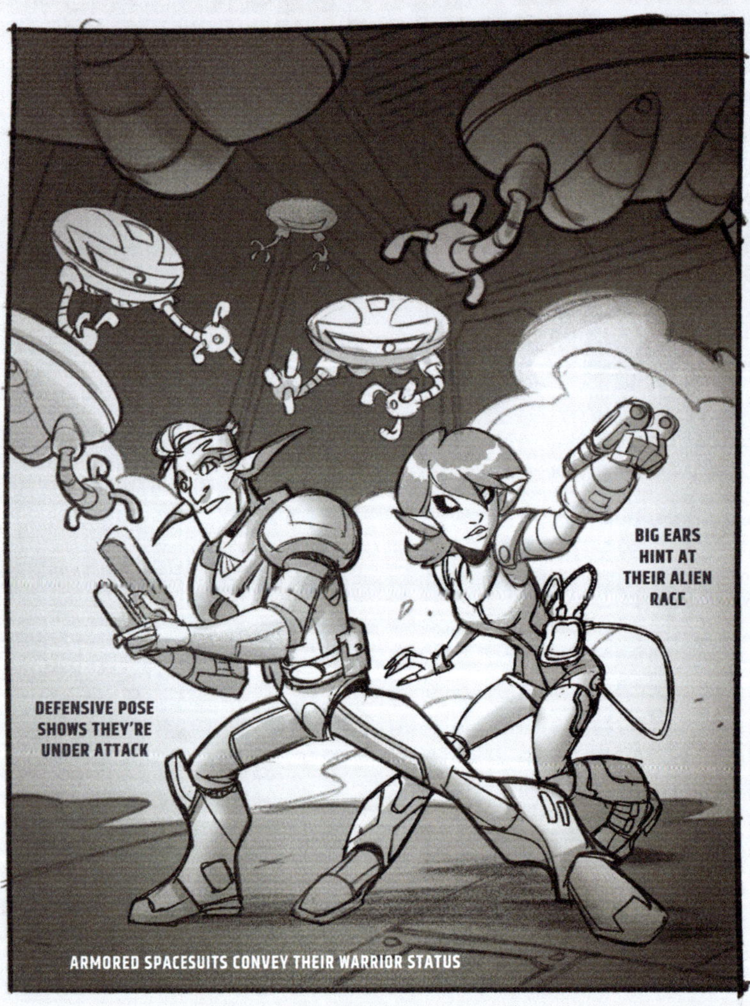

▶ To create a story for your character, consider questions such as: where are they from, what kind of experiences have they had, and how might these have affected them? Once you've created a story for the character, it will affect their shape language, pose, and gesture, as well as the attitude with which they face situations. Certain elements of their life can be reflected in how they dress, such as through details in their clothing and props.

▶ If you're developing a story with a complex narrative, take the time to plan this carefully. Consider how you can put together the character or vehicle's design to help show the viewer who they are.

▶ If you're not concerned with story, but simply wish to give context to your character, you can enrich their design with memorable details. This can include elements that draw attention and intrigue the viewer, leading them to wonder why that specific detail is there and what it says about the character's personality and purpose.

MOTIVATION

The life of an artist isn't always easy. No matter your experience or skill level, there will always be moments of despair that lead you to believe you can't progress. The following tips are here to provide encouragement and motivation on your artistic path.

▶ Try to take the drawing process lightly and don't get too upset if you don't get the desired results right away. In moments of frustration, take a break and relax, returning when you feel calmer. Every creative pursuit requires a great deal of practice and patience. Be intentional about making time to practice the aspects you struggle with.

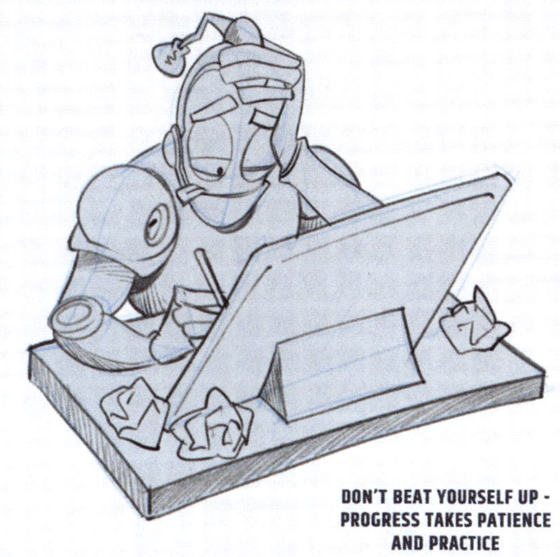
DON'T BEAT YOURSELF UP - PROGRESS TAKES PATIENCE AND PRACTICE

▶ Don't compare yourself to other artists and try not to be disheartened if they are creating artwork that seems impossible for you to achieve. Professional artists will have put in a lot of time and effort behind the scenes to reach their current success. Also, some artists manage to achieve their goals sooner than others. Don't let this discourage you. Everyone has their own path.

▶ Set yourself specific artistic goals, even when drawing for fun. Pursue these with determination and a constant desire to learn. Only with the right attitude will you be able to progress and achieve excellent results.

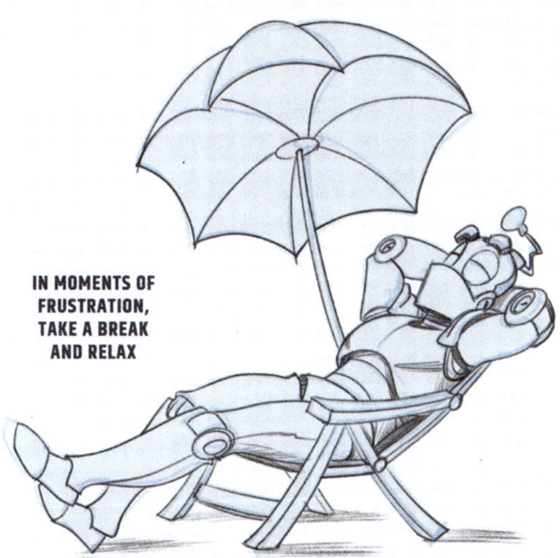
IN MOMENTS OF FRUSTRATION, TAKE A BREAK AND RELAX

▶ Don't fall into the trap of believing that you have reached your best and have nothing to improve on. There will always be more skills and techniques to learn and ways to progress.

▶ Practice working on elaborate projects. Give backstory and context to what you draw – this will make your work richer and more memorable, and may even bring new opportunities you didn't consider.

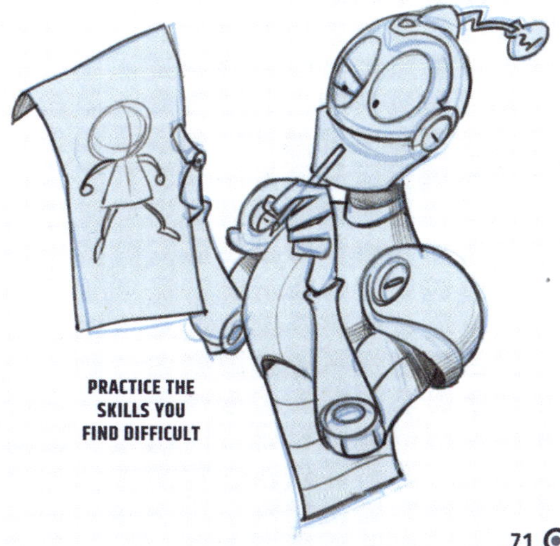
PRACTICE THE SKILLS YOU FIND DIFFICULT

TUTORIALS

Now that you have an understanding of drawing tools, design techniques, and the sci-fi genre, it's to time start putting your newfound knowledge into practice. The following section contains ten tutorials by ten leading artists, each guiding you through how to design a variety of different characters, robots, and spacecrafts. Each tutorial follows a similar process, though some of the artists offer variations on this example workflow. The tutorials demonstrate a wide range of styles and approaches, so follow each one in turn to find the workflow and style best suited to you and your own creative process.

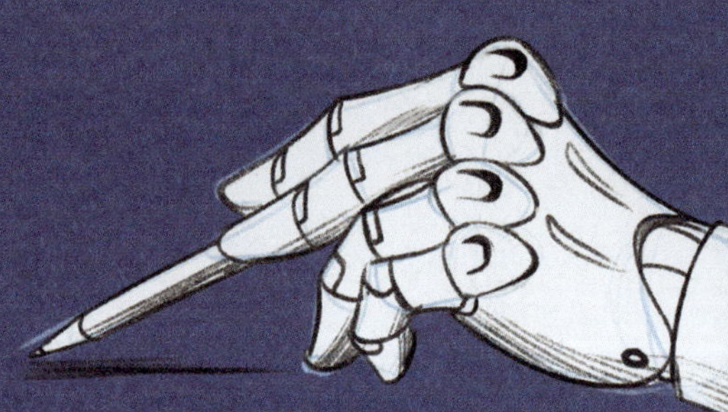

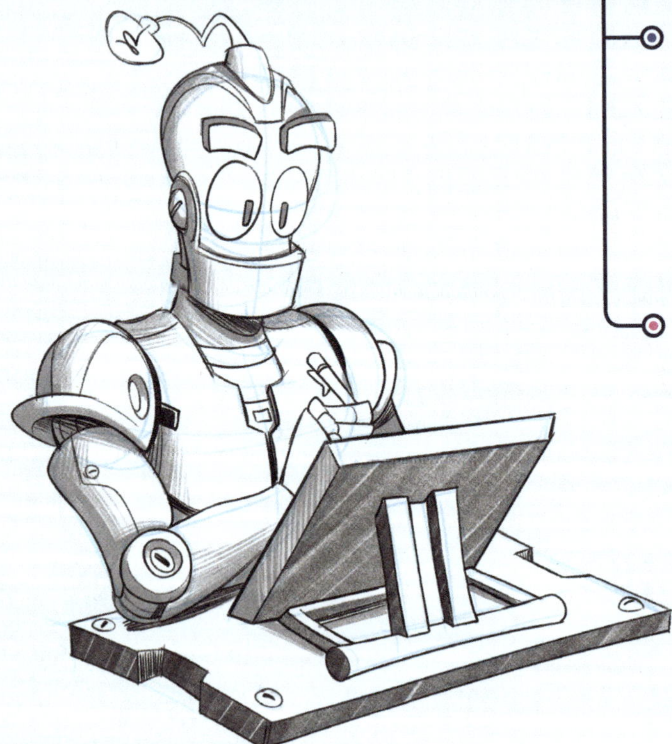

RESEARCH

Every successful character or craft design begins with research. Working from a wide range of reference material will enable you to produce a much more interesting and plausible design. Use what each artist researches to inspire your own reference collection.

THUMBNAILS

Creating rough thumbnail sketches allows you to explore a variety of different concepts, compositions, proportions, and silhouettes before choosing which design elements to take forward. Observe how each artist uses this stage to refine their ideas and choose one to progress with.

DOWNLOADABLE RESOURCES

Drawing can be challenging and it's not unusual to face situations where you need a little extra help and guidance. Visit **3dtotalpublishing.com/resources** and discover a selection of downloadable resources to help as you work through the following chapters. The resources include line work for each tutorial plus several anatomy sketches (human and robot), all of which can be printed out to provide helpful guides as you draw. Once you've completed the ten tutorials in the book, you can download an exclusive bonus project that will take you a step further in terms of complexity and skill. Plus, we've provided some exciting project briefs to inspire your own futuristic sci-fi drawings.

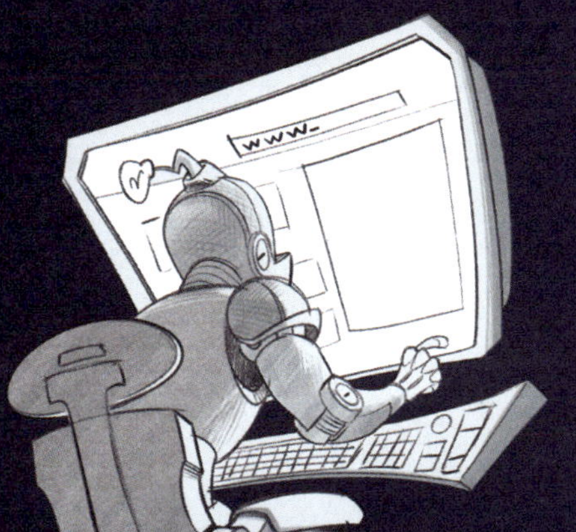

FOUNDATIONS

A strong drawing requires a strong foundation. Watch how each artist uses this stage to sketch the simple building blocks of the design, providing a solid base for drawing detail on top of later.

BUILDING UP

With the foundation in place, a full-size pencil sketch can be drawn on top. Read the tips each artist offers for drawing specific areas of the design and adding initial details.

IDEA INVENTORY

Before drawing a final sketch, take the time to explore different design variations that could develop the concept. Watch how the artists use this step to spark a new idea or put a new spin on their current design.

FINAL SKETCH

Once all variations have been explored, a final pencil sketch can be drawn. See how the artists use this step to clean up the design in preparation for inking.

INKING

The inking process involves creating clean line work of the final design, in preparation for adding color. Follow how the artists refine their drawing, while also varying the line weight to add depth and interest.

COLORING

Whether using colored pencils, markers, or watercolor, finish by bringing your drawing to life with color. The ten artists have used a variety of different media – step out of your comfort zone and experiment with some new tools, or follow along with the tools you have to hand.

SPACE GUN

BY KENNETH ANDERSON

Want to learn how to design a futuristic space gun? This tutorial will demonstrate a basic design process that takes you step-by-step from your initial idea through to a finished design, considering appropriate design choices along the way. Stylistically, the space gun will be fun and comical, rather than menacing or deadly. Avoid all thoughts of traditional guns and instead think along the lines of a space-slime thrower, a lightning-bolt ray gun, or even a cosmic stardust launcher!

This tutorial will be created using traditional media, including colored pencils and watercolors to finish. Col-Erase pencils are perfect, as they are designed to be erasable. Plus they are waxy and soft, which makes for versatile line work.

TOOLKIT

▸ Black pencil

▸ Eraser

▸ Light box or thin paper

▸ Colored pencils

▸ Watercolors

RESEARCH

While it's impossible to research the future, you can draw on the past and present for inspiration. Familiarize yourself with the basic functionality of a gun and look up reference material. Sketch studies of fifties-style ray guns, children's water pistols from the nineties, and even archaic pirate pistols! Your goal is to understand the ergonomics of a gun, while getting a feel for how you can change and exaggerate it in your own sci-fi design.

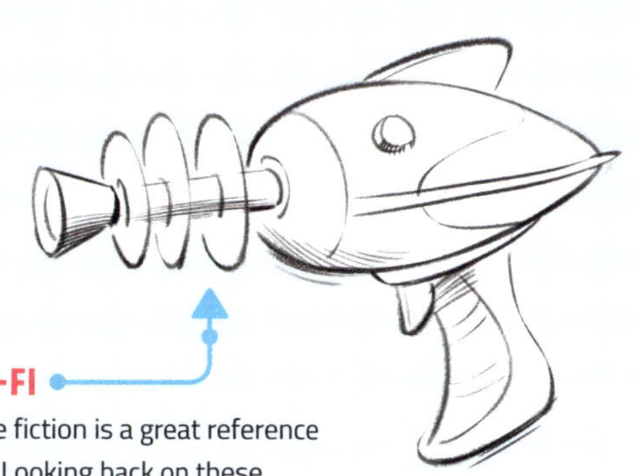

RETRO SCI-FI

Fifties science fiction is a great reference for this topic. Looking back on these designs, they look comical and fun, which is exactly the direction you want.

RAY GUNS

Look up various retro ray-gun designs to draw inspiration from. The organic forms and repeating tubes of this sketch work well.

WATER TANKS

Nineties water pistols are full of fun shapes, with tanks to store the water. Could a similar design be used to store space slime?

PIRATES

Historic pirate pistols often have ornate or interesting designs. Maybe this gun belongs to a futuristic space pirate!

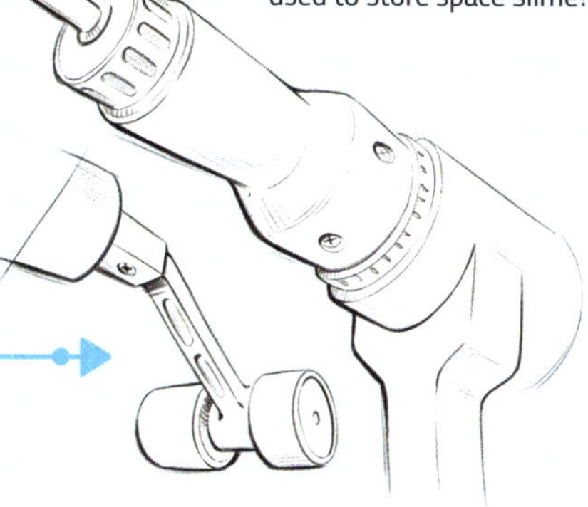

TECH & TOOLS

Consider researching present-day space technology too. These sketches are based on tools used to repair the Hubble Space Satellite.

THUMBNAILS

Once the research stage has provided sufficient ideas, it's time to start sketching. A blunt black pencil is a great tool for thumbnailing, as it will prevent you from adding too much detail too quickly. Experiment with shapes and general construction, not worrying about details just yet. Your aim is to find a design with fun shapes and a clear silhouette, while exploring different types of gun and their various functions. As you draw, keep in mind the direction you want to take your sketches in – retro, chunky, and over the top! Draw on the inspiration provided by your research.

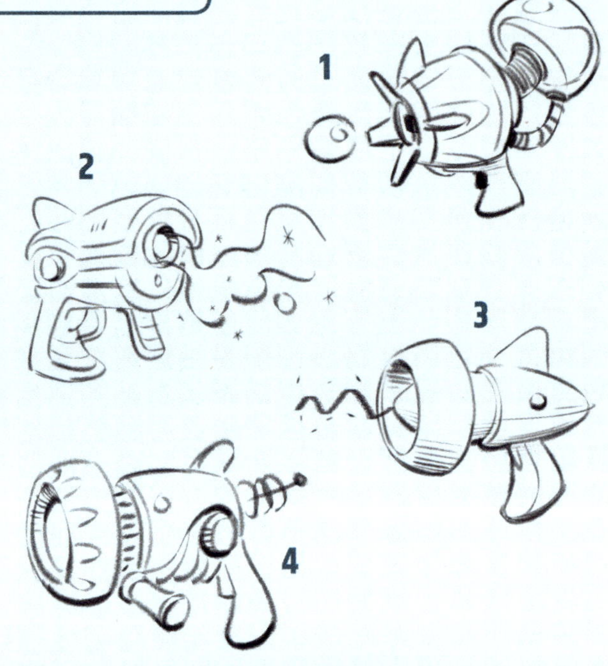

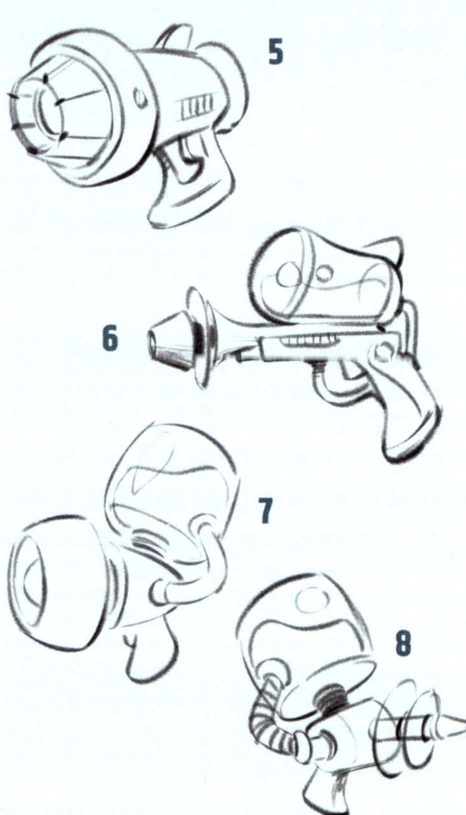

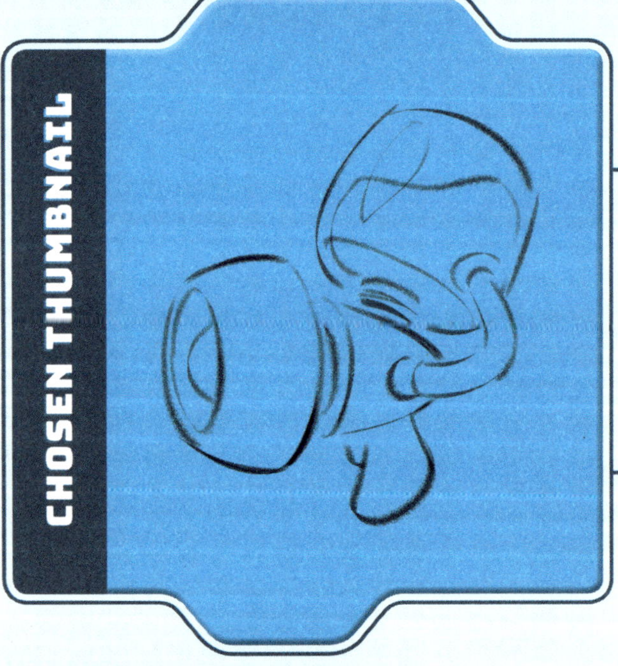

▶ The chosen thumbnail is funky and ray-gun-like, with an eccentric sci-fi style. The shapes work well together and it has a strong overall silhouette. It will work well as a space-slime launcher!

FOUNDATIONS

With a rough idea in place, you can begin to develop it further and properly establish its base forms and construction. While a loose thumbnail sketch suggests forms and construction quite well, it's important to establish the different volumes that make up the design and consider some more details. Continue using the colored pencils here; your goal is to take the rough sketch and clarify it further.

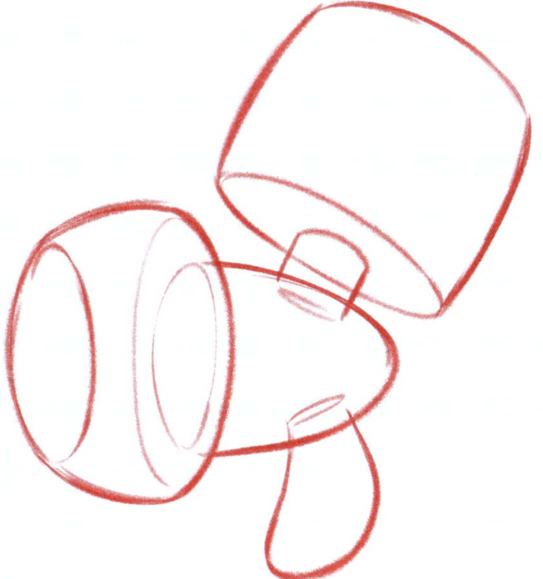

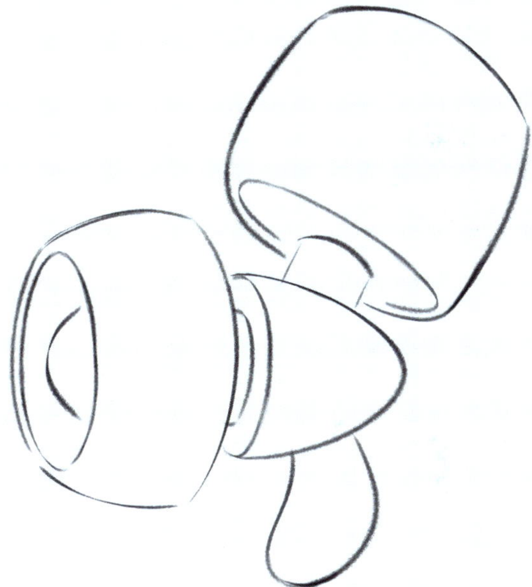

BASE

▶ This sketch is made up of simple shapes – mainly cylinders and cones. Note the subtle differences between them, which add variation.

▶ The shapes are chunky and slightly rounded, with no hard edges. This will add to the feeling that this space gun is fun and comical, rather than threatening.

▶ The gun's main structure comes from the cone-shaped body – everything else expands from that. Take care to draw in perspective and feel out the forms of the shapes as 3D objects on the page.

LINES

▶ With the simple geometry of the design broken down, it's easy to draw on top with a little more attention to detail. Begin to add more complexity to the forms.

▶ Break up the body of the gun – the cone shape – by cutting into it as it meets the rounded form at the front. This will make the design slightly more visually appealing.

▶ The front of the gun should have an indentation. Again, this will add visual interest to the design. Try to visualize the forms as you draw, observing how they go in and out and intersect with the other forms.

BUILDING UP

With the major forms now in place, begin to break them up with some medium-sized elements. The key is not to get too carried away. You don't want to add too much that it breaks the design or overcomplicates it. Start to add a few key features, such as the slime container on the top of the gun. Sketch the pipe coming out of the side of the slime container into the main body. Add detail around the trigger, nozzle, and the joints that connect the major parts.

▶ Experiment with the gun's front section to give it a nozzle-like look. It should look as though it is designed to shoot slime.

▶ The key idea of this design is that it shoots slime. The slime tank should look like a believable container – drawing lines on top to denote the slime level will sell the idea of transparency.

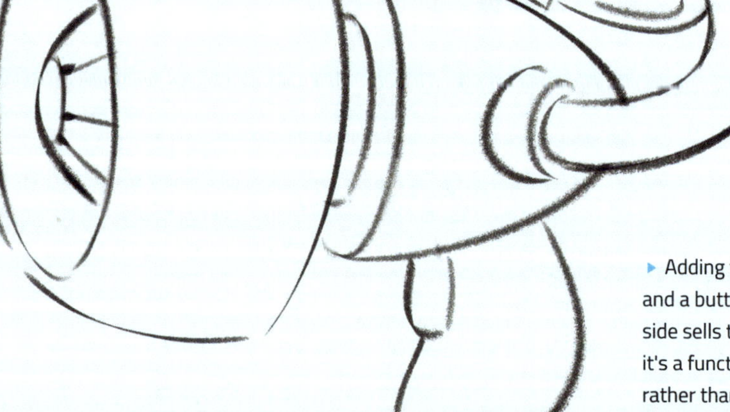

▶ Adding the trigger and a button on the side sells the idea that it's a functional object, rather than some kind of ridiculous joke gun.

DESIGN FOCUS

NOZZLE

Creating the feeling of the indentation at the front of the gun is quite simple. By drawing the nozzle shape underneath the circle opening, the overlapping of shapes will sell the idea of depth.

TUBE

It can help to think of the tube that connects the slime tank and body of the gun as a bendy rectangle. To make it feel tubelike, pay attention to how it curves at both ends to connect to the other forms. Sketch curved lines along the body of the shape to emphasize this further.

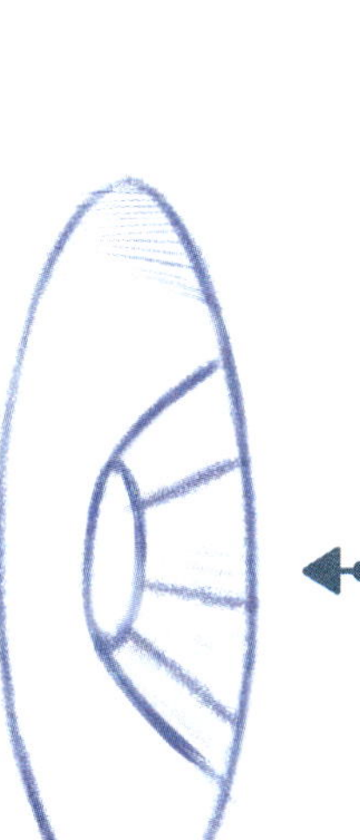

HANDLE

The handle of the gun needs to feel ergonomic and suitable for its purpose: to be held in a hand. The shape of this handle is more complex than the others; slightly tubelike, but with more organic forms and a wider base.

IDEA INVENTORY

SLIME TANK

Experiment with variations of slime tank. Perhaps there are two tanks, each holding a different type of space slime? Or maybe the tank is a different shape – a little more streamlined with no tubes?

FRONTAL NOZZLE

Play around with ideas for the frontal nozzle to find something that is visually appealing but still functional. The big cone shape could open as slime is fired! The more nozzle-like shape suggests a stream of slime.

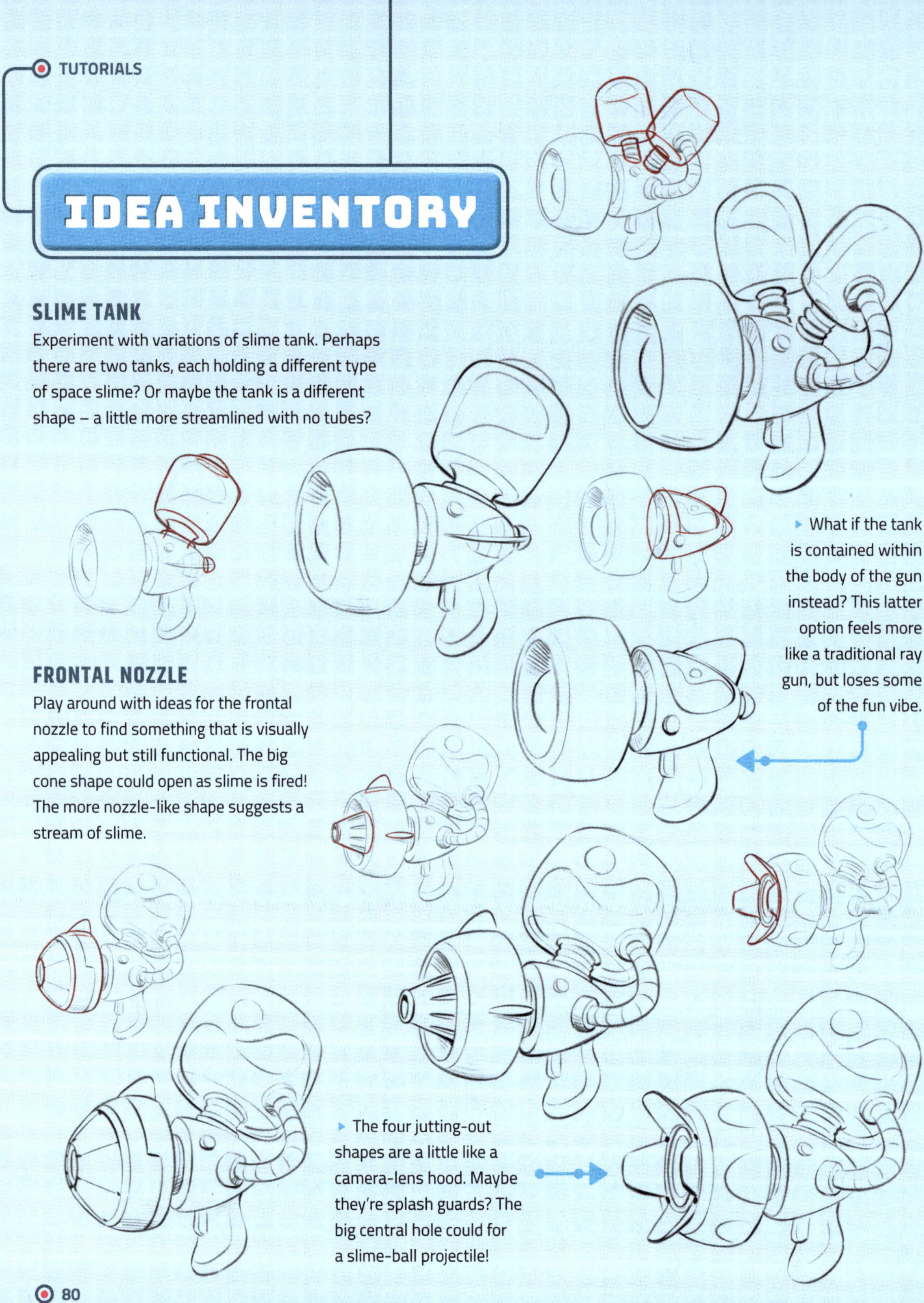

▶ What if the tank is contained within the body of the gun instead? This latter option feels more like a traditional ray gun, but loses some of the fun vibe.

▶ The four jutting-out shapes are a little like a camera-lens hood. Maybe they're splash guards? The big central hole could for a slime-ball projectile!

FINAL SKETCH

Create a final sketch using your rough designs as reference. One approach is to trace over your image – placing thinner paper on top or using a light box. If you don't have a light box, try using masking tape to attach your sketch to a window, with a new piece of paper placed on top. The daylight will allow you to trace your design.

Explore what idea inventory designs you can carry over into your final sketch. This sketch keeps the big slime tank, as well as including a tank in the main body of the gun. It also adds the four projecting hoods onto the nozzle to break the design up a little.

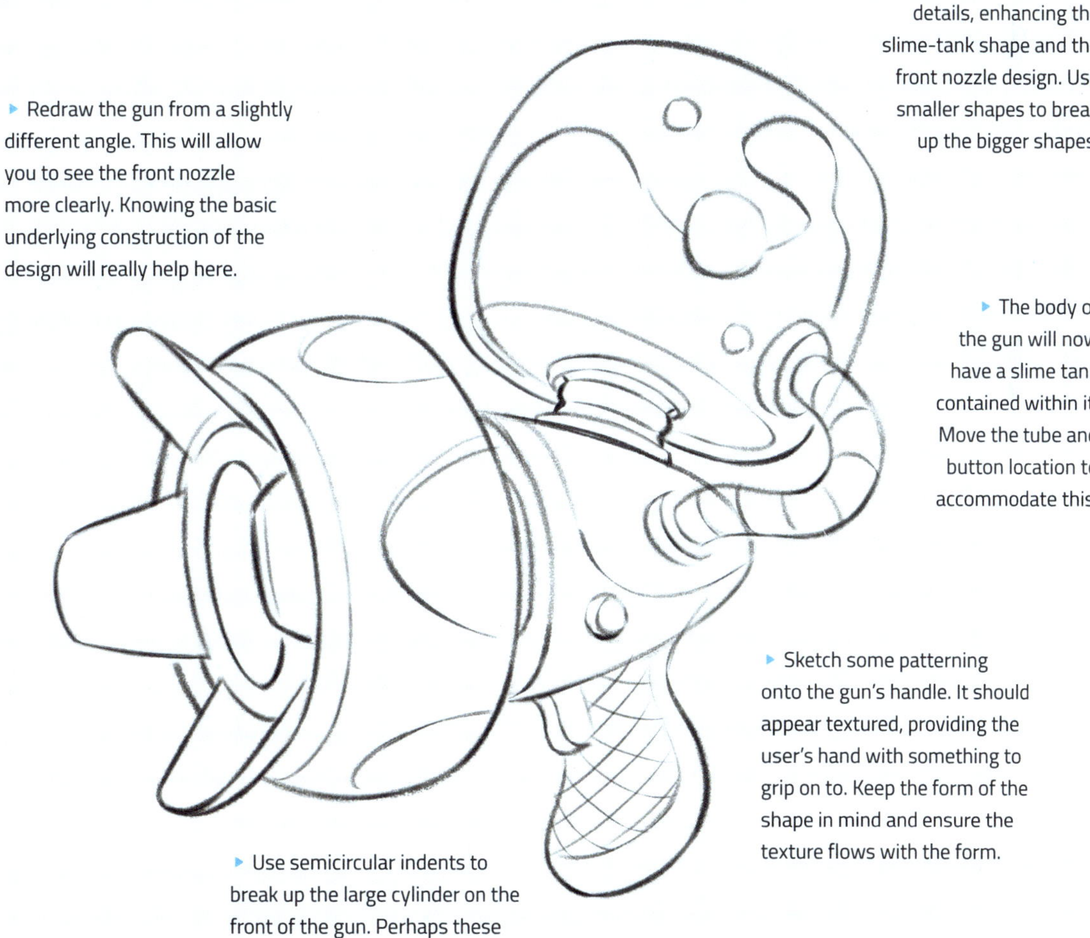

▶ Start to introduce more details, enhancing the slime-tank shape and the front nozzle design. Use smaller shapes to break up the bigger shapes.

▶ Redraw the gun from a slightly different angle. This will allow you to see the front nozzle more clearly. Knowing the basic underlying construction of the design will really help here.

▶ The body of the gun will now have a slime tank contained within it. Move the tube and button location to accommodate this.

▶ Sketch some patterning onto the gun's handle. It should appear textured, providing the user's hand with something to grip on to. Keep the form of the shape in mind and ensure the texture flows with the form.

▶ Use semicircular indents to break up the large cylinder on the front of the gun. Perhaps these could glow with neon light.

FINAL LINE ART

Use a sharper black pencil to draw the final line art. Draw over the sketch, working into the lines, refining and clarifying them. Make the lines on the underside of the forms darker and thicker – this will create the idea of shadows and can really improve the line work. Avoid using the same line thickness everywhere, but vary the line weight to create the impression of the different materials and construction.

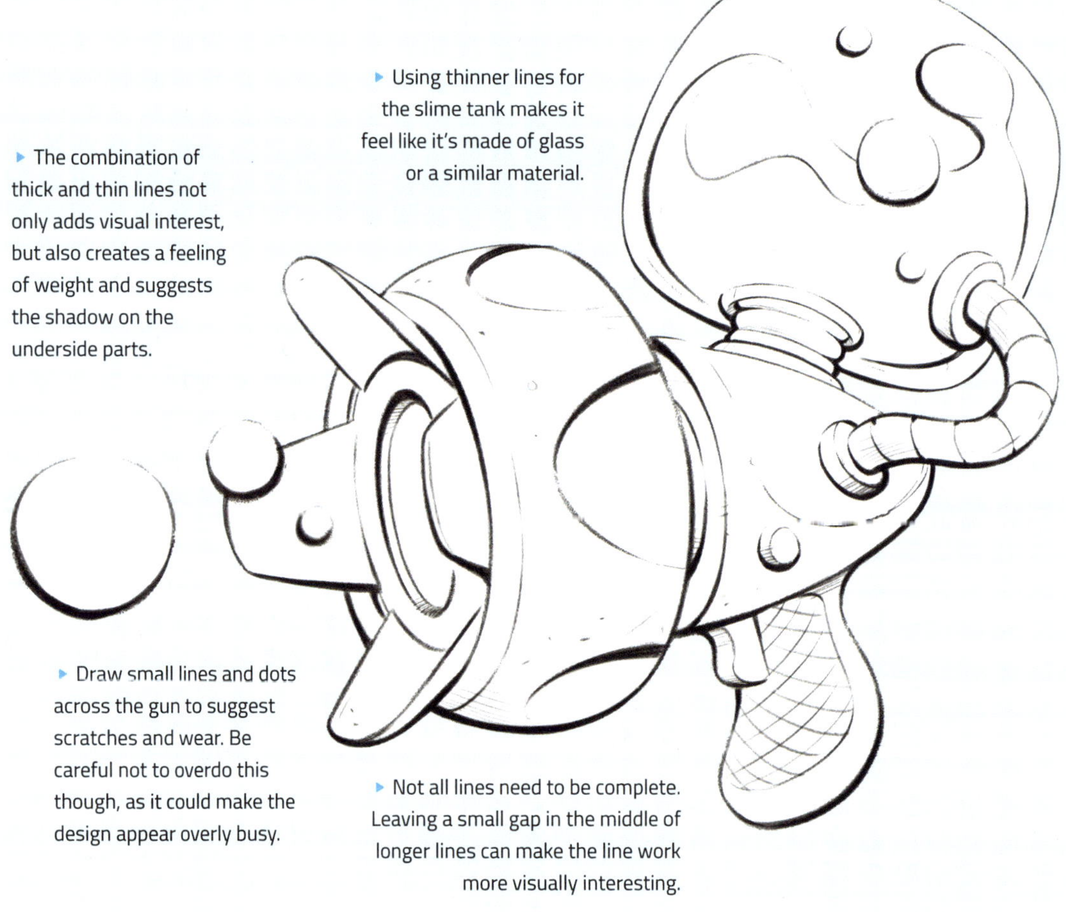

▶ The combination of thick and thin lines not only adds visual interest, but also creates a feeling of weight and suggests the shadow on the underside parts.

▶ Using thinner lines for the slime tank makes it feel like it's made of glass or a similar material.

▶ Draw small lines and dots across the gun to suggest scratches and wear. Be careful not to overdo this though, as it could make the design appear overly busy.

▶ Not all lines need to be complete. Leaving a small gap in the middle of longer lines can make the line work more visually interesting.

COLORING

Use colored pencils to build up color and form using a simple cross-hatching technique. Select a bright pink for the space slime, as this is fun and striking, then base your other color choices around this. For the rest of the gun, use a combination of warm orange-yellow tones, broken up with neutral grays and black for the metallic parts, and a complementary blue for the glass sections.

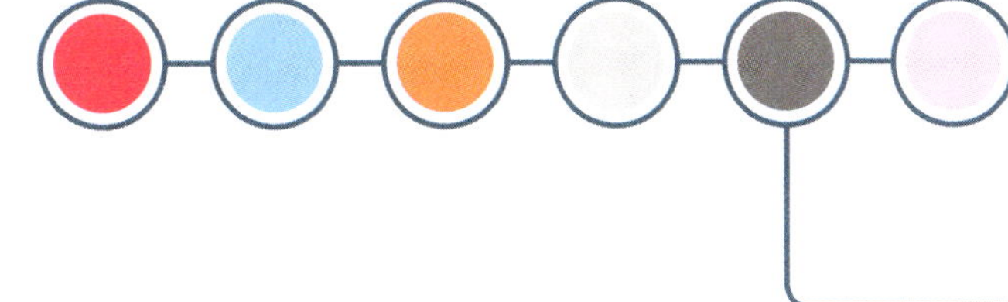

▶ Ensure your pencil lines follow the forms of each shape and section; for example, on the handle and around the large round nozzle.

▶ Use cross-hatching to gradually build up the colored pencil lines.

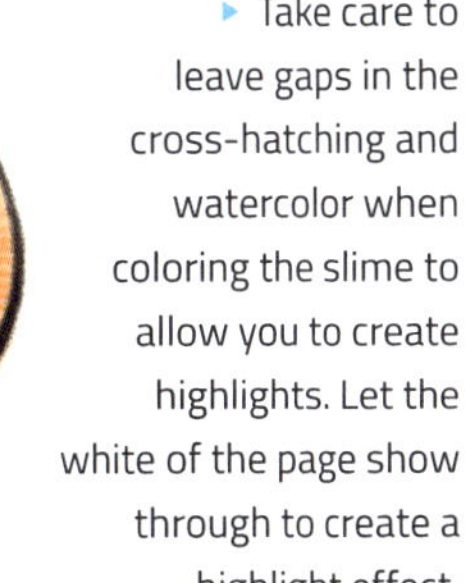

▶ Use a light watercolor wash to fill in any gaps in the cross-hatching and strengthen the colors of the space gun.

▶ Take care to leave gaps in the cross-hatching and watercolor when coloring the slime to allow you to create highlights. Let the white of the page show through to create a highlight effect.

▶ Final image © Kenneth Anderson

SOLARPUNK BIKER GIRL

BY MARGAUX KINDHAUSER

This tutorial will guide you through how to draw a solarpunk biker girl. Our heroine is young, confident, smart, and dynamic, traveling across the country with her eco-friendly solar-powered bike as her only companion. Her fashion sense mirrors her love of nature through green colors, while her wild punk hairstyle and the bold accent colors in her clothing show off her fiery character. You will learn how to make her personality shine through the use of sharp design silhouettes and lines, what features to exaggerate, and how to create a detailed yet clear costume design that combines both futuristic and classic punk features.

TOOLKIT

- ▸ Colored pencil
- ▸ Mechanical pencil with B and 2B lead
- ▸ Click eraser
- ▸ Ballpoint pen
- ▸ Watercolors
- ▸ Watercolor brush

RESEARCH

Two important parts of the character will be her costume and hairstyle, both drawn in a solarpunk style. Punk fashion is immediately recognizable and features a wide range of clothing and props, meaning reference photographs are easy to find. You will then need to introduce futuristic sci-fi features to these. As the character loves nature and sustainability, and her bike is solar-powered, it could be useful to explore nature-themed symbols such as leaves, trees, water, stars, and the sun, as well as the color green.

HAIRSTYLE

A flamboyant hairstyle for a flamboyant personality! The hair is shaven on one side, with spiky strands on the other. This conveys her wild and feisty persona, while also nicely balancing the head's overall design.

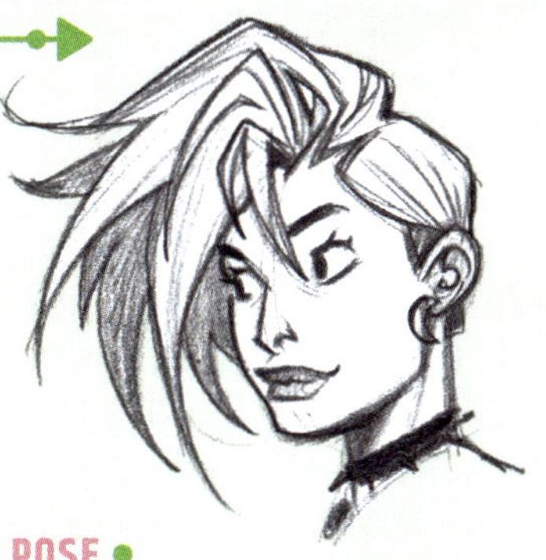

POSE

Researching an appropriate pose helps to define the character's silhouette. Before exaggerating other features, it can be useful to choose one element to "pop" out from the drawing. Here it's the hair!

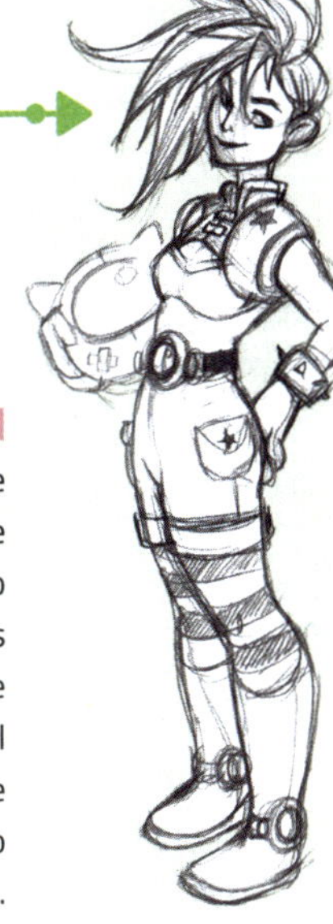

COSTUME DESIGN

Exploring different costume ideas will help to define the character's personality. Go with the flow, adding lots of little details that can be kept or discarded in the final design. It's always best to have more details than you need to experiment with.

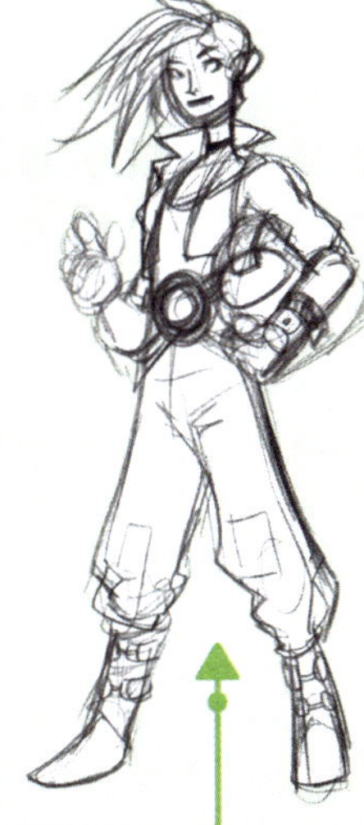

CLOTHES

Designing different clothing options can help with finding strong shapes and volumes. Here the baggy pants add an interesting shape to the overall character.

PROPS

Props can help with world-building, adding story and personality to the character. These designs suggest a futuristic, yet slightly vintage form of ecological energy supply. Note the sun motif on the central piece of the belt.

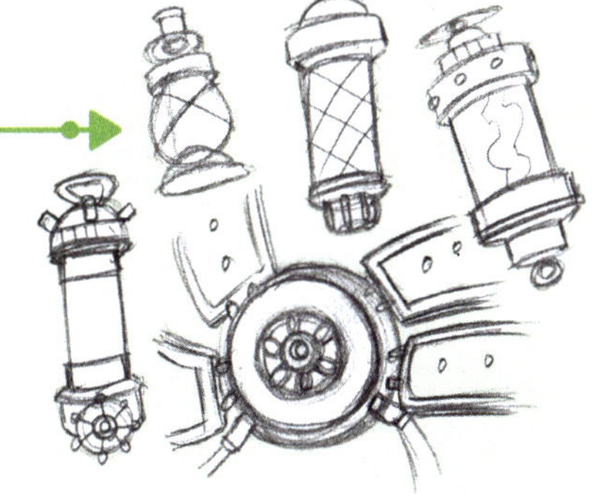

THUMBNAILS

Thumbnails help to define clear shapes and contrast in your character's design. The silhouette must be dynamic, sharp, and flow seamlessly, all at the same time. Contrasting the slender figure of the biker girl with large details from her costume and props will make the design look more striking, balanced, and visually pleasing.

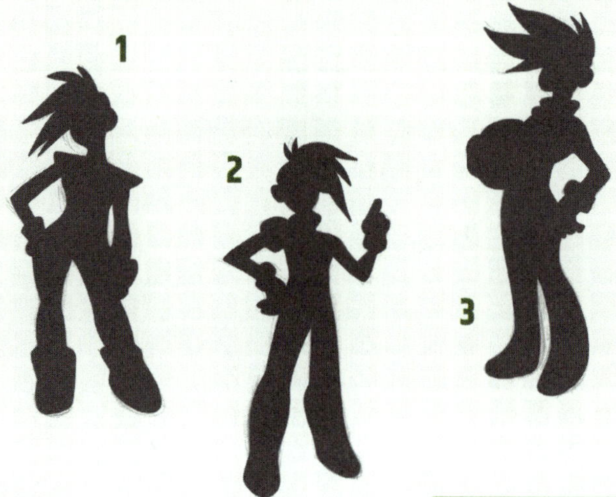

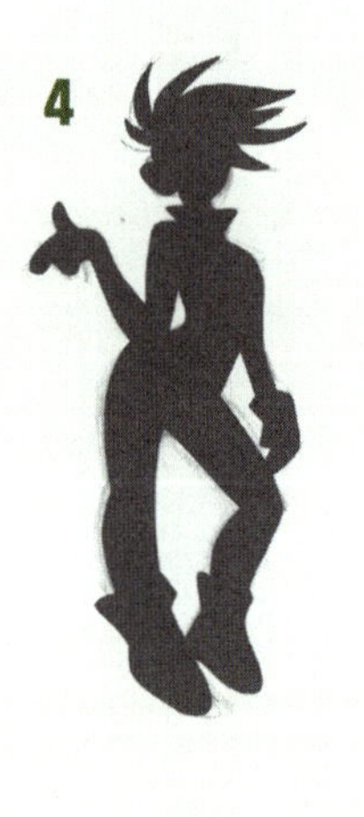

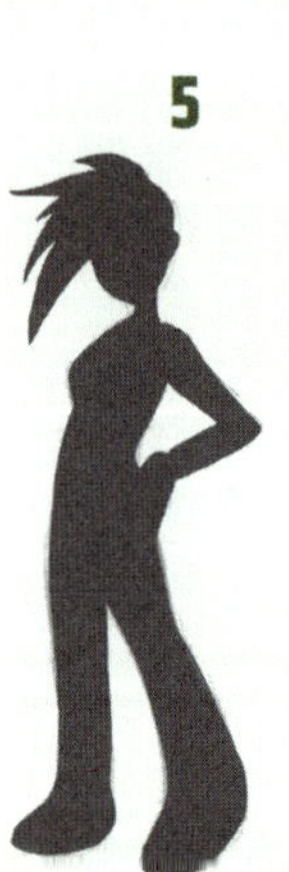

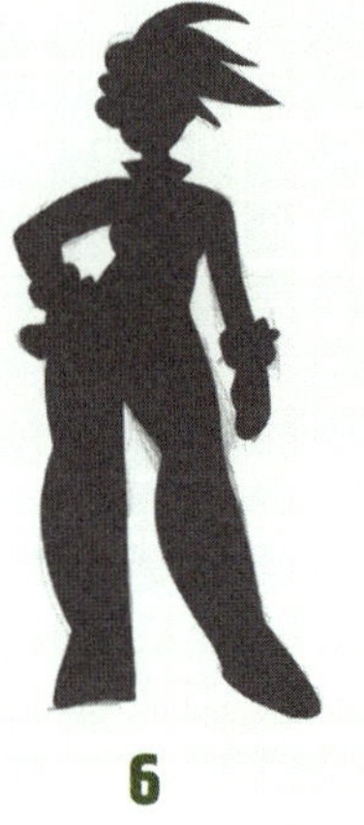

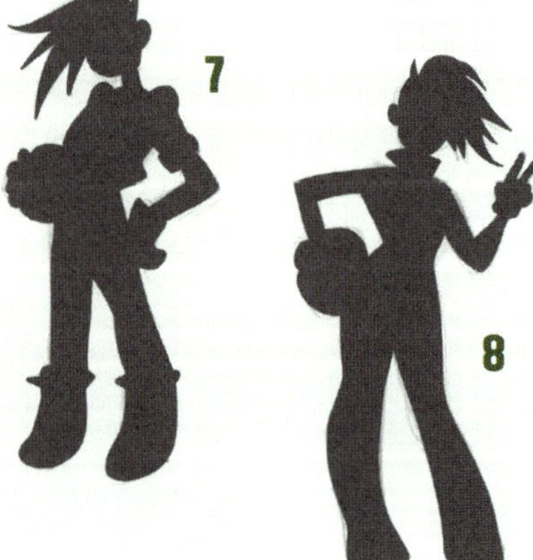

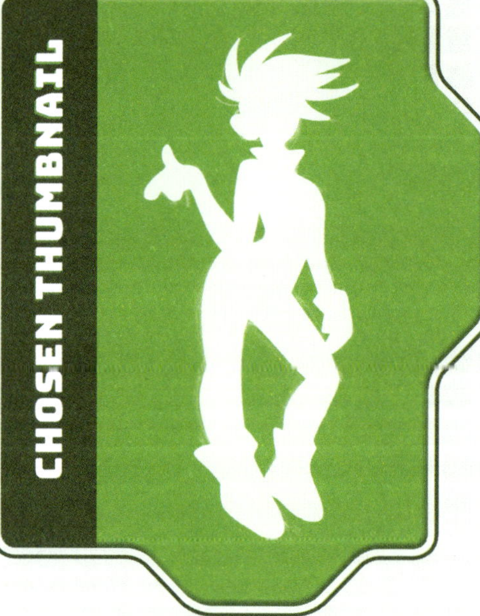

▶ This thumbnail is the most interesting; the pose is action-packed, flows well, and conveys the character's confident, sassy personality. The large boots and big hairstyle balance one another nicely. Slim characters with oversized features – such as gloves, hat, hair, or shoes – work well from a design perspective.

FOUNDATIONS

With a thumbnail chosen, the next stage is to transcribe the small silhouette into a larger sketch. First, break down the main components of the thumbnail (head, torso, hips, arms, hands, feet, and legs) into basic geometric shapes. A colored pencil will allow you to draw light lines that will be perfect for laying out the foundations of the illustration. The aim is to capture the proportions accurately. From this base, you will be able to add details as you go, without losing the strong design features that will make your character stand out.

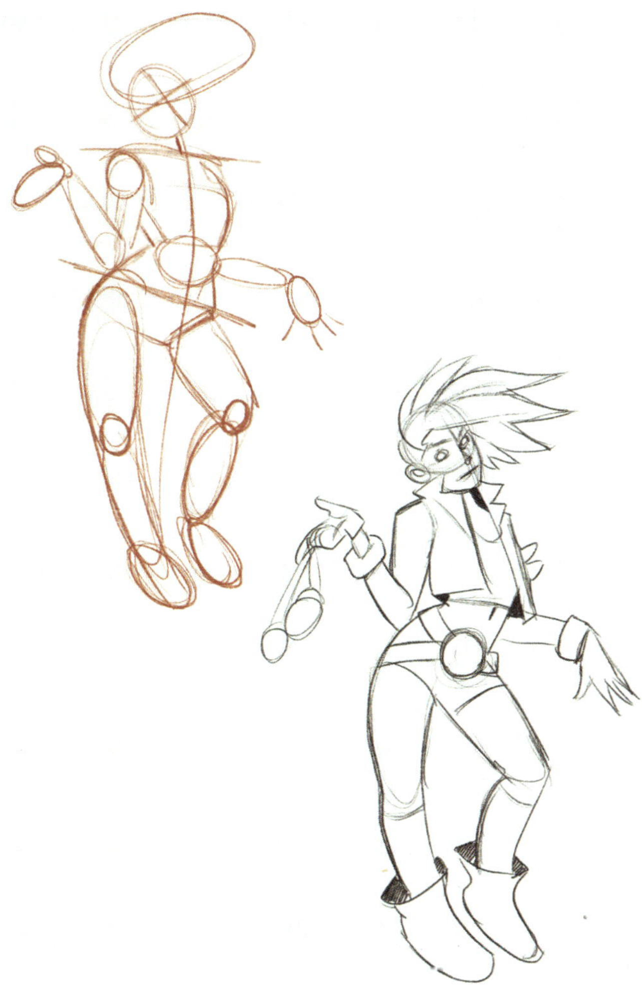

BASE

▶ Draw mostly round shapes to match the smooth design of the chosen thumbnail. Starting with the head, sketch shapes of different sizes to help find balance in the design, such as drawing big round shapes for the hair or shoes.

▶ Sketch a line of action that starts at the head and ends between the legs to add dynamism to your drawing. Next, draw tilted lines for the shoulders and hips. Drawing these lines in slightly opposite directions will help the character's pose look more dynamic.

▶ The torso will be hourglass-shaped. Sketch joints for the shoulders and hips within the torso. Using round shapes for these joints will help to define volume and angles in key parts of the body.

LINES

▶ Starting with the head, trace a line for the eyes that follows the tilt of the chosen pose. Place the eyes, nose, and lips fairly loosely at this stage. The face is very important to get right early on, as it will help to define the general feel and emotion you want to convey throughout the rest of the design.

▶ A clever design trick is to place straight and broken lines in opposition to one another. For example, look at the character's right leg — the inner line is almost completely straight, whereas along the outer edge there is an indent at knee-level. Playing with opposites brings a nice balance to the design.

▶ Start placing some costume elements. Consider how you can use certain lines to help define volume. For example, the boots shape the roundness of the legs, while the jacket wraps around the character's torso.

BUILDING UP

With the proportions defined by geometric shapes, you can now begin to refine the basic anatomy. This stage involves defining the eyes, facial expression, and body shape, plus a few elements of the costume that will be worked on more closely in the following step. The aim is to decide on the main features of the character without going into too much detail.

FACE

Start with the face and expression. The character is sassy, smart, and outgoing. This should be reflected with lively eyes, arched eyebrows, and a smile that is wider on one side of the face.

HAIR

The character's hair is a prominent feature of her design. Adding details will help to convey its volume. Show the top side of some strands and the underside of others. This will add depth to the face.

COSTUME

Introduce a few details to the costume and props, taking care to prioritize shape design. Be aware of their size in comparison to the rest of the drawing. Always take the time to step back and look at your drawing from afar to put things into perspective. Is the belt too small? Are the shoes too big?

DESIGN FOCUS

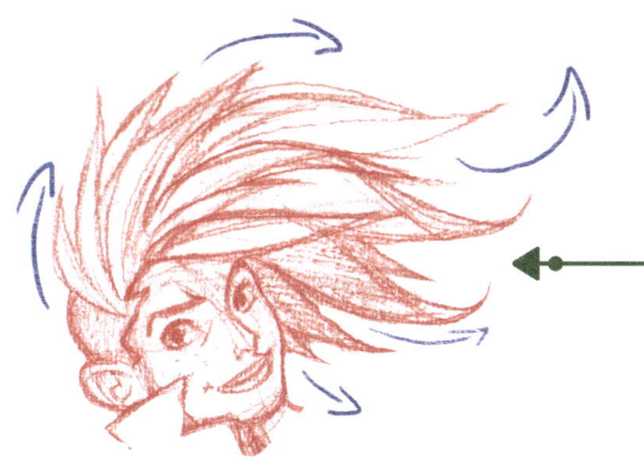

HAIRSTYLE

The hairstyle needs to be immediately recognizable as punk. The shapes can be exaggerated, with sharp, flame-like strands to emphasize the character's fiery personality. This also balances out the whole silhouette nicely.

HANDS

Wristbands are a great way to break up the shape of small, slender arms and hands. This is a classic design trick, bringing contrast to the general shape of the silhouette.

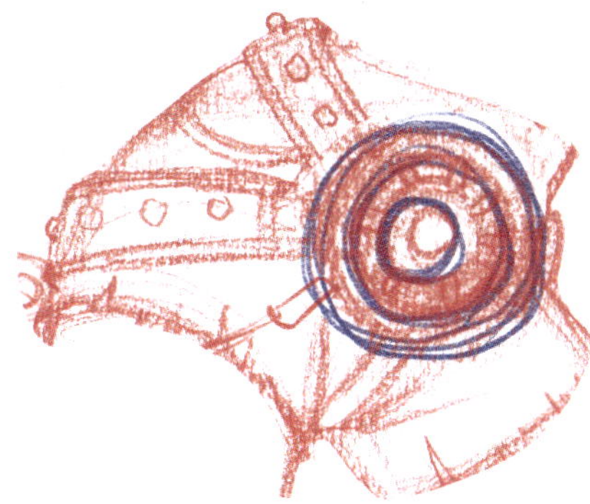

BELT

The belt buckle, with its sun-inspired design, is a good prop to exaggerate in size. Not only will it be eye-catching, but it will add a touch of retro-futurism to the character's costume.

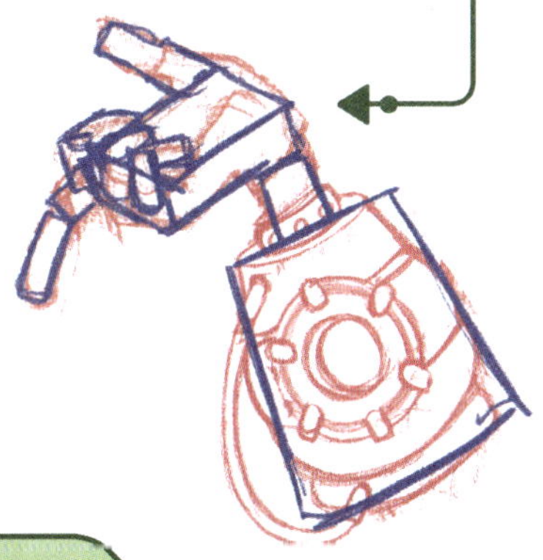

IDEA INVENTORY

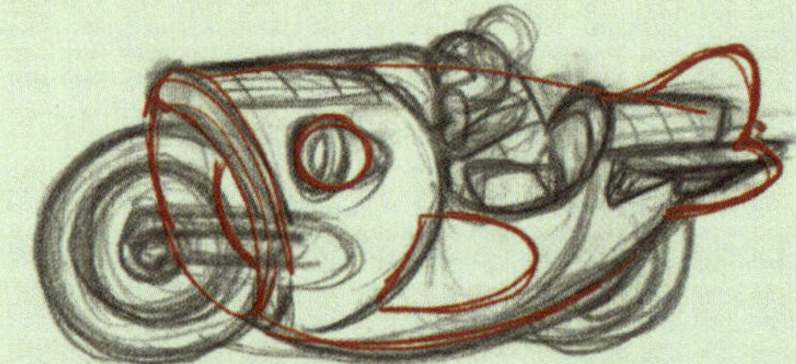

VEHICLE

The character's bike should complement her personality and core eco values. Some shapes, lines, and volumes can mirror her general design, with details and props also carrying over. For the overall design of the bike, continue the eco theme by exploring references of natural imagery. The fish-inspired motorbike (top) has clean, aerodynamic lines and a distinct urban, futuristic vibe.

Expand your research and draw inspiration from retro scooter brands, such as Vespa, combining these with sci-fi details. This will better fit the character's solarpunk theme. Making the shapes rounder and less aerodynamic makes them appear less urban and cold.

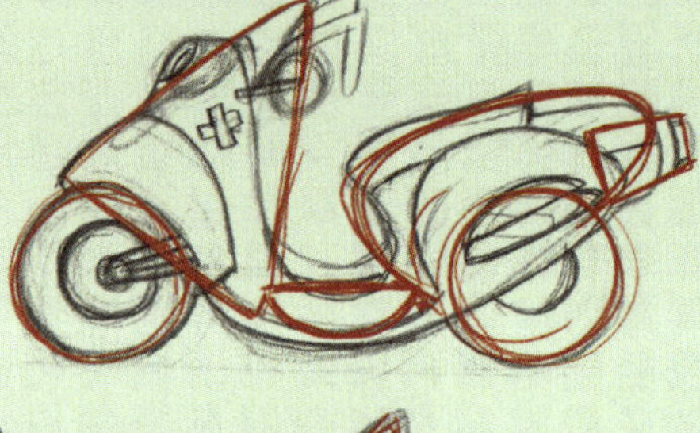

▶ Details like celestial stickers, solar panels, and battery compartments show the bike's solar-powered engineering. This third design reflects the character's punk personality best.

BOOTS

The first boot design has a strong punk aesthetic, with thick soles and numerous buckles. Though interesting and fun to draw, it lacks the sci-fi look and needs to include more futuristic details. Try to match prop designs together. For example, the second boot sketch mirrors the fishlike vehicle. The lines are clean, there are no heels, and the buckle matches the power-cell design from the bike.

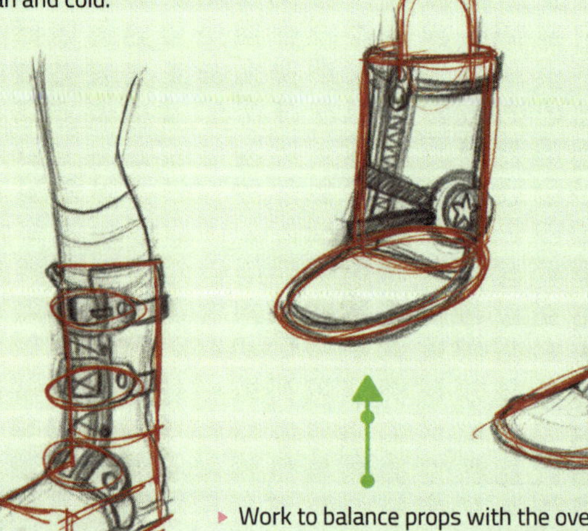

▶ Work to balance props with the overall silhouette. Bulky shoes contrast with the character's slim legs, while also mirroring her large hairstyle.

FINAL SKETCH

In the final sketch, the drawing is almost ready to be inked. The proportions are correct, all of the props are included in the costume design, and the pose is well-balanced and dynamic. The lines are soft and will disappear once the ink is applied. Erasing these first sketch lines is not always necessary if they are light. Keeping these soft lines a little visible can give the artwork more life, which can sometimes be lost in the inking stage.

▶ The head and facial expression are probably the most important elements to get right, as it's the area the viewer will look at first. Take your time on the eyes and expression. Consider the little details, such as the shape of eyebrows, and how to create the illusion of bold, punk makeup that echoes her costume design.

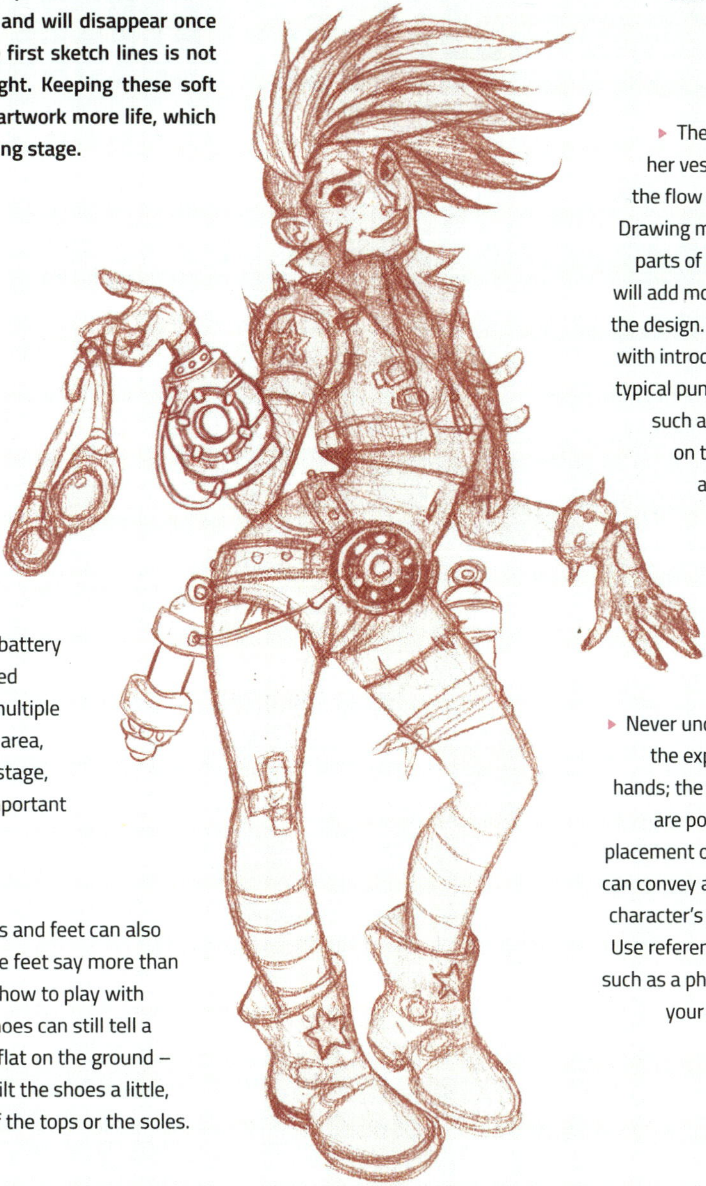

▶ The volumes of her vest top match the flow of the pose. Drawing movement in parts of the clothing will add more action to the design. Experiment with introducing a few typical punk elements, such as the spikes on the shoulder and bracelet.

▶ The central solar-powered battery on the character's belt will need cleaning up. When there are multiple details that overlap in a small area, things can get messy. At this stage, simply make sure all of the important lines are there.

▶ Never underestimate the expressivity of hands; the way fingers are posed and the placement of the wrists can convey a lot about a character's personality. Use references to help, such as a photograph of your own hands.

▶ Just like hands, shoes and feet can also be very expressive. Bare feet say more than shoes, but if you know how to play with volumes and angles, shoes can still tell a story. Never draw feet flat on the ground — consider how you can tilt the shoes a little, either showing more of the tops or the soles.

INKING

The inking stage involves selecting the final lines for a clean design and making the sketch underneath disappear. While a ballpoint pen isn't a traditional inking tool, it has the advantage of keeping the artwork spontaneous. Pen retains the character of a sketch while tidying up the mess, creating a much cleaner drawing. It won't smudge when used with watercolors or water-based paints, but note that it doesn't work well with markers.

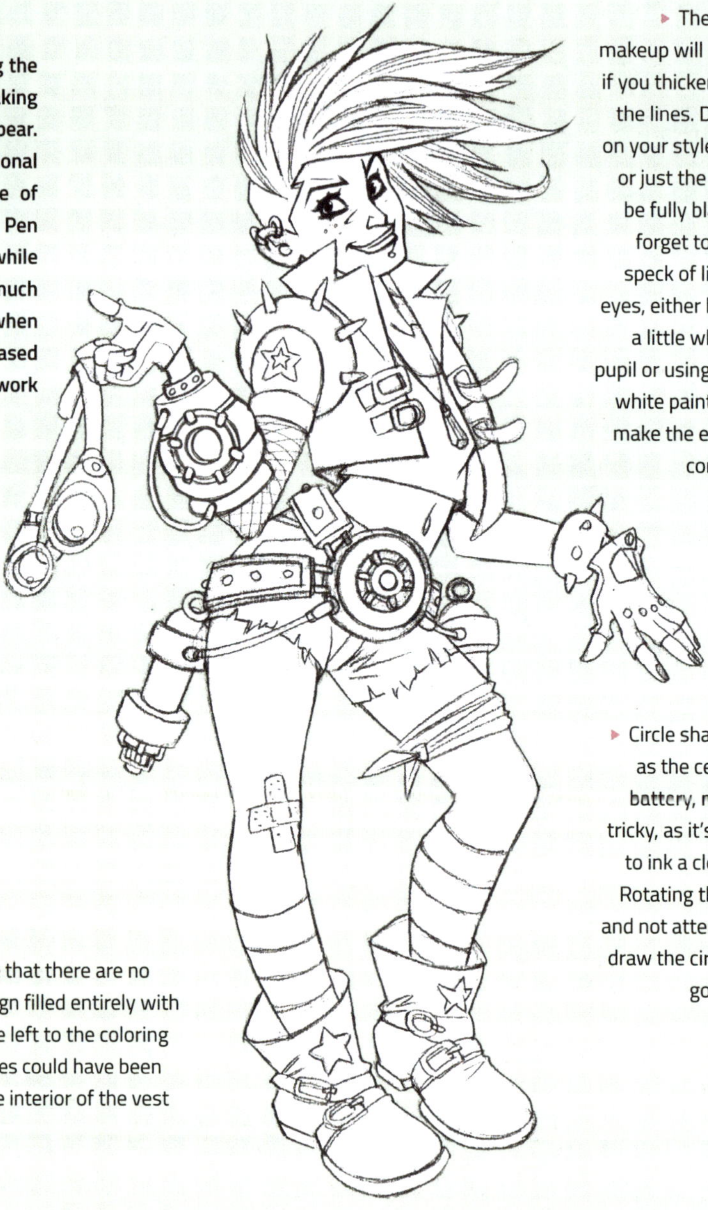

▸ Using this method of inking, the lines stay generally the same size as the sketch, keeping the loose, spontaneous, and dynamic style intact. The art will still look cleaner and more refined than the sketch. Try to mimic the movements you use with a sketching tool and forget you are inking!

▸ You will notice that there are no areas of the design filled entirely with black. This can be left to the coloring stage. Some zones could have been filled, such as the interior of the vest or the shoes.

▸ Start refining the hair, inking the lines from the base to the tip in a single, quick movement. The base will always be a little thicker, giving the illusion of light hair strands.

▸ The eyes and makeup will really pop if you thicken some of the lines. Depending on your style, the eye, or just the pupil, can be fully black. Don't forget to include a speck of light in the eyes, either by leaving a little white in the pupil or using a drop of white paint. This will make the expression come to life!

▸ Circle shapes, such as the central belt battery, may prove tricky, as it's not easy to ink a clean circle. Rotating the canvas and not attempting to draw the circle in one go will help.

The character is colored with two layers of watercolor: one for flat colors and a second for simple shadows, giving the artwork a cell-shaded feel. The color palette matches the character and her eco-friendly, solarpunk style. Two major colors define the overall palette: pink and green. Pink is a punk-themed shade, while green is associated with the ecological values of the character. All of the other colors in the final drawing will have either a hint of pink or a green in them.

▶ Test the shade of each color on a separate piece of paper first. Not only will this help you to find the perfect palette, but it will also make selecting a color for the shadows easier later on.

▶ The bold hair color is tricky to get right, as watercolors generally produce muted tones. Make the pink as flashy as possible, as this shade will help determine the overall saturation of the other tones.

▶ Once the hair color is complete, work on the skin tone. The color should be slightly saturated to match the pink hair. Skin tones are very important to get right – experiment as much as possible!

▶ For the simple shadows, apply a light, reddish-brown mix to the entire drawing. Watercolors are very transparent; your shadow tone will work with every color already used if you have tested them on the colors already on your test paper.

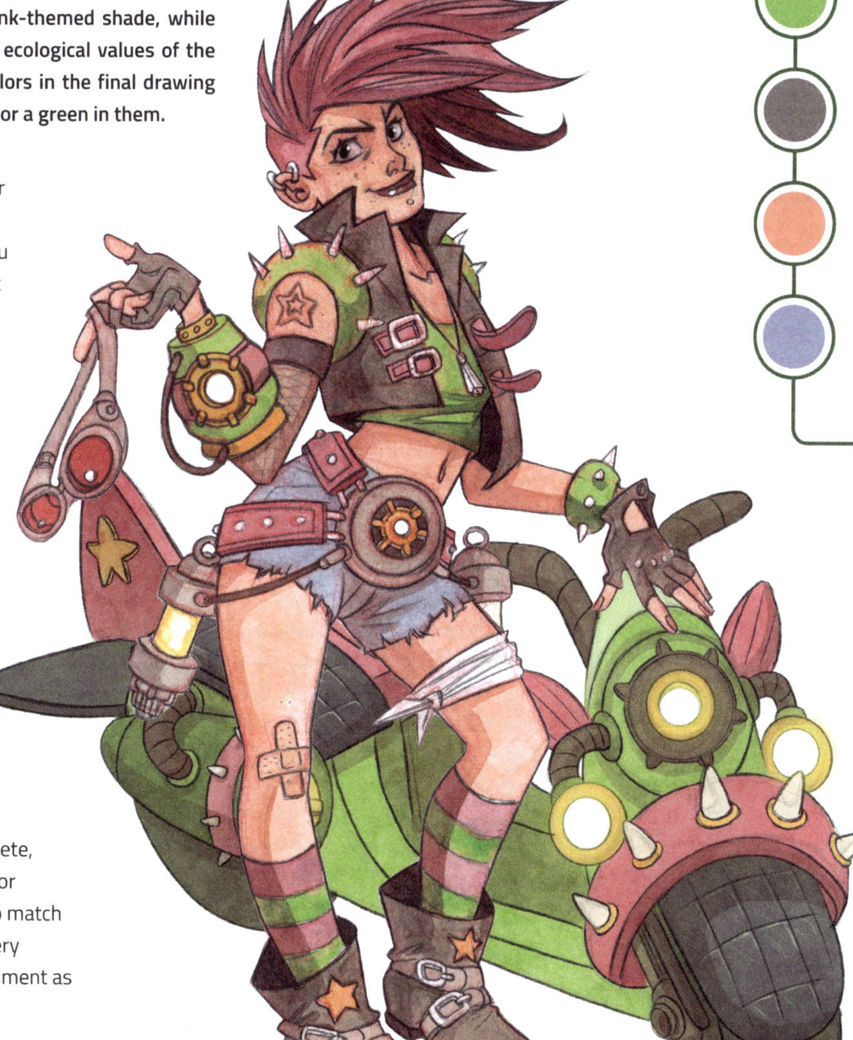

BUTLER DROID

BY BRETT BEAN

This tutorial will walk you through how to design a comical butler droid. This lovable bot should feel alive, have a fun stylized look, and a cool retro vibe to its design. The design process will explore the importance of clean lines and a readable silhouette, as well as a task to occupy the droid and help tell his story. Once you have a direction for the character, it's time to dive in!

TOOLKIT

- ▶ Zebra brush pen
- ▶ Brown or neutral paper
- ▶ Pigma Micron pen
- ▶ Colored marker pens
- ▶ White gel pen
- ▶ White pencil
- ▶ Colored pencil

RESEARCH

Begin by grabbing your trusty brush pen, or any pen that can't be erased, and get your ideas down on paper. Explore various concepts and discover the key components you want to focus on. Once you have run out of ideas, start to gather references. Experiment with the stereotypical shapes associated with butlers and their trade. Draw anything and everything that brings to mind retro robots and the classic butler image.

METAL

Robots are made of metal – rivets, bolts, and cool edges. Finding easily recognizable designs for every component will be key for a quick read.

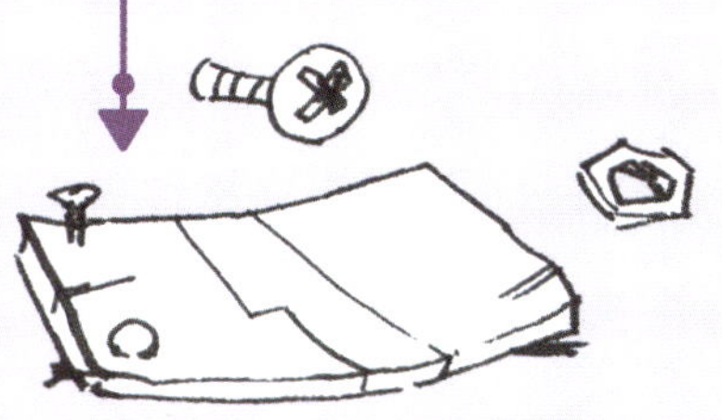

PERSONALITY

What kind of personality will this butler droid have? Is he happy with his lot in life? Maybe he's tired and cranky, or simply just overworked!

RETRO

Taking inspiration from existing movies, video games, and TV can add elements that offer a new take on classic retro designs.

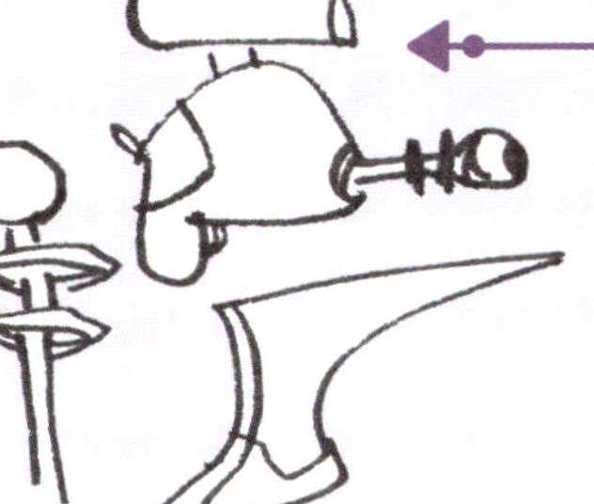

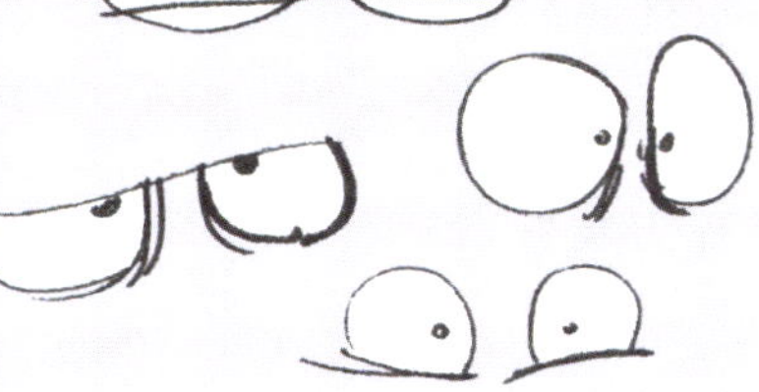

ROBOT PARTS

A robot doesn't have to have two hands and two feet. Maybe they have pincers, wheels, or bendy tubelike limbs. The character has no frame of reference, so let your imagination run wild!

BUTLER

Determining the key elements that define a butler will allow you to incorporate them into the droid's design. For instance, butlers are always seen in their formal uniform.

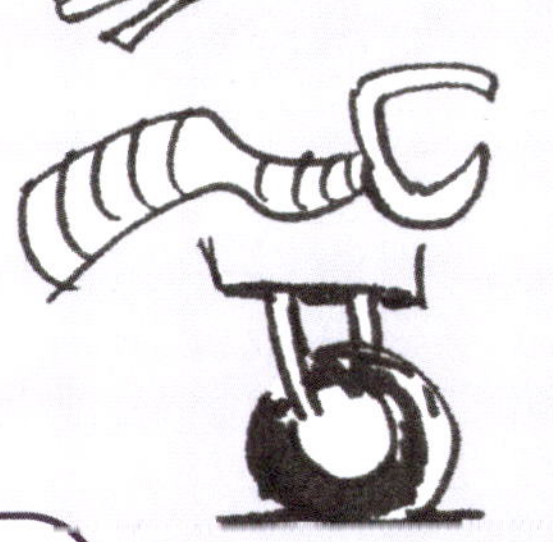

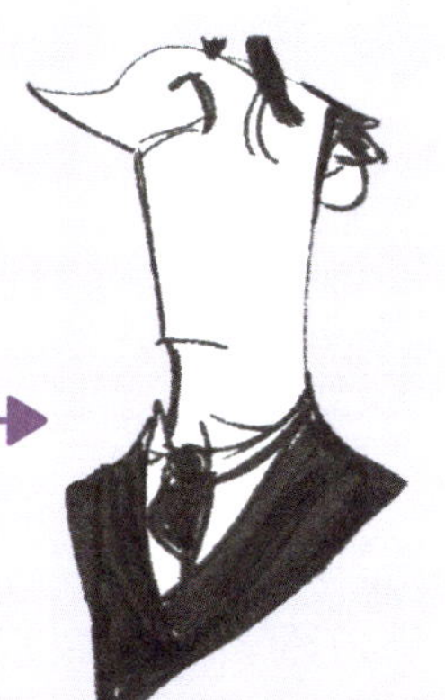

THUMBNAILS

With the research stage complete, you can now start to thumbnail more thought-out designs. Aim to draw with enough detail to create well-defined characters – this will allow you to feel confident that your initial design decisions will work later on in the process. With a brief as broad as this one, it's the perfect opportunity to think outside the box and make the design truly unique. What can you personally add to the overall idea? Thumbnails are your way to shoot for the moon!

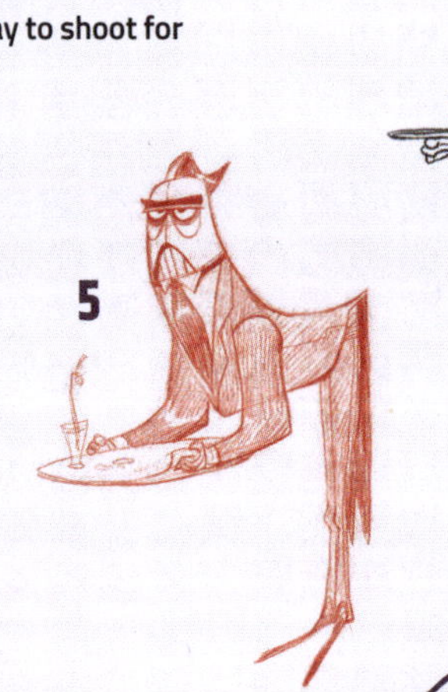

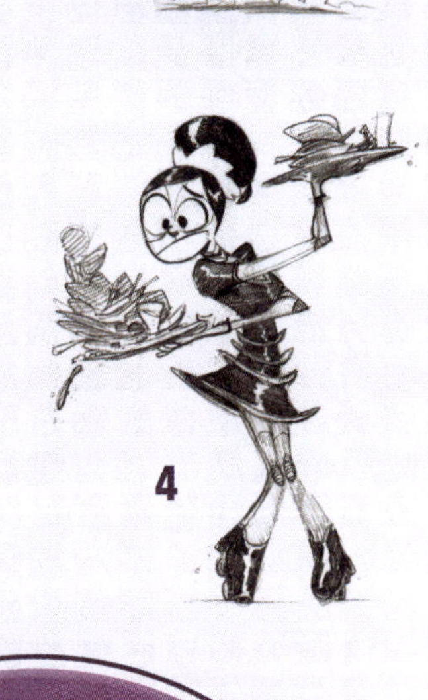

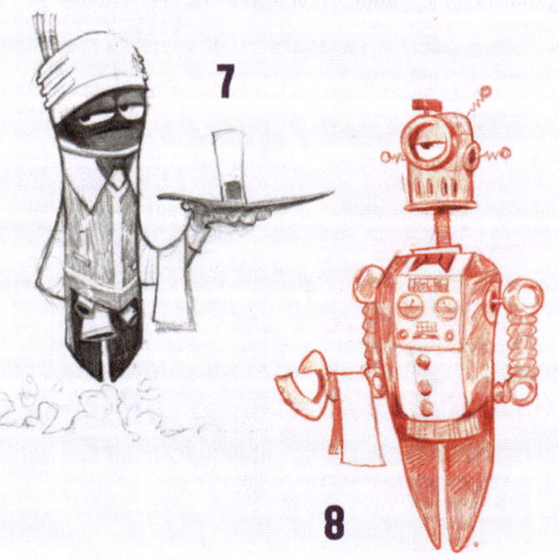

Try not to be discouraged if you don't have a favorite thumbnail, or if they don't possess that special something you're looking for. Rarely do you hit it out of the park on your first go. Sit with the designs for a while and consider which parts you like enough to use. Rather than choosing only one thumbnail, you may decide to draw inspiration from all of them. Use them as a collection of ideas that will inform your final design.

FOUNDATIONS

The next step is to take your favorite parts from the thumbnails to create a foundation to work from. Incorporate all of the key ideas at this stage. A clear silhouette, pushed with style, and a strong concept embedded in the design will help create a story, drawing the audience into the droid's sci-fi world.

BASE

▶ Continue to work with pencil, applying more pressure to define your final lines. From time to time, look at your drawing while squinting to check that the overall shape is still easy to read.

▶ Start with the line of action – a single line that captures the basic energy and movement of the character. While the base is essentially just a wonky cylinder, it still needs to have some life. Sketch in contour lines to get a feel for how it moves and bends.

▶ The droid has spindly arms that flail about in a comical manner. Be mindful of how the arms interact with the body and ensure you maintain a clean read and solid silhouette. Maybe even try tying one of the arms in a knot!

LINES

▶ Start to cut out pieces of the cylinder to create shapes within shapes that reference a butler, such as a face, hat, and suit. Consider the size of each element in relation to one another.

▶ Begin to draw in the arms and be mindful of your contour lines. Imagine how the limbs wrap around the body and in what direction they can move. Sketching rivets and lines is an easy way to add three-dimensional depth to a static, flat drawing.

▶ Adding shadow will help to ground the character and place them in a livable space. Smoke adds a good base, plus a little movement and mayhem.

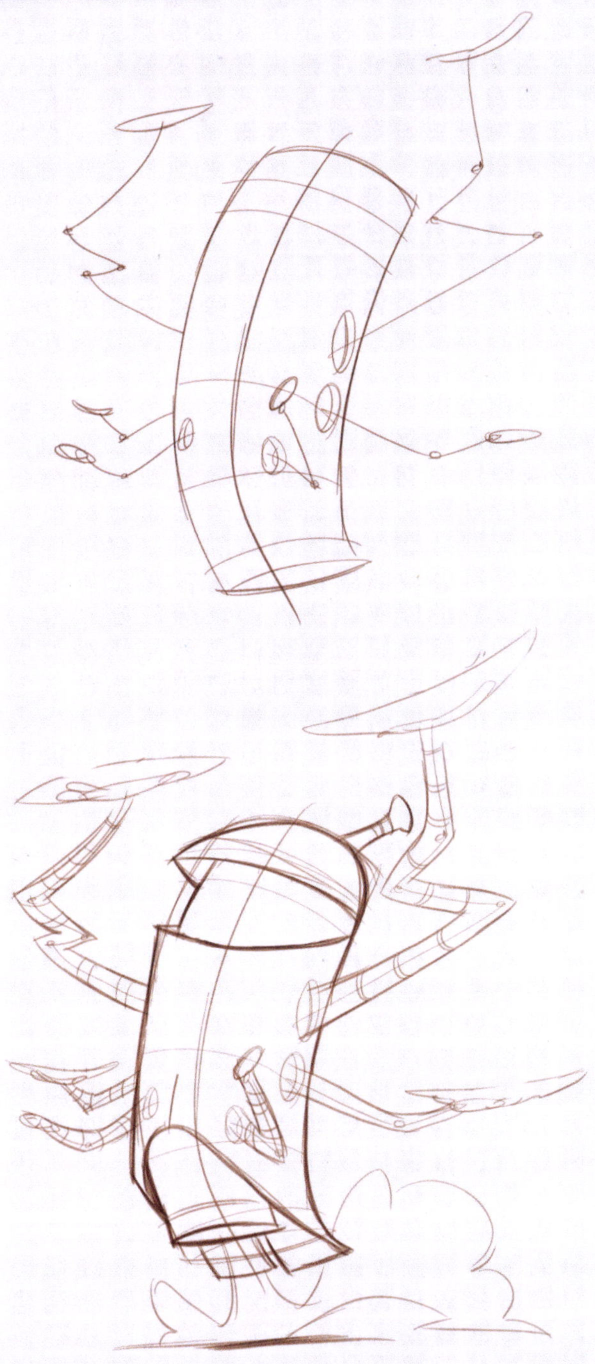

BUILDING UP

This stage will allow you to start adding some real personality to the butler droid. The design should read as fun, humorous, and engaging. As you are still only working with big shapes, any smaller elements you add should complement the overall design, not overreach and take away from the main object.

PROPS

Refer back to your thumbnails and add props that bring to mind a butler, such as dishes and a serving cloth. Props help to tell a story quickly and efficiently – you can instantly see how busy and flustered he is!

FACE

As the face is generally the first place the viewer's gaze is drawn to on a character design, sketch big, comical eyes and a wide mouth to set the tone for the rest of the image.

UNIFORM

A butler's uniform clearly displays their role, so sketch on a tailcoat suit and metal bow tie. These are recognizable as real-world clothing, but drawn in a style to suit the futuristic character.

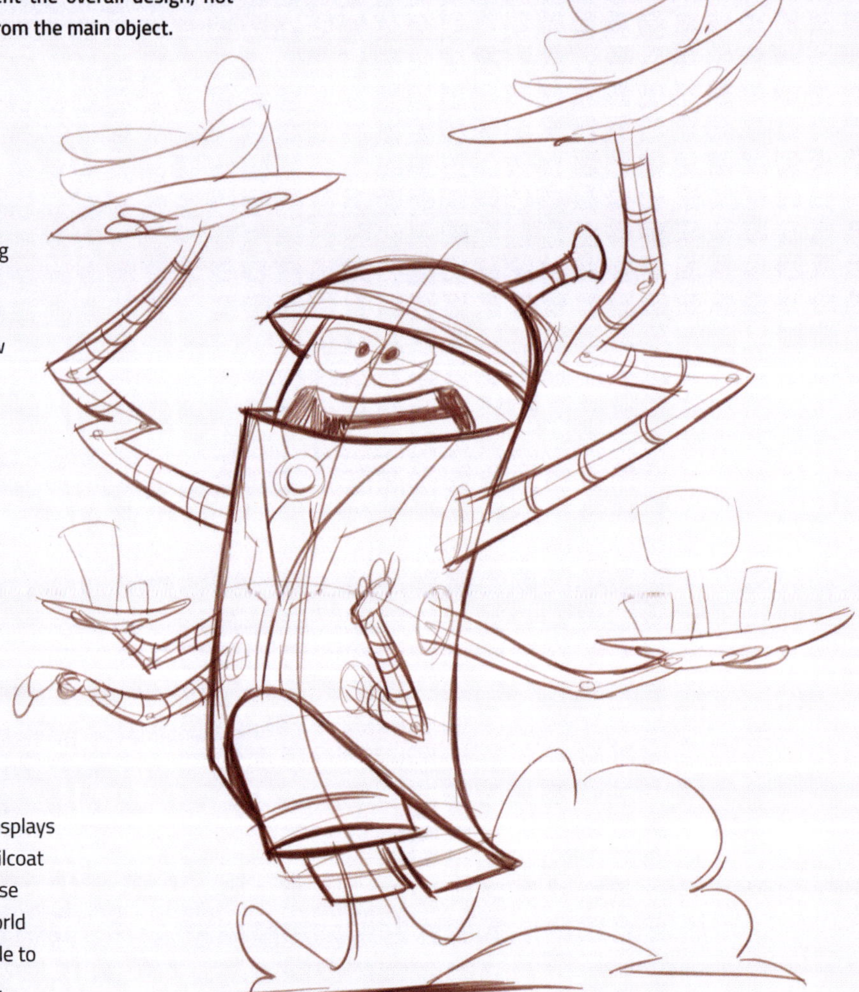

DESIGN FOCUS

BODY

Following the outer cylinder's middle line, ensure the butler's tie and metal lining wraps around the form, adding depth to the design.

FACE

The droid is a shape within a shape, so make sure your breakdown shows this. The inner cylinder's middle line – where the mouth and eyes are drawn – won't align with the center line of the outer cylinder's body.

ROCKET

The rocket he uses to putter about should be in perspective and angled toward the viewer. Drawing his suit to wrap around the rocket shows how the droid is built, adding complexity to the base cylindrical shape. You should aim for variety, while still keeping the design relatively simple.

IDEA INVENTORY

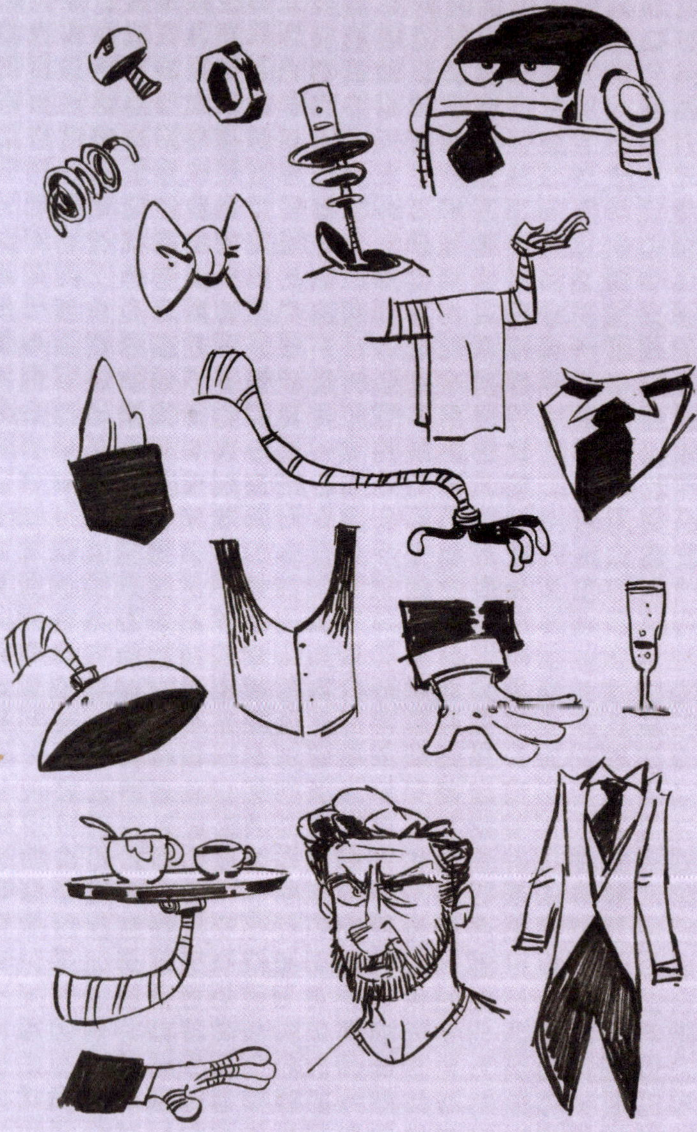

THEMES

Before progressing to the final drawing, sketch out some ideas inspired by the keywords "butler" and "robot." Experiment with the themes and let your mind wander across the page. This is a big component of design that leads to individuality shining through. Leave room to surprise yourself! Creating these ideas using pen means it doesn't matter if they are clean, dirty, or truly legible. This is the behind-the-scenes art and design that will influence and inform the final piece.

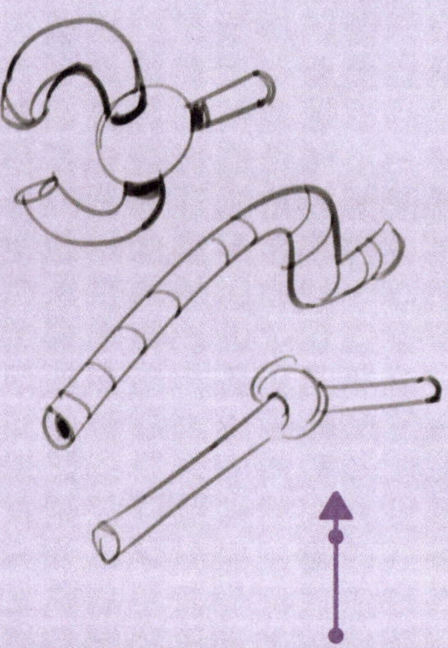

▶ The arms and other mechanical elements chosen to carry forward into the final sketch.

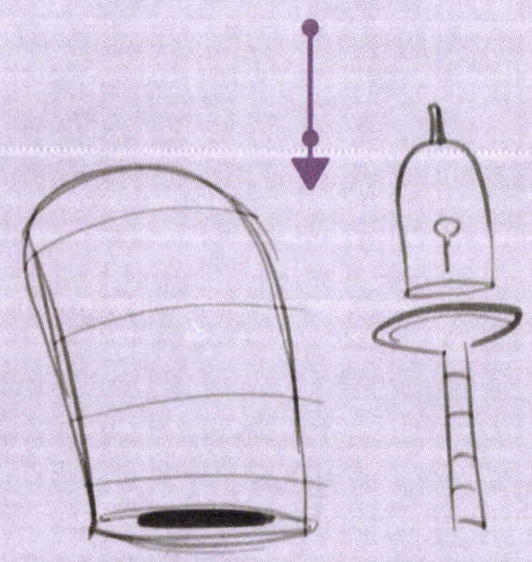

FINAL SKETCH

It's now time to start cleaning up and locking in some final decisions for your butler droid. Add some extra movement with smoke trails, falling forks and food, and liquid spilling onto the floor. Draw small rings at the points where the arms connect to the body, some extra details on the head, and suit sleeves at the end of the extendable arms to convey the butler look.

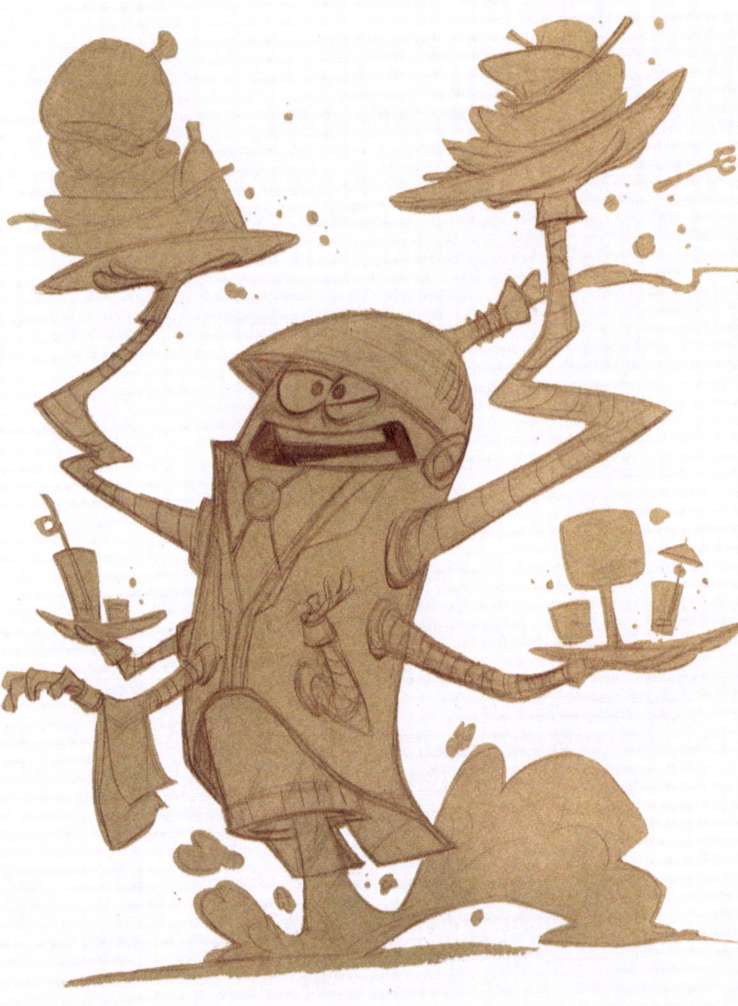

▶ Googly eyes and a crazed expression help to define the story of a robot butler who's losing control. Keep it light, however. While he should appear flustered, avoid anything too dramatic that could make the viewer feel upset.

▶ Draw the glasses and dishes in motion, flying from the plates, to reinforce the idea of chaos. They are big shapes, but hopefully won't prove too distracting when inked and colored.

▶ Decide whether to give the butler a proper suit or a simple metal body. If you had time to tell a story over several stages, you may be able to leave some iconic elements out, but this design needs to be instantly recognizable as a butler.

▶ Steam pouring out of the top of his head adds variety, movement, and narrative to the piece – and it looks funny too! It's ok if your design decisions are geared toward aesthetics over functionality. Never lose focus on the purpose of the art you're creating.

▶ Leaving a few open spaces in the image, such as the rocket and headpiece, will allow you to make spontaneous decisions during the inking and color stages. Think of this as controlled chaos – spontaneity is important!

INKING

Using a medium brush pen to ink will produce visually pleasing thick-to-thin lines. The amount of pressure you apply dictates how wide the lines will be. The advantage of brush pens is that you don't have to pause to dip a brush in ink all the time – plus, there's no mess to clean up! Once you've added color, you can go back over your design with a large brush pen, adding a few more chaotic lines and contours to further reinforce the theme.

▶ Determine how each object will wrap around the form you've created. This is why you penciled in the contour lines, to provide a visual representation of dimensional space as you ink.

▶ Be sparing when adding the blackest blacks and biggest ink shapes. You want to add complexity to the overall design without distracting from the face. It's a balancing act!

▶ Don't forget to apply pressure for thicker lines and release as you ink thinner ones. Different brushstrokes will add variety and lead the eye around your design.

▶ For tighter, cleaner lines, use a Pigma Micron 2.0, or equivalent. This will put a good variety of line weights at your disposal as you ink, helping with elements like contour lines and the robot's eyes.

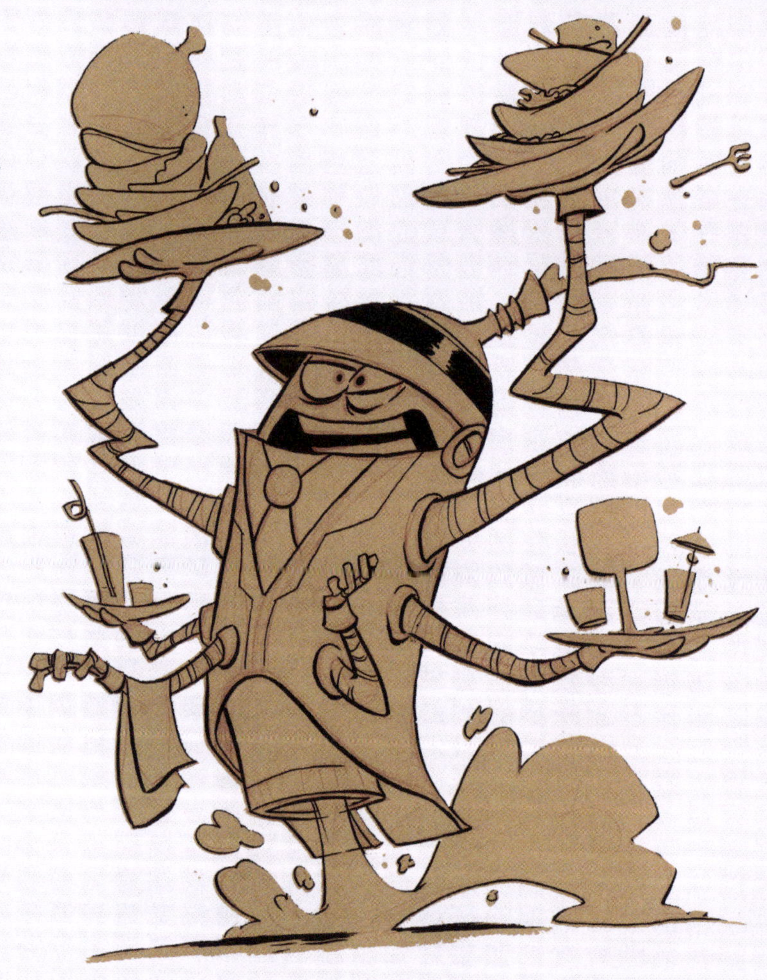

The color palette should suit both a butler and a robot, as well as mixing well with tonal paper, if used. Using brown or gray paper can make for a much quicker and easier coloring process, as you won't need to go as dark or light in a medium base. When using watercolor markers, always work from light to dark. By applying different amounts of pressure, one color can work across an entire area, creating different gradients. Cool grays and purples are used for most of the butler droid's final design.

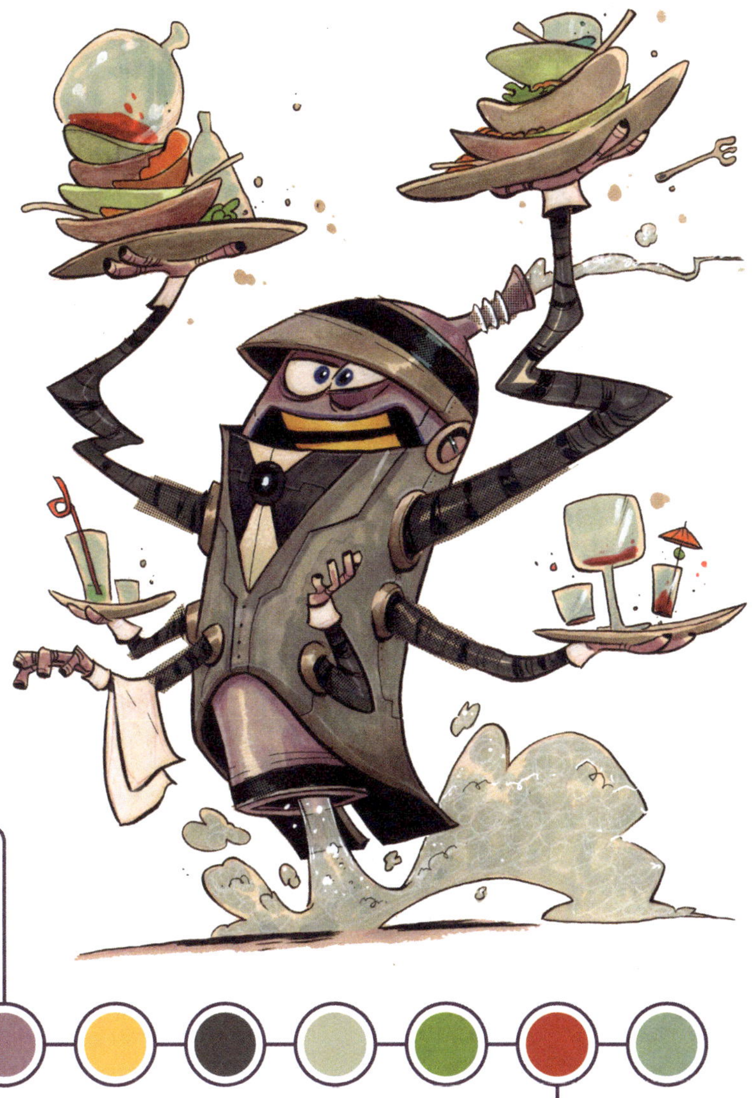

▶ Using watercolor markers, apply light and medium purples to show the rounded shape of the eyes and the droid beneath the suit. Leaving some of the brown tone of the paper beneath can add variety.

▶ As the dishes and plates are secondary and third reads, their colors and shapes shouldn't be too eye-catching, nor draw too much attention away from the droid. They are there to reinforce the story, not distract from it!

▶ Duotones are a way to show shadow in comics. Use them to add texture and a little chaos if the design is looking too clean. Spontaneous decisions can add freshness and life to a design.

▶ Stay close to a classic butler color palette for the suit and arms. As butlers typically wear black, which can look a little boring, introduce some blue to the cool grays to help the arms stand out from the body.

▶ Final image © Brett Bean

LIFESAVING DROID

... BY ADAM FORD

This tutorial will walk you through how to design a lifesaving firefighting droid. We'll begin by exploring many different ideas and directions, both serious and silly. Be open to experimentation, allowing your style to evolve based on the direction of your early concepts. The tutorial will cover how to narrow down your chosen idea, how to pose the droid, and finally, how to apply colors and shading to bring your design to life.

TOOLKIT

- ▸ Mechanical pencil
- ▸ Kneaded eraser
- ▸ Erasable colored pencil
- ▸ 0.5 mm fine-tipped pen
- ▸ Watercolors
- ▸ Watercolor brush

RESEARCH

Learn to "fail fast" and make your mistakes early in the idea exploration stage, rather than later on in the design process. Don't spend too much time on your early sketches, but get your rough, messy ideas down on paper quickly with your pencil. If you spend too much time on any one sketch, you might become too attached to an idea that may not work. Take some time to think about symbols and imagery early on. People often think of water when it comes to extinguishing fire, so explore what comes to mind when you think of water and firefighting.

WATER

Most people are familiar with the common watercooler. While not typically a firefighting tool, it would be fun to consider how the tank could be incorporated into a robot's kit.

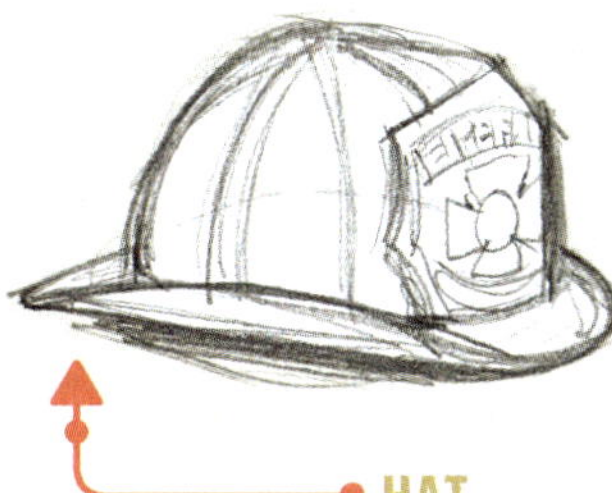

HAT

A firefighter's hat has a distinct shape and could potentially lead to some fun motifs.

SHAPE

The firefighter's hat has a similar dome shape to that of a sea turtle's shell. They have a nice crossover and it could be fun to see how this reptile could be incorporated into the design.

SEA CREATURES

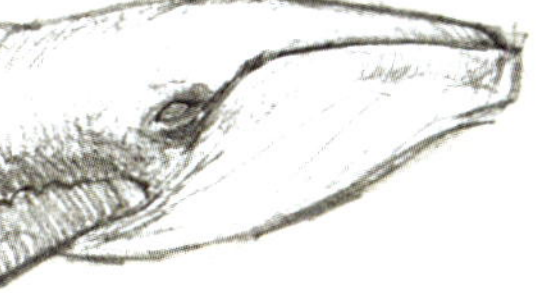

When you think of water, you might think of the sea. The curved shape of a whale is instantly recognizable and could be used to inspire the design of our droid's anatomy.

FIRE TRUCK

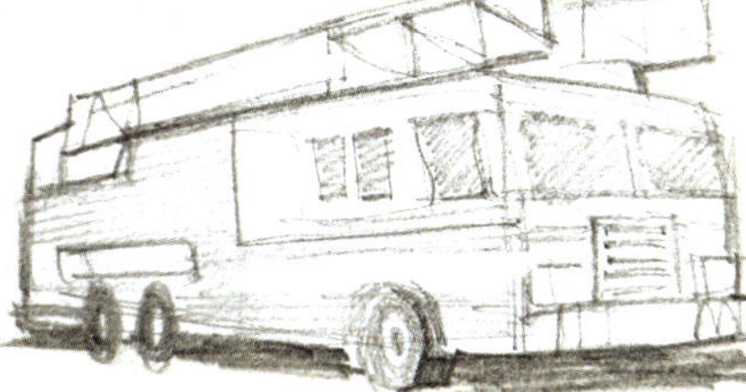

Nothing is more iconic to firefighting than the fire truck, with its almost universal colors, stripes, and shape. Research mechanical references like these to inform the equipment the droid could use.

CONCEPTS

Once you've explored different references and ideas, begin to combine them in ways that make sense and cross over into fun new concepts. Any parallels in themes can create stronger design combinations. Continue to work quickly, not spending too much time on any one sketch. This stage is like taking notes in image form. It can be tempting to spend time polishing, but getting your ideas down on paper fast will prove more beneficial.

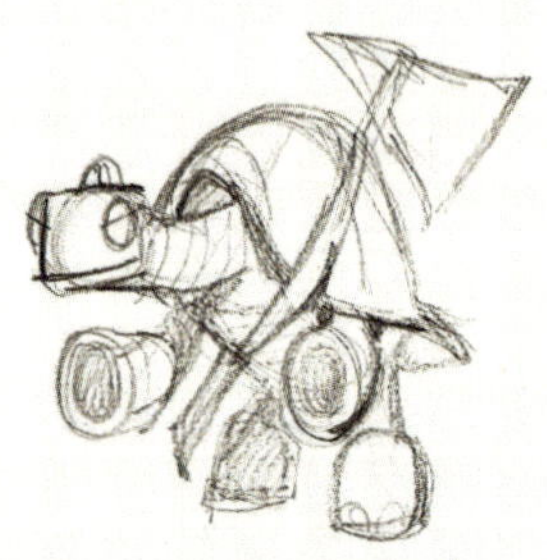

▶ Everyone loves turtles! You could design a nifty little yellow- or red-shelled robot turtle to look like a firefighter's hat. Sketching a mini hat on the robot turtle's head adds a fun touch.

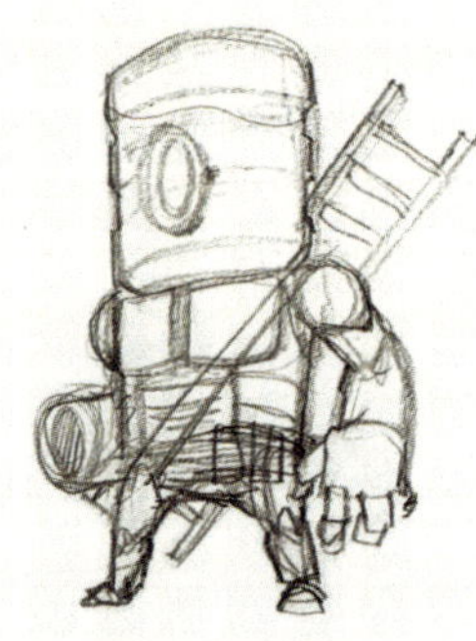

▶ This droid has a watercooler for a head. Every time he shoots water out to extinguish a fire, the water level on the tank drops.

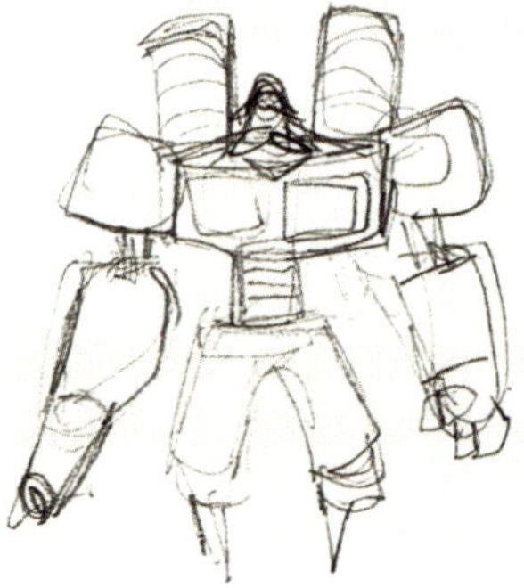

▶ This sketch shows a more heroic-looking robot with two watercoolers on his shoulders. The bulky armor echoes a muscular physique and it has a strong anime mecha vibe.

CHOSEN CONCEPT

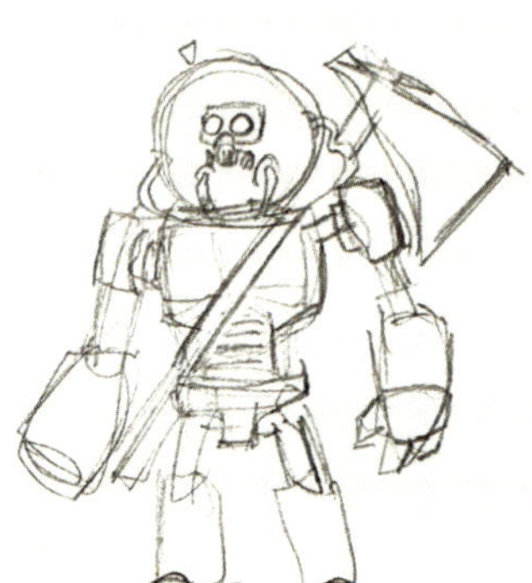

▶ Water balloons are a fun way to throw water, and balloons in general can seem a little goofy. This balloon robot deflates his head as he sprays water to put out fires.

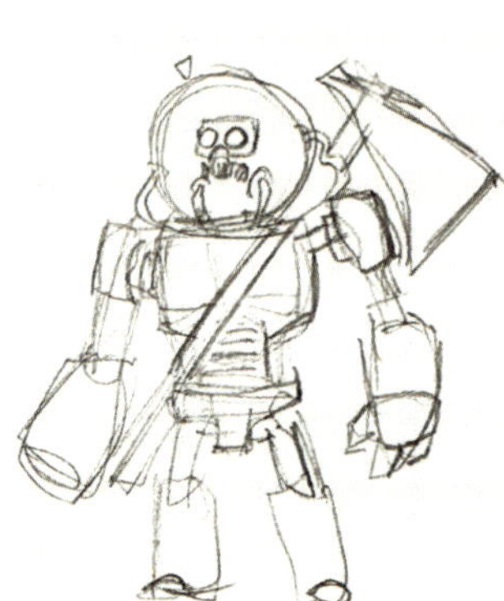

▶ The heroic design works well. It's aspirational and cool, and has the potential to be drawn in all kinds of dynamic action poses. This lifesaving firefighter droid will be someone to look up to, not laugh at.

▶ This sketch combines the fun water-balloon-headed robot with the more muscular mecha robot. It can be fun to contrast super heroic designs with silly themes.

THUMBNAILS

Still using your pencil, lightly sketch thumbnails based on your chosen concept. Light, soft sketches are easier to erase. It's okay if your thumbnails are just as loose and sketchy as your starting concepts. Again, try to get the shapes down fast without worrying too much about refinement. Polishing comes at the end, whereas this step is about exploring poses that feel fluid and alive. Look for an interesting silhouette that doesn't lose who the character is.

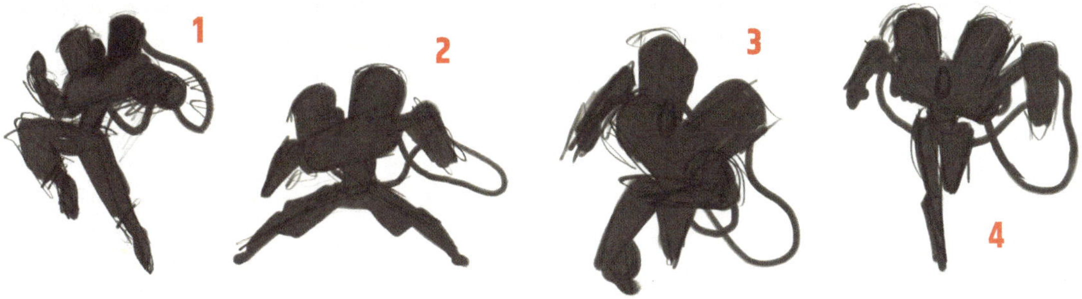

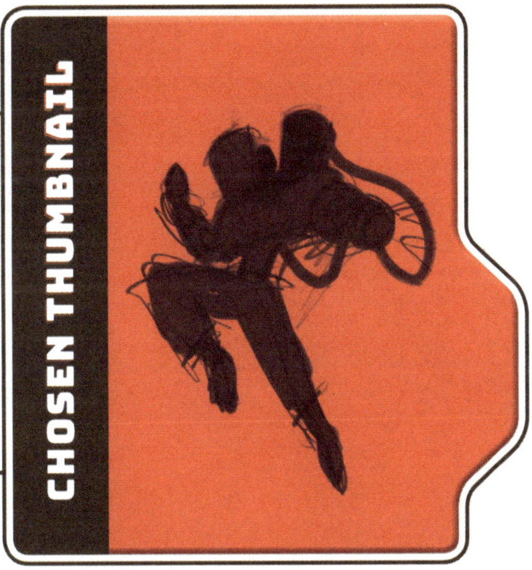

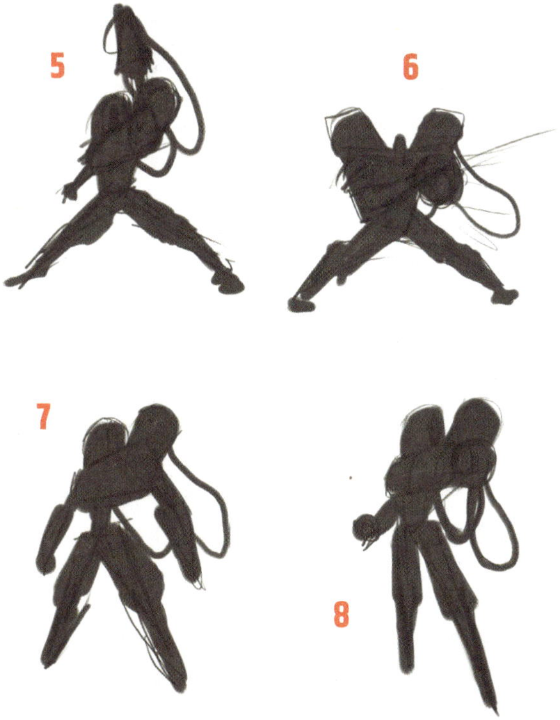

CHOSEN THUMBNAIL

▶ When designing a character that has multiple parts, sketching an exaggerated pose can sometimes prove more confusing. The first thumbnail works well, as it is heroic without losing the details or clear silhouette. The droid is poised to extinguish a fire, and the negative space adds interest to the design.

FOUNDATIONS

Drawing volumetrically involves taking the three-dimensional world around you and translating it into a two-dimensional image. Use a light-colored pencil that will be easy to distinguish when you go over the sketch with a darker color later. Consider the various mechanical parts that will make up the droid and how you can capture the volume of these. It must look three-dimensional for it to be believable.

BASE

▶ Sketch simple, volumetric shapes that make up each part of the droid. Draw a cuboid for his chest and a cylinder for his outstretched arm. These shapes will inform the final sketch and inking stages.

▶ Draw over your thumbnail pose with the colored pencil, keeping it as close to the loose sketch as possible. Try to keep the proportions close to your original direction.

▶ Break the mechanics down into bite-sized pieces. Keeping the shapes as simple blocks and cylinders will prevent you feeling too overwhelmed.

LINES

▶ Using a darker pencil, build up the foundation sketch layer by layer. Begin to place a few more details to bring it to life.

▶ Add details to the fire-hose-nozzle arm. Give the droid firefighting clothes to capture a contrast of soft and hard surfaces. Protective gloves are a practical addition. Sketch folds on the pants to make them look more realistic.

▶ Begin to hint at liquid in the water containers, as well as sketching support lines around the barrels. Ensuring those lines echo the foreshortening of the cylinders is critical to helping it feel volumetric.

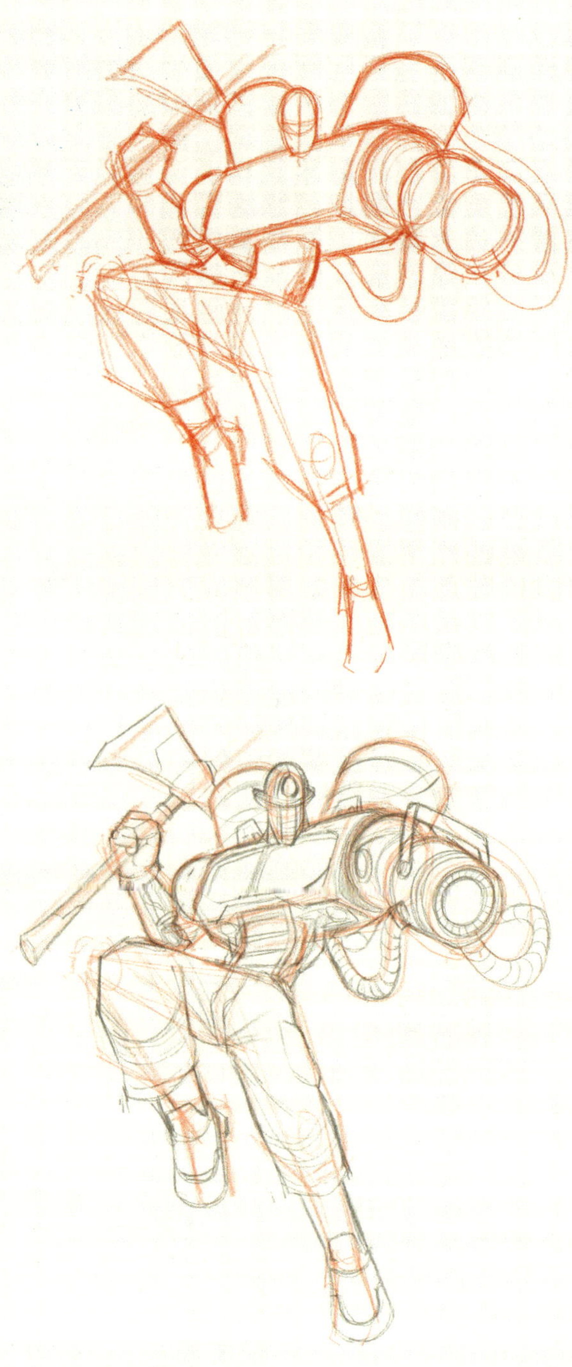

DESIGN FOCUS

ANATOMY

Work out how the droid will move and bend his waist and joints. Drawing inspiration from real-world anatomy can help to make robot designs feel more relatable.

LAYERS

Build up your sketch in layers, creating a sense of depth by showing how the different mechanical parts overlap. Mechanical designs should contain overlapping shapes that stack on top of each other, as opposed to looking like they were placed on top of a skintight suit. Consider how the volumes might look if you had x-ray vision: do the parts have volumetric integrity below the surface?

DETAIL

Mechanical detailing can prove challenging, so start to draw in some of the small details that will make the design more believable. The stomach, chest piece, and joints are all important. A thinner lead pencil, such as a mechanical pencil, can make it easier to create tight details. Make good use of references for any elements you are not familiar with.

FINAL SKETCH

In the earlier stages, it's best to stay broad and conceptual, experimenting with as many ideas as possible, but now you can begin to refine the details. Polish the sketch with your pencil and leave very few questions to be answered. This will mean that when you start to ink, you won't have to work things out on the fly. Break the design into small, medium, and large shapes – the most visually interesting designs are those that have shape variety. The simple pants, for example, strike a great contrast against his more detailed mechanical torso.

▶ Foreshortening (see Design Techniques, page 50) can be tricky to master, but it will make your design feel much more exciting and alive. Practice sketching extreme angles and poses as much as possible.

▶ The fabric folds should point to where the most tension is. In a split pose like this, folds will radiate out from below the waist as it is stretched by the bent knee and extended leg. Understand how fabric works, then use it to add movement.

▶ Avoid settling for two round eyes and a slit for a mouth. Introduce a few plate lines on the side of the head to break up the space. The plate lines echo how muscles work on a human face.

▶ The hoses provide another opportunity to break up the silhouette, while also adding depth. Banded metal is great for showing volume, shown here as the hoses twist with the movement.

▶ The suspenders add additional depth and motion to prevent the metal from looking too flat on the chest. If you can make it feel like there is a breeze on your character, as opposed to static gravity, you will end up with a little extra magic.

INKING

There are almost as many ways to ink as there are art styles. A popular approach is to ink a combination of thick and thin lines to create variety and depth, ensuring the lines that are closer to the camera appear thicker. To create the anime mecha aesthetic, however, the lines should be more uniform in thickness. Anime-style line work often looks better when inked using a thinner pen, such as a 0.5 mm tip pen or smaller.

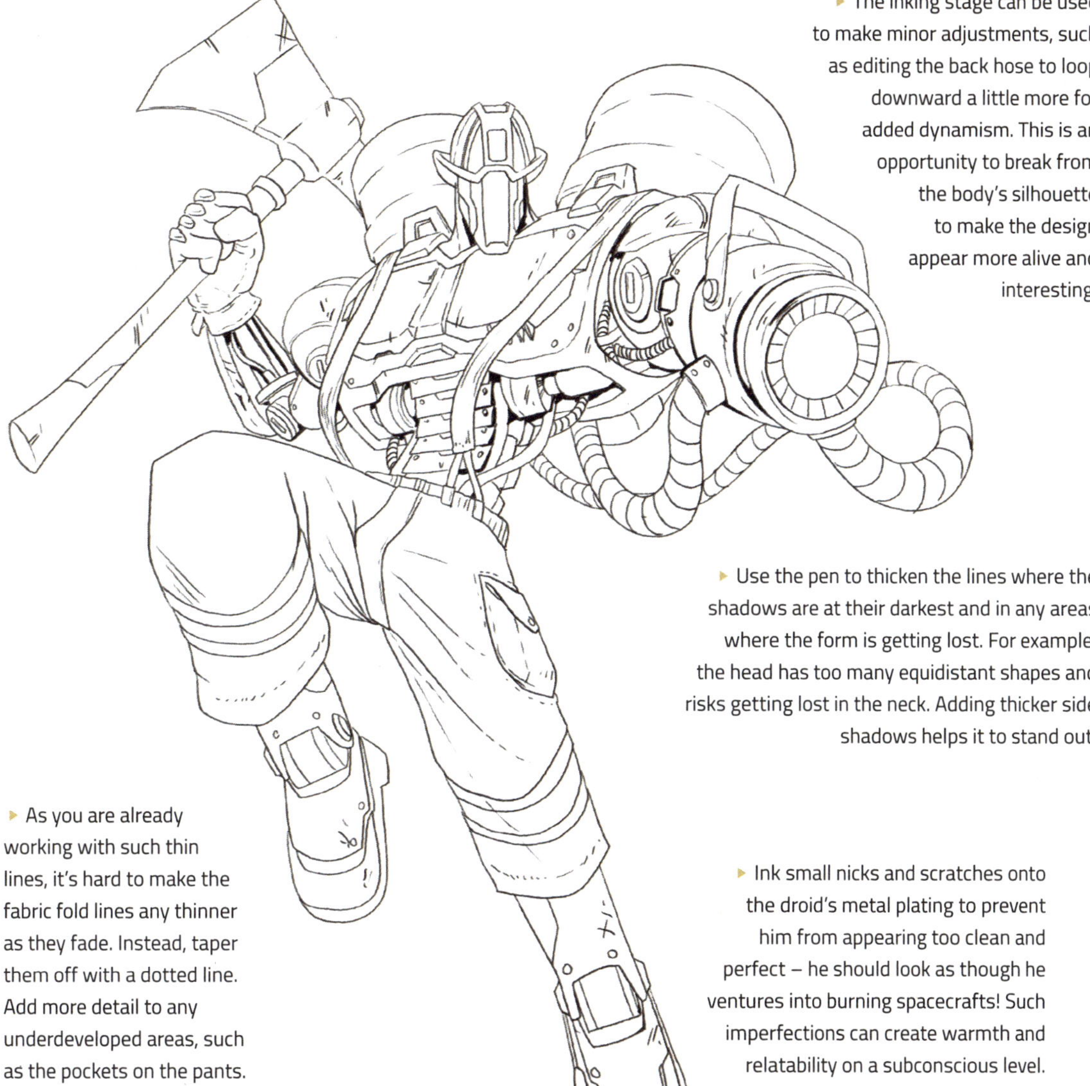

▶ The inking stage can be used to make minor adjustments, such as editing the back hose to loop downward a little more for added dynamism. This is an opportunity to break from the body's silhouette to make the design appear more alive and interesting.

▶ Use the pen to thicken the lines where the shadows are at their darkest and in any areas where the form is getting lost. For example, the head has too many equidistant shapes and risks getting lost in the neck. Adding thicker side shadows helps it to stand out.

▶ As you are already working with such thin lines, it's hard to make the fabric fold lines any thinner as they fade. Instead, taper them off with a dotted line. Add more detail to any underdeveloped areas, such as the pockets on the pants.

▶ Ink small nicks and scratches onto the droid's metal plating to prevent him from appearing too clean and perfect – he should look as though he ventures into burning spacecrafts! Such imperfections can create warmth and relatability on a subconscious level.

COLORING

The shading and coloring phase is where the design comes to life. Pay attention to surface types, shadows, and lighting, including where the light source is and how it reacts with each of the materials that makes up the design.

▶ Draw inspiration from your reference materials when deciding on a color palette, then use watercolors to group areas into simple color regions. The colors will be relatively flat at this stage.

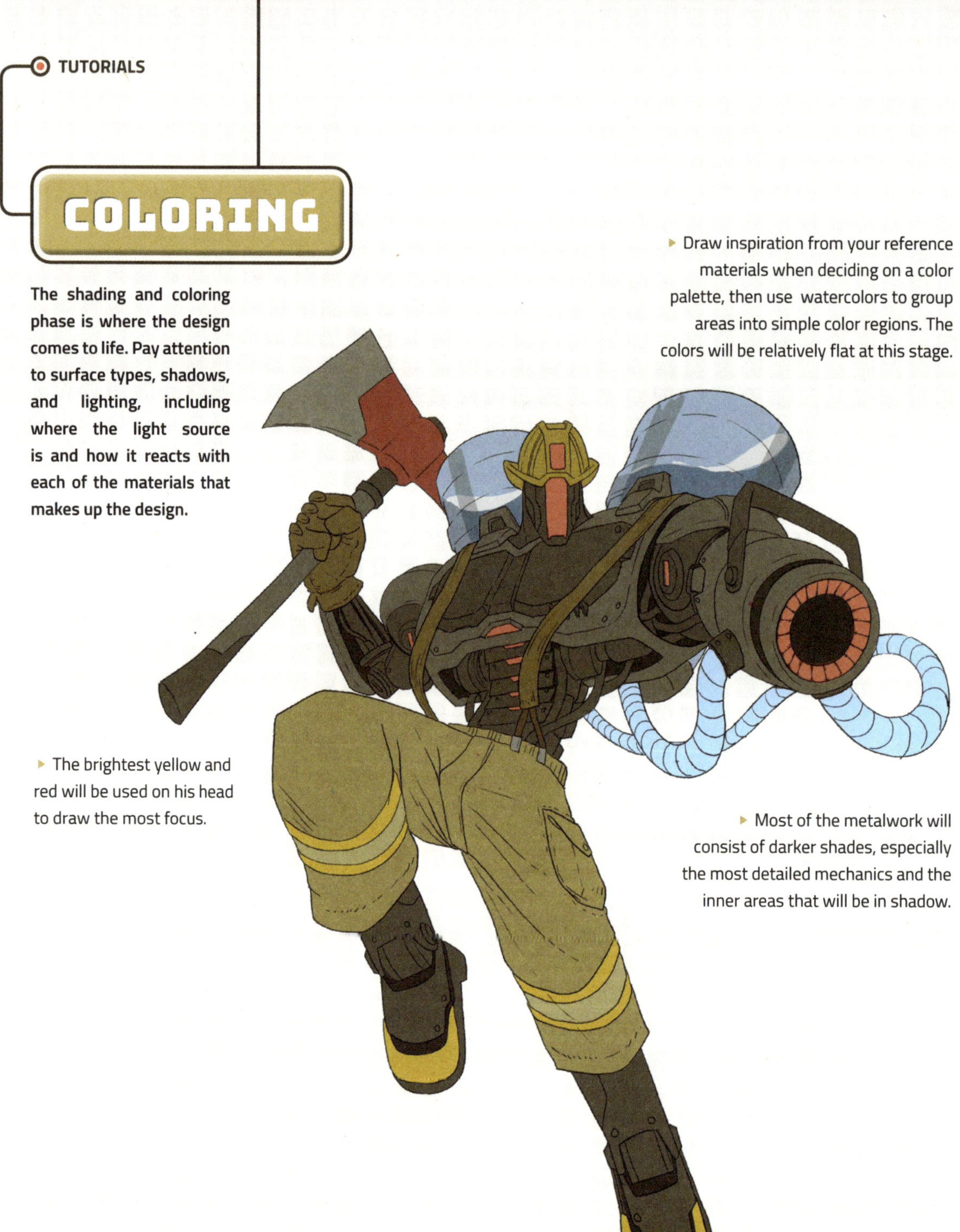

▶ The brightest yellow and red will be used on his head to draw the most focus.

▶ Most of the metalwork will consist of darker shades, especially the most detailed mechanics and the inner areas that will be in shadow.

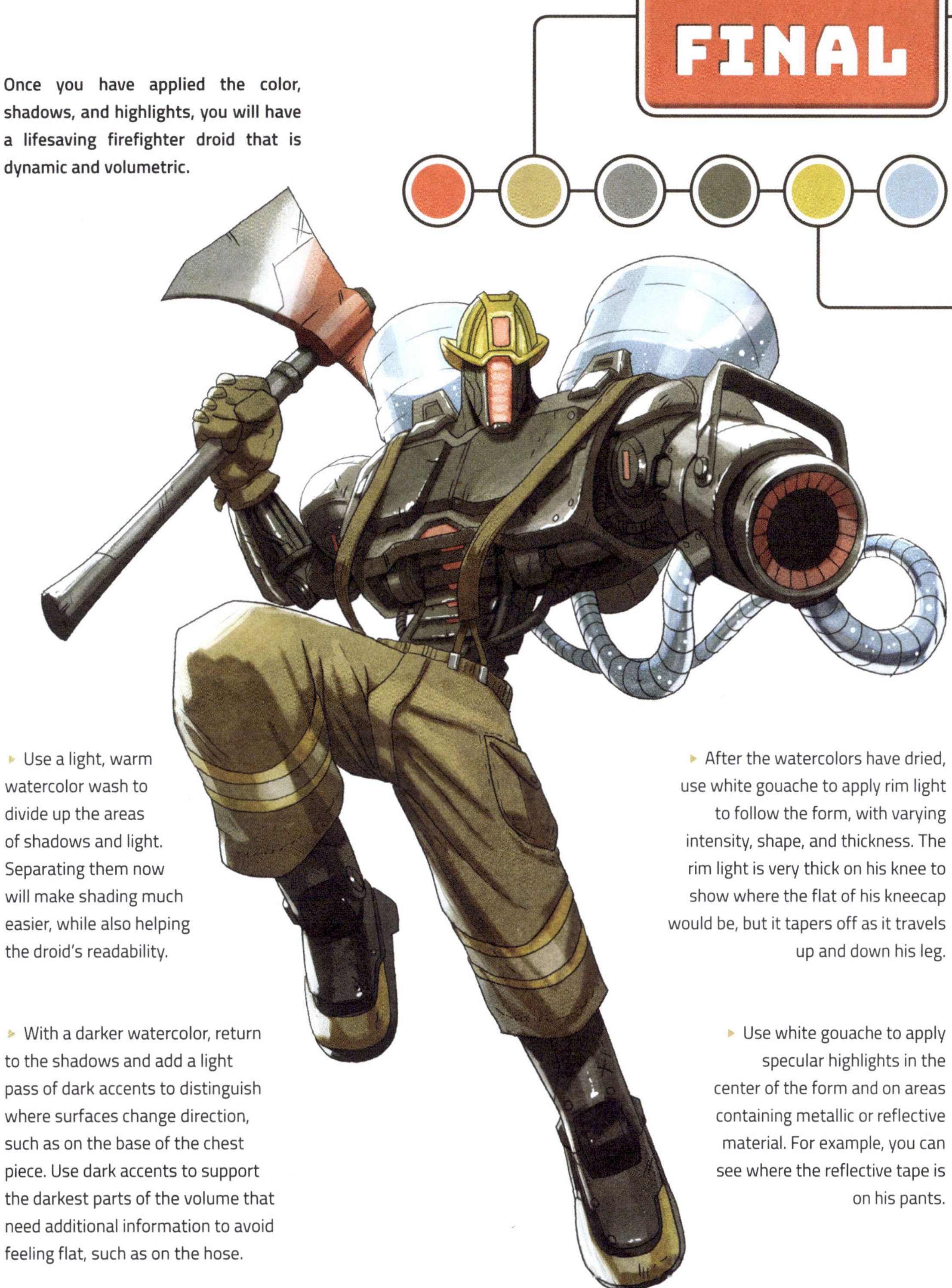

Once you have applied the color, shadows, and highlights, you will have a lifesaving firefighter droid that is dynamic and volumetric.

▶ Use a light, warm watercolor wash to divide up the areas of shadows and light. Separating them now will make shading much easier, while also helping the droid's readability.

▶ With a darker watercolor, return to the shadows and add a light pass of dark accents to distinguish where surfaces change direction, such as on the base of the chest piece. Use dark accents to support the darkest parts of the volume that need additional information to avoid feeling flat, such as on the hose.

▶ After the watercolors have dried, use white gouache to apply rim light to follow the form, with varying intensity, shape, and thickness. The rim light is very thick on his knee to show where the flat of his kneecap would be, but it tapers off as it travels up and down his leg.

▶ Use white gouache to apply specular highlights in the center of the form and on areas containing metallic or reflective material. For example, you can see where the reflective tape is on his pants.

▶ Final image © Adam Ford

DRILLER SPACESHIP

... BY DOFRESH

This tutorial will demonstrate how to design and illustrate an industrial driller spaceship. It will be a heavy, reliable, and bulky machine, with angular shapes and vibrant colors. Perhaps it's used to mine asteroids in remote areas of the solar system. The following pages will explore the creation of the spaceship, from the first sketches through to final render.

TOOLKIT

- ▸ Graphite pencil
- ▸ Eraser
- ▸ Ink marker
- ▸ Brushes
- ▸ India ink
- ▸ Gouache paint
- ▸ Watercolor paper

RESEARCH

The spaceship has a clear industrial function that should translate into its design. It will be reminiscent of existing drills and machines, such as excavators. The spaceship will also have a slight retro feel, rather than looking super fancy or high tech. Think of heavy-duty machinery rather than sleek sports cars. Look up references online, draw inspiration from your surroundings, and let the inspiration flow.

DRILLER

The drill will be the main element of the ship. Maybe it could have a huge mobile mechanism.

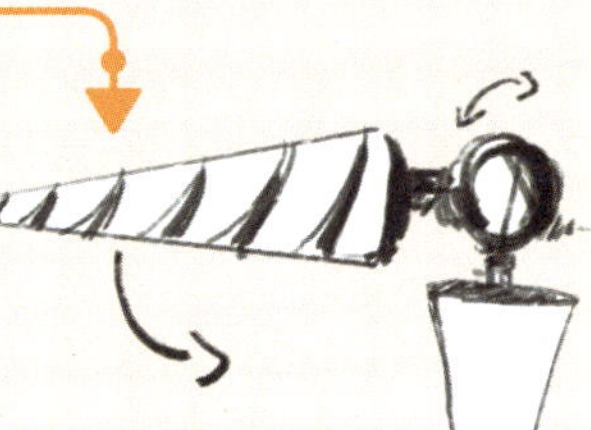

EXCAVATOR

The ship's design will be inspired by heavy machinery used in construction operations, particularly the shapes and colors.

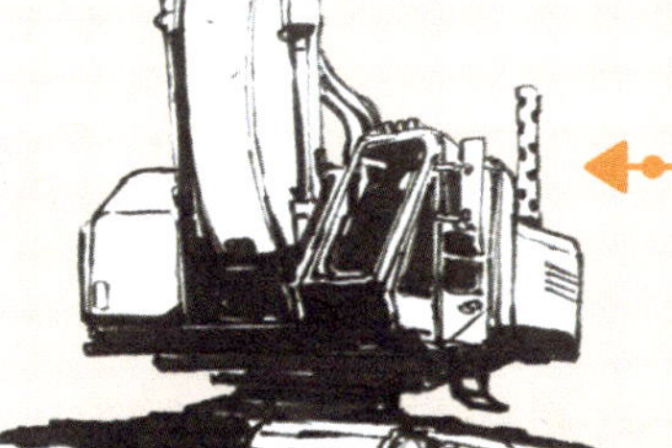

SPACESHIP

The spaceship will have a strong silhouette and a slightly "old-school" look, inspired by classic sci-fi illustrators.

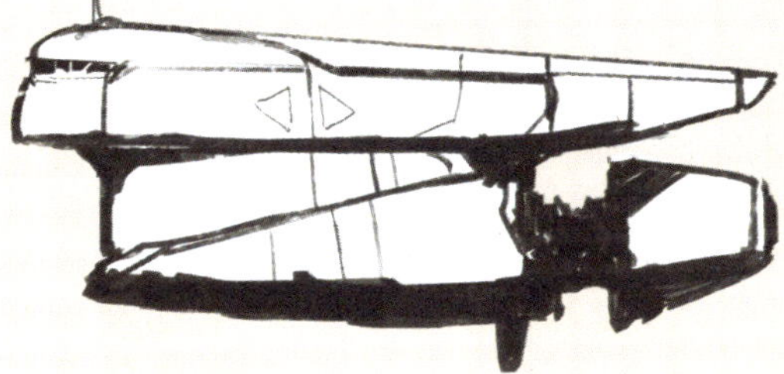

EXHAUSTS

As the ship will be powered by massive fusion reactors, it will need to have giant exhausts at the rear.

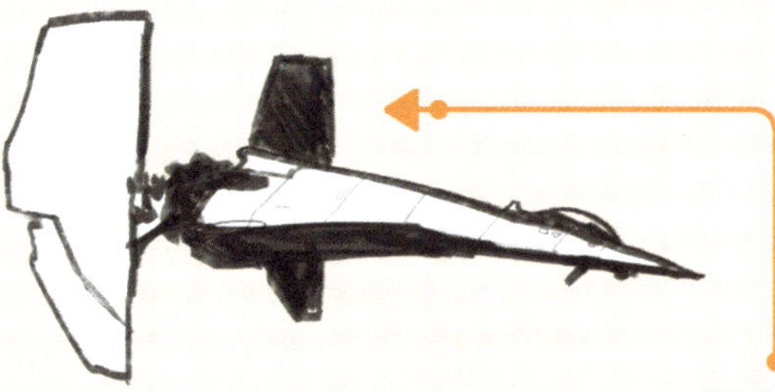

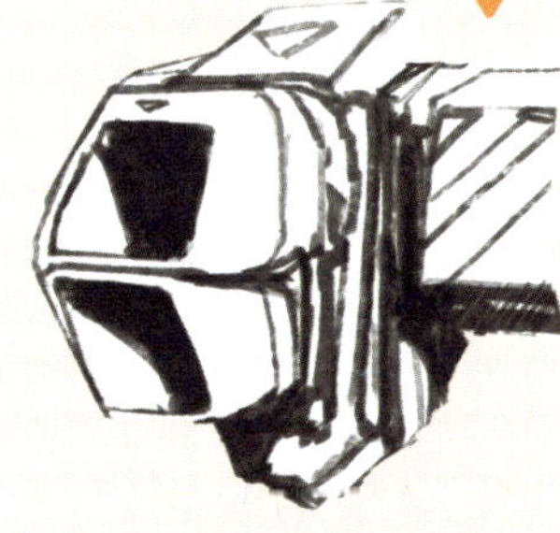

WINGS

Inspired by WWII airplanes, these wings will create an interesting contrast with the fuselage of the ship. They will also be a good area to add decals, numbers, or stripes.

THUMBNAILS

Before creating a clean, polished painting, start by drawing small thumbnail sketches to quickly explore shapes and ideas. It's not about creating a neat drawing at this stage – you will refine and add details later. Using a large ink marker will allow you to draw large shapes quickly. The most important factor at this stage is to find an interesting silhouette.

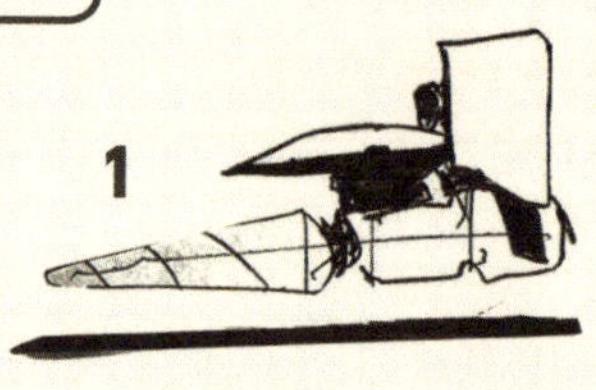

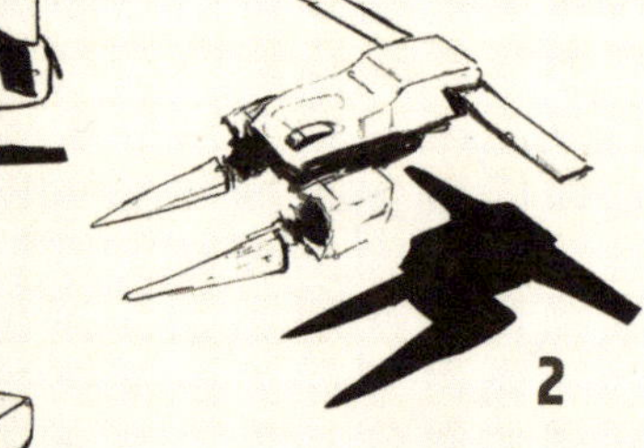

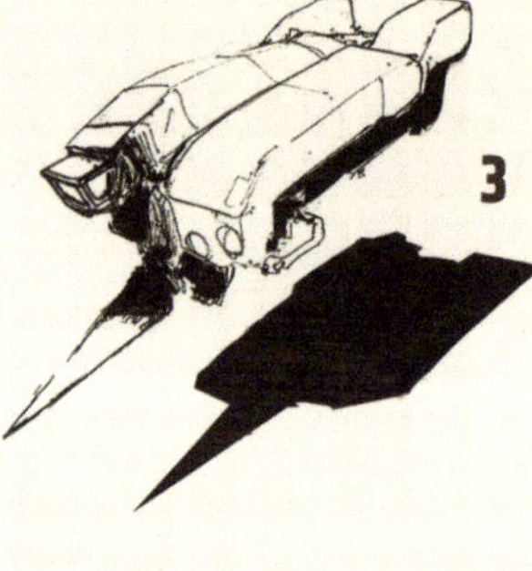

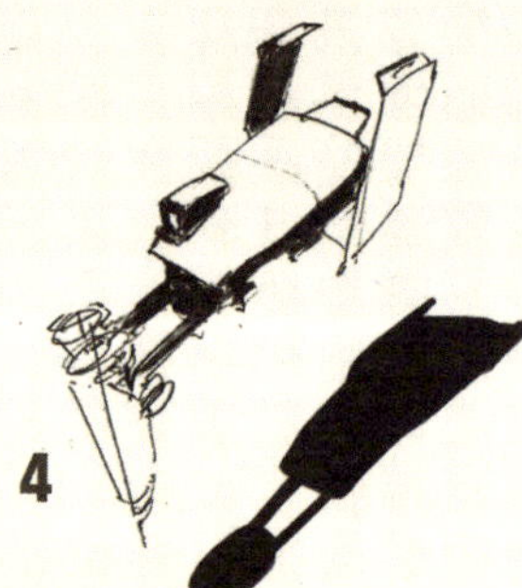

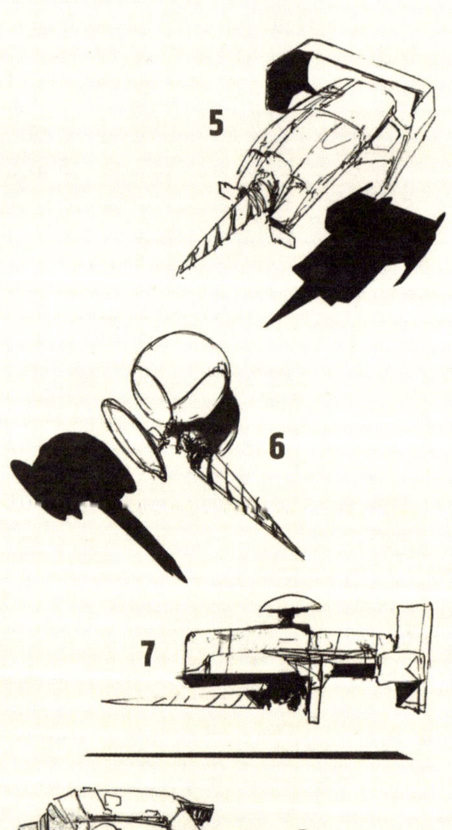

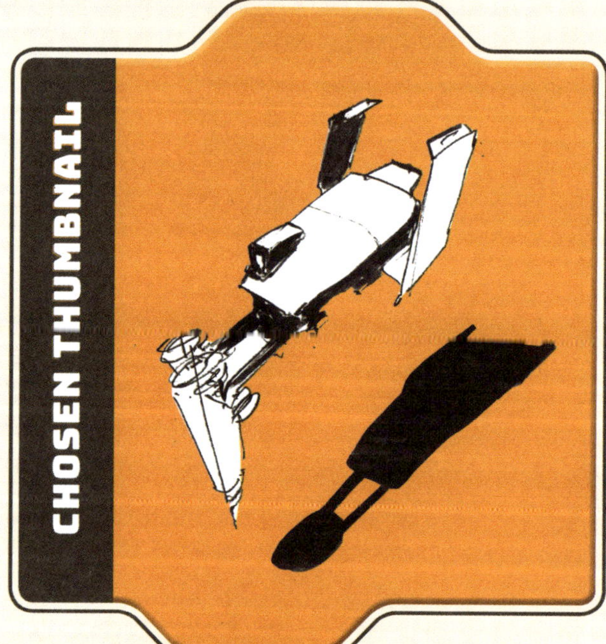

▶ This vehicle has a strong overall shape and clear silhouette. The driller remains the main element of the design, while the wings provide a vertical contrast.

FOUNDATIONS

Once you have your chosen thumbnail, it's time to turn it into a more refined drawing. Use a graphite pencil to start creating simple geometrical shapes – these are much easier to draw and will provide a good foundation for the next steps of your creation. Try to visualize and convert each element of your design into these simple shapes.

BASE

▸ The fuselage is a kind of flattened cone. Try to keep a sense of tension in the shape. The thrusters, located at the rear, are more cuboid in design.

▸ The drill is a big cone attached to the main hull of the ship by two simple boxes. The rotating elements are cylinders.

▸ The two wings are simple planars. They are attached to the ship by large arms. Keep each element very simple – detail will be added later.

LINES

▸ Building on the previous steps, draw in lines to give the ship its main structure. The shapes may still change a little – allow yourself to discover new possibilities.

▸ Flesh out the mechanical structure of the ship a little more and block out the main elements, such as the fuselage and wings. Next, spend more time detailing the driller.

▸ Start to add smaller details, such as panels, thrusters, exhausts, and other mechanical elements.

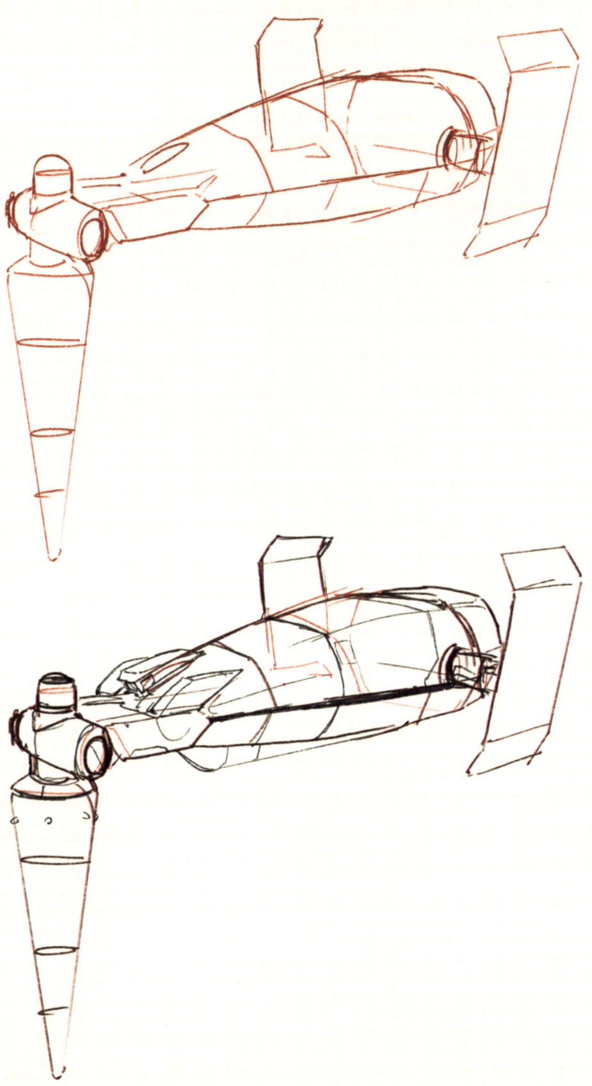

DESIGN FOCUS

WINGS

Both of the wings are made of articulated panels. At this stage you can explore various patterns for them. The articulated arms are made of pistons, wires, and moving components.

COCKPIT

The cockpit and surrounding areas also need more attention. Since the fuselage is rather simple, it's a good idea to create highly detailed areas too. Producing a pleasing design is often a matter of rhythm.

DRILLER

The driller and its points of articulation require a lot more detailing. This is one of the key areas of the ship, so it must catch the eye of the viewer. Add joints and other elements.

IDEA INVENTORY

FUSELAGE

Explore elegant, streamlined shapes for the main fuselage. A good method to design this kind of form is to draw an overall shape, then "cut" it into smaller elements.

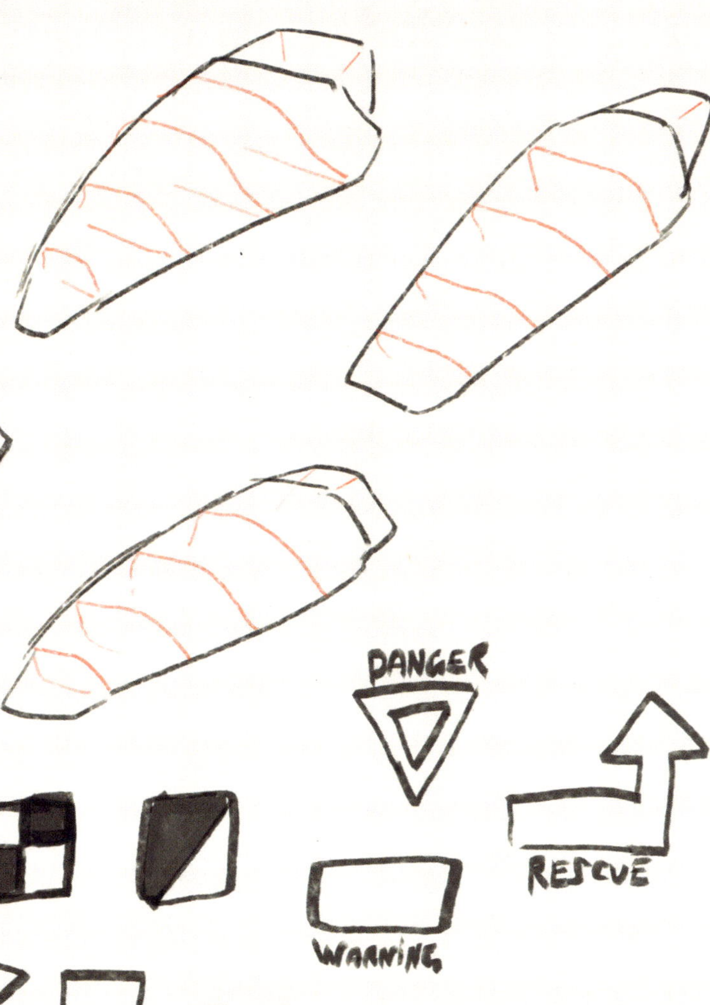

DECALS

Adding warning decals will introduce a more industrial and technical feel to the ship's hull. Decals are also very graphical elements that can be used to enhance the look of your design. Try to find inspiration from real-life jet planes or machinery.

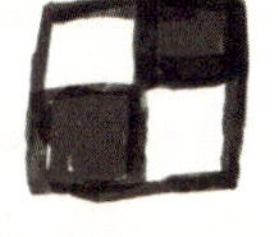
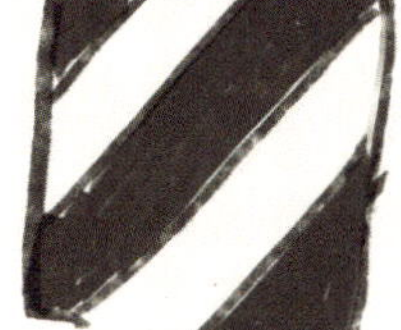
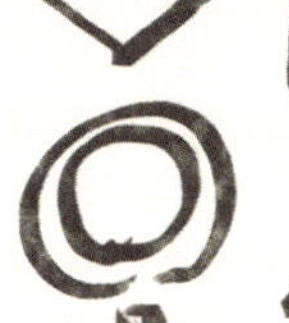
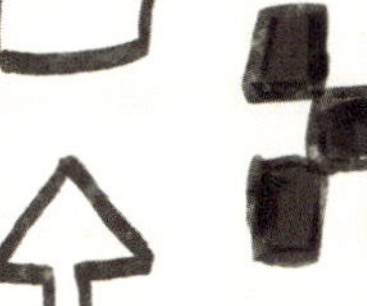

FINAL SKETCH

Pull together all the elements you have worked on to complete a final sketch. Using the previous steps as a guide, use a graphite pencil to start to refine and polish the spaceship design, adding details and complexity to the overall drawing. Keep your lines loose and light, as these graphite lines will need to be erased during the inking stage.

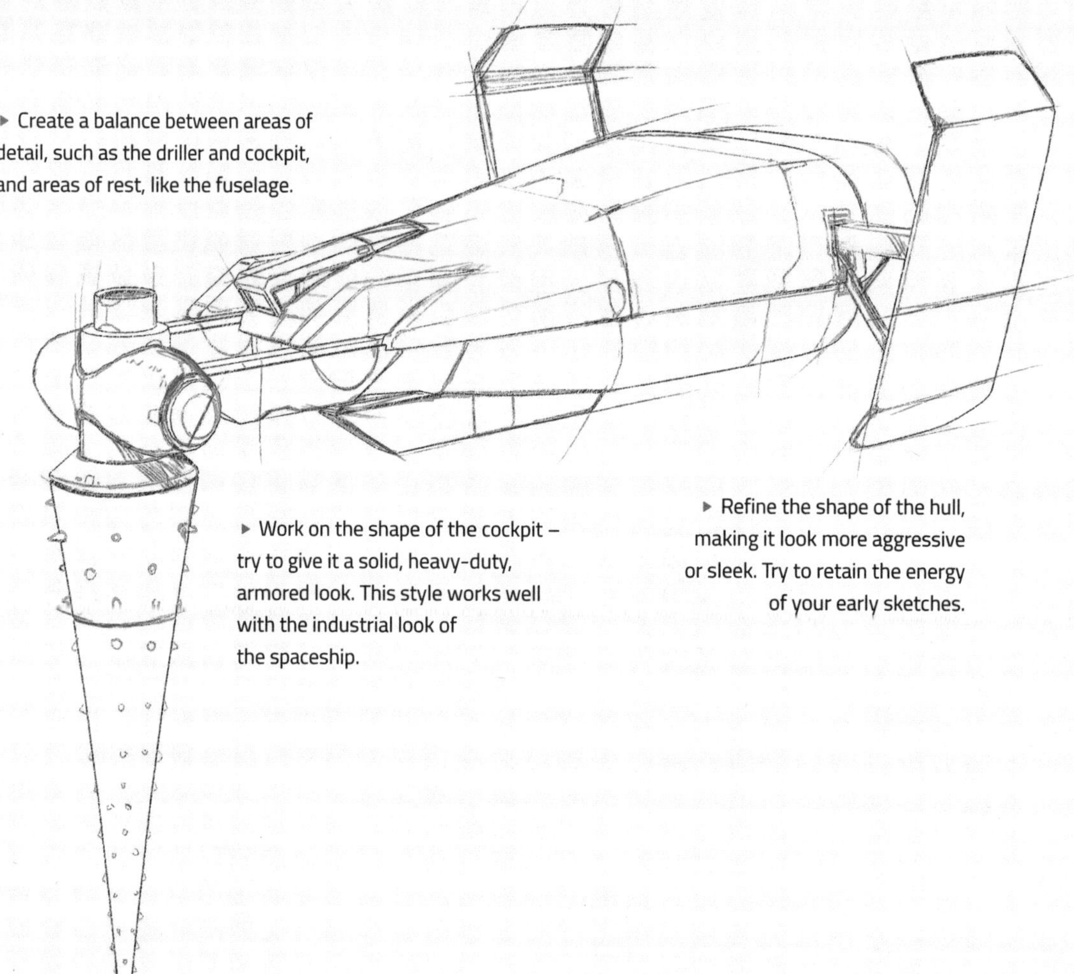

▸ Create a balance between areas of detail, such as the driller and cockpit, and areas of rest, like the fuselage.

▸ Work on the shape of the cockpit – try to give it a solid, heavy-duty, armored look. This style works well with the industrial look of the spaceship.

▸ Refine the shape of the hull, making it look more aggressive or sleek. Try to retain the energy of your early sketches.

INKING

Using a fine brush, apply India ink over your pencil sketch. Be patient and careful; this is not a forgiving process and it might take time before you feel confident. Nevertheless, keep in mind that minor mistakes can be fixed and try to apply the ink fluently. It may be a good idea to practice before starting on your final piece.

▶ Don't worry about trying to create perfectly straight lines. Small imperfections will add variety to your design.

▶ Don't erase all of the pencil lines right away — you can remove them later, once the ink is dry. It's much easier to work this way.

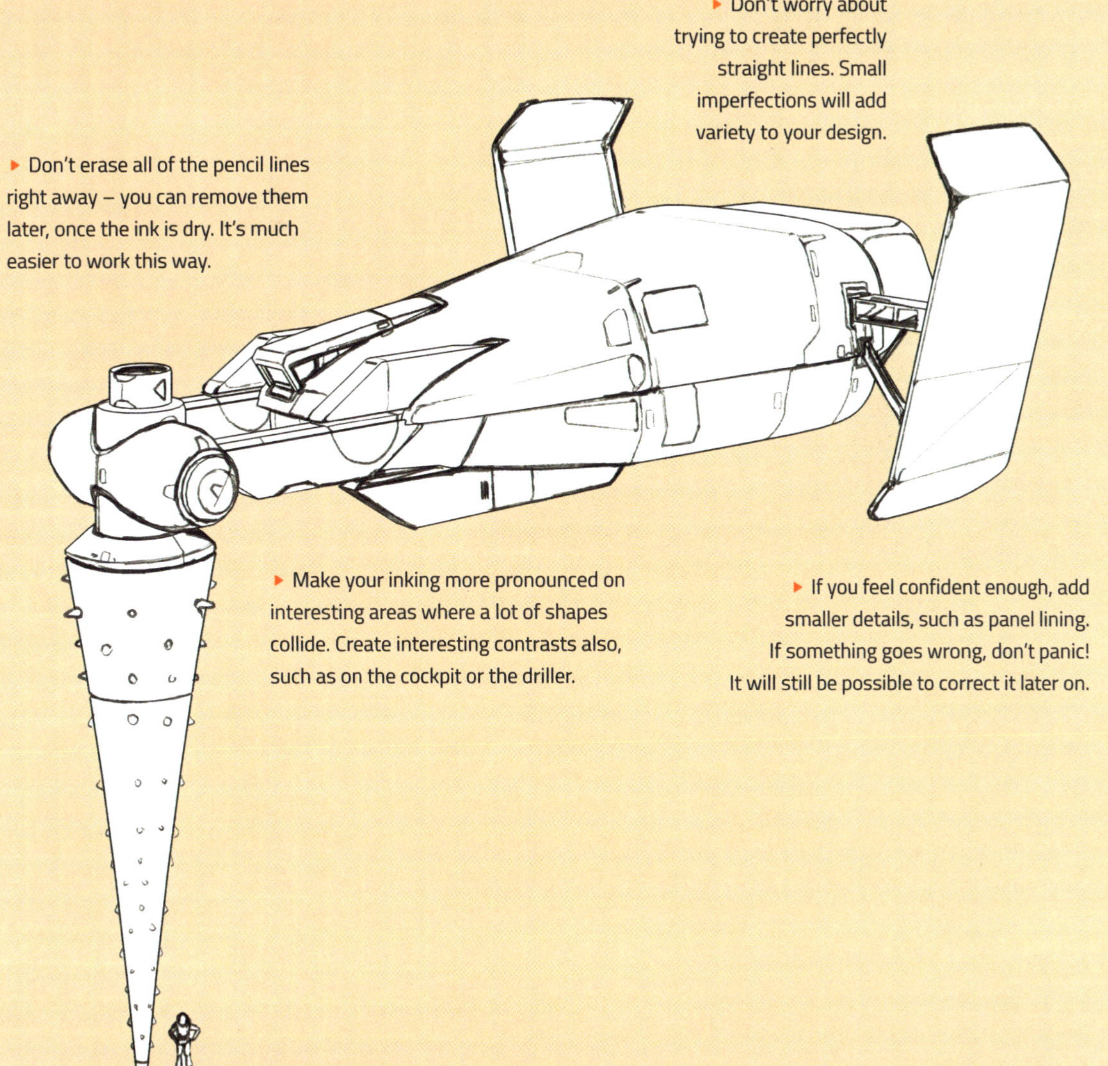

▶ Make your inking more pronounced on interesting areas where a lot of shapes collide. Create interesting contrasts also, such as on the cockpit or the driller.

▶ If you feel confident enough, add smaller details, such as panel lining. If something goes wrong, don't panic! It will still be possible to correct it later on.

COLORING

Once you are happy with how the spaceship design looks, it's time to bring it to life with color. Gouache paint allows you to use vibrant colors and is easy to handle. Start with the medium tones before applying darker shades, then add the light colors, such as highlights, afterward. When choosing your color palette, stick to a few colors to prevent the image looking overly busy.

▶ Paint large areas with your main color. Inspired by construction machines, an orange shade works well. Don't try to create a perfectly smooth finish – small imperfections will add interest.

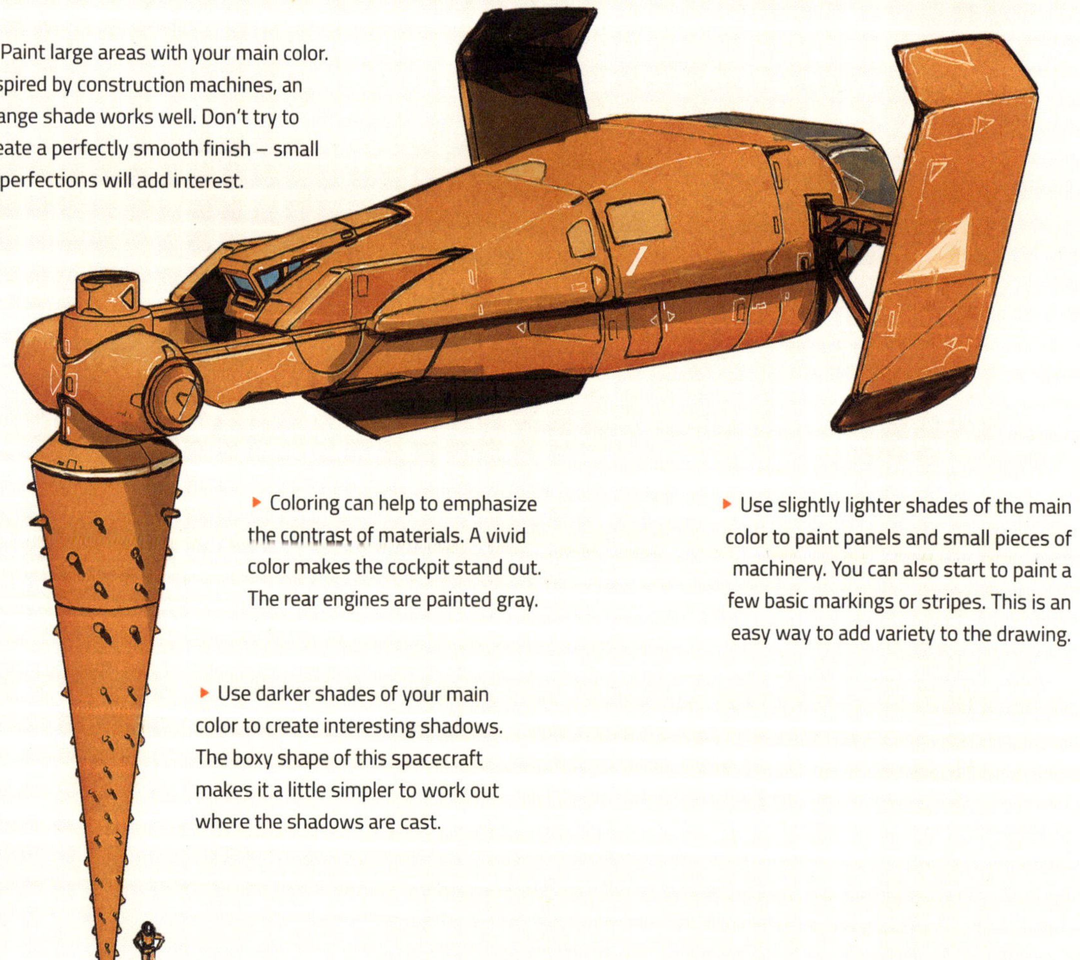

▶ Coloring can help to emphasize the contrast of materials. A vivid color makes the cockpit stand out. The rear engines are painted gray.

▶ Use slightly lighter shades of the main color to paint panels and small pieces of machinery. You can also start to paint a few basic markings or stripes. This is an easy way to add variety to the drawing.

▶ Use darker shades of your main color to create interesting shadows. The boxy shape of this spacecraft makes it a little simpler to work out where the shadows are cast.

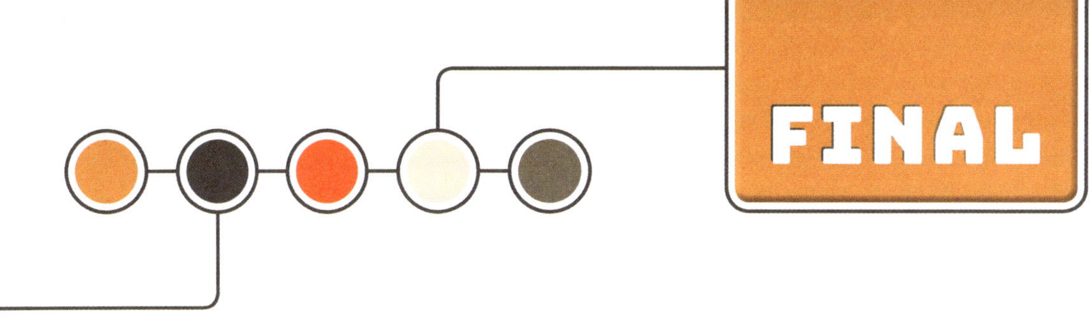

Now the main color palette has been established, it's time to polish the render. This spaceship will benefit from a weathered, battle-worn look, with dust, rust, and paint chipping away to show that it's a hardened workhorse operating in extreme conditions. This is an easy yet very effective way to add visual richness to an image.

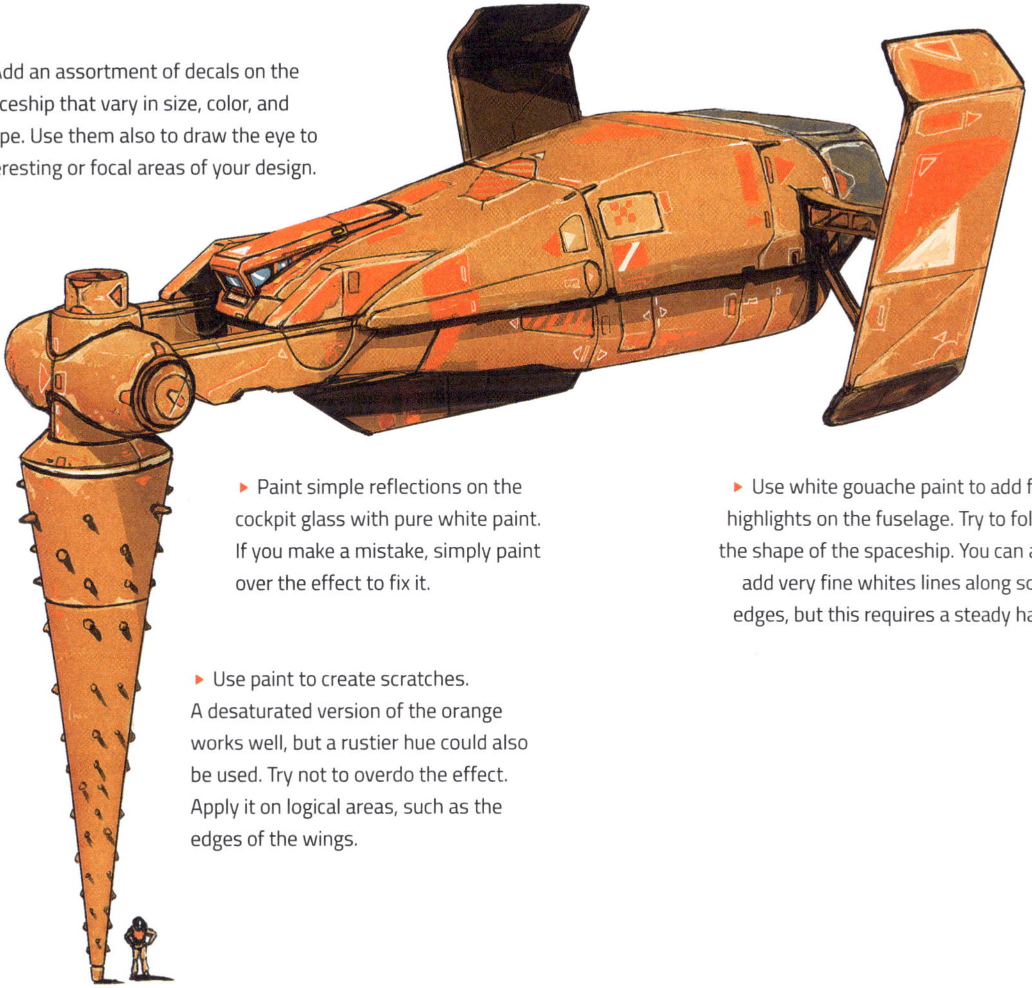

▶ Add an assortment of decals on the spaceship that vary in size, color, and shape. Use them also to draw the eye to interesting or focal areas of your design.

▶ Paint simple reflections on the cockpit glass with pure white paint. If you make a mistake, simply paint over the effect to fix it.

▶ Use white gouache paint to add final highlights on the fuselage. Try to follow the shape of the spaceship. You can also add very fine whites lines along some edges, but this requires a steady hand!

▶ Use paint to create scratches. A desaturated version of the orange works well, but a rustier hue could also be used. Try not to overdo the effect. Apply it on logical areas, such as the edges of the wings.

CLEANING BOTS

... BY JAKE PARKER

This tutorial will demonstrate how to draw a small gang of cleaning robots. They won't be humanoid in shape, but instead will have designs that support the specific task they are intended for. Each bot will be based on a different basic shape to give them distinct personalities and unique looks. There will be a consistent design language across every robot to ensure they still form a cohesive group.

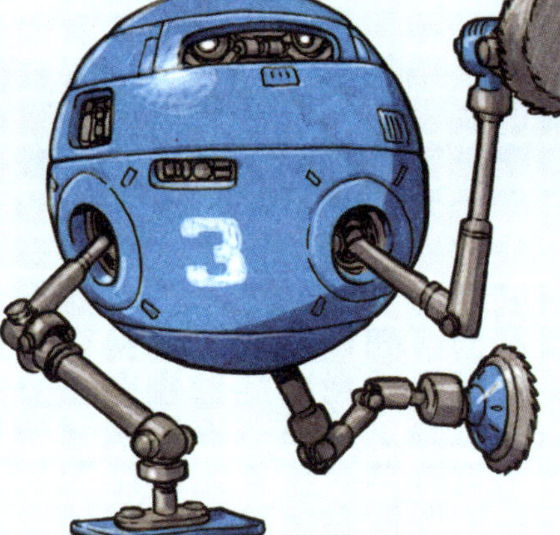

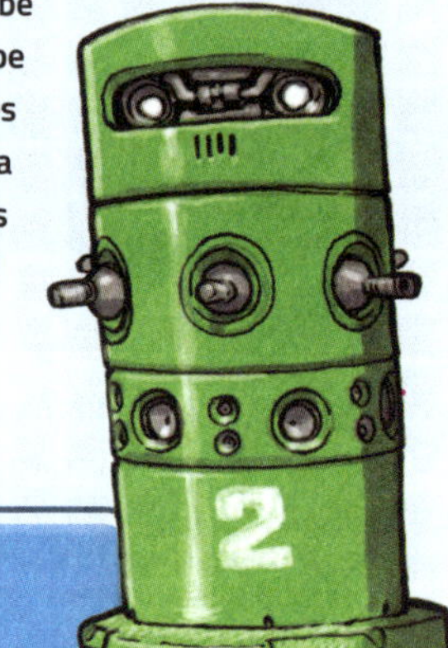

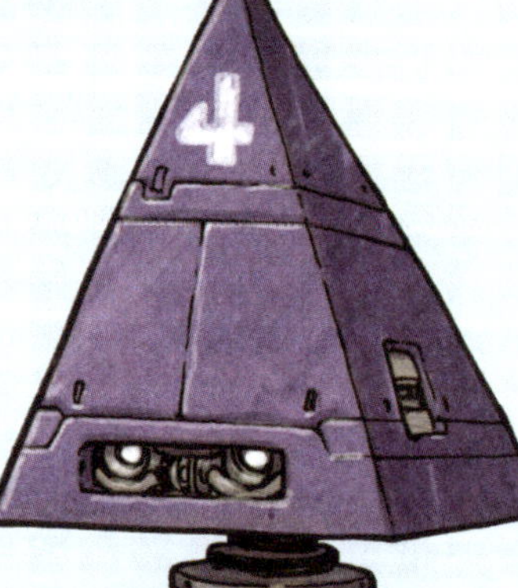

TOOLKIT

- ▸ Bristol smooth paper (400 series)
- ▸ Graphite pencils, HB
- ▸ Erasers, rubber and kneaded
- ▸ Fine brush pen
- ▸ Alcohol markers
- ▸ White colored pencil

RESEARCH

It's essential to base your robot designs on real-world objects in order to ground them in reality. Including elements from industrial items will make your bots look like they were designed by human engineers, to do tasks they would rather not do. Look at appliances and objects around you and use online search engines to build up a reference library of imagery.

CLEANING SUPPLIES

What supplies and tools would the gang of cleaning bots use? Take note of the different categories these items fall into – each robot could be designed to do a different cleaning task.

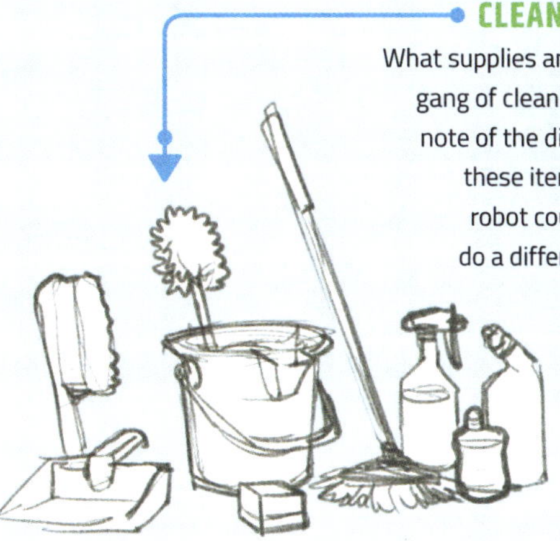

EQUIPMENT CRATES

Crates and carriers used in the military and for film productions can provide an insight into what makes something look utilitarian and sturdy.

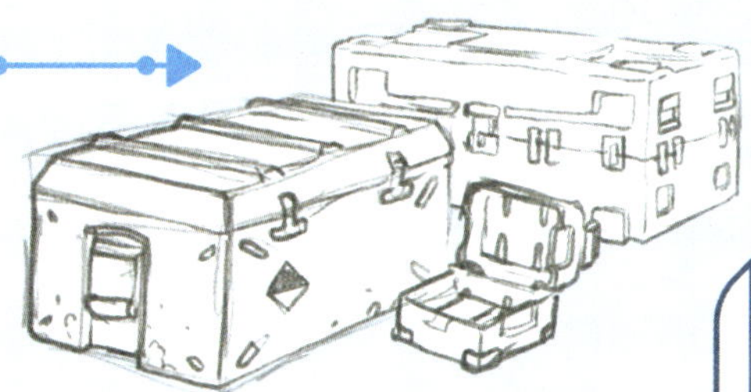

ROBOT FACTORY ARM

Factory machinery is functional and looks interesting too! A futuristic take on an industrial robot arm will work well with the cleaning bots.

VACUUM CLEANER

Research vacuum cleaner designs, taking note of the shapes, textures, and details that give each their unique look.

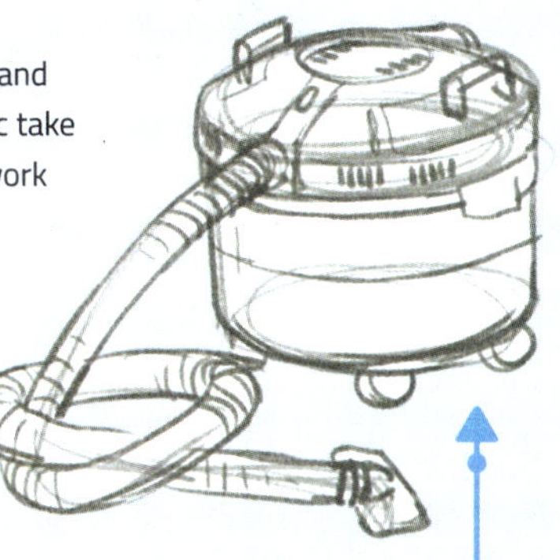

OLD COMPUTER

Studying old computer designs can provide ideas for how to give the bots a retro look, while also remaining somewhat realistic.

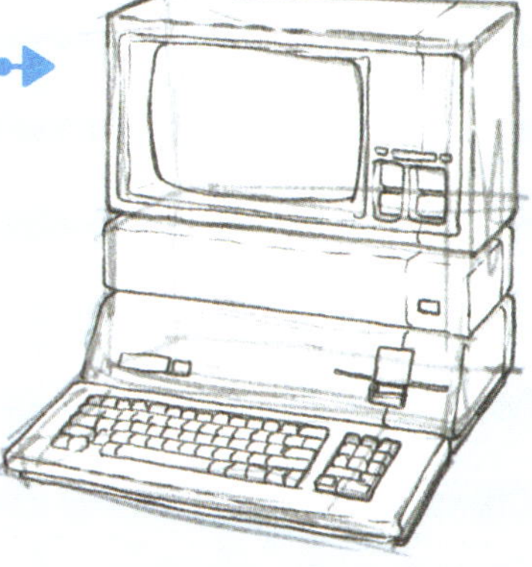

THUMBNAILS

The thumbnail process is all about finding a basic shape and clear silhouette for your design. Each cleaning bot should have its own unique shape that reflects its individual duties. By using similar basic shapes, the gang of bots also need to form a cohesive group and look like they come as a set.

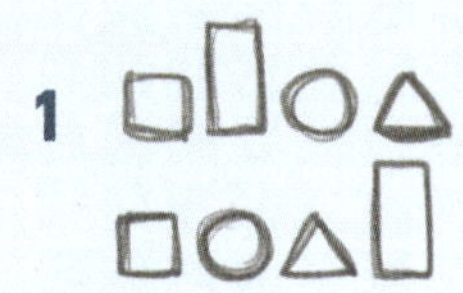
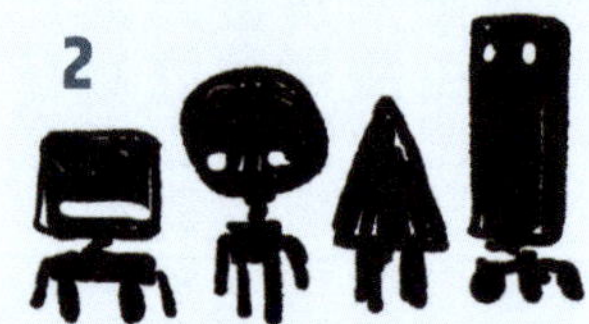
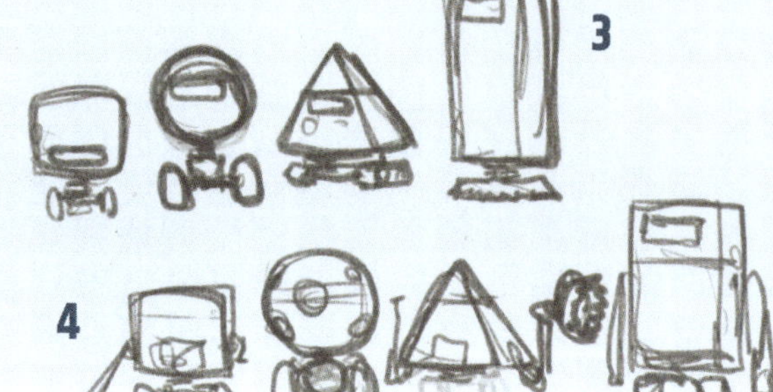
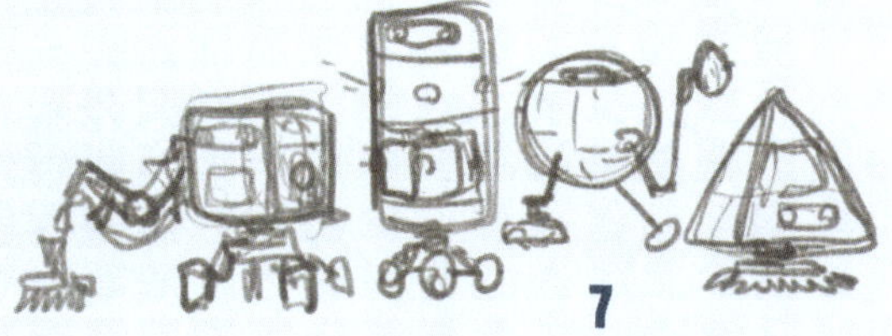
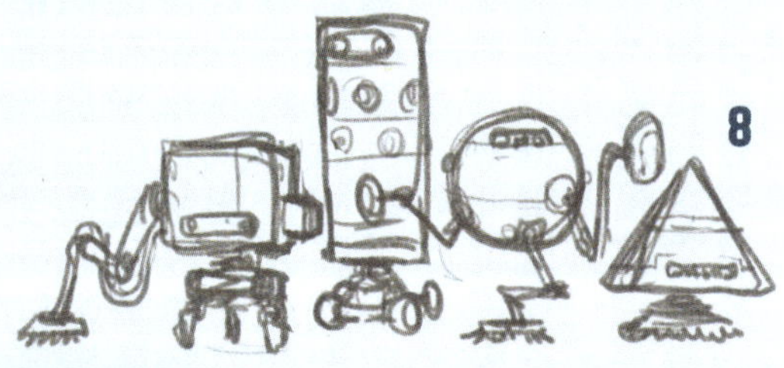
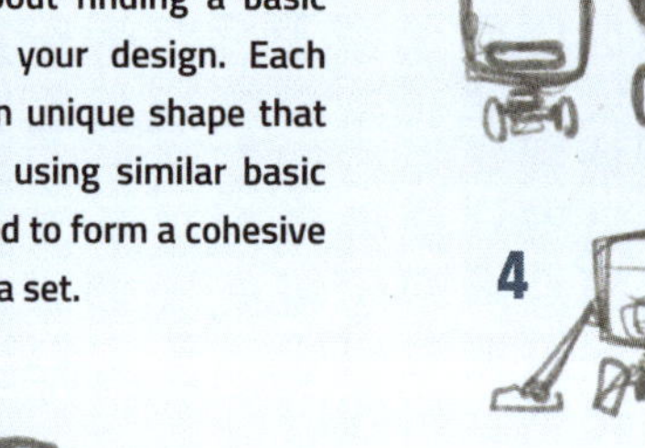
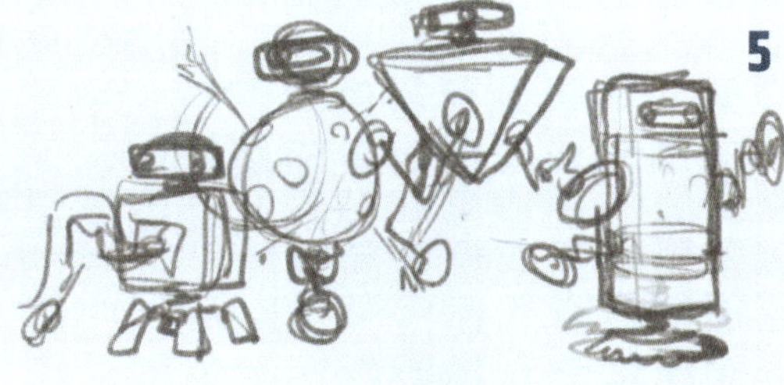
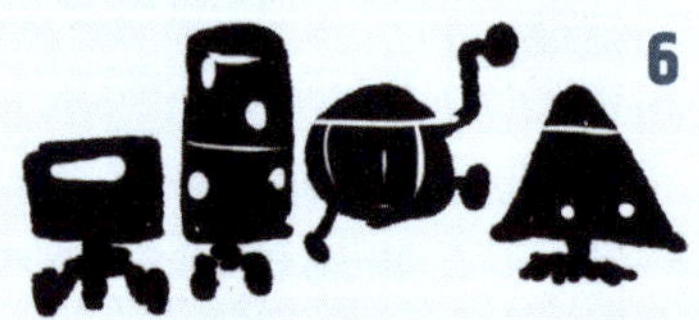

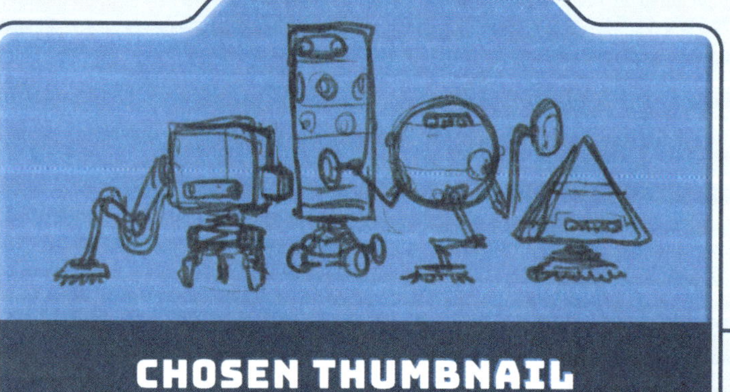

CHOSEN THUMBNAIL

▶ The shapes and proportions work best together in this thumbnail. The position of the smaller details works well and would be worth fleshing out a little more in the subsequent stages.

FOUNDATIONS

It's time to take your thumbnail to the next level and lay down a foundation you can build a great drawing on. At this stage, keep the sketch fairly loose and lively – avoid nailing anything down just yet. Think about structure first and design second. One approach is to draw the foundation in vermilion to ensure the sketch will be hidden under the ink and color added in the final stages.

BASE

▶ Start by drawing the basic three-dimensional shapes. To check the shapes are structurally sound, draw through the designs to show what the rear sides will look like.

▶ Don't worry about creating a good drawing at this point in the process. For the bots' limbs, it's fine to sketch in basic lines as placeholders.

▶ Pay close attention to drawing clear silhouettes. Any limbs and extensions shouldn't overlap too much – keep the design open and easy to understand.

LINES

▶ You may wish to lighten the drawing slightly using a kneaded eraser. This will make it easier to see details as you begin to build up the drawing.

▶ It's okay to stick with a vermilion color for this stage of the drawing. You want to add more detail while still keeping the design fairly basic.

▶ Make sure some design elements are repeated on each bot to tie them together, such as the style of their eyes or joints.

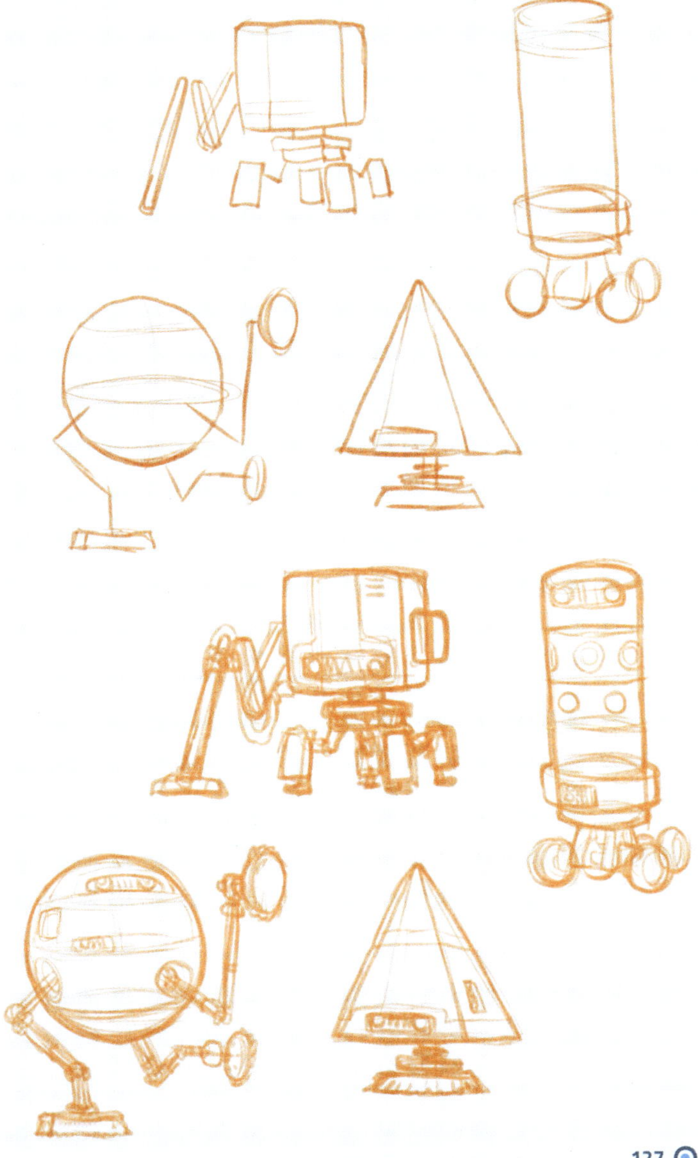

BUILDING UP

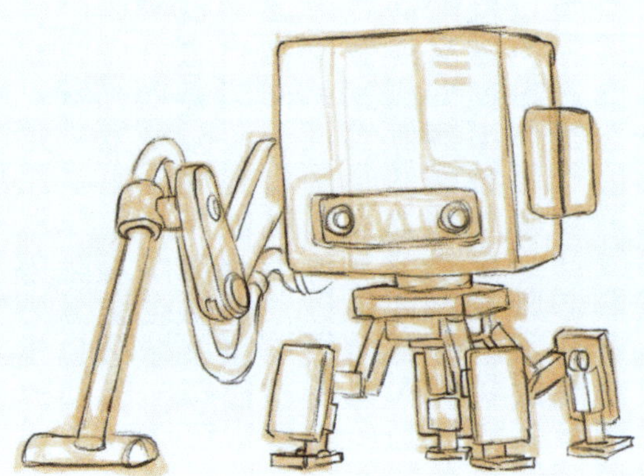

Now that the basic shapes and sketches are complete, you can begin to figure out the details. Switch to a graphite pencil, as this will allow you to see the design more clearly on top of the vermilion lines underneath.

LINES

Keep your lines light and lively. There's no need to apply pressure at this stage, as you may need to erase sections of the drawing as you figure out what works best.

SHAPES

Use simple shapes to figure out the smaller components of each robot. Features such as joints, wheels, and eyes should already be established in your drawing before detail is added.

DETAILS

Add panel lines, vents, and openings. Think compositionally – where do you want space in the design, and where do you want lots of interesting detail? Aim to create a balanced look across each bot, with not too much or too little detail in one area.

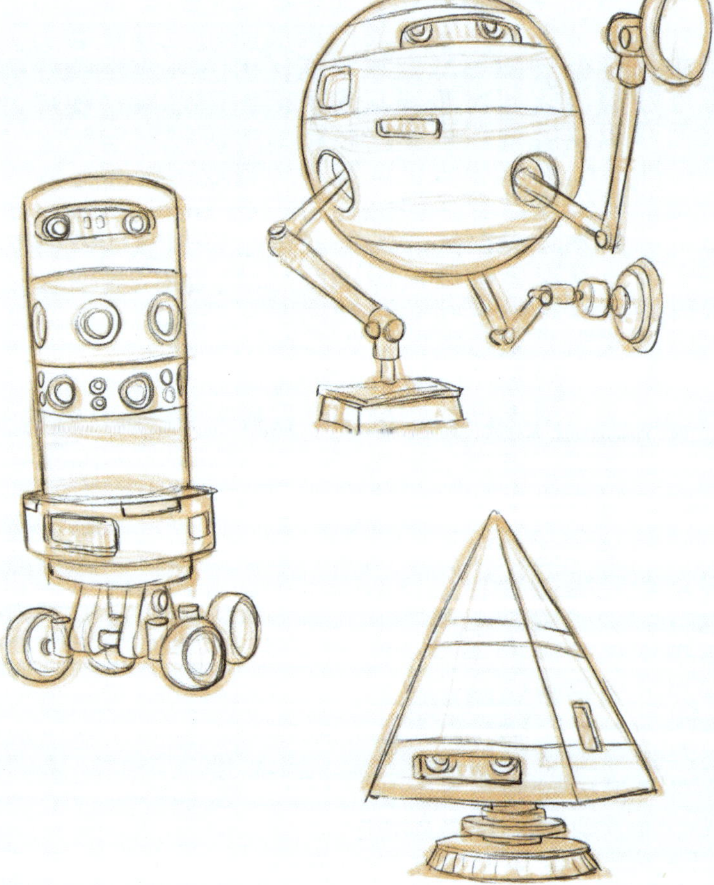

DESIGN FOCUS

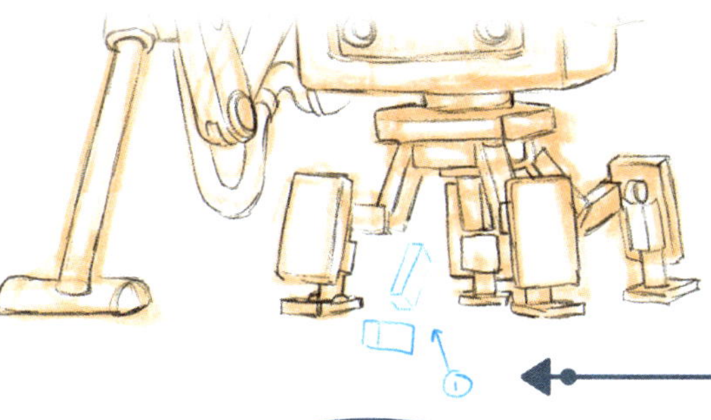

CUBES

Use rectangular cubes as the foundational shape for the robot's legs, as this is a simple shape that can easily be drawn from different angles. Leave details until later. For now, focus on capturing the basic components to make each bot look structurally sound.

CYLINDER

If you have long, uninterrupted shapes, like this cylinder, it helps to add a contrasting shape to break up the silhouette, making the overall design more visually appealing. Add a second cylindrical shape that protrudes from the robot halfway down their body, smoothing the transition into the lower section of the design.

LIMBS

When adding extruding shapes, such as limbs, be sure to leave plenty of open space around them. The design can look messy if the shapes overlap, making it harder to work out which piece of the body goes where, and does what.

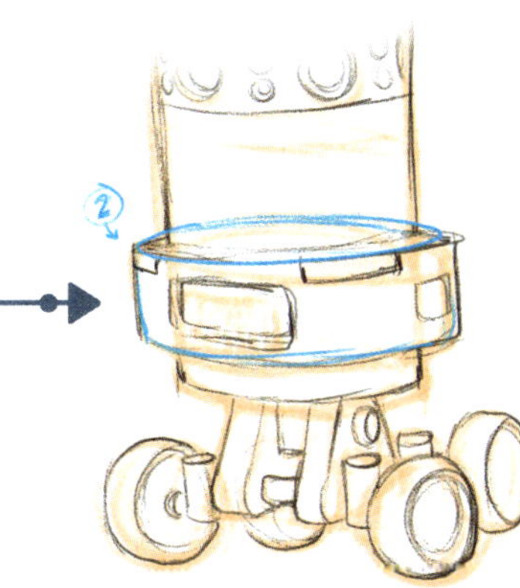

IDEA INVENTORY

EYES

The robots need to be able to see, especially as their job is to clean! It makes sense that they would use an array of sensors and receptors to detect dirt and navigate terrain. Sketch out a few variations of cameras and other sensors, studying how symmetry and asymmetry affect their design. Symmetry will make the robot look more approachable, and asymmetry more alien.

TOOLS

To create cleaning tools for the bots, draw different shapes that look interesting when placed together. Keep the amount of components to a minimum for simple-looking tools, and add more shapes for something a little more complex.

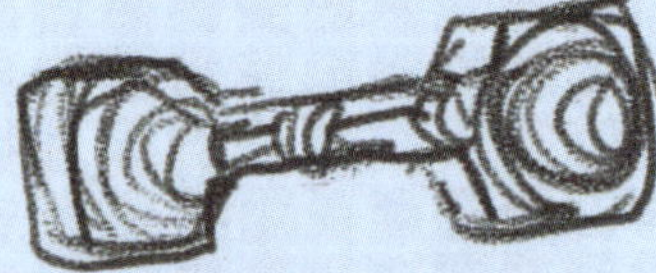
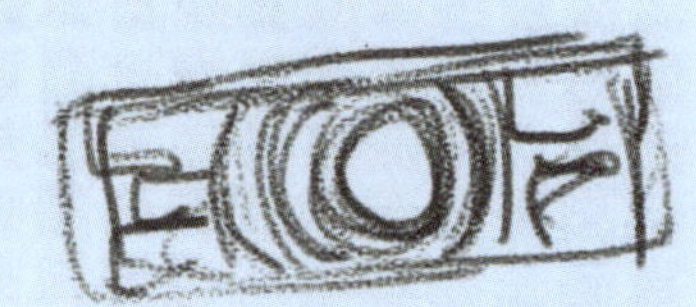
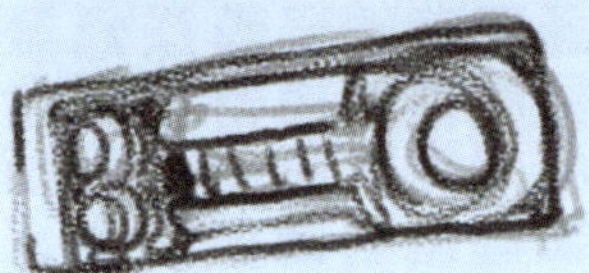
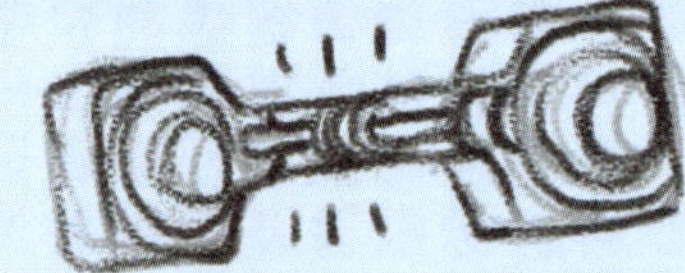
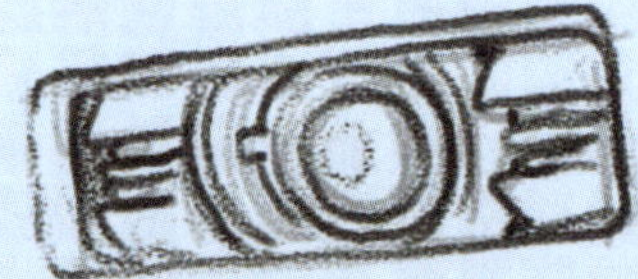
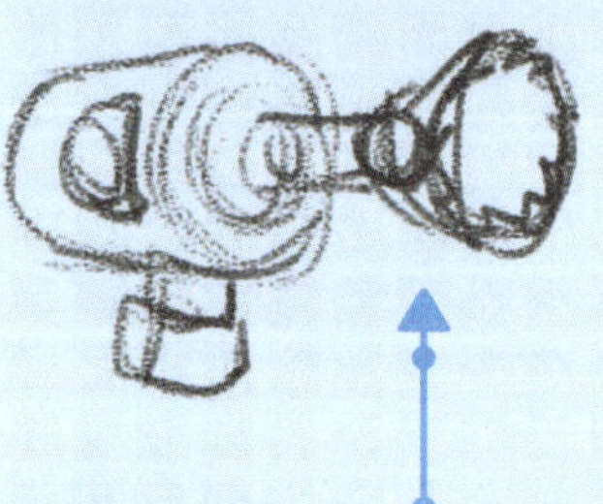
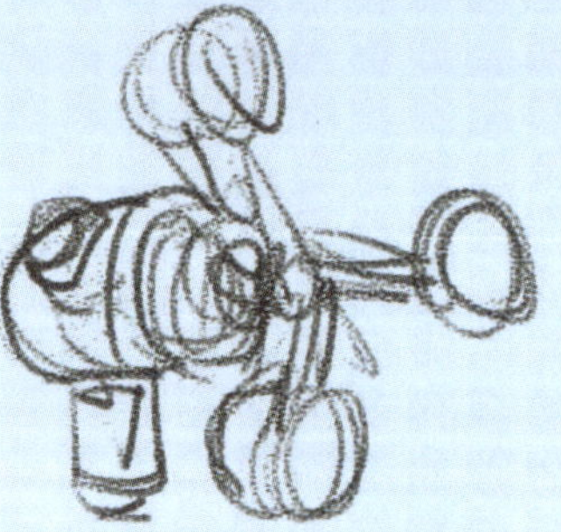
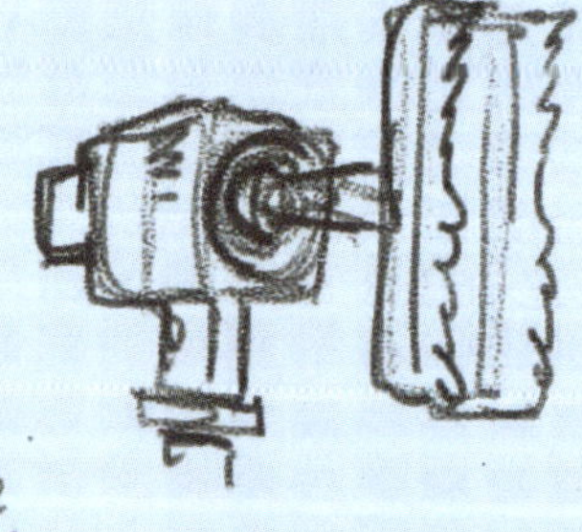
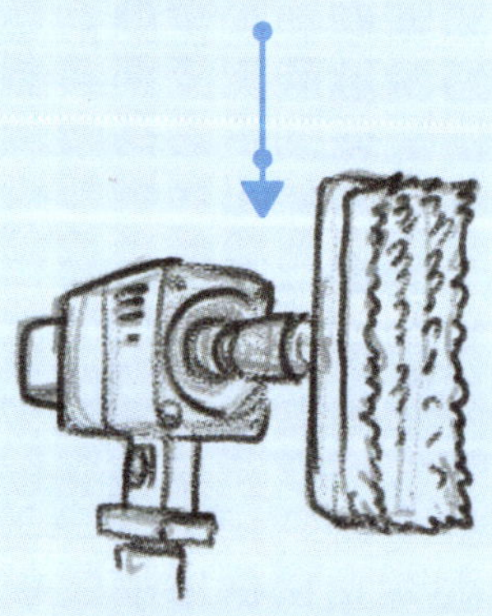
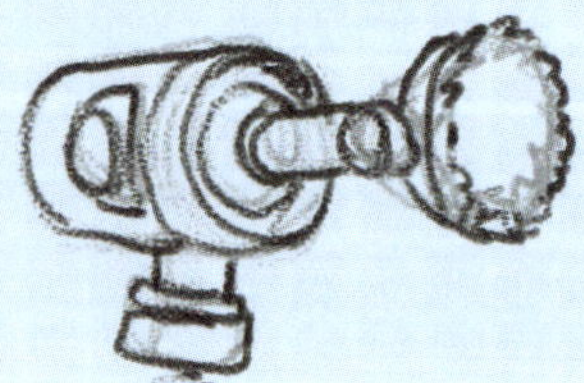

▶ Try both rectangular and round shapes, then decide which fit better with the robot's overall design.

FINAL SKETCH

Using stronger, more defined lines, draw all of the detail and design elements into one cohesive drawing. With the explorations for the eye components as inspiration, feel free to create a new design that fits better. You aren't tied to the decisions made earlier – allow yourself to experiment at this stage and let new ideas surface as you draw. Just make sure that the important details are worked out before you progress any further – it will make life much easier when you begin inking.

▶ Add little notches and indents to enhance the industrial look of the robots. Keep these details small, placed in the corners, and around larger design elements. This will imply the robots are constructed from mechanical components, giving your design a greater level of believability.

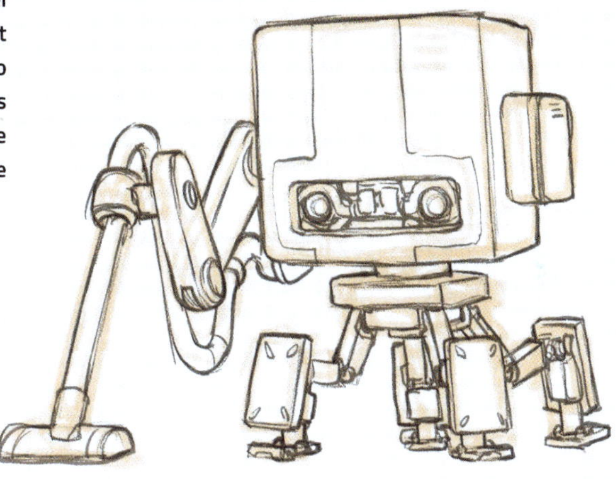

▶ Sketch little wires and tubes inside the openings of panels and in-between panels to suggest the quantity of technology hiding beneath the outer shell.

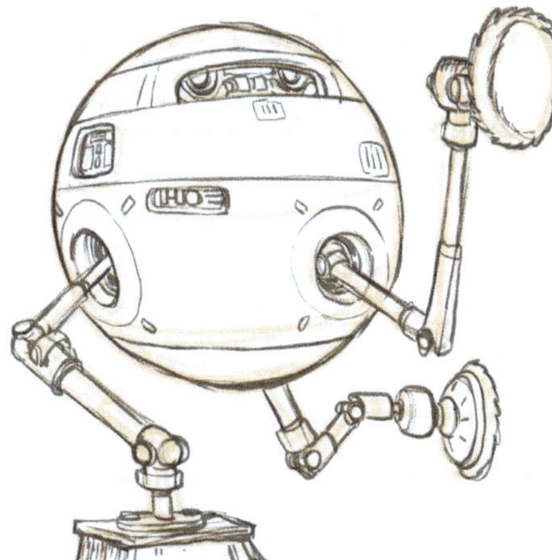

▶ Keeping in mind how joints and components fit together, add screws, bolts, and fasteners to make them look more believable.

▶ Add vents by drawing three or four parallel lines in blank spaces on the body of each bot. This is another element that will add to the overall credibility of the design.

INKING

It's understandable if you feel a little nervous about inking over your beautiful sketch – it's so much harder to correct an inked line! Try to relax and let the lines be themselves. Even if they're a little off, it will give your drawing an organic look. While some artists prefer to use rulers, it can be nice to let your lines have a little natural warp to them.

▶ Use a 0.1 mm or 0.2 mm technical pen for the interior lines. If using a felt-tip pen with a nice sharp point, press lightly, letting the tip gently brush the page.

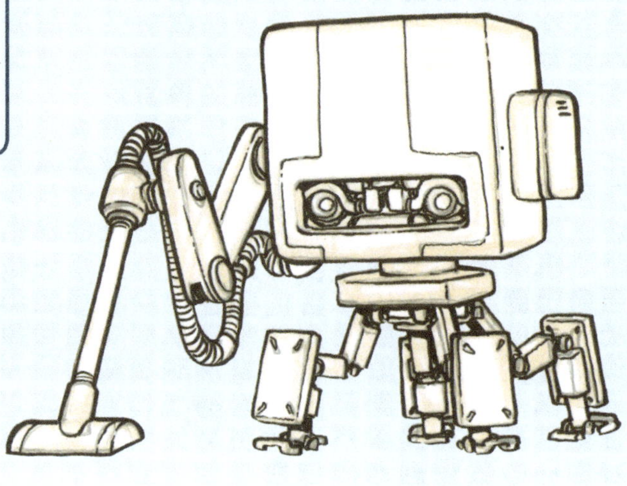

▶ Outline the drawings using a sharp felt-tip pen, or a 0.8 mm technical pen. These lines should be thick, as they define the outer edge of the drawing and hold the rest of the lines together.

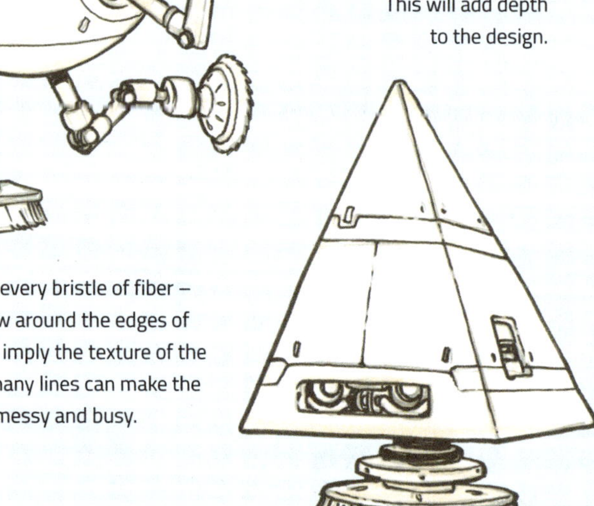

▶ Wherever there is a nook, cranny, or overlapping shape on a robot, fill it with black. This will add depth to the design.

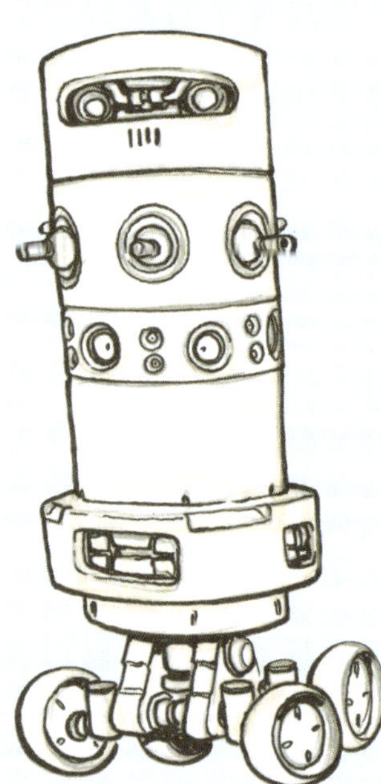

▶ Don't draw every bristle of fiber – just draw a few around the edges of each shape to imply the texture of the surface. Too many lines can make the drawing look messy and busy.

COLORING

Just as each of the cleaning bots has a different shape, it would be visually interesting for each to have a different color also. Apply these colors on each of the robots' paneling, with a second cool gray color for the mechanical parts working beneath the surface. Having this contrast in value and color will make the robots stand out from each other.

▶ Using your design markers, lay in a base color first. Don't worry about light or shadow at this stage. Just color within the lines.

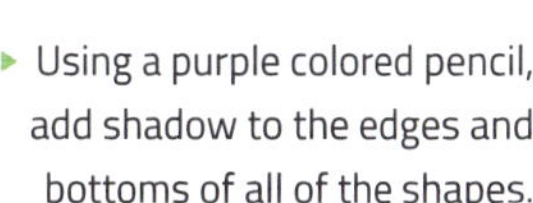

▶ Using a purple colored pencil, add shadow to the edges and bottoms of all of the shapes. For anything underneath another shape, make the purple darker by going over the area multiple times. Lightly color in the purple for horizontal sides and vertical facing planes.

▶ Don't forget to add shadow and light to each of the panels to create extra dimension.

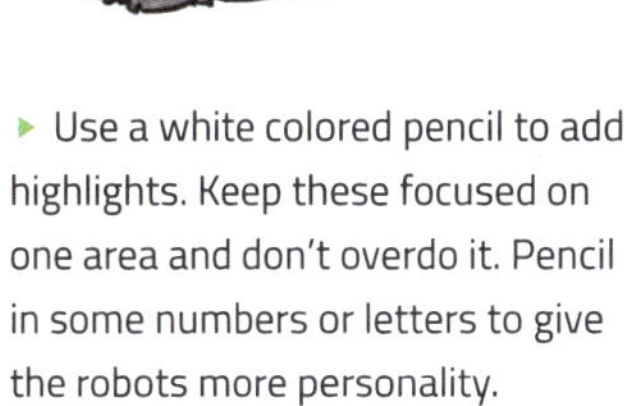

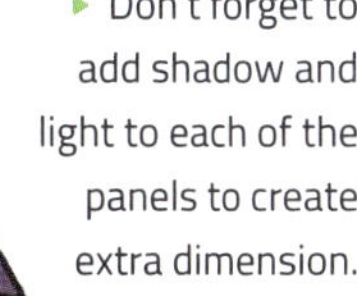

▶ Use a white colored pencil to add highlights. Keep these focused on one area and don't overdo it. Pencil in some numbers or letters to give the robots more personality.

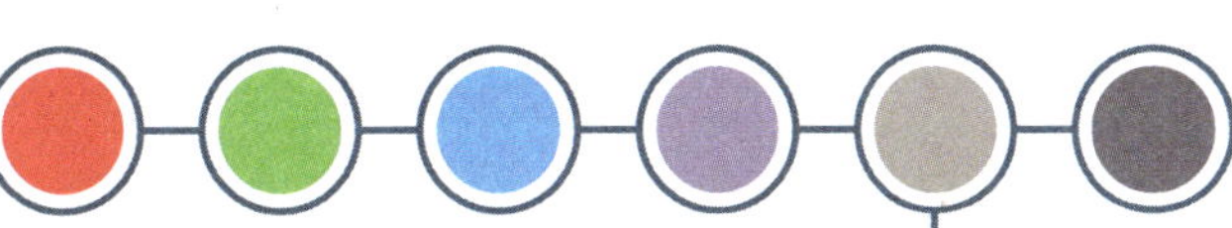

SPACECRAFT

... BY JEREL DYE

This tutorial will guide you through how to create a spry little spacecraft. With room to seat only the pilot, the ship is designed to be fast and agile for short trips around the solar system. It can fly in most atmospheres. Perhaps it's part of a small fleet docked on a carrier, or is used as a patrol ship for an orbital defense web. Go wherever your imagination takes you! Following this tutorial, you will learn the basics of vehicle design and discover the skills you need to create the coolest spacecrafts in the galaxy.

TOOLKIT

- ▶ Bristol smooth paper (400 series)
- ▶ Graphite pencils, HB
- ▶ Erasers, rubber and kneaded
- ▶ Fine brush pen
- ▶ Alcohol markers
- ▶ Gouache paint, white

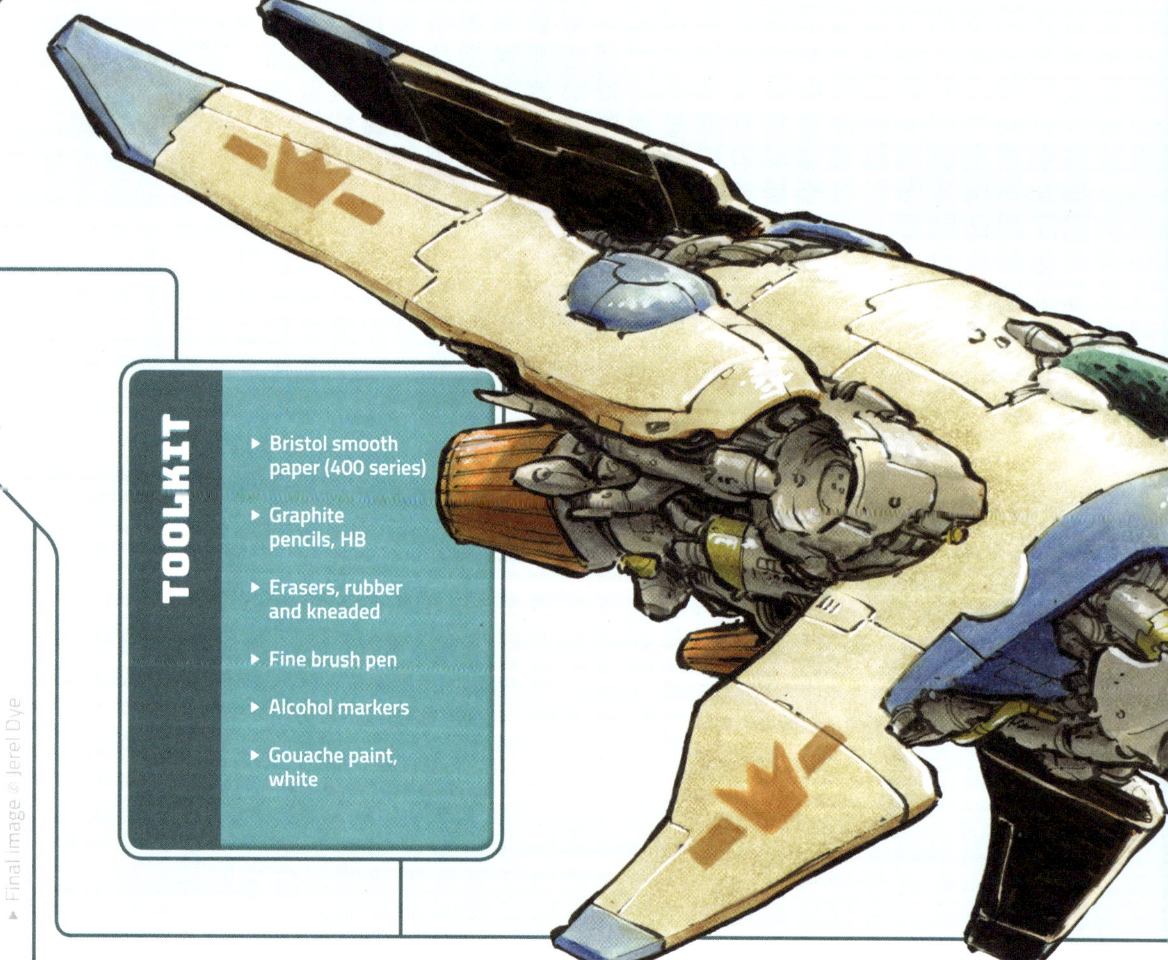

RESEARCH

While it may seem like sci-fi spacecrafts are born from pure creativity and imagination, grounding such designs with real-world references will provide them with a sense of reality. Science-fiction design is best when it's imaginative but feels like it could be real. Take the time to study some real-world tech that can be incorporated into the spacecraft, both historical and present-day.

ROCKET ENGINES

The spacecraft will be powered by rocket engines. This sketch is from a NASA liquid-fuel design – check out the pipes feeding into the main thrust cone!

RETRO

There is something retro and appealing about the aircraft designs of WWII. This Corsair is about the right relative size to the design and function for the spacecraft.

FUSELAGE

Let's take a closer look at the fuselage of a similar WWII aircraft. The subtle curve of the surface of the body is constructed from multiple metal plates riveted together.

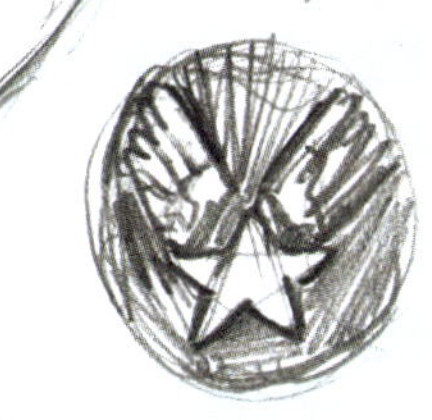

WING DESIGN

The spacecraft's wing design should be more modern than those of a WWII aircraft. Straighter lines and sharper angles will give the spacecraft a futuristic feel and more aggressive edge.

INSIGNIA

The spacecraft should have some kind of iconography or insignia incorporated into its design. Such symbols will give it a subtle sense of story.

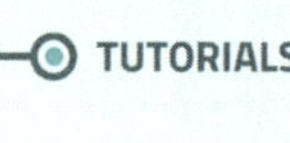

THUMBNAILS

It's a good idea to work in pen when creating small thumbnail sketches. While this may seem a little daunting at first, pen will help you just go for it and try different ideas without editing them straight away. There will be time to perfect the shapes later. The aim is to get your ideas down on the page, only allowing a couple of minutes for each sketch. The thumbnailing process will train your hand and generate new ideas. One leads to the next, which leads to the next, and so on.

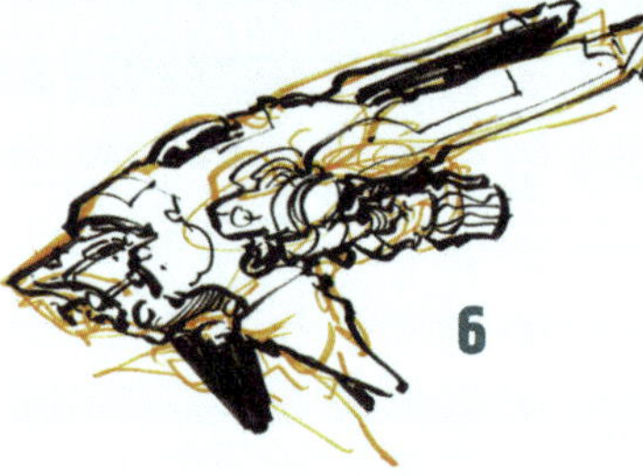

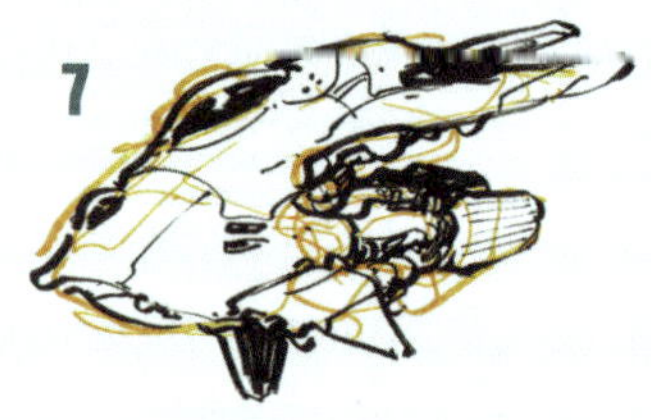

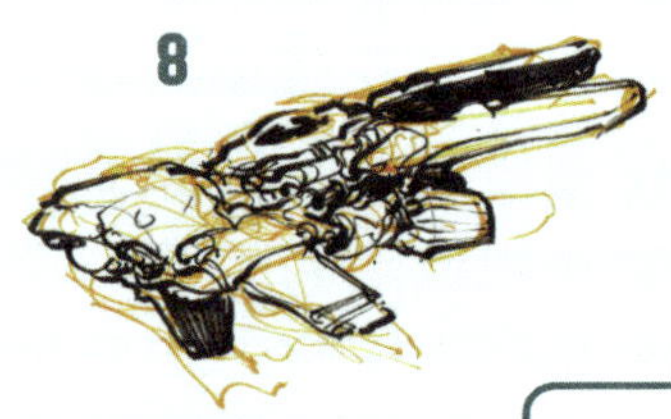

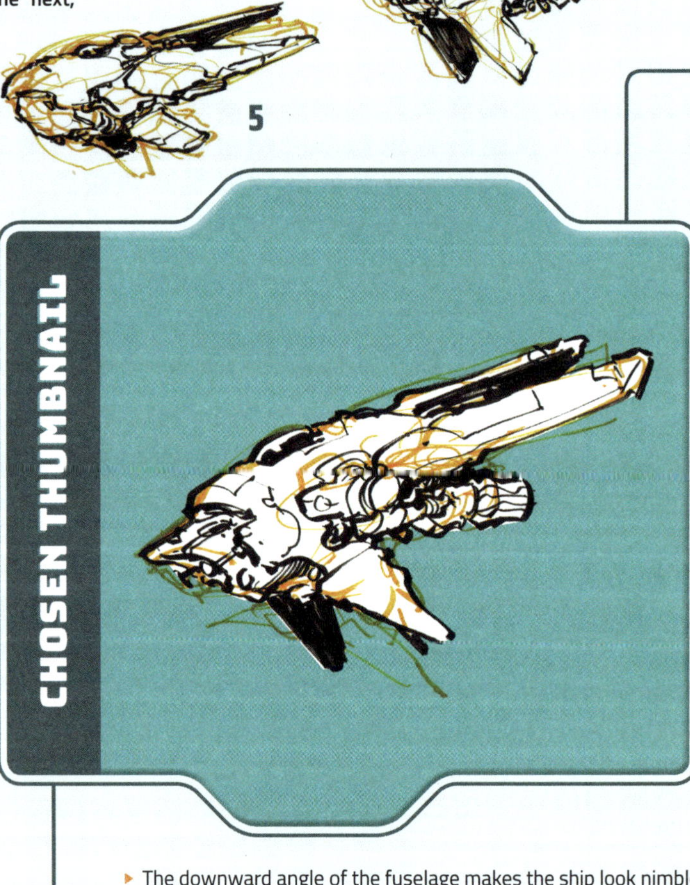

▶ The downward angle of the fuselage makes the ship look nimble and the swept-back wing element is most successful here.

FOUNDATIONS

The next stage is to build the spaceship's basic volumetric form, which is crucial for creating a ship that looks three-dimensional. While the individual shapes are fairly simple, having a good grasp of these underlying volumes will make many of the following steps much easier. This kind of design benefits from a good sense of three-dimensional space. Some people have this sense naturally, while others need to learn it by drawing basic volumes over and over.

BASE

▶ The fuselage is a slightly curved cylinder with a dome for a cockpit. The thruster is another cylinder attached to the underside of it.

▶ While the wings, or fins, are simple planes, their shape and the angles with which they attach to the fuselage makes the design interesting. Push those elements as far as they can go.

▶ Sketch lines that move across the spaceship's form, almost like the horizontal ridges on a can of soup. Not only will these lines help you to draw each form, they will inform the viewer of the different volumes that make up the design.

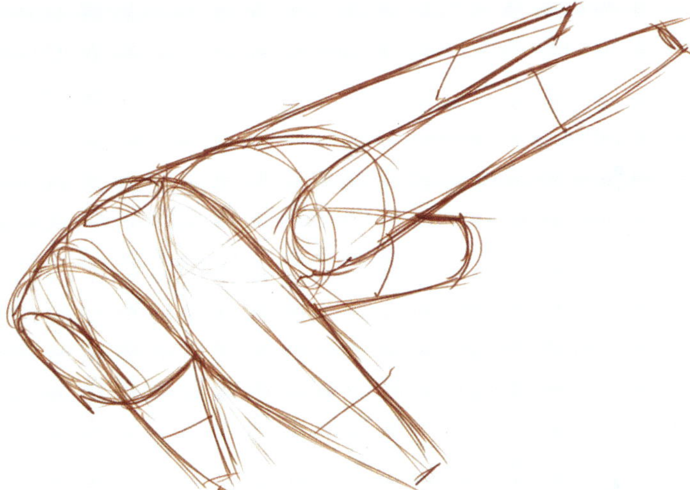

LINES

▶ Try to keep your sketch fairly loose at this stage. Nothing is locked in. You may discover new ideas you wish to include in the design.

▶ Develop the forewings to give them an almost hook-like shape to imply greater mobility. Rework the nose with some added mechanical technology, even if its purpose is unknown just yet.

▶ Start to sketch in surface details. Simple lines and ovals can indicate metal panels, thrusters, and various other kinds of greeble (see page 139) that will add interest to the spaceship's design.

DESIGN FOCUS

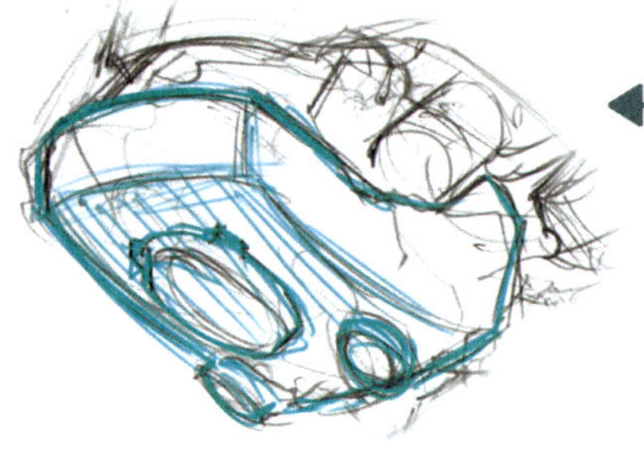

NOSE

The nose of the spaceship includes mechanical details that indicate some sort of function. This could be high-tech weaponry, futuristic sensors, or maybe it's a hatch that opens up to pull goods or space-cattle inside... You don't have to know its exact function to make the design interesting.

ENGINE

This section of the spaceship is by far the most complex. Just like the research sketch of the rocket engine, it should have lots of pipes and tubes leading into it.

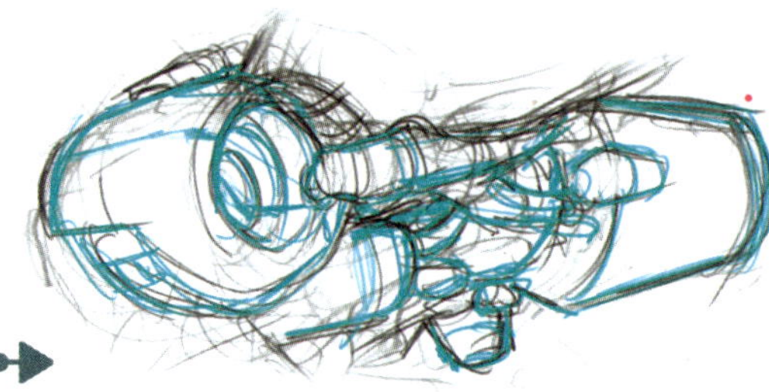

WINGS

When drawing the swept-back wings at the rear, make sure the angles of the planes are correct. This is one of the trickiest parts of this kind of design. Use measuring lines – like those used between the wing tips – to ensure the angles line up.

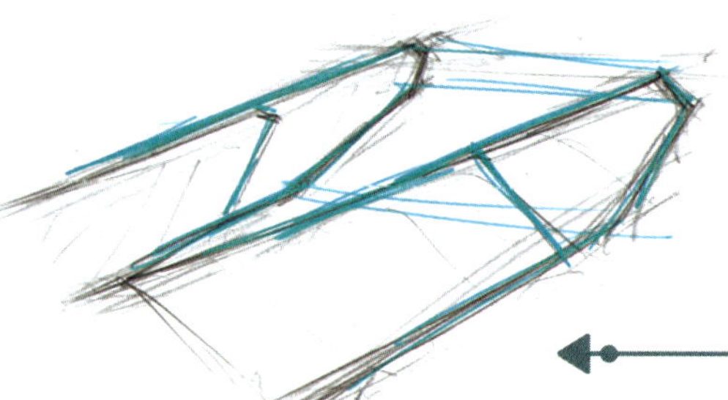

IDEA INVENTORY

▶ Explore different three-dimensional shapes that could make up this high-tech piece of machinery.

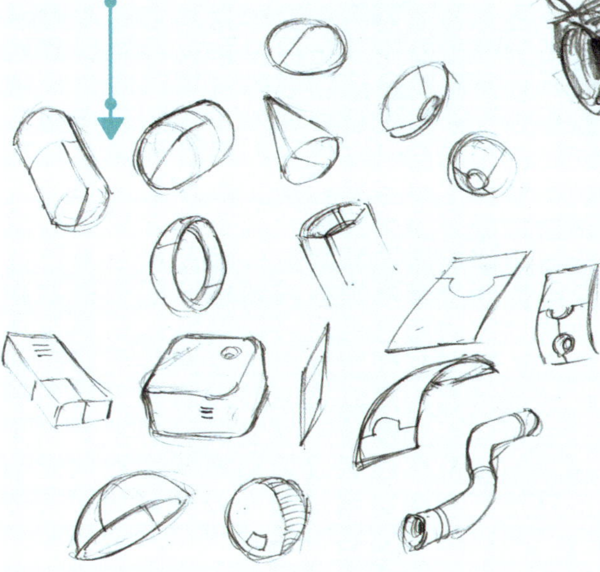

GREEBLE

"Greeble" is the term used to describe any technological bits and pieces that might be incorporated into the body of a science-fiction spaceship, vehicle, or machine. It's made up of many basic shapes, such as cylinders, cones, boxes, and domes. Practice drawing greeble from different angles. It's an awesome tool in a sci-fi designer's toolkit for adding interest to their designs.

INSIGNIA

Including some kind of insignia will give your spaceship a sense of backstory. Made up of basic shapes, these emblem designs are inspired by the initial research of historical aircrafts dating back to WWII.

▶ The crown design hints that the spaceship has an important purpose or royal owner. Perhaps it is part of an elite fleet owned by a grand space monarchy.

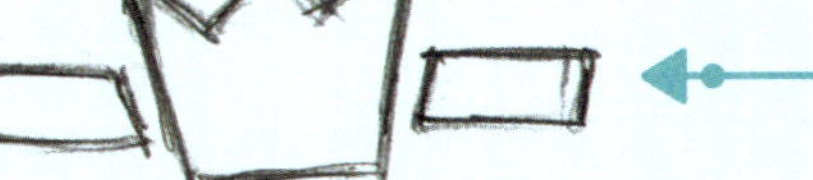

FINAL SKETCH

Begin to lock in the various design elements that have been developing. Keep thinking about the different volumes as you draw. You should also aim to vary the complexity of the drawing, creating some areas that are full of details, with lots of lines and shapes, while also creating simpler areas where there isn't as much happening. This will make the overall drawing more pleasing to look at.

▶ Refine the shape of the cockpit. The retro science-fiction bubble look is always popular. Consider adding some complexity to the shape with a slight bump where the glass meets the metal.

▶ Draw in the basic layout of the metal plate seams on the hull and wings. The angle of the seams should always move with and reinforce the three-dimensional volumes established in previous steps.

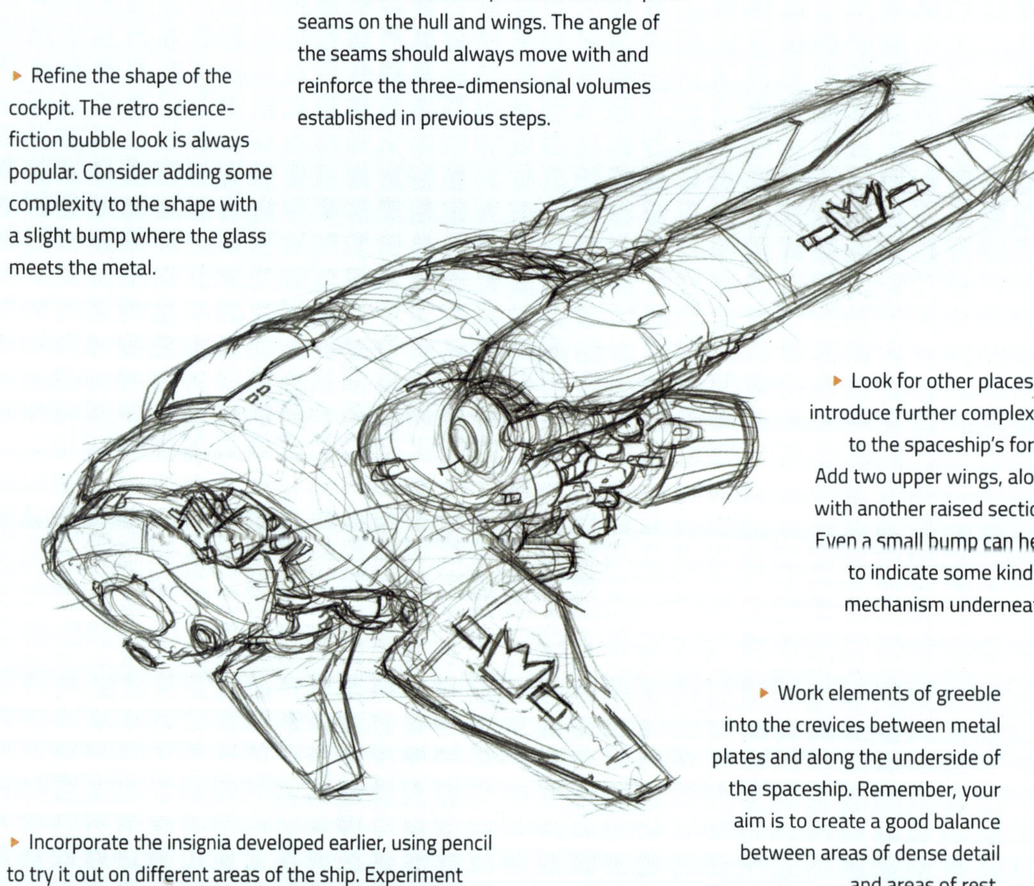

▶ Look for other places to introduce further complexity to the spaceship's form. Add two upper wings, along with another raised section. Even a small bump can help to indicate some kind of mechanism underneath.

▶ Work elements of greeble into the crevices between metal plates and along the underside of the spaceship. Remember, your aim is to create a good balance between areas of dense detail and areas of rest.

▶ Incorporate the insignia developed earlier, using pencil to try it out on different areas of the ship. Experiment with placing it on the side of the hull, or on top, though here it works best with a traditional wing placement.

INKING

Use a fine or very fine rubber-tip brush pen for the inking stage. A brush pen is ideal for creating lines with a varied line weight (the thickness of the lines). Inked lines look most effective when they transition from thin to thick and back to thin in one stroke. Another great way to add line weight is by drawing thicker outlines along the outside edge of your volumes – or any element that obviously overlaps with another element – then using thinner lines on the surface of the ship.

▶ Before applying any ink to the page, use your kneaded eraser to very gently lighten some of the graphite, making sure you are still able to see your drawing clearly. This will help the ink to penetrate the paper.

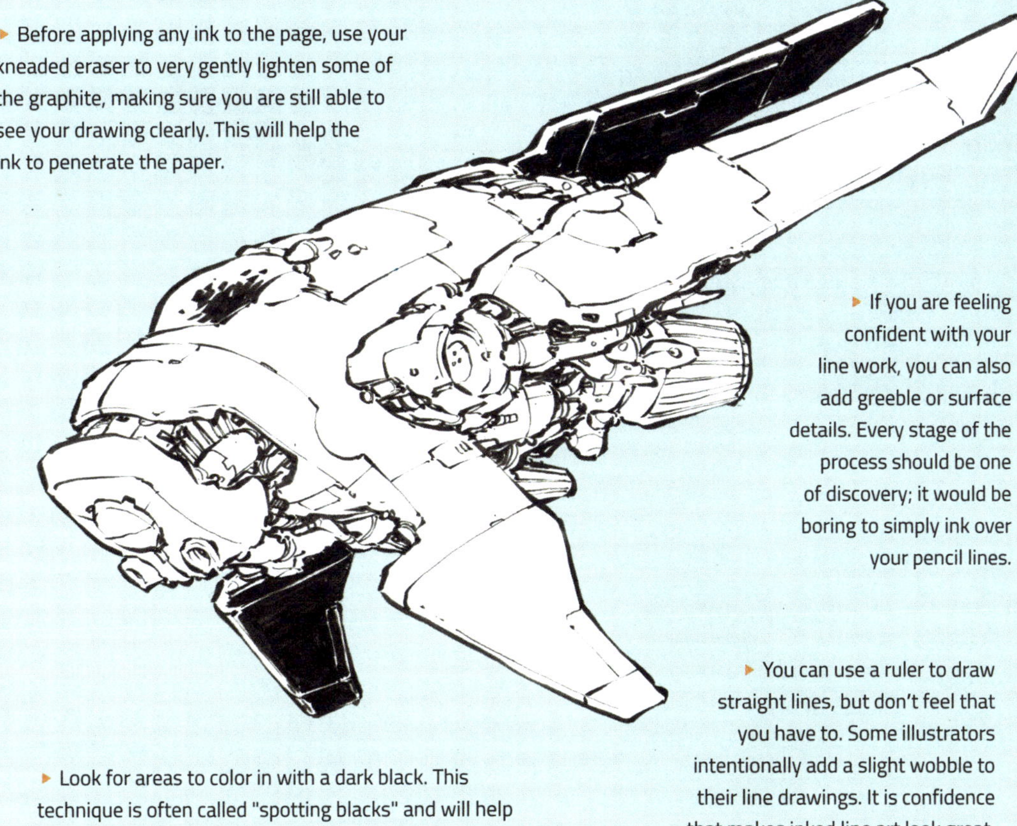

▶ If you are feeling confident with your line work, you can also add greeble or surface details. Every stage of the process should be one of discovery; it would be boring to simply ink over your pencil lines.

▶ Look for areas to color in with a dark black. This technique is often called "spotting blacks" and will help establish contrast and lighting, adding weight to your finished drawing and creating an overall more polished look. Start with the underside of the wing and cockpit, then look for any other areas that are in shadow.

▶ You can use a ruler to draw straight lines, but don't feel that you have to. Some illustrators intentionally add a slight wobble to their line drawings. It is confidence that makes inked line art look great, and this confidence only comes from practice.

COLORING

When adding color, start by establishing the base tones. Work with very light colors to block in what goes where. Using light colors at this stage will help you to establish the color palette, as well as allowing you to make slight changes.

Markers can be very unforgiving and are hard to edit once you color anything with rich or dark colors. For this reason, it's a good idea to try out your colors on scrap paper before coloring your inked spaceship.

▶ Creating a base tone will help prevent the markers from looking excessively streaky in the final image.
• The more pigment that is used, the less streaks will be an issue.

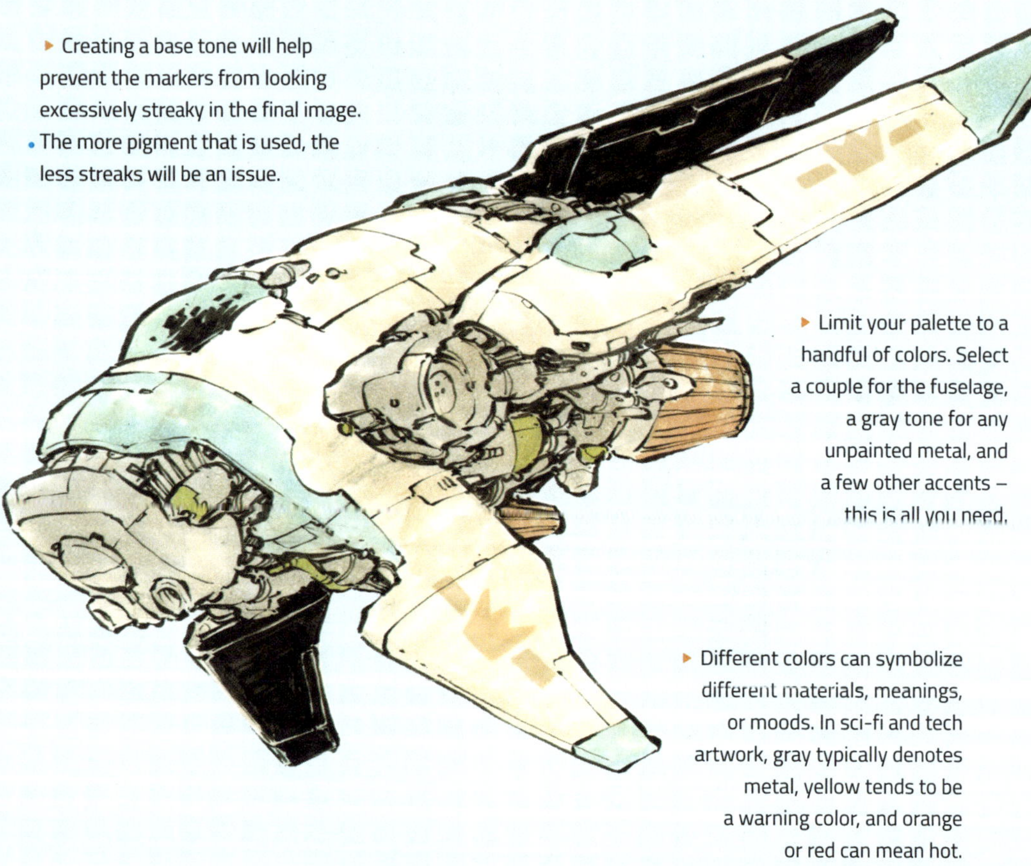

▶ Limit your palette to a handful of colors. Select a couple for the fuselage, a gray tone for any unpainted metal, and a few other accents – this is all you need.

▶ Different colors can symbolize different materials, meanings, or moods. In sci-fi and tech artwork, gray typically denotes metal, yellow tends to be a warning color, and orange or red can mean hot.

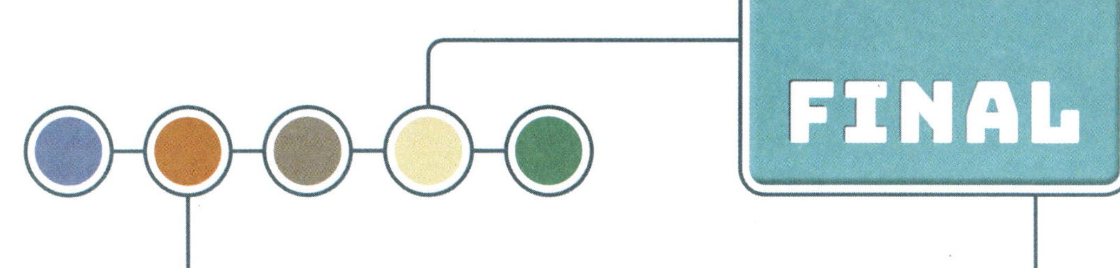

▶ Start to build up the base colors with richer tones. As the spaceship is almost entirely crafted from metal, its surfaces will be smooth and shiny. Leave highlighted areas virtually untouched by anything but the lightest colors to create this metallic sheen.

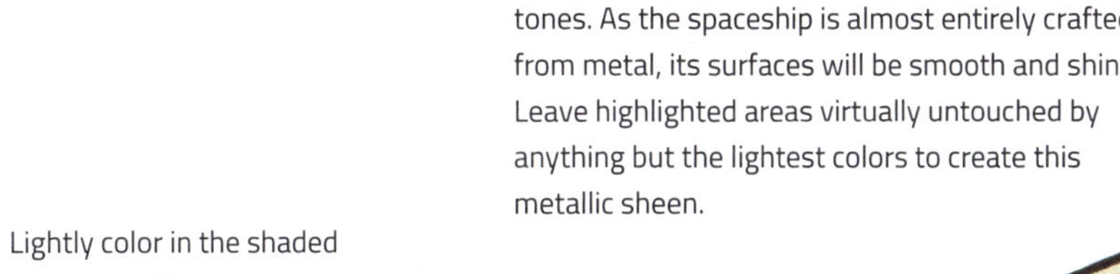

▶ Lightly color in the shaded areas with a different light gray to the one used for the base tone. Fill in any areas that lie in shadow. This is a simple guide that will help you as you introduce more color.

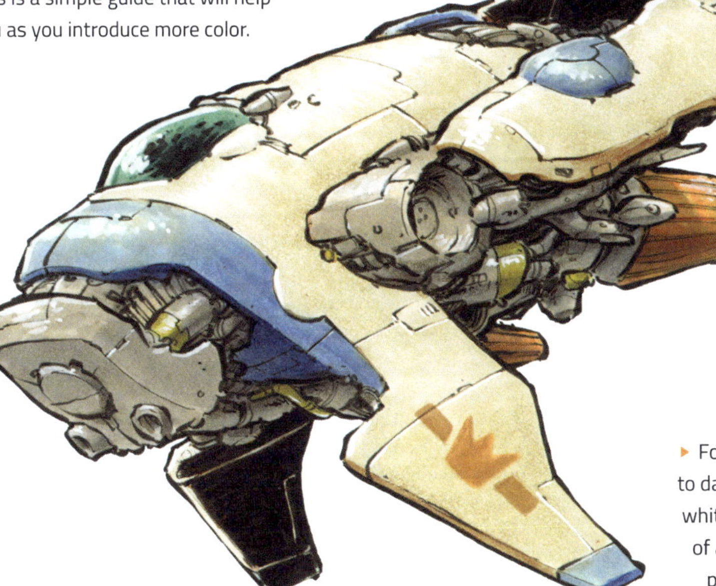

▶ Color in any areas that lie in deep shadow, such as the underside of the ship and in the crevices of the areas of greeble. Don't overdo it, however; the darkest colors should not be overly dark.

▶ For the final step, use a light hand to dab white gouache paint, or other white pigment, on the highest parts of any curved shapes. You can also paint on thin highlights along the panel seams of the fuselage.

Coloring with markers is all about implementing gradual changes and building up color. Start light and work toward the dark. It's a good idea to have two, three, or even four markers of a similar hue but differing darkness. Again, once you apply a dark tone, it's almost impossible to lighten it, so it's important to have a gentle hand when coloring. Skilled illustrators can create effective gradients by varying the pressure with which they apply the markers – experiment with this technique for yourself.

SPACE SOLDIER

...BY CÉSAR VERGARA

This tutorial will guide you through how to create a futuristic human space soldier. The character will be male, with a cartoon style that's cool and heroic. With this kind of character design, there are four main areas to explore: stylizing the face, designing the body and pose, the armor design, and finally, any props and weapons the soldier will use for his missions. You will start with ideas and sketches, before working up to the final design to ensure this sci-fi hero is as badass as he can be!

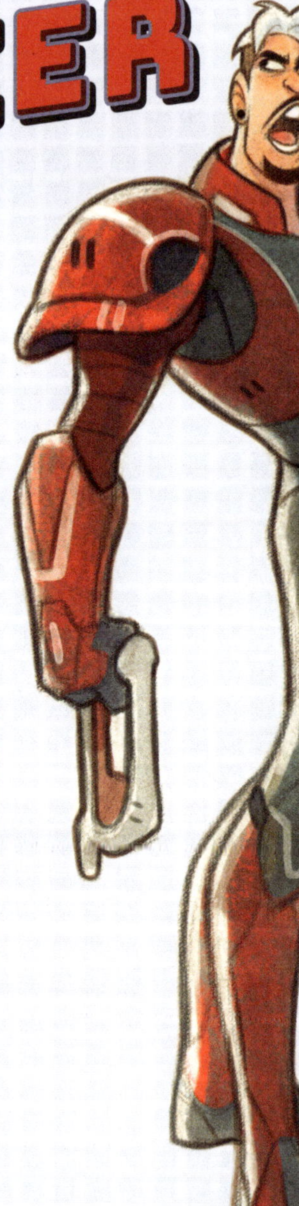

TOOLKIT

- ▶ Blue pencil
- ▶ Graphite pencil
- ▶ Eraser
- ▶ Light box
- ▶ Colored pencils
- ▶ Watercolors
- ▶ White marker

RESEARCH

Start by researching the four areas of design. Drawing sketches based on young, contemporary rock stars can help you to find the type of handsome face you're after. Next, study references of weapons and armor, exploring the different components. It's important to understand the volume and shape of these elements for when you stylize the design later on. If your character is wearing gloves or other hand props, it's crucial to understand those also.

HANDS

Hands are difficult to draw, even more so if they have props or armor. Whatever you add to your design, don't forget to draw the basic anatomy underneath.

WEAPONS

Stylize your weapon references to fit the character design. Think about proportions – how long will the barrel of the gun be compared to the grip? How will the character hold the weapon? Will the trigger fit their finger?

ARMOR

When drawing armor, it's important to break the overall design into individual elements. First, decide on a basic shape, and then consider how decorations, symbols, and other details will fit on top.

FACE

The space soldier will be almost entirely encased in armor, except for his face, so you may wish to add lots of detail here. Consider his hairstyle, and maybe piercings, or tattoos, to add character.

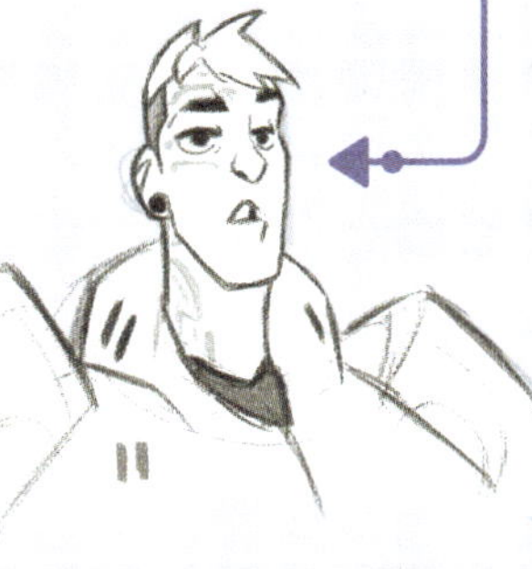

EXPRESSION

Along with the design elements of the face, start to explore expressions also. The facial expression and pose will need to convey almost all of the soldier's personality.

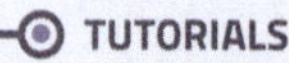

THUMBNAILS

The space soldier will wear sleek sci-fi armor that fits tightly to his body, but elements like shoulder pads, a belt, and boots can break up the silhouette. Use the thumbnail process to focus on finding the body design and pose. Experiment with the shapes that make up the body, going from slim to thick, long to short, and straight to curved. With the pose, try out different options that match the story, personality, and mood of the character.

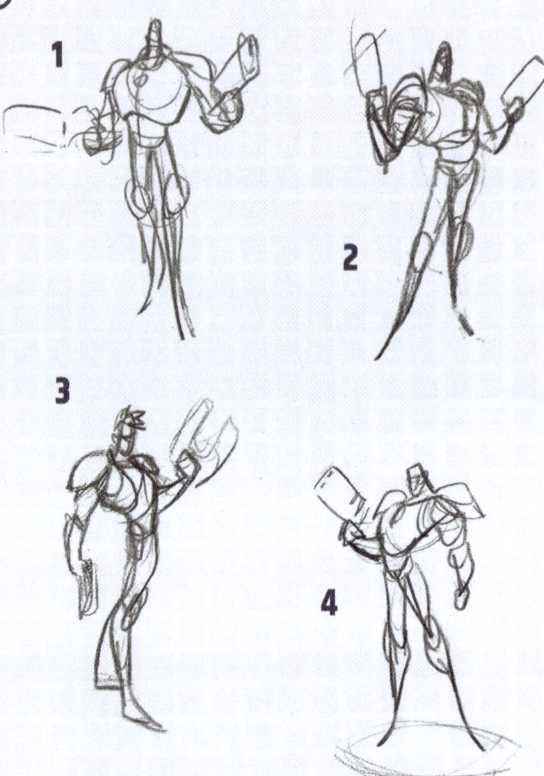

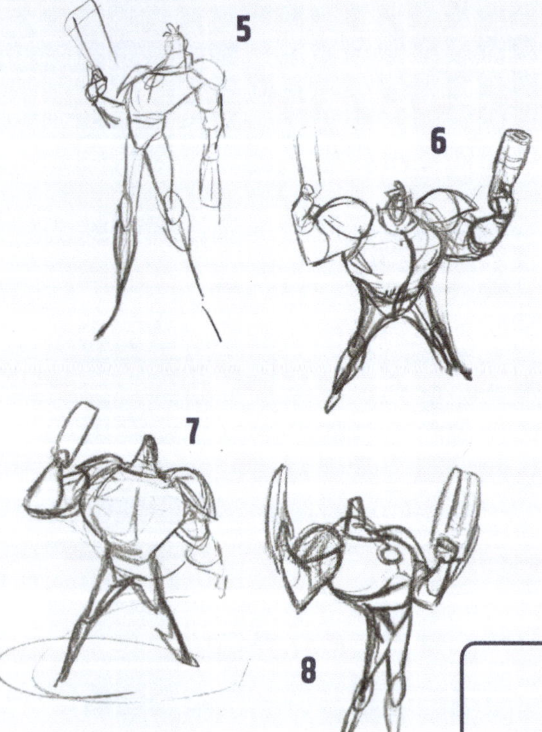

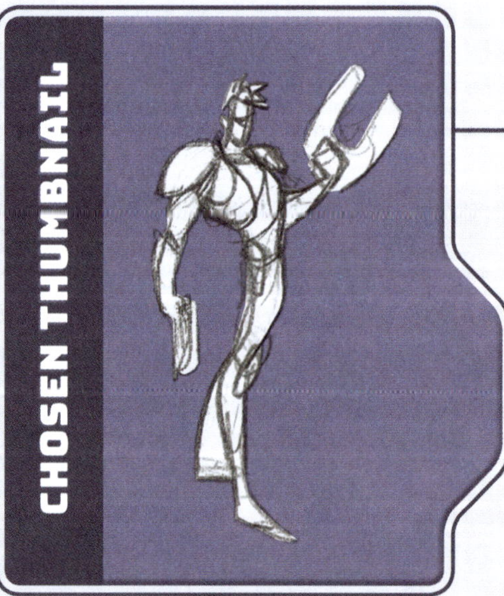

▶ The pose in this thumbnail looks natural yet heroic. The space soldier isn't smiling for the camera – he looks strong and dynamic.

FOUNDATIONS

Use blue or red colored pencils for sketching. They have a lower value than black, so the sketches are softer and leave room for cleaning up later on. During the thumbnail process, the design is not yet solid and most of the volumes are not quite right. The next step is to create a solid structure that retains the pose, gesture, and action lines of the chosen design.

BASE

▶ Even if parts of the character's volume aren't visible in the final design (such as the top left arm) it's still important to draw every large element to allow you to understand the entire structure. This will also help avoid future mistakes when adding medium or small details.

▶ To simplify the hands, think of them as oven mitts! For the feet, it's helpful to draw the base like the sole of a shoe, or a footprint.

▶ Draw circles to establish the joints. Later, those circles can be treated as spheres so you can mark the direction of movement and easily understand the position of the limbs.

LINES

▶ By refining the silhouette, the contours of the basic geometric shapes will start to look like muscles and real anatomy. It's important that you already understand the human body for this step.

▶ Visualize the limbs as if they are cylinders and the joints as spheres. This will help to establish the axes of the body and to make sure the structure is solid.

▶ Draw an inverted triangle shape on the face to determine where the eyes and eyebrows will be placed. Think of it like a superhero mask!

BUILDING UP

Now you've established the basic shapes of the body, you can continue to build up the design by adding the different elements of the armor, such as the shoulder pads, bracelets, and more. Having the finalized anatomy underneath guarantees the character will look solid and believable. It's important to introduce the soldier's facial expression now to determine if the jaw will be open or closed, as well as deciding the position of the eyebrows. Using a light box can prove very useful at this stage.

GEOMETRY

Make sure you understand the geometry of each new element added to the design. Think of imaginary lines cutting across the main axes of the character.

EXPRESSION

You can polish the expression in later steps, but it's important to nail down the three most important elements early: the eyes, eyebrows, and mouth.

WEAPONS

You don't need to wait for the final design to add the weapons. Include their basic shape now to make sure they aren't breaking the silhouette or creating tangents. When you reach the design stage, you can use this base shape as a reference.

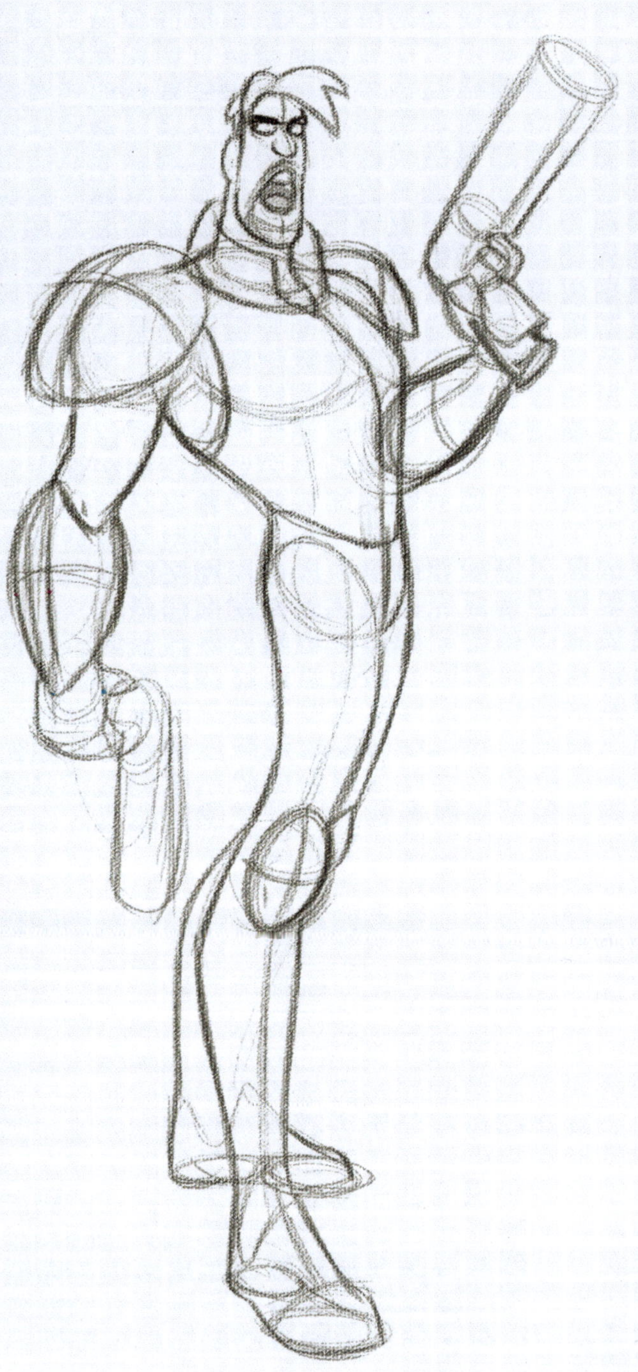

DESIGN FOCUS

EYES

"The eyes are the windows to the soul" is a common expression for a reason. Eyes are incredibly expressive, so think carefully about how they will look. Angling the eyebrows downward and the lower eyelids slightly upward will give the space soldier an air of determination.

HANDS

While the finger on the gun's trigger is mostly obscured, you still need to draw all of the volumes to ensure everything lines up right, and the weapon design fits the proportions of the character.

WEAPON

Weapons can have unusual designs, but they still need to be ergonomically practical. The handle and the trigger must fit the proportions of the soldier's hand, regardless of how large the rest of the weapon is!

IDEA INVENTORY

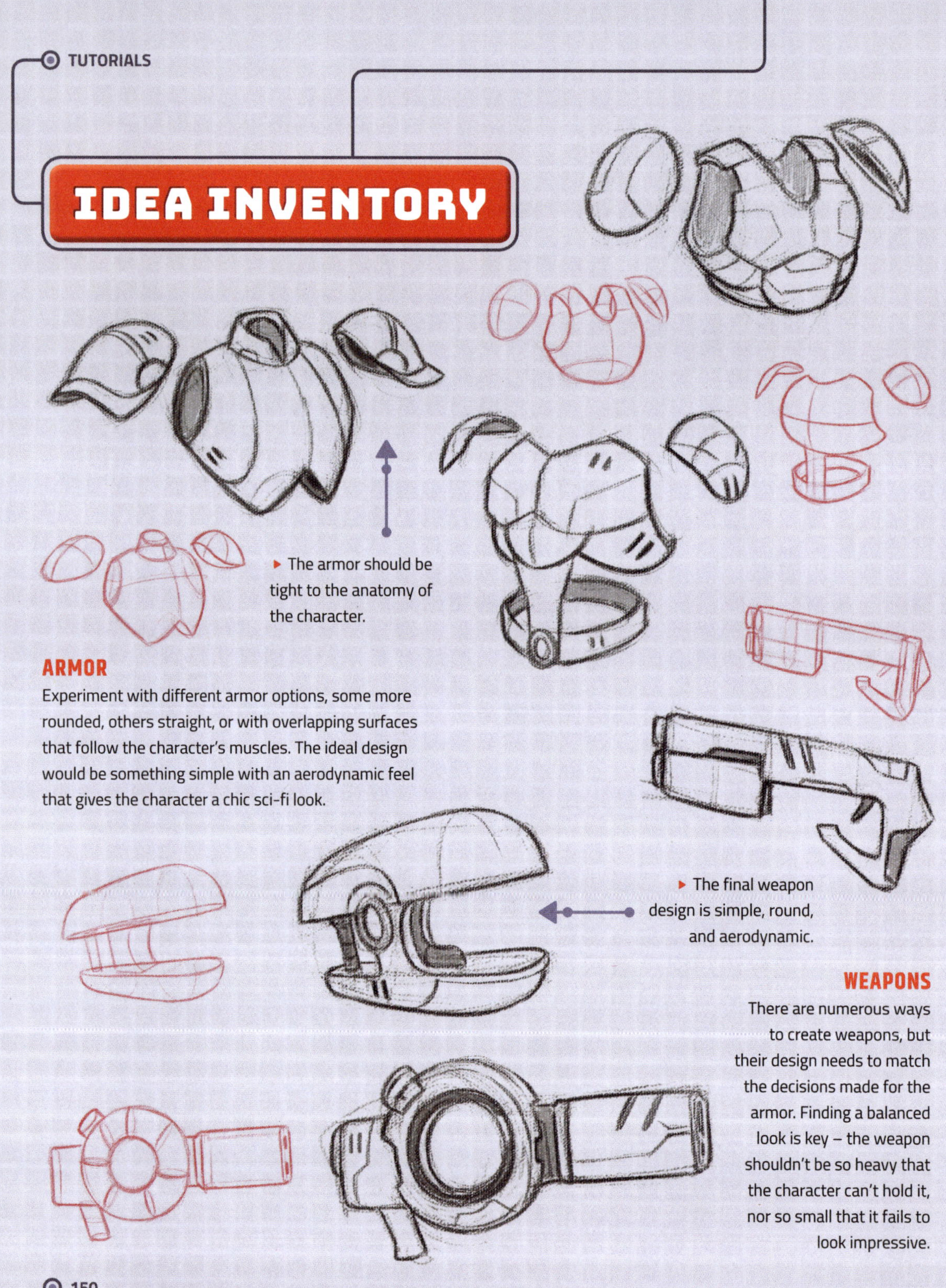

▶ The armor should be tight to the anatomy of the character.

ARMOR

Experiment with different armor options, some more rounded, others straight, or with overlapping surfaces that follow the character's muscles. The ideal design would be something simple with an aerodynamic feel that gives the character a chic sci-fi look.

▶ The final weapon design is simple, round, and aerodynamic.

WEAPONS

There are numerous ways to create weapons, but their design needs to match the decisions made for the armor. Finding a balanced look is key – the weapon shouldn't be so heavy that the character can't hold it, nor so small that it fails to look impressive.

FINAL SKETCH

For the final sketch, define the armor geometry using details that run along the entire surface. The lines will create the impression of multiple assembled pieces, while also keeping the character's silhouette clear and clean. The armor lines follow the volumes of the body, reinforcing the solid structure defined earlier. The line weight of the sketch is slightly wider along the borders to produce a silhouette for the major elements and for the character itself.

▶ The lines along the armor are not placed randomly – most follow places of potential movement. For example, there are circles on the shoulder pads that mimic joints. Think of the armor as if you were looking at an articulated action figure.

▶ Create consistency throughout the design by repeating simple patterns, such as the pairs of short lines across the weapons and armor. Maybe they are ventilation ducts to keep the soldier cool in heated situations.

▶ Although the weapon design is unusual, the shape reinforces the action line of the character's arm. You can imagine electric waves blasting from the barrel!

▶ When creating armor, consider the mobility and comfort of the character. The space soldier needs to be ready for action, so the chest and waist should be free of hard elements in case he needs to bend or twist his torso.

▶ While the tattoos across the soldier's face were striking, they would prove too noisy given the limited space and the technique used for coloring. Sometimes, less is more.

LINE WORK

When working with watercolors, you don't need to add too much strong line work to your designs. Instead you can preserve some of the rough line work underneath, which can add texture and liveliness to the character. To clean the lines and dark flat areas, refine them using a black pencil, so the drawing benefits from more contrast and sharpness. Try to use quality materials – black lines can sometimes react badly with watercolors.

▸ Make sure the tip of your pencil is always sharp to ensure the line quality is consistent throughout, otherwise you will lose the effect of inking and the character will start to look like a rough sketch again. This is especially important with facial details.

▸ Reinforcing the silhouettes of the larger elements creates a shape hierarchy and better readability of the character.

▸ As the coloring stage will involve watercolor, avoid the use of hard shadows to prevent dirty colors when mixing with water. The quality of the materials is so important – make sure to test them first!

▸ To prepare for the watercolor stage, you may choose to use warm color pencils – such as red, brown, or orange – for the sketch and inking steps. This will give your character more vibrant tones.

COLORING

Avoid hard lights and shadows when coloring with watercolors. Instead, aim to create soft gradients that reinforce the cartoon style, while preserving lighting information. The warm tones of the soldier's skin should contrast with the cold, dark armor that covers his body. The saturated red on the armor creates a more appealing look, while the dark blues look elegant and cool. Use different tones to define the separate shapes of the armor.

▶ When using watercolors, start with the lightest colors and work toward the darkest, little by little, and layer by layer. Be patient and let colors dry, otherwise you may dirty the water with darker tones.

▶ When painting dark values, never apply the color directly. Instead, apply a lighter version of the same tone first to make the colors appear more vibrant. For the armor, paint a layer of light blue before applying the darker tone.

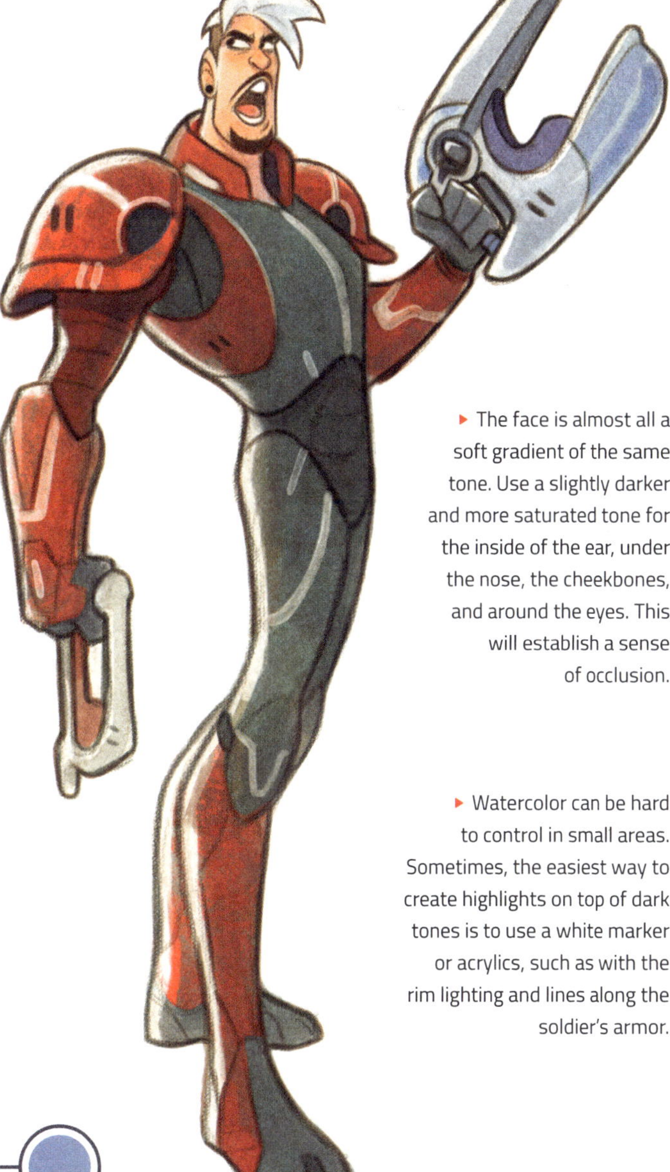

▶ The face is almost all a soft gradient of the same tone. Use a slightly darker and more saturated tone for the inside of the ear, under the nose, the cheekbones, and around the eyes. This will establish a sense of occlusion.

▶ Watercolor can be hard to control in small areas. Sometimes, the easiest way to create highlights on top of dark tones is to use a white marker or acrylics, such as with the rim lighting and lines along the soldier's armor.

SCI-FI SUSHI BAR

BY ALEX VEDE CABALAR

This tutorial will demonstrate how to draw a sci-fi sushi bar in outer space. The idea is to create a floating food stall that evokes a traditional Japanese street restaurant as well as a futuristic spacecraft. Begin by considering the reason for the sushi bar's existence. Maybe it's a wandering establishment, drifting from one place to another? Perhaps it's been traveling through space for several decades, serving food to all manner of aliens, and so is a little battered and in need of repair? Let's find out!

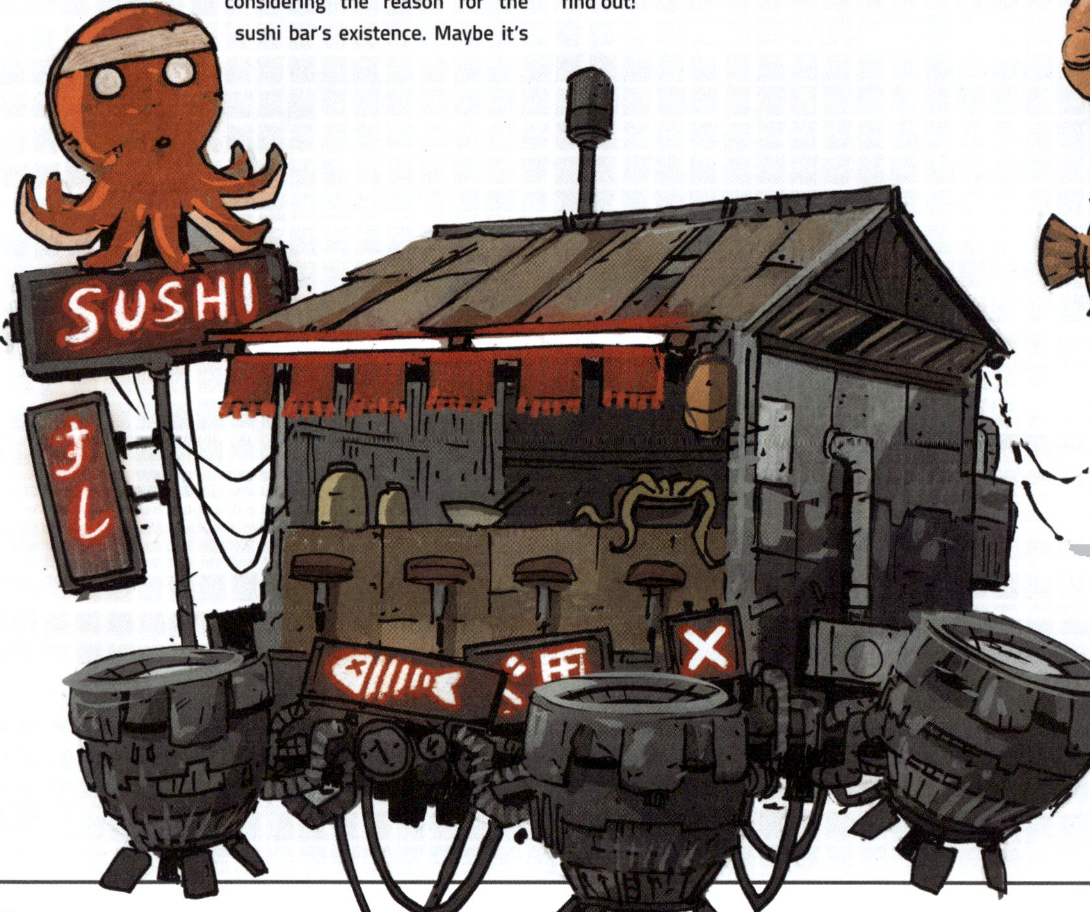

RESEARCH

There are two main elements to explore. Firstly, typical Japanese street restaurants, both their structure and decoration. And secondly, sci-fi spacecrafts and the various futuristic or mechanical objects these entail, such as pipes, fans, and airplane engines. The key is to acquire an interesting mix of objects to strike the right balance between traditional and futuristic design.

KITE

Fish-shaped kites, known as *koinobori* or carp streamers, originate in Japan. They inflate when a breeze blows through them.

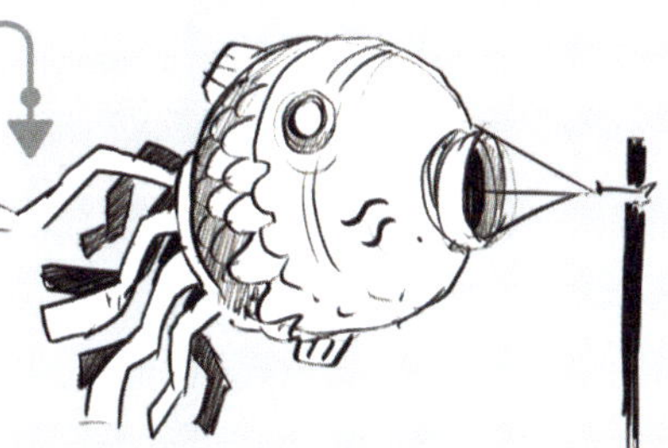

SUSHI BAR

Sushi stands can be found throughout Japan's city streets. Study their structure and decoration.

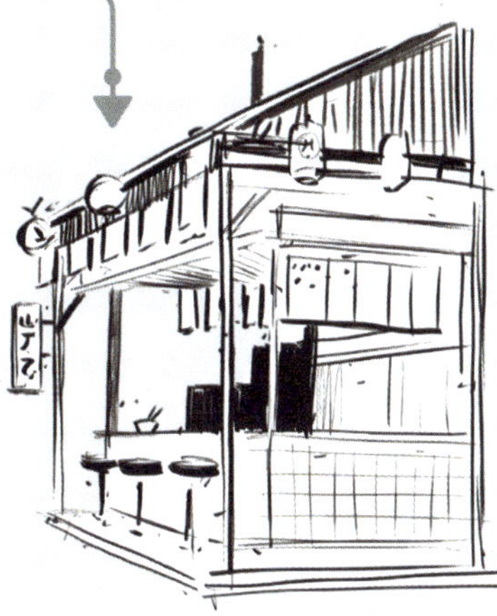

AIRCRAFT ENGINE

This is the inside of a jet engine – study its shape and the details that make it recognizable. This will be one of the sushi bar's main elements.

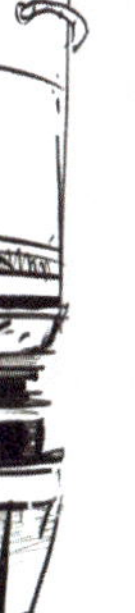

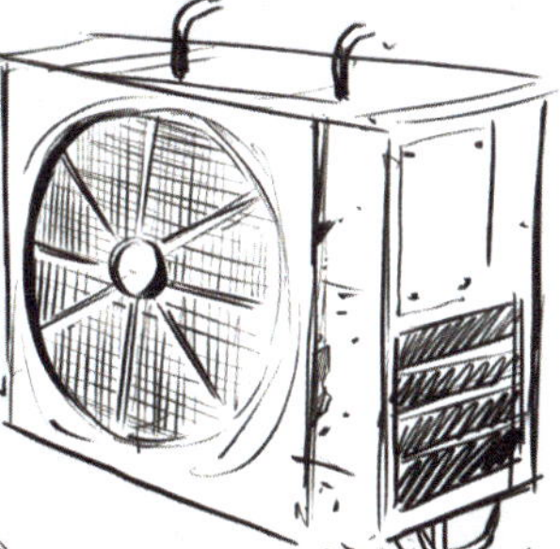

FAN

Everyday objects, like this fan, can also serve as inspiration for a futuristic design. Adding familiar elements will make the final creation seem more believable.

OCTOPUS

This cartoonlike style of octopus is typical of Japanese poster illustration. Including this element will help the sushi bar to read as Japanese, while also adding character to the design.

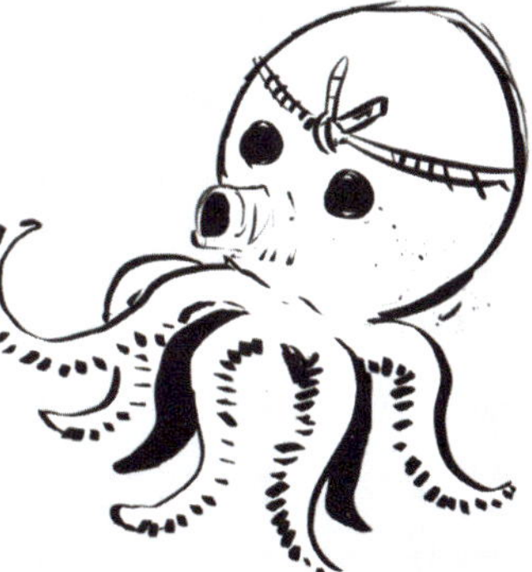

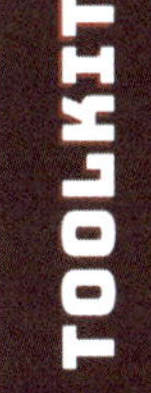

TOOLKIT

- ▶ Pencil
- ▶ Calligraphic pens (size 0.7 and 0.8 mm)
- ▶ Watercolor brush
- ▶ Gouache paint

THUMBNAILS

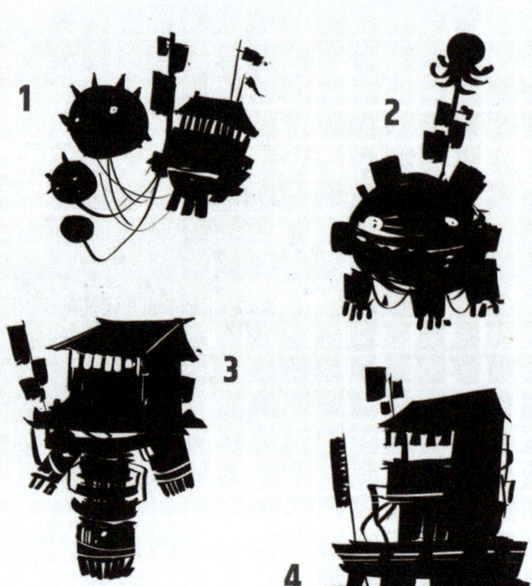

When sketching thumbnails, it's important to look for a strong silhouette. The basis of any good design lies in its most basic structure. The sushi bar's silhouette should be recognizable and easy to read. Experiment with designs that are futuristic, but wouldn't seem out of place in a junkyard! Details matter little at this stage in the process – look for a shape that sparks your imagination and catches the eye.

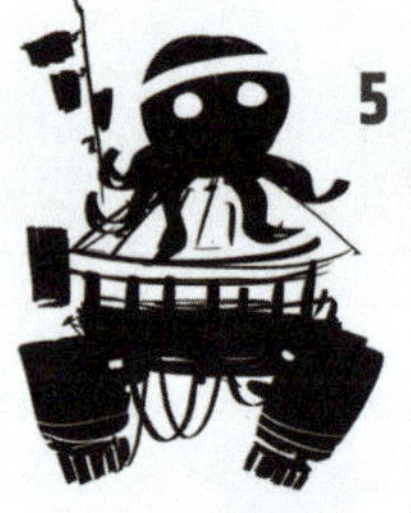

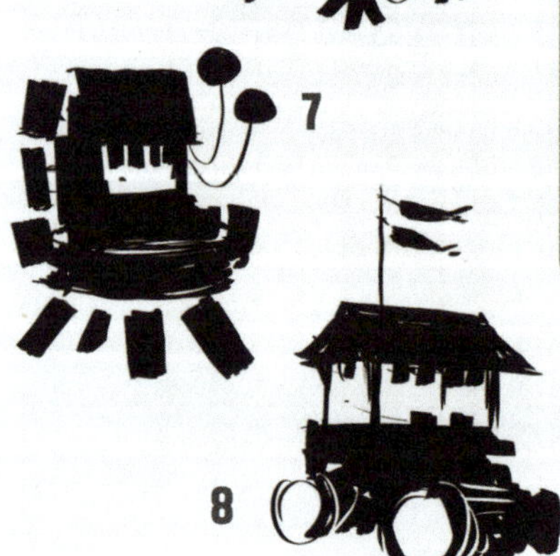

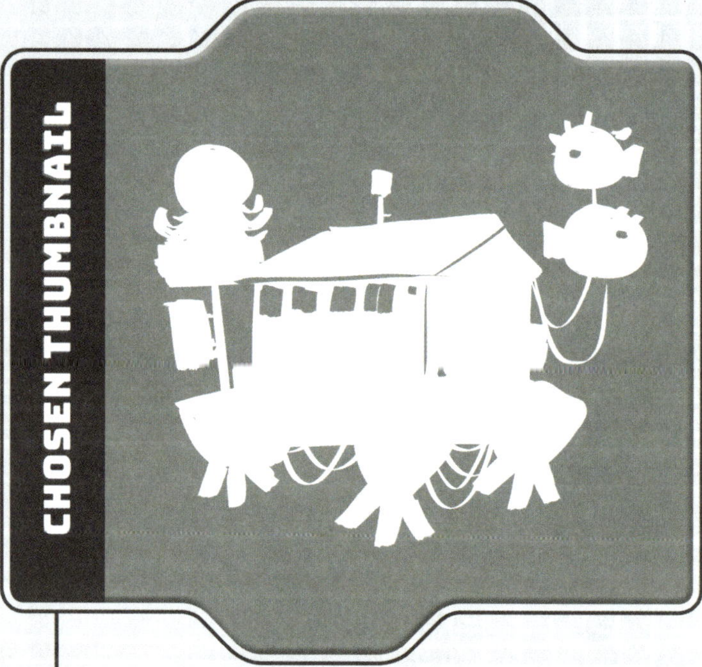

CHOSEN THUMBNAIL

▶ This thumbnail works well, as it is reminiscent of a traditional Japanese food shack and the design is easily readable at a glance. The futuristic elements come through in the large motors that support the structure.

FOUNDATIONS

Use a colored pencil and a graphite pencil to lay down the foundations of the drawing. With the chosen thumbnail as a guide, build the structure of the sushi bar using simple geometric shapes, such as cubes, spheres, and cylinders.

The goal is to develop your initial idea, starting with a simple shape, then adding volume and detail. Think of each step like the stages of building a house; this stage involves laying the foundations.

BASE

▸ Start with a cube for the main structure and add a roof by sketching a triangular shape above it. It's important to maintain a coherent perspective. The central cube will help to position other shapes appropriately.

▸ Next, add a few cylinders that will be the engines. Don't draw them parallel to the cube, but with a slight tilt for a more interesting, off-kilter look. Sketch curved horizontal lines across the cylinders to accentuate their volume.

▸ Introduce additional details, such as the post with the octopus sign and the two puffer fish floating to the right. These two elements frame the main structure.

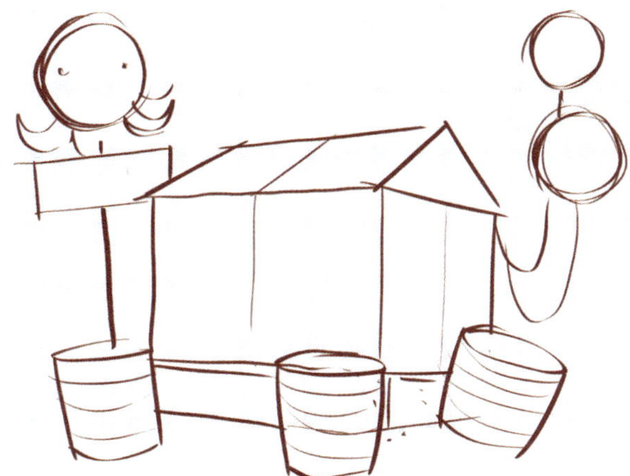

LINES

▸ Sketch parallel lines onto the roof, then draw a small chimney and various neon signs. Add a few pipes here and there, especially surrounding the engines.

▸ Shape the secondary elements: the engines, the floating puffer fish, and the pole with the octopus. Draw small legs on the underside of the engines to give them an original look.

▸ Introduce a repetitive motif throughout the design to ensure the new details have a coherent overall look. For example, draw cables connecting all of the signs and structures.

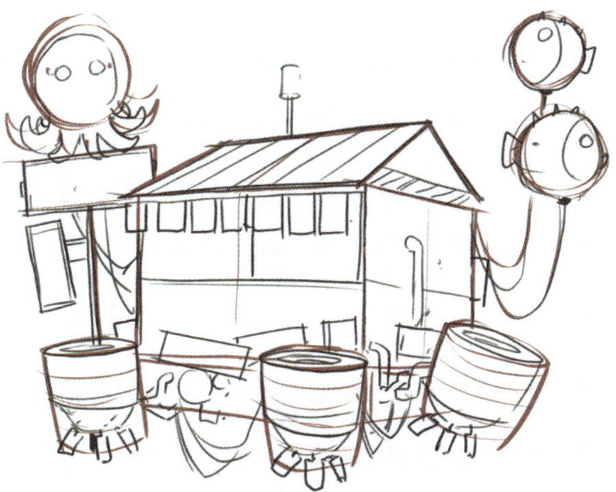

BUILDING UP

Once you have defined the main elements, begin to sketch in extra detail and medium shapes. Inject personality into every aspect of the sketch, while also carefully choosing which areas to add emphasis to. At this stage, you also need to pay special attention to perspective. This is possibly the most important step of the entire process – a good sketch contains the essence of the final drawing!

SIGNS

Add eyes to the octopus and start planning the text for the other signs. These signs are how the restaurant will attract customers, so they need to be exciting and eye-catching!

BAR

Sketch a few elements on the bar, such as bowls, chopsticks, plates, tentacles... anything you can think of! Draw some stools for patrons to sit at as they enjoy a bite or two.

FISH

Give the floating puffer fish a little more personality. Opt for a cartoonish yet recognizable look, adding a few spikes and lines that show how they are constructed from metal and bolts.

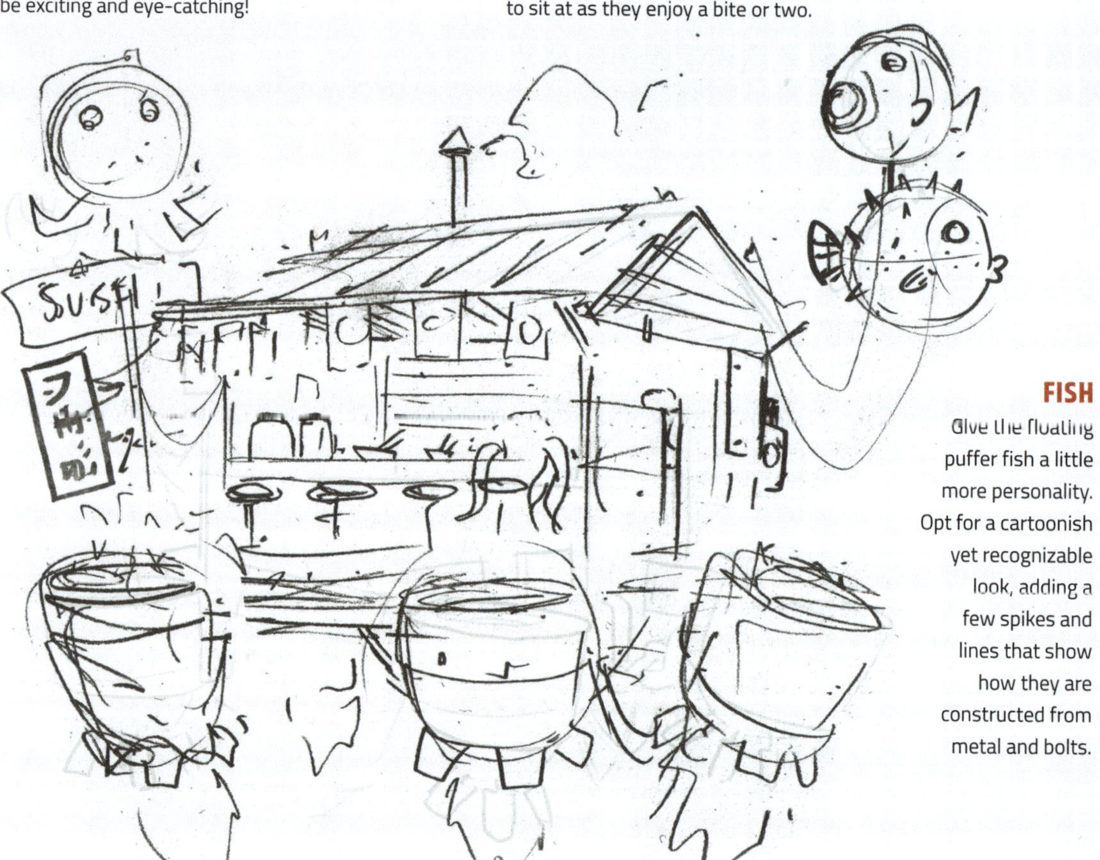

DESIGN FOCUS

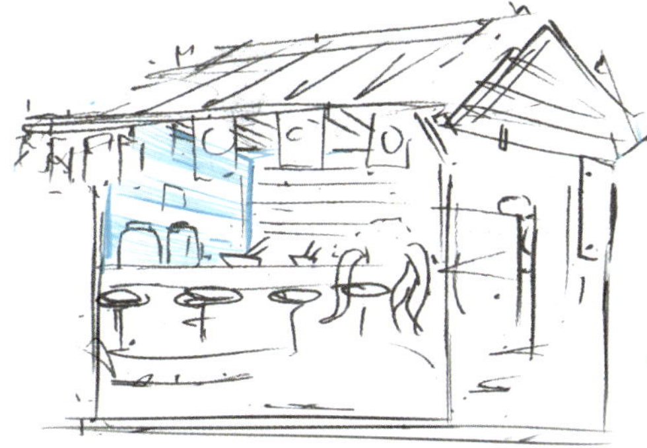

PERSPECTIVE

It's very important to keep the perspective consistent throughout the drawing. In this case, you should consider not just the outside of the building, but the internal walls too. The straight lines of the wooden slats will help to show the perspective is correct.

SIGNS

Draw the pole with the octopus and the text signs a little off-kilter to suggest movement. A design that consists only of parallel lines can become very boring – a little slant will make it appear more quirky and fun!

WIRES

When sketching wires, pay attention to how gravity pulls them downward. It's this sort of seemingly insignificant detail that will give your drawing credibility.

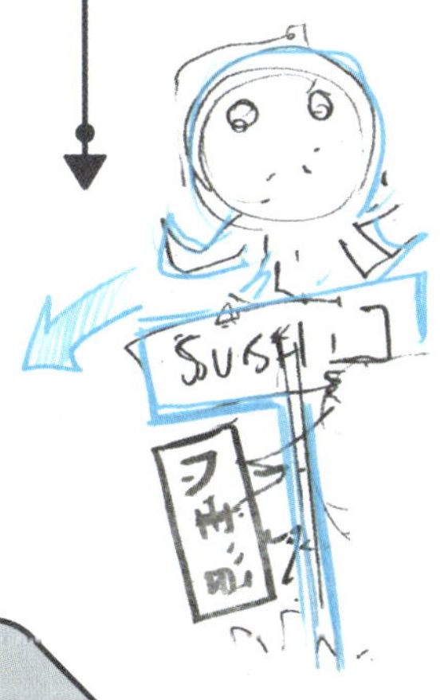

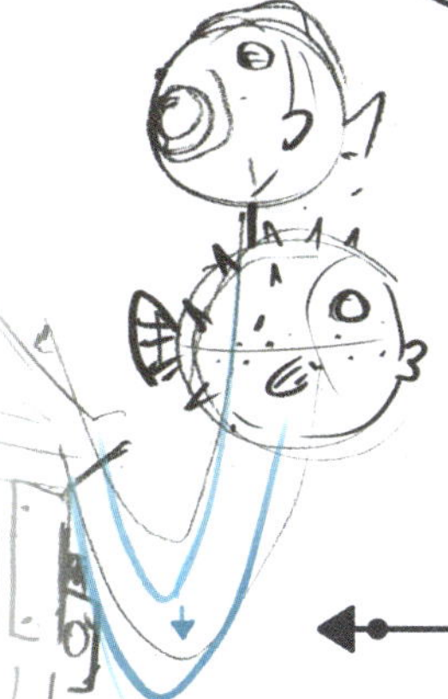

IDEA INVENTORY

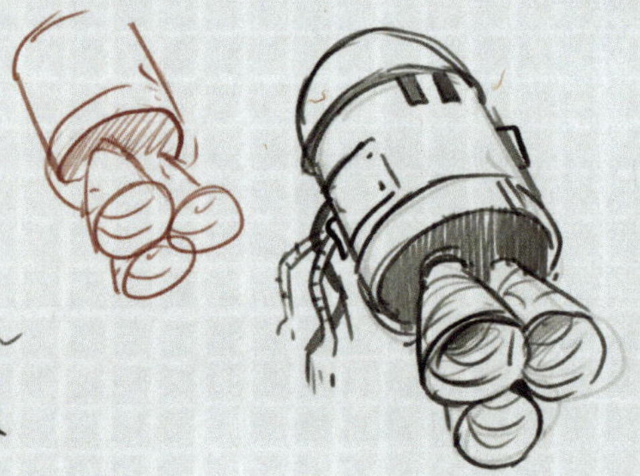

ENGINES

Explore variations of the engine design, experimenting with shape, size, and mechanical detail. It's important to keep elements that reference real objects in your fictional designs for credibility.

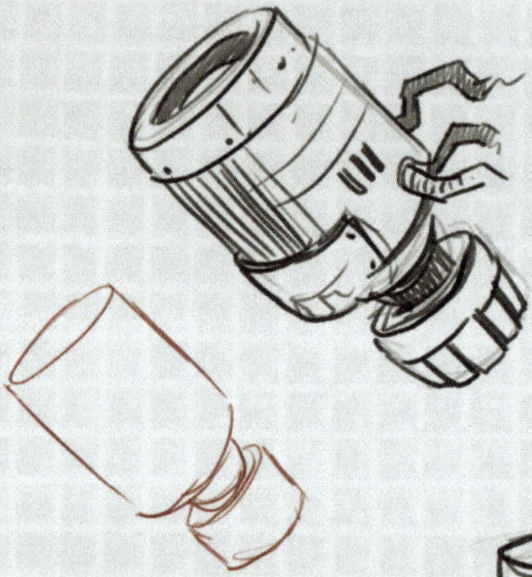

▶ Starting with an idea faithful to realistic airplane engines, then mixing in an inverted vase shape typical of aerospace rockets, will create a new design.

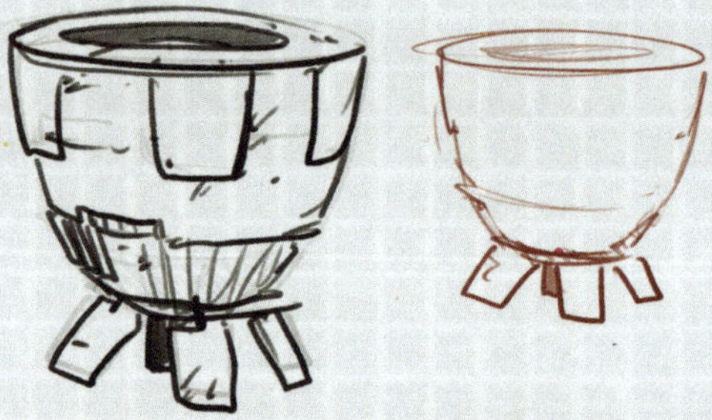

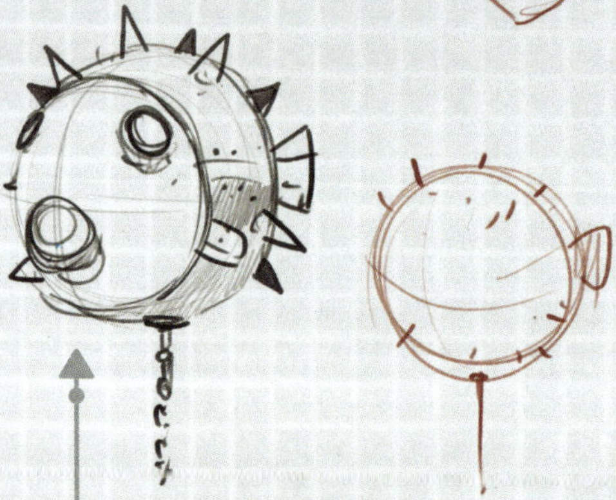

KITE

For the floating kite fish, experiment with several different species of varying shapes and sizes. Adding a twist on a familiar design can add to the futuristic aesthetic.

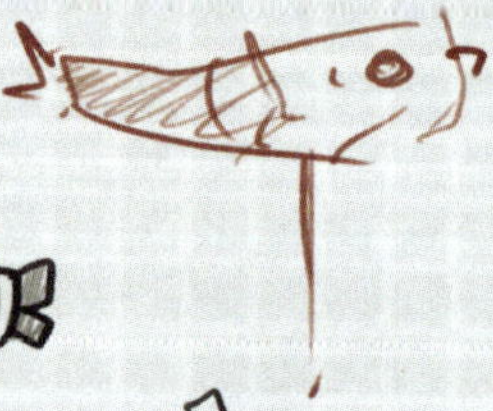

▶ While the Japanese traditionally use a carp in a long windsock design, here a round puffer fish with spiky protrusions may prove more comical.

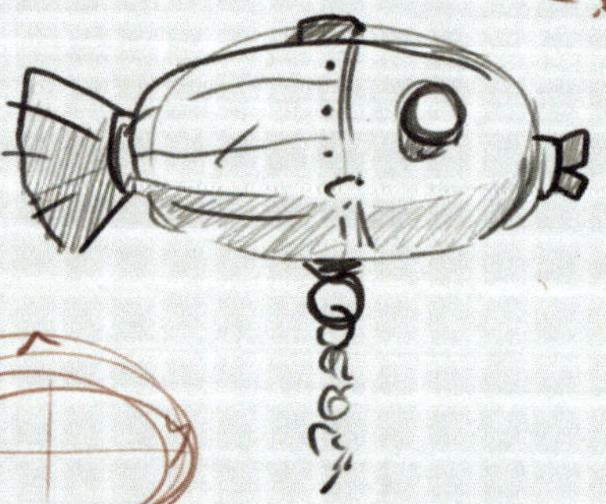

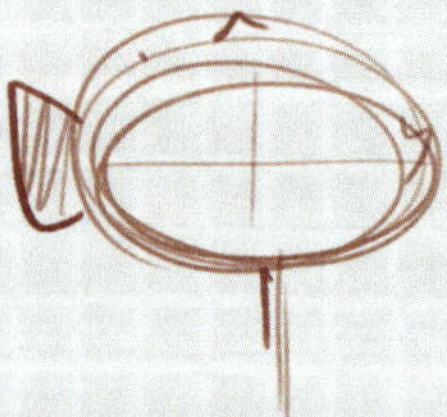

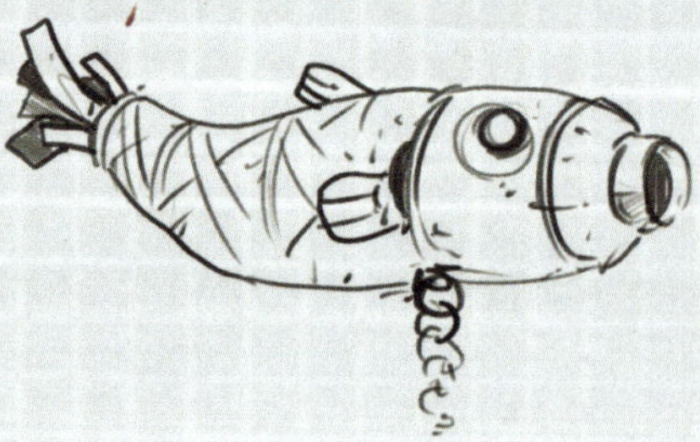

FINAL SKETCH

Start to reinforce the lines of the design by applying more pressure with the pencil. Be sure to erase any lines you no longer need. Add any extra details where needed, such as the lettering on the signs and the haphazard pipework surrounding the engines. These lines will help when inking in the next step, so they must be clear and accurate.

▶ Draw a headband on the octopus's head, like the type often worn by traditional sushi chefs. Adding simple features to the face adds personality, without looking too busy.

▶ Add detail to show the materials the bar is built from. The main structure is constructed from metal, but adding wooden repairs adds to the quirky character of the building.

▶ Draw in traditional Japanese pendants and lamps hanging from the top of the bar.

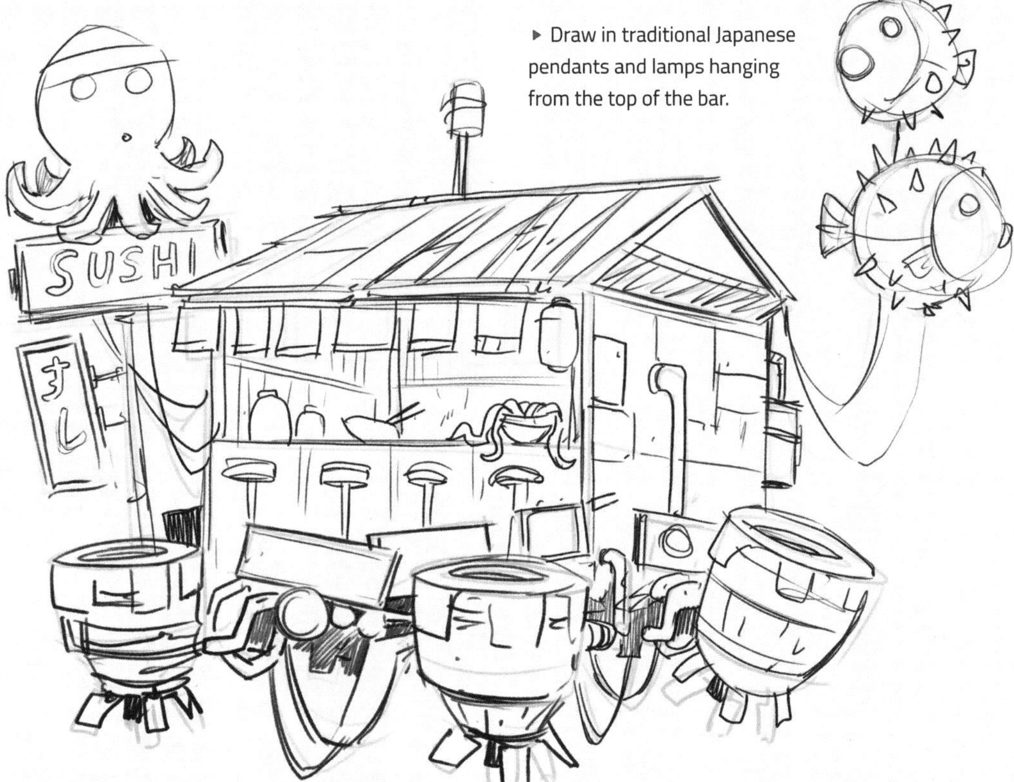

▶ Be careful not to add too much detail where it isn't necessary. Darken the underside of the sushi bar, as this section of the structure sits in shadow.

▶ Adding just a few lines can suggest details that you don't actually need to draw in full. Just a hint of an idea can be enough to tell the audience what they're looking at.

INKING

Inking adds weight to the drawing. Making some areas completely black will allow the more detailed sections of the drawing to stand out much more. Ink the design using calligraphy pens with 0.7 and 0.8 mm width. These are quite thick pens – the key is to control the pressure with which you draw, to achieve different line thicknesses.

Inking very quickly can create strokes that feel energetic and spontaneous. Drawing a perfectly clean line is not always the best option. Another fun approach is to use a watercolor brush with India ink. The stroke variation created is unmatched by any other tool.

▶ Adding small details will give the drawing texture. Nails in the planks, gaps between metal plates, the occasional scratch – these all make the design feel more believable.

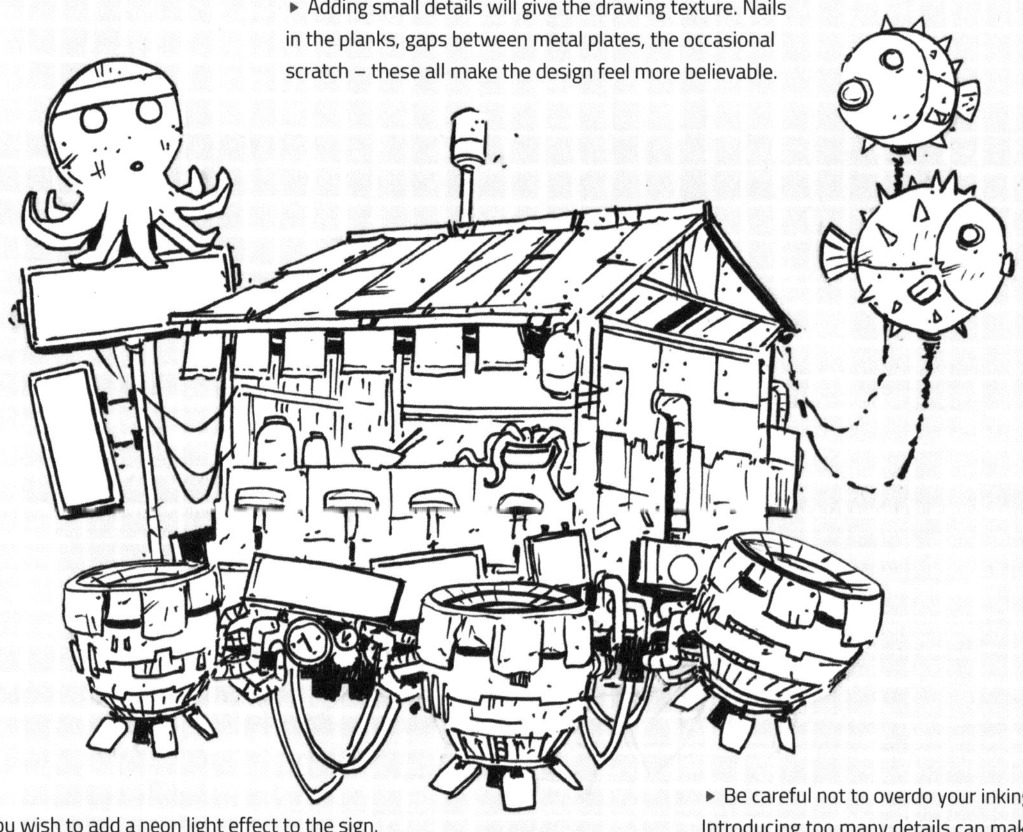

▶ If you wish to add a neon light effect to the sign, leave it blank for now. Always consider the next steps you may want to take and how color will interact with ink.

▶ Be careful not to overdo your inking! Introducing too many details can make the drawing look confusing and over-busy. Carefully choose which lines to mark and which to leave implicit.

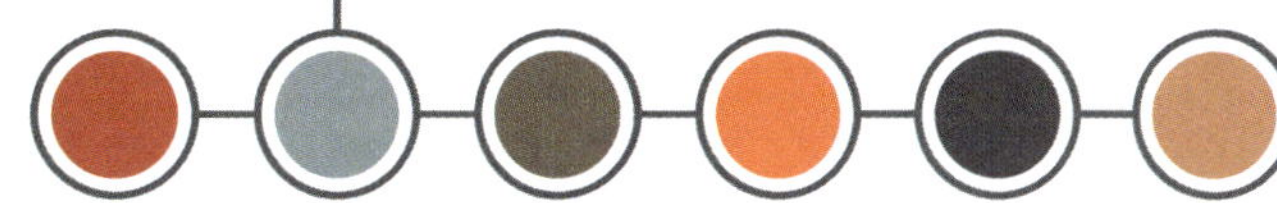

When adding color, start with lighter shades before moving through to darker tones. Using watercolor, or gouache, you will color every section of the drawing. Select a largely gray palette, with touches of brown for the wood, plus accents of red. The color will help to differentiate between the materials that make up the sushi bar. The octopus and fish will require more orange colors to make them appear a little rusty. Be sure to use a brush that is neither too big nor too small.

▶ To create a neon light effect, keep the letters completely white and paint a deep red around them.

▶ Add brushstrokes to the ink lines, well-loaded with paint, to ensure the lines are completely covered. This is just a finishing touch – don't overdo it or the drawing may start to look messy.

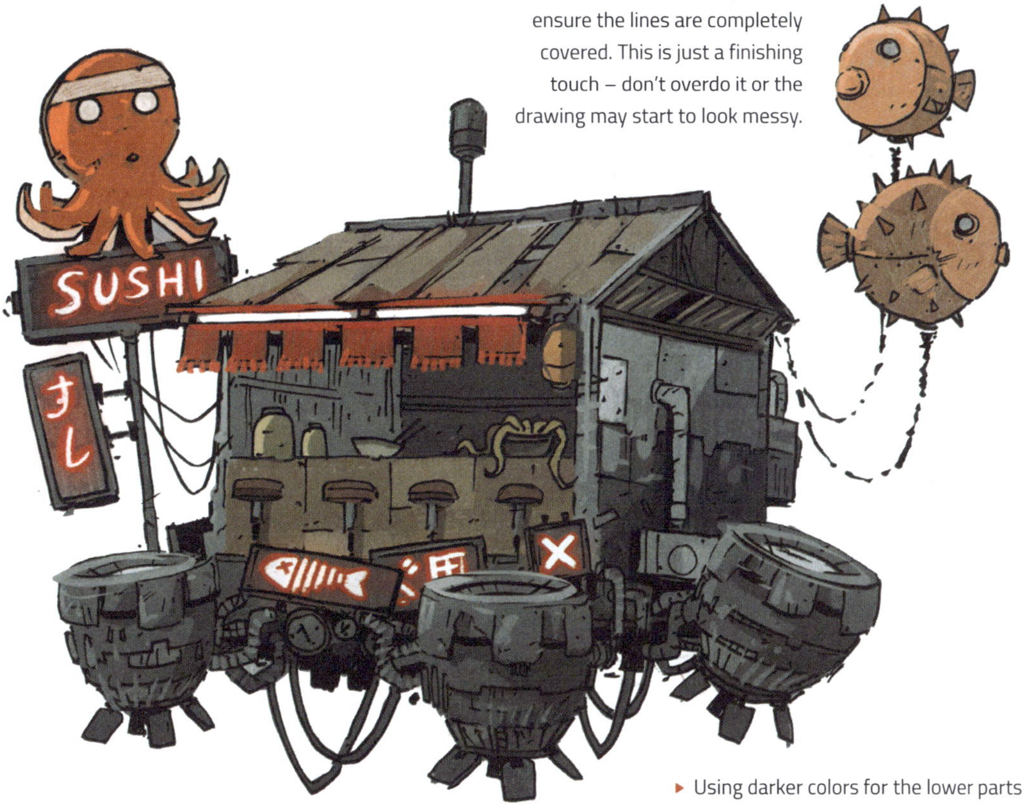

▶ Start coloring softly. Always begin with the lighter colors and finish with the darker ones. It can be very difficult to cover a dark color if you make a mistake.

▶ Using darker colors for the lower parts of the image and lighter colors higher up gives the sushi bar a pleasing rhythm and balance.

MARTIAN TRANSPORT

... BY ELIJAH MCNEAL

This tutorial will teach you how to design a shuttle-service carrier for inhabitants of the red planet. Don't let its lumbering appearance fool you though – this rugged rumbler has an approach angle any monster truck would envy. By following the steps, you will learn what makes a red-rock crawler like this look convincing.

TOOLKIT

- ▸ Bienfang paper
- ▸ Copic markers
- ▸ Prisma color pencils
- ▸ Staedler HB pencils
- ▸ Faber Castler kneadable eraser
- ▸ Micron pen/marker

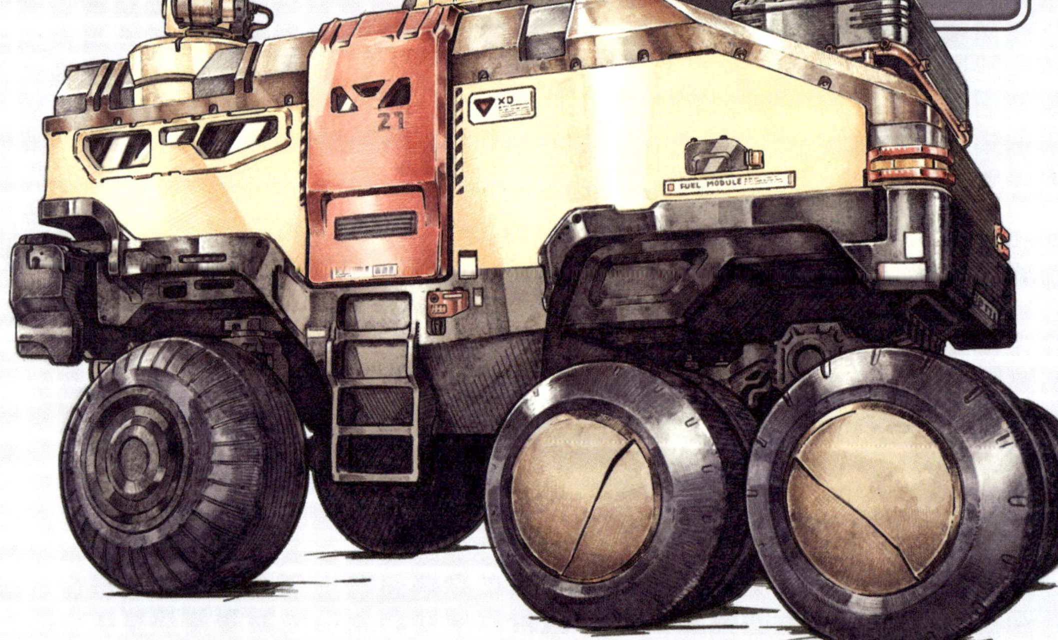

▲ Final image © Elijah McNeal

RESEARCH

Start by trying to understand what makes this vehicle move. Think about the kind of tires, corporate branding, optics for automation, suspension system, and so on. While the vehicle should have an exaggerated sci-fi look, a key ingredient for a successful design is to convince the viewer it could be real.

RIDE HEIGHT

How will the vehicle ride? Is it a smooth roll over moderate obstacles, or a harsh rumble across the terrain? Its large size means it will need strong suspension to support its weight. These details are critical in communicating the idea to your audience.

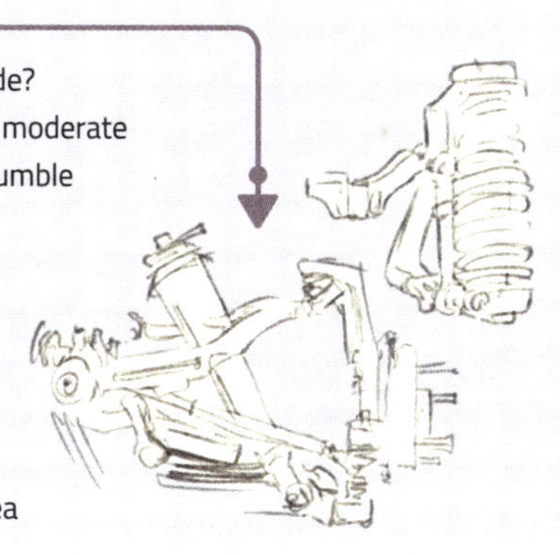

ALL TERRAIN

Traveling over the surface of Mars will be no small feat. Draw inspiration from NASA, modern military vehicles, and consumer SUVs to form an idea of the type of tires required. Transporting dozens of passengers over a rocky surface will require some hefty rubber!

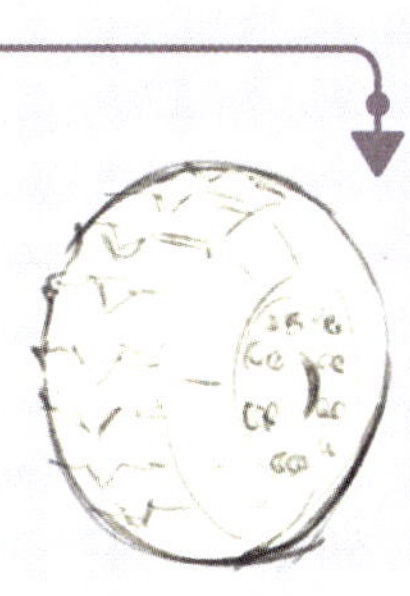
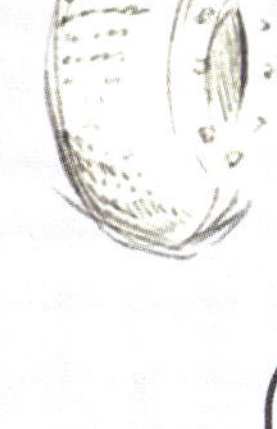

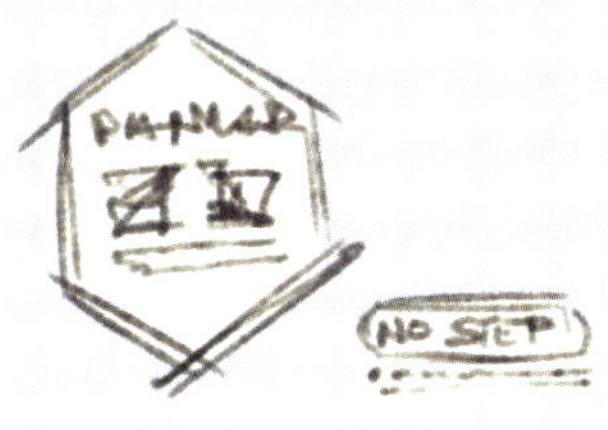
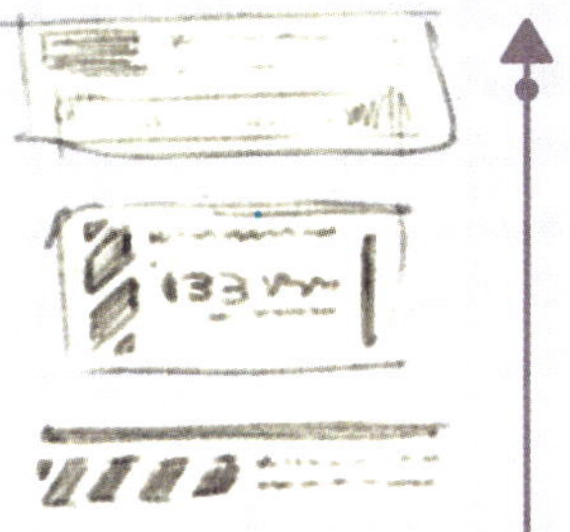

CAMERAS

What if the driver wants to put their feet up and grab a carton of space juice? Cars equipped with driver assist and autopilot are already on the road in real life, but this vehicle will require some heftier cameras for the journey.

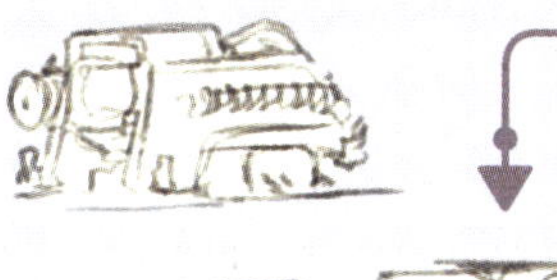
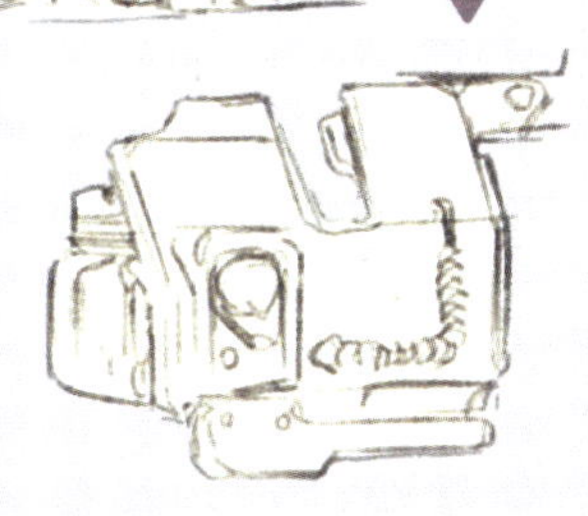

BRANDING

Another important detail to make the vehicle feel familiar is branding. Watch any automotive sports event, or look at most commercial vehicles, and you will notice stickers everywhere – warnings, company logos, even personal messages. While this transport vehicle may be out of this world, these little details will make it more believable.

HEAVY LOAD

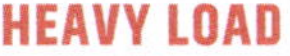

A heavy vehicle needs heavy support. Vehicles are built in layers, so considering how your Mars rover is assembled will help you all the more. This also functions as another way to convince the viewer this concept could actually exist.

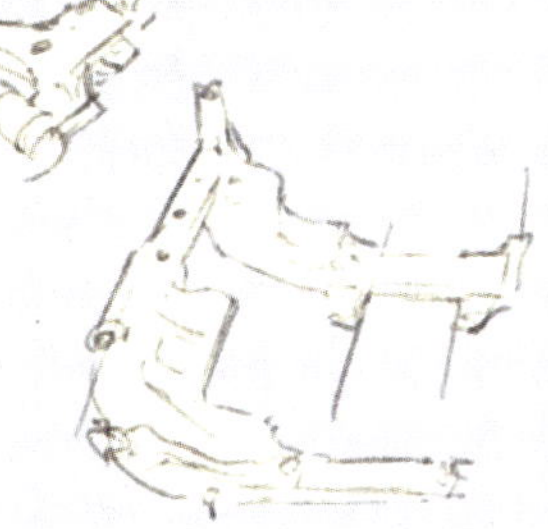

THUMBNAILS

Even if you already have a good idea of the direction you want your design to take, sketching thumbnails will help you to weed out the "bad" ideas before you move on to adding detail. Stopping and starting later on will only hinder your motivation and negatively impact the design. Also, thumbnails allow you to quickly develop the presentation if you already have an idea you like.

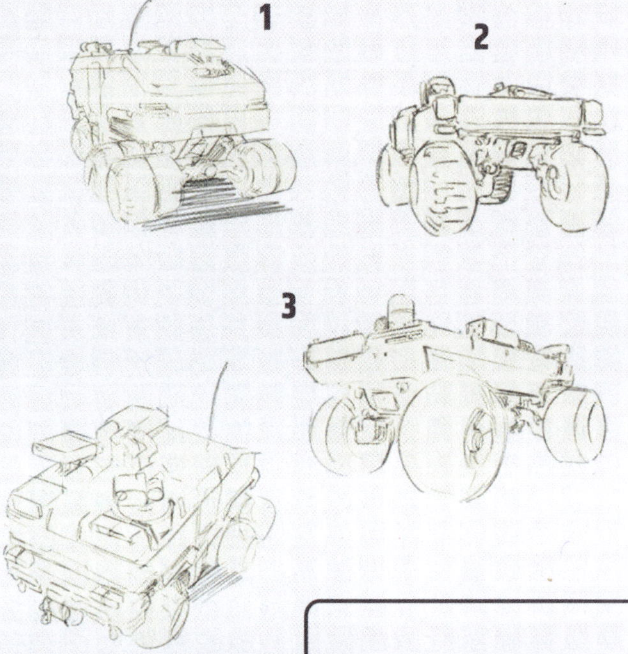

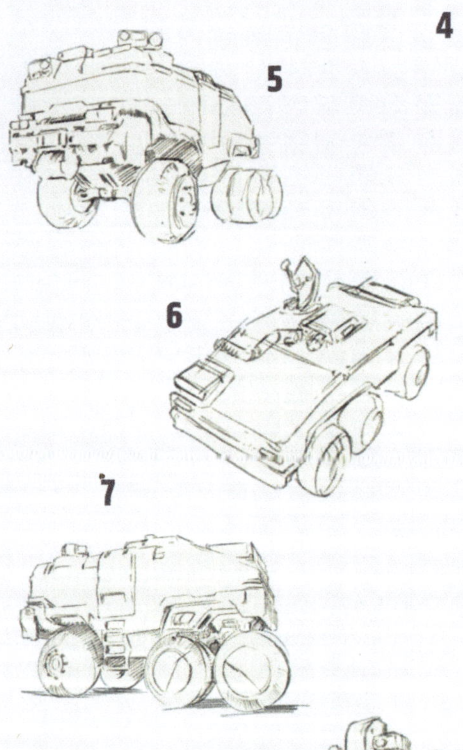

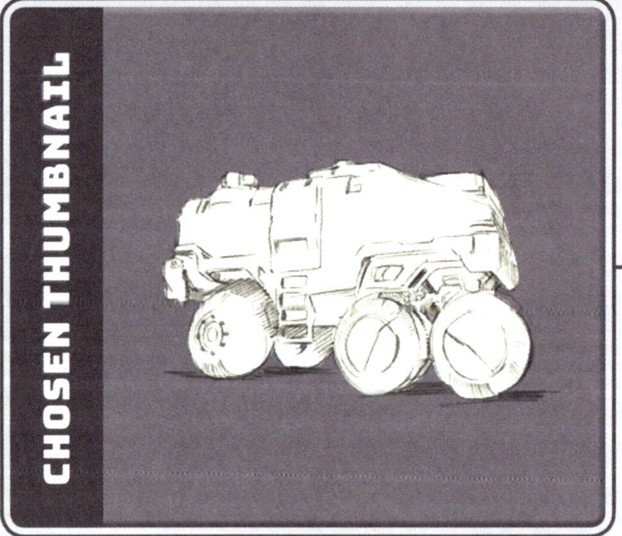

▶ The eye-level view helps to place the viewer in the scene, plus it's an ideal position for the retro commercial-illustration style. Viewing a subject from the front is quite common, but from the side creates a little more attitude. It also provides the potential to use the details you sketched earlier.

FOUNDATIONS

The next step is to begin to model the idea into an actual design. Start to think more carefully about how things are laid out. Where do you want to exaggerate the design? How will you balance the minor and major details? How can you draw the viewer's attention to key areas? You can also begin to think about the colors and inking that will come later. Use an HB pencil to create a clean graphite sketch. You may choose a softer or harder pencil if you prefer, but HB strength won't wear down as quickly as a soft pencil, while still being dark enough to see through the marker paper for the final sketch.

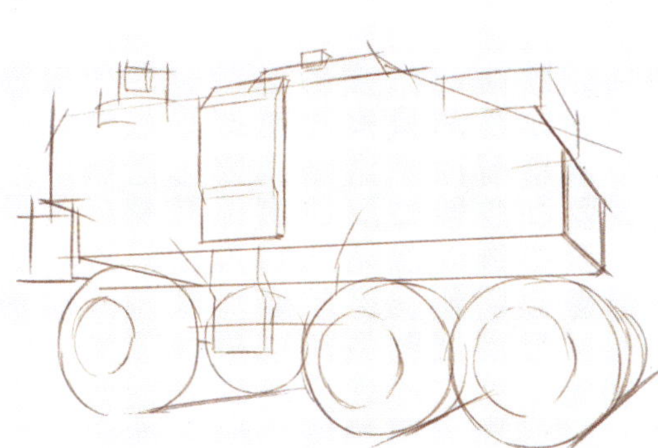

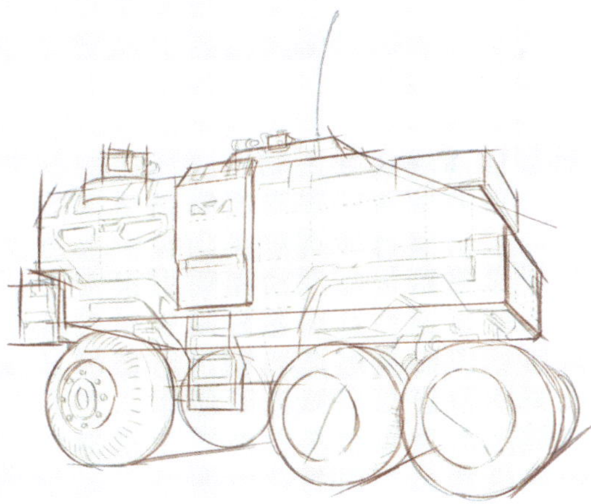

BASE

▶ It may seem like there is a lot going on, but you are simply layering big shapes in an interesting way. Good design at scale is a thoughtful combination of shapes.

▶ While still early in the design, take a look at how to manipulate the perspective. Why might you want to change the perspective? Style! You can ever-so-slightly exaggerate some areas to enhance the feel of the design.

▶ Big tires, a big frame, and a big cabin emphasize the weight of this vehicle and the load it can carry – you want the vehicle to look heavy. Move some elements around to convey this.

LINES

▶ While initial sketches work best when they are kept loose, you can now begin to clean the sketch up as more ideas for minor details arise. If you have access to a scanner, one approach is to scan your chosen thumbnail and enlarge it, then create a cleaner sketch for drafting the final design.

▶ Start sketching in window placement. Leave the aft section empty so there is a large area of rest to contrast with the detail to be added. Aim to create bursts of detail that blend into the large, plainer areas that allow the viewer's eye to rest. Focus more on material type for the emptier areas to ensure they don't feel completely flat.

▶ Give some more thought to the minor details on the optics system and the front wheels. You want this vehicle to be heavy, but not so industrial that it looks like a work truck.

BUILDING UP

DETAIL

Add more details to the minor areas, such as developing the shapes for the detachable window frames, extrusions on the entry door, and adding a luggage case on the back.

CONTRAST

You may notice that some areas of the design are darker than others. This is early contrast placement and can be used to experiment with focus and form. Areas that feel less important could be filled with graphite, and marker could be used in places with less line work.

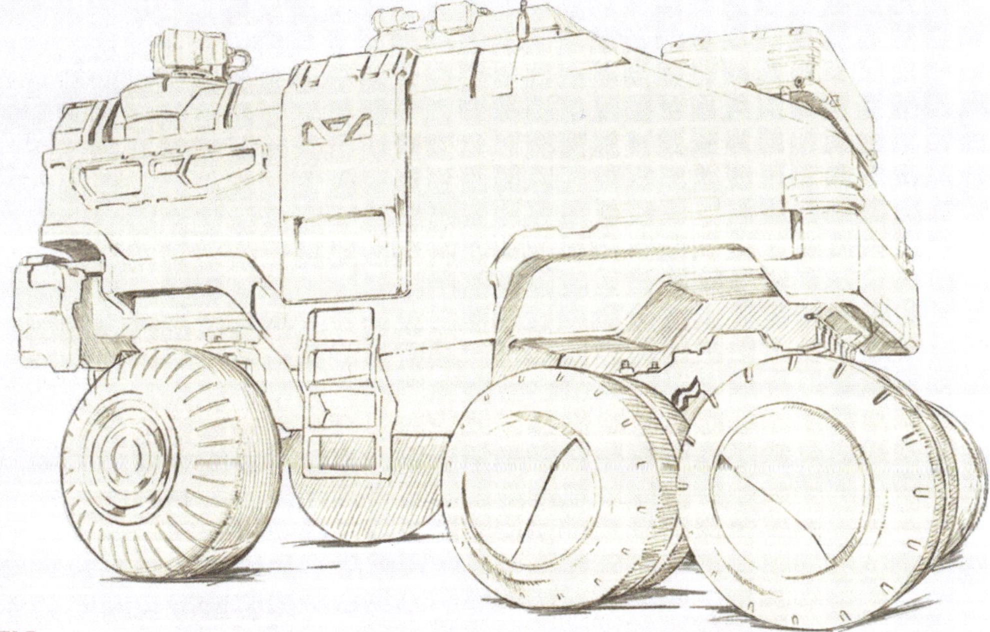

WHEELS

The wheels are an important, prominent element of the design, but also a contrasting shape. While you can create more balancing and contrast with color later, lay the groundwork for this by sketching the primary details that will be present in the final image.

DESIGN FOCUS

ENTRYWAY

This is a key area that needs a bold design with some minor details to break up the shape. You can use color to highlight this area later, so the simplicity of the shape is not an issue at this stage.

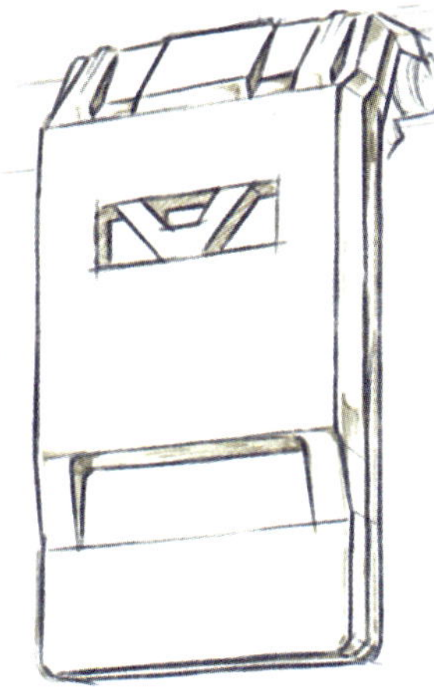

LUGGAGE

It might not seem that important, but showing luggage helps define the rover's purpose. It also provides an area on the vehicle's periphery that grabs attention and leaves the design feeling less like a big, empty truck.

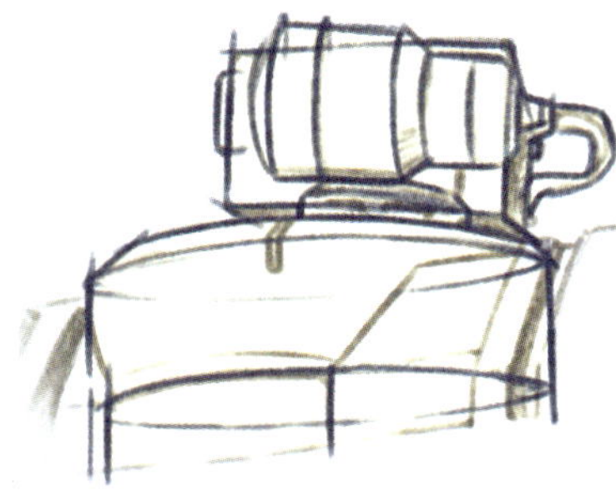

OPTICS

For the forward optics, keep the shapes simple and bold, with a few small details. While the other optics system will be more detailed and will draw more focus, use less render emphasis and contrast here so this one fades into the background.

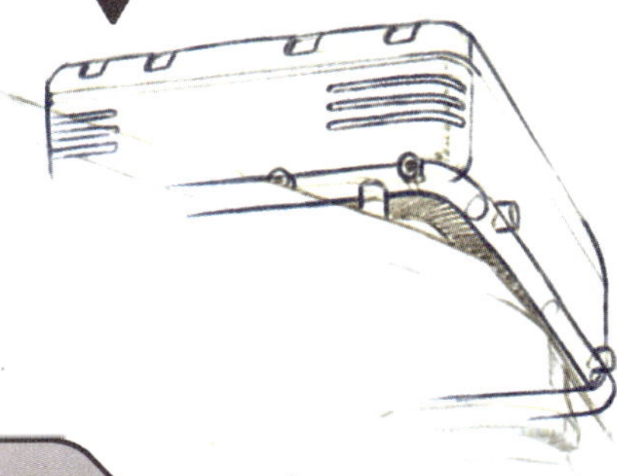

IDEA INVENTORY

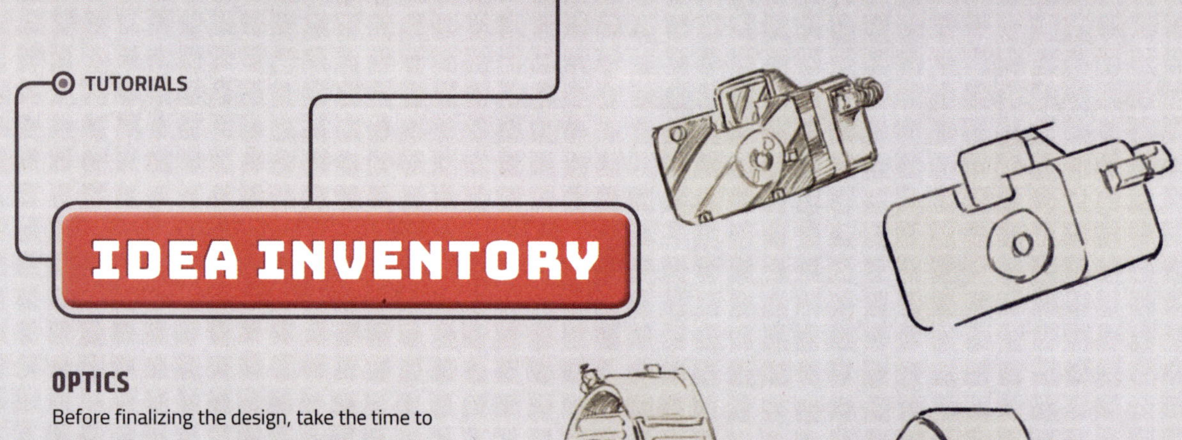

OPTICS

Before finalizing the design, take the time to explore the optics some more. Sketching out the details will really help before experimenting on the final image. There are some cool shapes here, but the newer sketches upstage the vehicle and other details. You want to make sure that the viewer's eye is drawn to the main body, not distracted by a support mechanism.

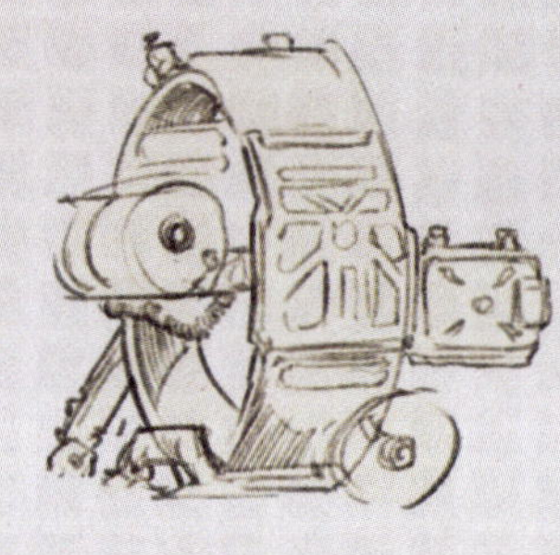

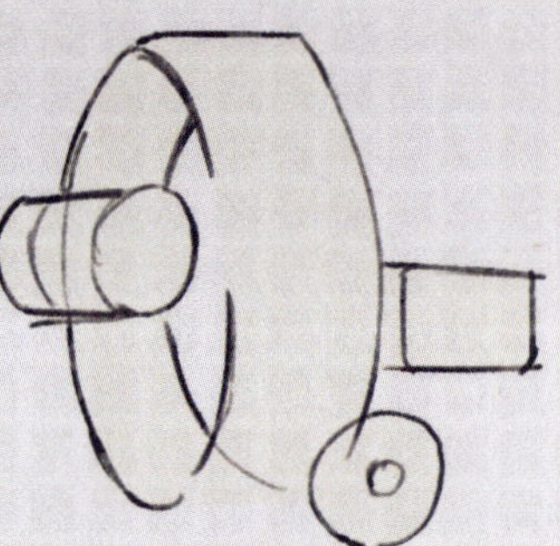

FUEL

A large vehicle like this will need a reliable fuel source. Including a port where the rover can be refueled will go a long way toward making the design feel real. Sketch out some rough ideas: one for the fuel port and another for the entryway keypad.

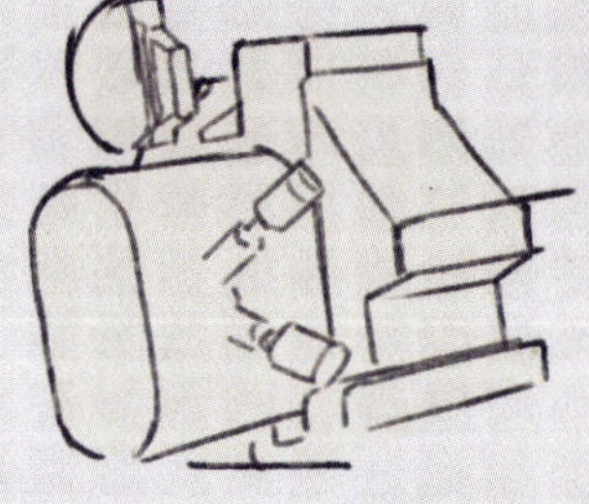

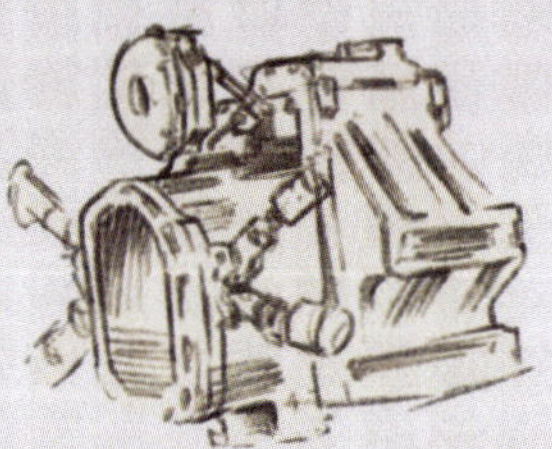

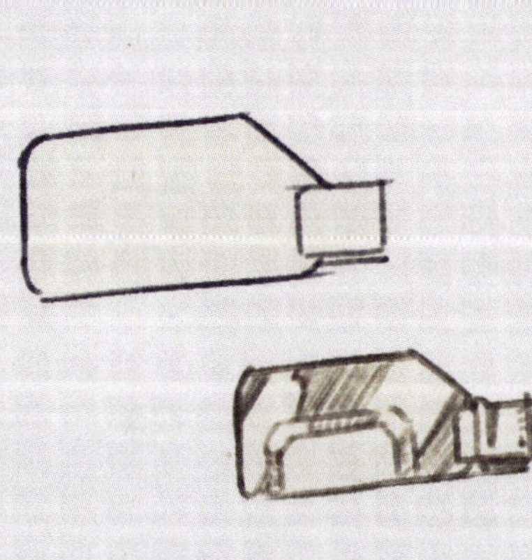

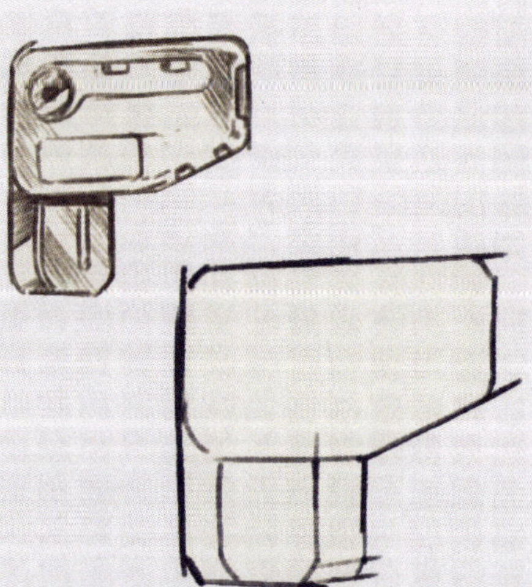

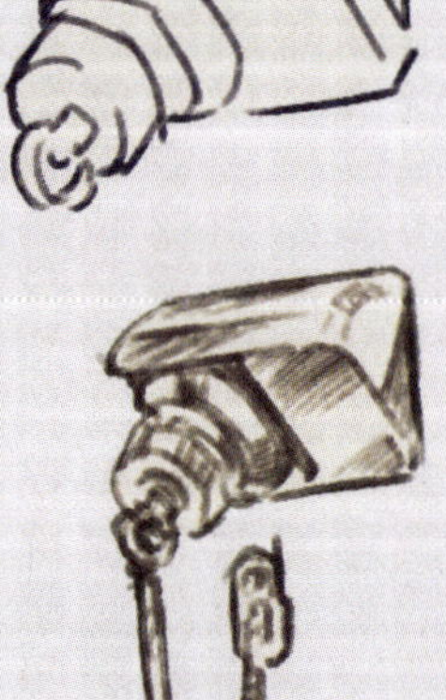

FINAL SKETCH

For the final sketch, begin to implement the full suite of details. Consider how the panels will connect to the main body, where the branding will be placed, and what parts of the vehicle are interactive. Think about how to improve the lighting as well. Notice the shading on the rear face is drawn with a heavier hand, pushing the corner forward. The fuel port, entry panel, and branding elements are in place, where you would expect them to be. Every element should enhance the design, not upstage it.

▶ Ensuring the line work is relatively clean will allow you to keep the graphite when moving into color and ink, creating a distinct, hand-drawn feel. It will also keep up your momentum – erasing all of the rough lines can be very distracting.

▶ Add the minor details on the optics systems so there is something to hold the interest when the viewer passes over this area. Keep them a little on the loose side, however, so they aren't an active distraction from the more important areas of the design.

▶ The fenders will likely be a bare metal, so including cutouts and insets will add interest and potential for lighting. Leaving them as these simple structures may risk the design feeling toylike or crude. This also breaks up the shapes enough that they feel lighter.

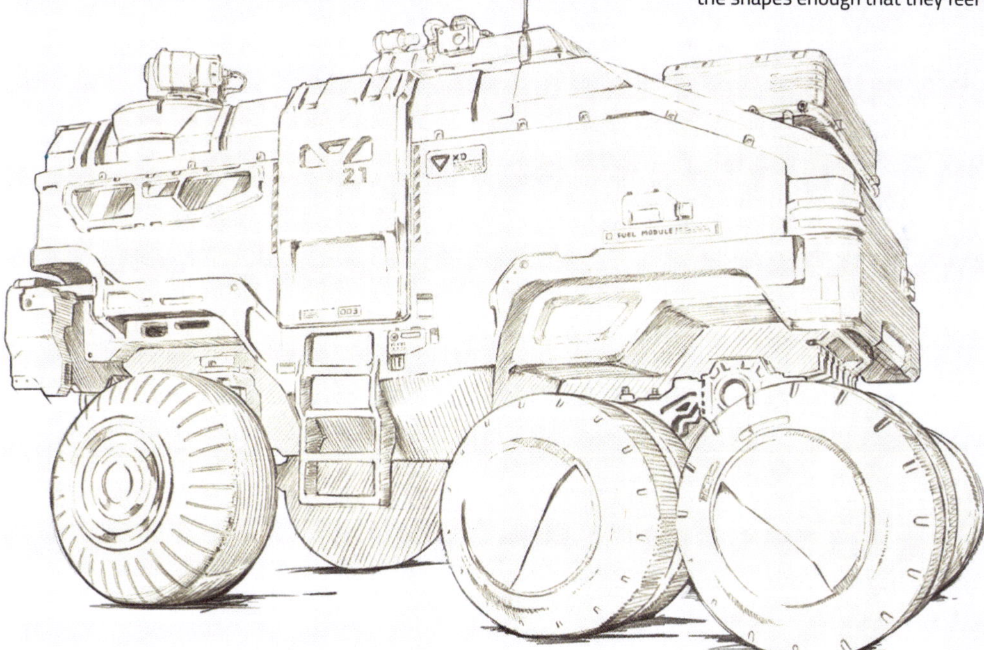

▶ Start to suggest the materials the vehicle is built from. Some parts will have a matte finish, while others will be metallic or semigloss. Work out where each material will be so you can push the graphite around the appropriate areas once you color with marker.

▶ Look for nondescript corners to exaggerate with light or heavy shading. Areas such as the edges of the entryway door, the fenders, the quarter panels, or the roof. What are the surface details of the luggage carrier or the axels?

COLORING

Coloring on top of your final sketch, enhance the materials hinted at earlier and use color depth to emphasize areas of focus. Use Copic markers and Prisma color pencils, with very light touches of gouache. The colors will give the design a place in time, while also indicating its intended function. Use this stage to fix minor details, such as the shape of the front end tire.

▶ The red door is the central focus. Opting for a semigloss metallic material helps to separate it from everything else. Start with a 20% gray marker to push the values, followed by vermilion for the undercolor, then top this with various reds. To create a semigloss look, use soft, gradual tones for the lit areas and place the darkest where there is a distinct lighting point. This gives the door a reflective look.

▶ The upper panels of the roof should be a copper-gold color; the kind of material often used for NASA vehicles. Use light violets and yellow, bringing some graphite through, with orange and gray color pencils for the final layer. To create a harsh reflective quality, use the high contrast of lights and darks to push this area from the rest of the body. This will guide the viewer from the edges of the design toward the door, and back again.

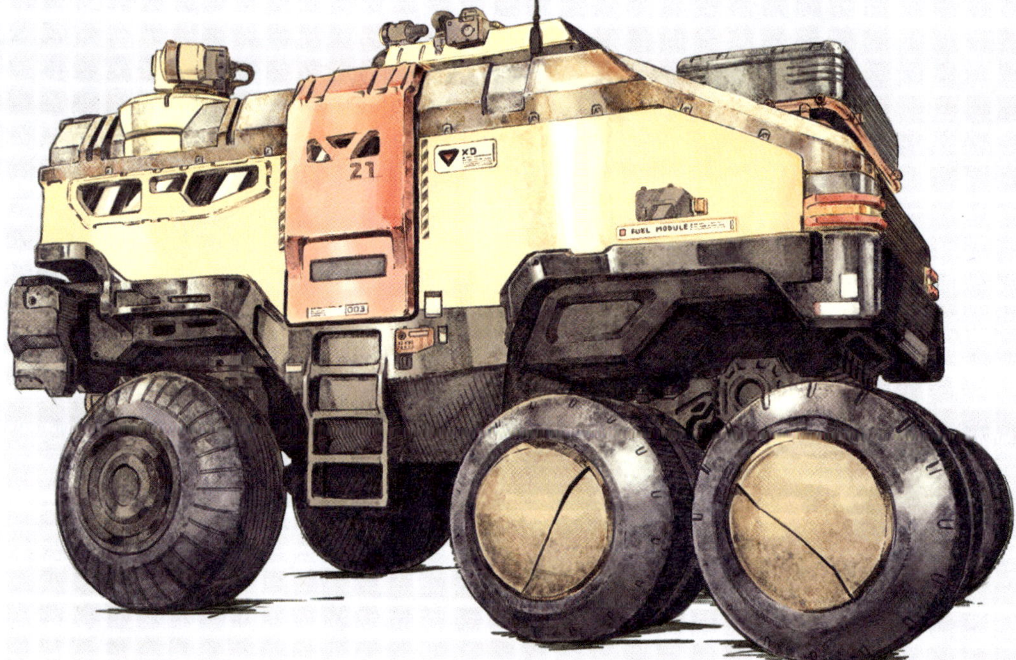

▶ The main body will be yellow with a semimatte finish, so it isn't completely flat, but won't become a distraction from the key areas. Place a few orange shades near to the rear quarter panel so it doesn't dramatically drop off from the dark values. Add some hatching in the center of the body to complement the lighting established with the door.

▶ The fenders will be a non-distracting gray. A few layers of 10% gray, followed by 60%, works well for the base and contrast areas. Top this off with white pencil. The tires will be violet, but you will need to rely more on pencil here to separate them from the fenders and manage the forms.

For the final stage, use a large, dark Copic marker and varying sizes of Micron pen to ink more defined line work, focusing on contrast points and weight.

▶ The first areas to focus on are points of separation, such as the cabin window frame. It's made of the same material as the body, so looks like a simple extrusion. Keep most (or all) of the pen focused on the edges to create the feel of a modular piece bolted onto the body of the vehicle.

▶ There is minor detailing on the fenders and axels that's become a little messy. Push those areas forward with some heavy line work. Use a large Micron pen here with the dark base values previously established.

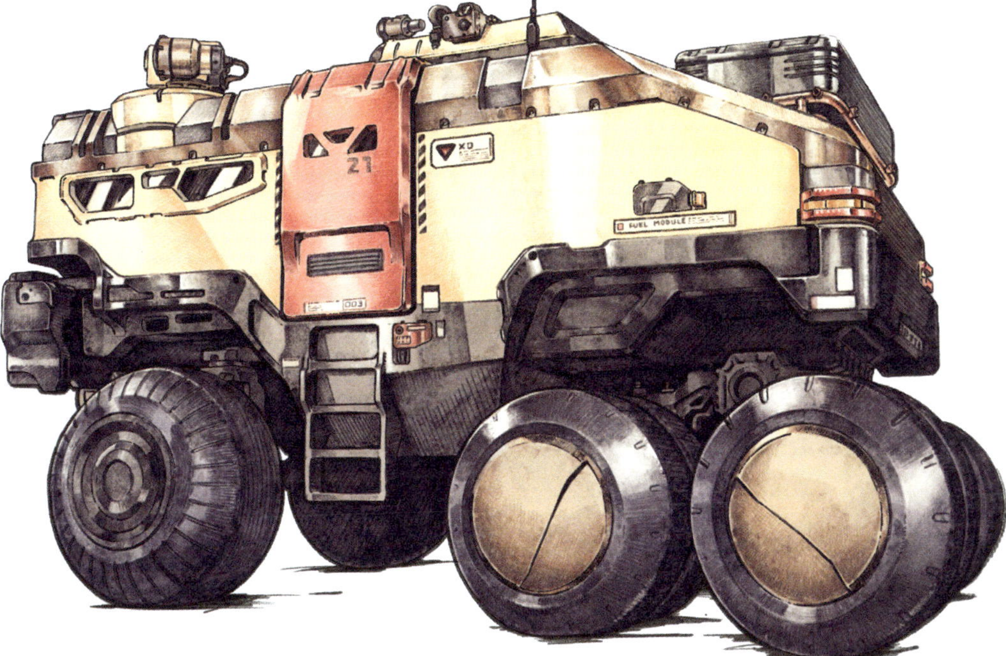

▶ Separate the fenders, fuel port, and branding using the same process. Use the smaller side of a 50-60% Copic for the branding to keep the edges soft. Save hard edges for the metallic objects.

▶ With all of the Micron and minor marker edges in place, begin to add the final touches. Use the larger edge of an 80% Copic to outline the design. Draw some marks on the undercarriage and axels to push those areas forward. Make each mark intentionally with a single long stroke, keeping the thickest edge toward the bottom of the placement. This will keep the design from looking like a 2D sticker.

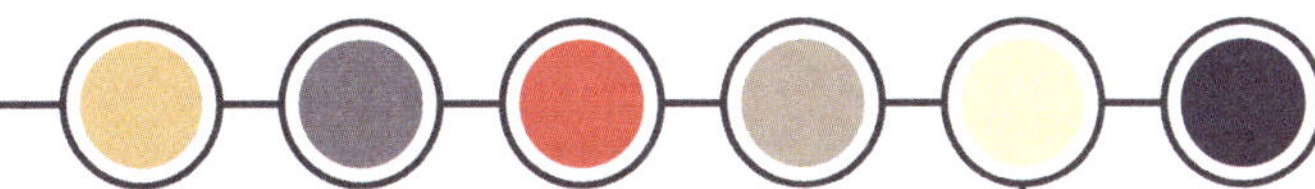

GLOSSARY

ANALOGOUS COLORS

These are colors that sit directly next to each other on the color wheel, creating a harmonious color scheme. For example, blue, blue-green, and green produce an analogous color palette.

COMPLEMENTARY COLORS

These are colors that sit directly opposite each other on the color wheel, creating a contrasting color scheme. Used to create visual impact, these include magenta and green, cyan and orange, and yellow and purple.

CONTRAST

The difference between parts of an image, such as bright highlights and dark shadows, small and large shapes, or different colors. Contrast can be used to create visual interest and focal points, drawing the viewer's eye to different areas of an artwork.

FLAT COLORS

Solid, uniform colors that are consistent in shade, depth, and texture. They create a clean, graphic look, typical of comics.

FOCAL POINT

The area of an image that is the most visually interesting and immediately catches the viewer's attention. It often includes a higher level of detail and contrast, such as a character's face.

FORESHORTENING

A technique used to convey perspective by making parts of the subject appear larger and closer to the viewer. Foreshortening can be used to ensure an image doesn't appear flat and lifeless.

HIGHLIGHTS

The brightest areas of an image, which are painted with the lightest values or colors. These may be the areas closest to the light source, or those made from a glossy material such as chrome.

LIGHTING

How an artwork is lit in order to create different atmospheres, moods, and emotions. A scene's lighting might be neutral, natural, artificial, or dramatic, depending on the setting or story.

LINE WEIGHT

The thickness or thinness of a line. An artwork drawn with the same line weight throughout may appear flat and a little boring, whereas an image drawn with varied line weight will have more depth, fluidity, and visual interest.

LINE WORK

Also known as line art. This is often the final line drawing of an image before color is added. It is a neater, cleaned-up version of the final sketch, though some artists may prefer to have rougher or looser line work.

MOOD

The feeling, atmosphere, or emotion an artwork creates, such as spooky and mysterious, or sunny and cheerful. Color, lighting, character, and composition can all contribute to an artwork's mood.

PERSPECTIVE

A technique used to create the illusion of three-dimensionality on a two-dimensional surface. You can plan out a scene's perspective using a horizon line and one or more vanishing points

PRIMARY COLORS

Magenta, yellow, and cyan; these are the three basic colors that can be mixed to create all other colors. Red, yellow, and blue are also considered primary colors, depending on the color theory you prefer.

REFERENCE

First- or second-hand research for an artist to refer to, such as photographs, videos, or real-life objects. Researching reference imagery is an essential first step in the design process, providing inspiration and ideas that can add interest, believability, and relatability to a design.

SCIENCE FICTION

Also known as sci-fi or SF, this is a popular genre of speculative fiction that explores the advancement of science and technology, space travel, alien life, robots, artificial intelligence, futuristic settings, and more.

SECONDARY COLORS

Purple, green, and orange; these are created by mixing different variations of the three primary colors.

SHADOW

The areas of a design that are not lit, perhaps because they are on the underside of an object, or are on the opposite side to the light source. Shadows are sometimes cast by an object blocking the light from reaching another object.

THUMBNAILS

Small preliminary, draft versions of your design, used to explore different ideas and compositions. By nature, thumbnails must be simple and quickly made, rather than highly detailed and polished.

VOLUME

This describes an object's three-dimensional depth, which can be created through perspective and shading. For example, a sphere has more volume than a flat circle.

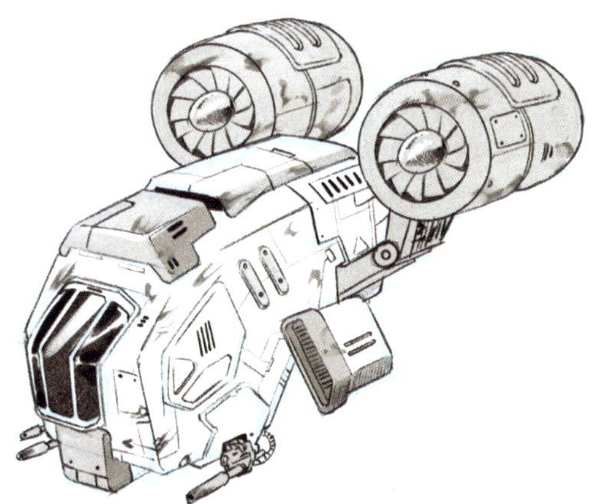

CONTRIBUTORS

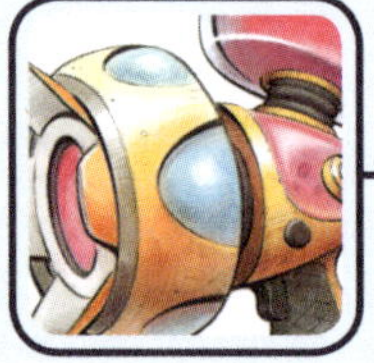 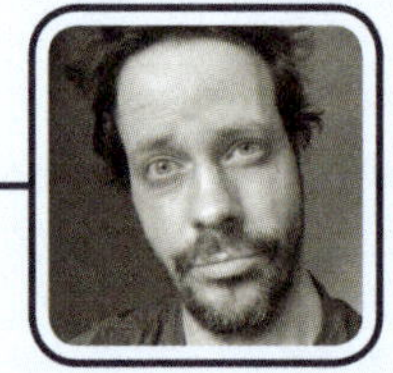

KENNETH ANDERSON

Character designer & illustrator | charactercube.com
Based in Glasgow, Scotland, Kenneth is an artist who specializes in designing characters for animation and illustrating for books and magazines.

 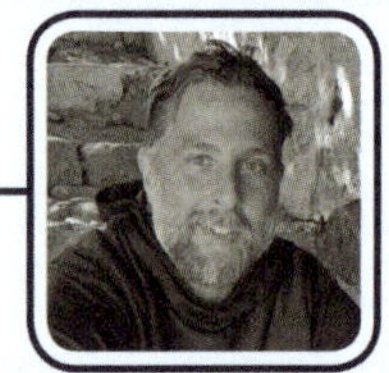

BRETT BEAN

Artist & author | brettbean.com
Brett is an author, character designer, and artist. His clients include Disney, Penguin, DreamWorks, Riot, Ravensburger Jim Henson, and Marvel. He also teaches at CGMA and at workshops around the world.

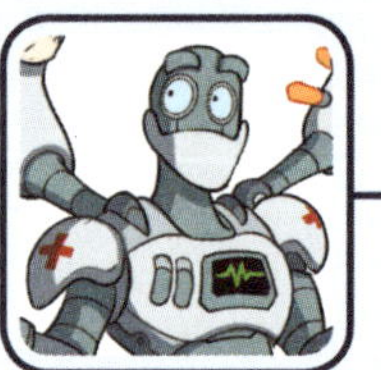 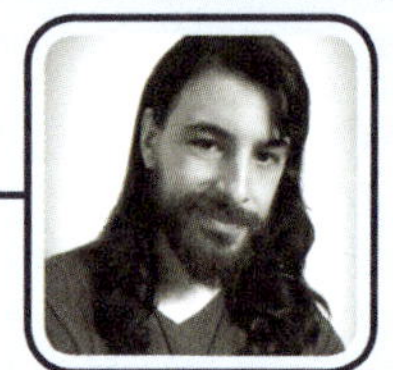

VALERIO "DREELRAYK" BUONFANTINO

Character designer | artstation.com/valeriobuonfantino
Valerio is a freelance artist from Italy. After studying at the Cartoon School of Palermo, he has worked on concept art, illustration, comics, traditional sculpture, and 3D modeling.

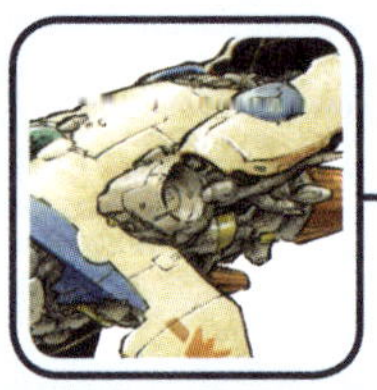 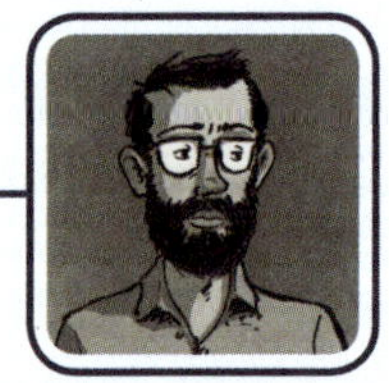

JEREL DYE

Illustrator & cartoonist | jerel-dye.squarespace.com
Jerel is an illustrator from Boston. His first graphic novel *Pigs Might Fly* was published in 2017. Jerel has been teaching courses in drawing, cartooning, and comics in Massachusetts since 2010.

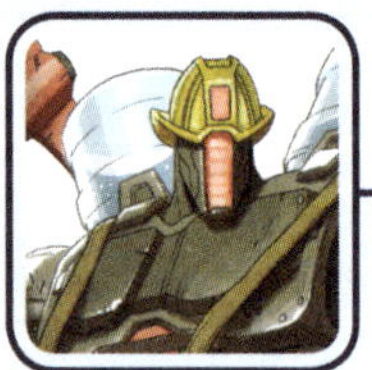 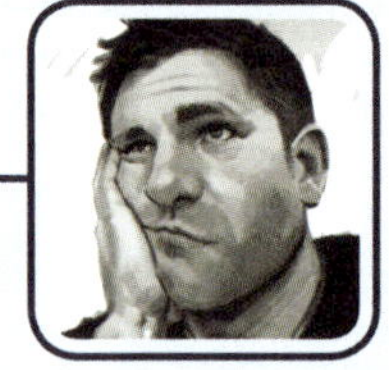

ADAM FORD

Art director | instagram.com/adamford_art
Adam has been an artist all his life. For the last two decades he has worked in the gaming industry as an environmental artist and art director. He lives in the Rocky Mountains in the United States.

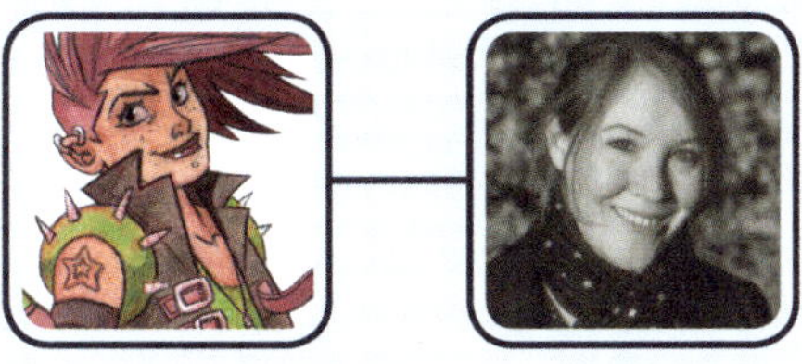

MARGAUX KINDHAUSER

Comic-book artist, writer, & art teacher | instagram.com/margauxmara

Margaux is a French character designer who has worked as a comic-book artist since 2008 and an art teacher since 2017. She loves creating characters with expressive, memorable designs and lots of hair.

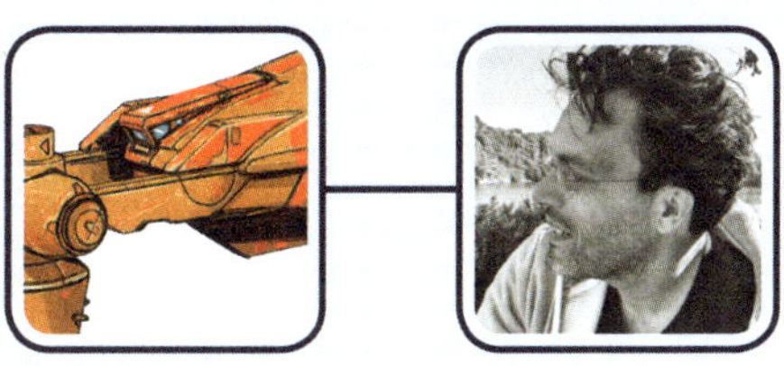

DOFRESH

Concept artist | artstation.com/dofresh

Dofresh, real name Ronan Le Fur, is a freelance concept artist and illustrator living in Brittany on the western coast of France.

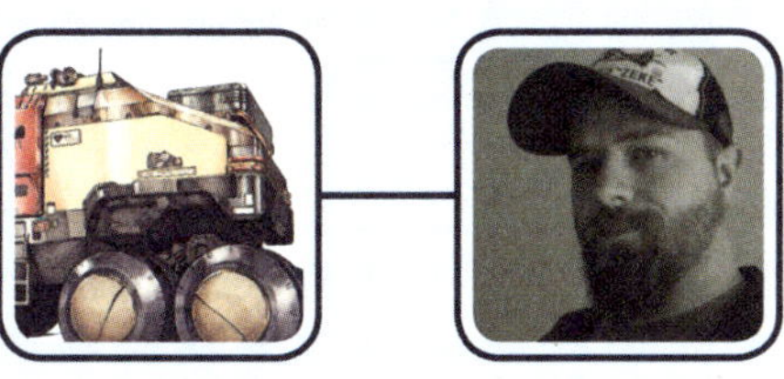

ELIJAH MCNEAL

Senior concept artist | el1j4h.artstation.com

Elijah has over ten years of experience working as a concept artist in the video-game industry. He has worked on franchises including Fortnite, Gears of War, Borderlands, and many others.

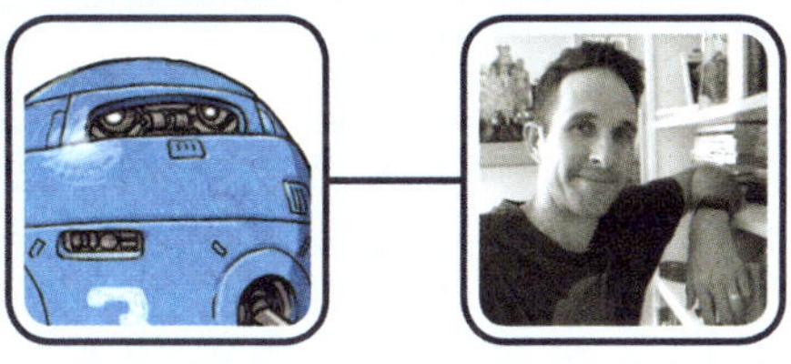

JAKE PARKER

Illustrator | mrjakeparker.com

Jake is a *New York Times* bestselling illustrator. He is a co-founder of svslearn.com, which teaches thousands of people how to become a professional illustrator. He works out of his home studio in Arizona.

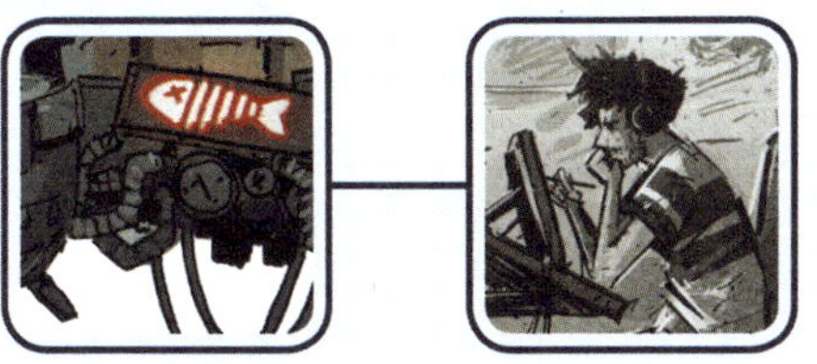

ALEX VEDE CABALAR

Illustrator | instagram.com/alexvede96

Alex is an illustrator and storyboard artist based in Galicia, Spain. He works on commercials and cover art for novels, as well as publishing his own art books and comics.

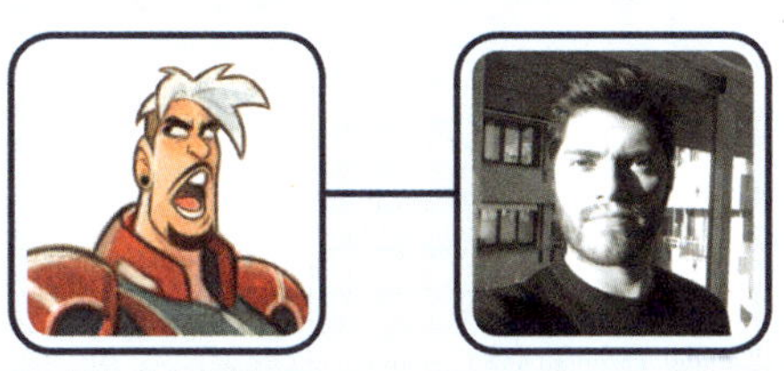

CÉSAR VERGARA

Character designer & illustrator | artstation.com/cesarvs

César is a 2D artist and character designer from Mexico City, with nine years of experience in the animation and games industry. He is a full-time studio employee by day and a brave freelancer by night.

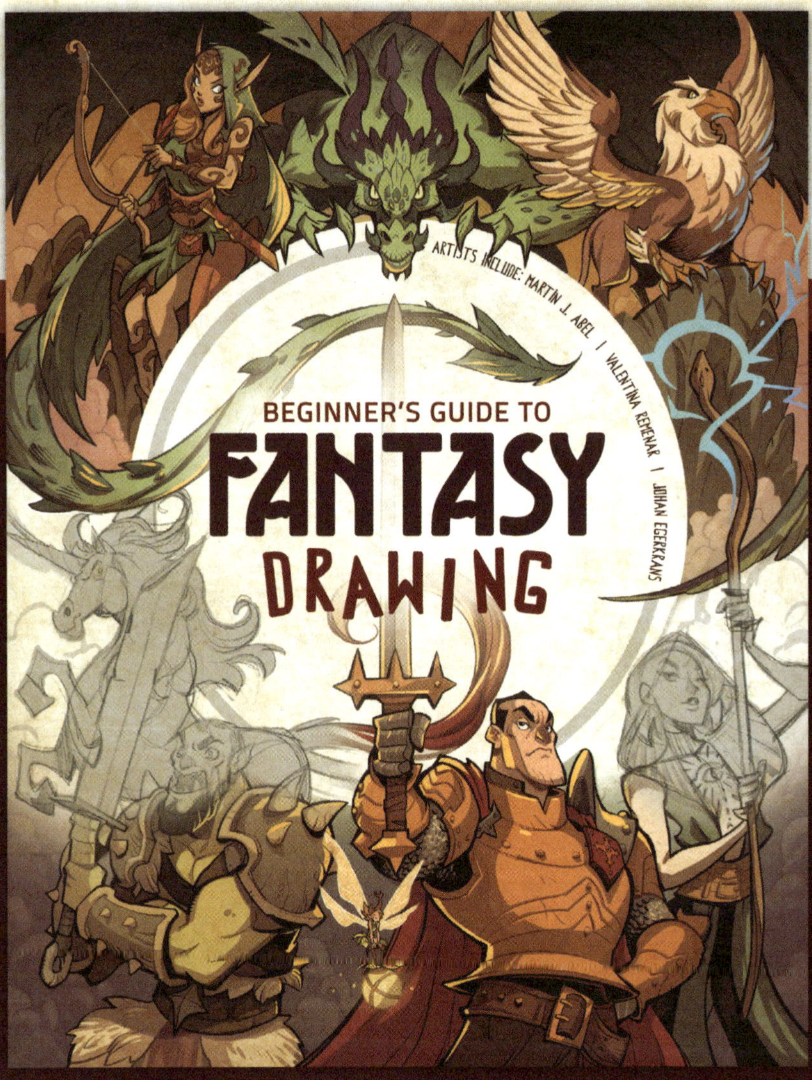

Delve into the enchanting world of dragons, wizards, and warriors with *Beginner's Guide to Fantasy Drawing* – an accessible, entertaining introduction to creating fantasy concepts, with only a few simple traditional tools and no prior drawing knowledge needed.

Available now at
store.3dtotal.com

Sketching from the Imagination

In each book of the *Sketching from the Imagination* series, 50 talented traditional and digital artists have been chosen to share their sketchbooks and explain the reasons behind their design decisions. Visually stunning collections packed full of useful tips, these books offer inspiration for everyone.

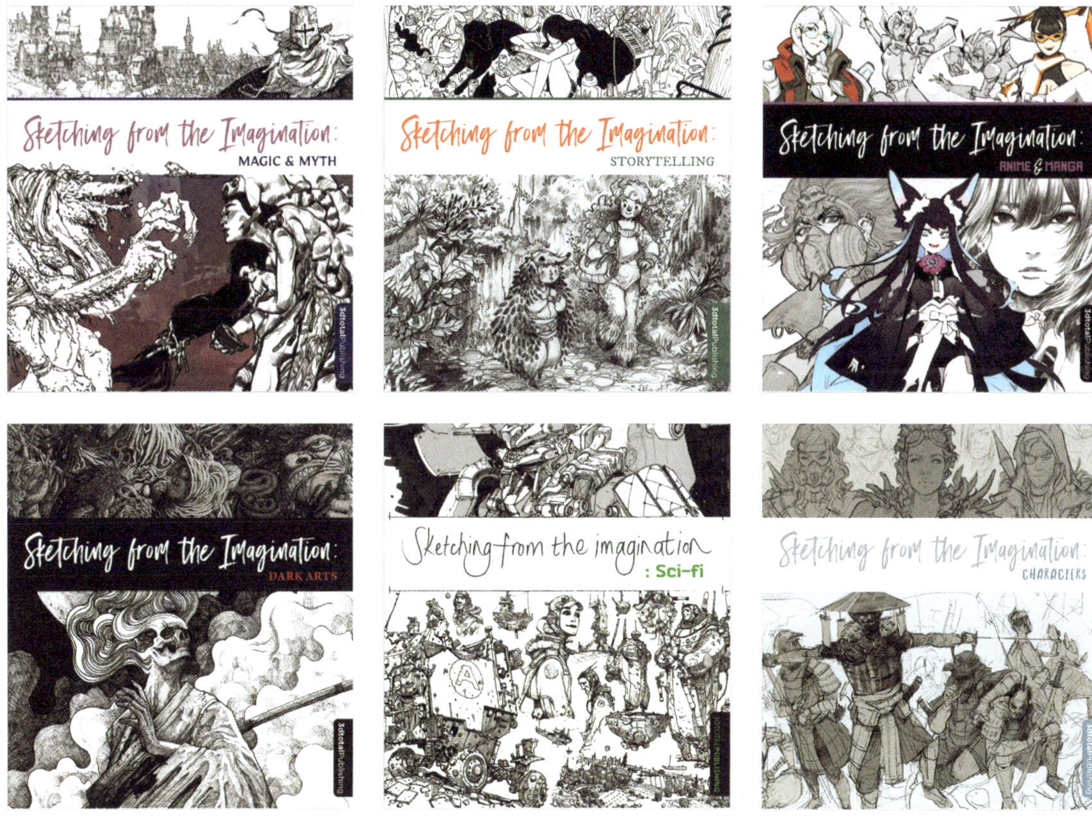

See the full collection at
store.3dtotal.com

3dtotalPublishing

3dtotal Publishing is a trailblazing, creative publisher specializing in inspirational and educational resources for artists.

Our titles feature top industry professionals from around the globe who share their experience in skillfully written step–by–step tutorials and fascinating, detailed guides. Illustrated throughout with stunning artwork, these best–selling publications offer creative insight, expert advice, and essential motivation. Fans of digital art will enjoy our comprehensive volumes covering Adobe Photoshop, Procreate, and Blender, as well as our superb titles based around character design, including *Fundamentals of Character Design* and *Creating Characters for the Entertainment Industry*. The dedicated, high–quality blend of instruction and inspiration also extends to traditional art. Titles covering a range of techniques, genres, and abilities allow your creativity to flourish while building essential skills.

Well–established within the industry, we now offer over 100 titles and counting, many of which have been translated into multiple languages around the world. With something for every artist, we are proud to say that our books offer the 3dtotal package:

LEARN ▪ CREATE ▪ SHARE

Visit us at 3dtotalpublishing.com

3dtotal Publishing is part of 3dtotal.com, a leading website for CG artists founded by Tom Greenway in 1999.